Writing Authority

Writing Authority

Elite Competition and Written Law in Early Greece

Jason Hawke

Published by the Northern Illinois University Press, DeKalb, Illinois 60115
Manufactured in the United States using postconsumer-recycled, acid-free paper.

Design by Shaun Allshouse

Library of Congress Cataloging-in-Publication Data
Hawke, Jason.
Writing authority: elite competition and written law in early Greece / Jason Hawke.
p. cm.
Includes bibliographical references and index.
ISBN 978-0-87580-438-5 (clothbound : alk. paper)
1. Justice, Administration of (Greek law) 2. Greek language—Writing. I. Title.
KL4345.H39 2010
347.38—dc22
2010041623

CONTENTS

Preface

This book is a contribution to a long-established subject of scholarly debate, the emergence of written law in the Greek world, beginning around the middle of the seventh century BCE. Despite the already immense bibliography on the topic, it continues to demand the attention of each generation of scholars, who find something new over which to puzzle in the fragmentary remains of most early laws and the interpretations of ancient writers regarding the significance of legislation in the formative period of Greek civilization. Even as I was revising the present monograph for a final round of reviews, two major monographs on the subject appeared in English alone, namely Michael Gagarin's *Writing Greek Law* and Zinon Papakonstantinou's *Lawmaking and Adjudication in Archaic Greece*, both published in 2008. The reader may then be forgiven for asking, why the need for yet another book examining the genesis of written law among the Greeks?

In my view, the best way to answer that is to state that there has yet to appear a study quite like the one the reader now holds. Like any scholar, I stand on the shoulders of giants to whom I and others owe an enormous intellectual debt, and this book would not have been possible without their many insights and inspirations; yet, I would argue that the scholarly examination of early Greek legislation has yet to embrace all of the tools at our disposal for understanding it in its complete context. Modern approaches to the study of law and legal theory—particularly in the realms of "legal culture" and "law-as-community"—have much to offer, as does the discipline of anthropology. The last generation or so has seen the resistance to a dialogue between anthropology and classical studies wane, but to date no one has engaged in a "thick descriptive" approach to our available evidence for early Greek law. Such a method necessitates an exploration of the juridical world of the Greeks before and during the process of committing laws to writing, so that we have a fuller appreciation of the cultural dynamics that compelled such a transformative event in the legal history of the Greeks. By considering the emergence of written law among the Greeks "in the round," I argue that we can not attribute it to popular or institutional forces, but rather to the elites whose competition for power and prestige encouraged them to seek new ways to enshrine legal authority in a rapidly changing social and cultural landscape, where new problems arose for which traditional norms and "rules" seldom had the answers.

But that is to anticipate. My hope is that in constructing the argument as I have, classicists, ancient historians, legal historians, theorists, and anthropologists will all find value in what follows. Writing about the ancient world so as to satisfy the demands of the specialist audience, while maintaining accessibility for those without Greek or a general background in Classics, is always challenging. I have sought to provide enough context to aid the nonspecialist while avoiding tedium for the classical historian. In the text of the argument, I have transliterated the Greek; quotations of the Greek itself I have consigned to the notes where the language of a particular passage, and my interpretation of it, may interest the reader with Greek. I beg the indulgence of the philologically inclined when it comes to translations: this being a treatise on law, I have preferred technical exactitude over aesthetic elegance. In terms of transliteration, I have opted for more familiar, Latinized spellings of the names of literary figures and characters and well-known toponyms, while choosing more direct transliteration from the Greek for individuals and places perhaps more obscure to a general reader.

This book has a long history of its own, and over the years I have incurred many debts of gratitude. I want to thank my many teachers over the years who selflessly gave much of their time and expertise in helping me become the scholar and educator I am today. Carol G. Thomas of the University of Washington offered invaluable guidance and advice when I was just beginning my serious study of early Greek law, and her encouragement at various stages of this project helped bring it to its completion. The suggestions and criticisms of Robin Stacey and Lawrence Bliquez, respectively of the History and Classics Departments at Washington, have improved this project significantly. To James J. O'Donnell, currently Provost at Georgetown University, I owe my abiding interest in the subject of the interface between orality and literacy. James D. Nason, an anthropologist at Washington, endured many thankless hours in conversation that immeasurably made of me a much more sophisticated thinker in that discipline than I otherwise would have been. I owe Robert Stacey, now a divisional dean of the College of Arts and Sciences at Washington, gratitude for his intellectual and professional guidance over the years. Sandra Joshel and Alain Gowing have also provided invaluable advice over the years, and I thank them. Last, but by no means least among my teachers, W. Lindsay Adams of the University of Utah was the person who inspired me to pursue an academic career in ancient history, and his tutelage and friendship I have found invaluable in the twenty years I have known him.

Two of my former colleagues in the Department of History at Northern Illinois University deserve special acknowledgment and thanks. James Schmidt and Sean Farrell read multiple drafts of this study as I executed substantial revisions, and their keen and critical observations at every stage of the process, regarding both substance and style, were extraordinarily helpful; in fact, this study would not exist in its present form if not for their urging to persevere with the project as a monograph rather than cannibalize its ideas for journal articles. Anne Hanley, also at NIU, strongly suggested the same course of action. Among others who read all or parts of the evolving manuscript were Valerie Garver of NIU, Peter and Carin Green and Craig Gibson of the University of Iowa, and Byron J. Nakamura of Southern Connecticut State University. I appreciate their time and their input more than I can adequately express.

I would additionally like to thank for their collegiality, friendship, and support the following former colleagues at Northern: in the Department of History, Stan Arnold, E. Taylor Atkins, Sandra Dawson, Heide Fehrenbach, Aaron Fogleman, Michael Gonzales, Robert Hagaman, Kristin Huffine, Eric Jones, Vera Lind, Ismael Montana, Brian Sandberg, and Andrea Smalley; and in Anthropology, Michael Kolb and Leila Porter. My former chair, Beatrix Hoffman, was a source of strength in what could have been an otherwise unbearable experience in my final years at Northern, which coincided with the completion of the book: again, words can not help but fail to capture my sense of gratitude. I also wish to thank Christopher Blackwell and Anne Leen of the Department of Classics at Furman University, where I have found a welcoming home away from home due to the kindnesses that they and many others at Furman have offered.

I am grateful as well to J. Alex Schwartz, Director of Northern Illinois University Press, for his extraordinary professionalism and plentiful advice in bringing the project from manuscript to monograph; I also want to thank all of the staff at the Press for their many contributions to this volume, including Susan Bean and Pamela Hamilton, whose careful evaluation of the manuscript saved me from various inconsistencies; Sara Hoerdeman, who helped guide the book through the press board; and Julia Fauci and Shaun Allshouse for their keen eye and taste in producing a beautiful monograph. I additionally owe Alex my gratitude for his efforts in securing three outside reviewers whose expertise and many helpful criticisms were invaluable, rescuing me from various oversights and errors, and offering insights and suggestions that have made this a better book. David Tandy's detailed and exacting analysis of both the initial and revised manuscripts was, for lack of any better description, above and beyond the call of duty. At the time of this writing, the other two readers remained anonymous: but their reviews were equally helpful, and I thank them for their criticisms and suggestions, positive and otherwise, which they will hopefully find reflected in what follows. Any errors that remain are, of course, my own.

No undertaking such as this, I believe, is truly possible without a support system. I have been very fortunate in my circle of friends over the years, something over which I have had at least some control, and want to acknowledge especially Lawrence J. Roseman of Seattle for his sage observations over the years about life, career, and the universe in general. My good fortune in my teachers I have already noted, but perhaps I have been most fortunate in that group in which we are all subject to Fate. My family—my late paternal grandfather, my parents and stepparents, aunt, and sister—have, I am certain, often puzzled over why someone would dedicate so much of his life to something as obscure as archaic Greek law in a profession once hilariously characterized by Henry Beard as "the fast-paced, high-paying world of the classics." Whatever their doubts, they have always been supportive and encouraging, and their faith at the darkest of times has been sustaining.

Finally, but most importantly, I express my heartfelt appreciation for my wonderful wife, Laura. The completion of this book was complicated by a variety of factors both professional and personal, and the combined weight of it all can not have made me an easy person to live with, much less love. Throughout everything, she exhibited a constancy, patience, and devotion to make Penelope herself proud. And, as if all this were not enough, just as this project went out for the final round of peer reviews, she brought into the world our beautiful son, Trajan. For these things and so much else, Laura, you will always have my love and gratitude. Thank you.

Writing Authority

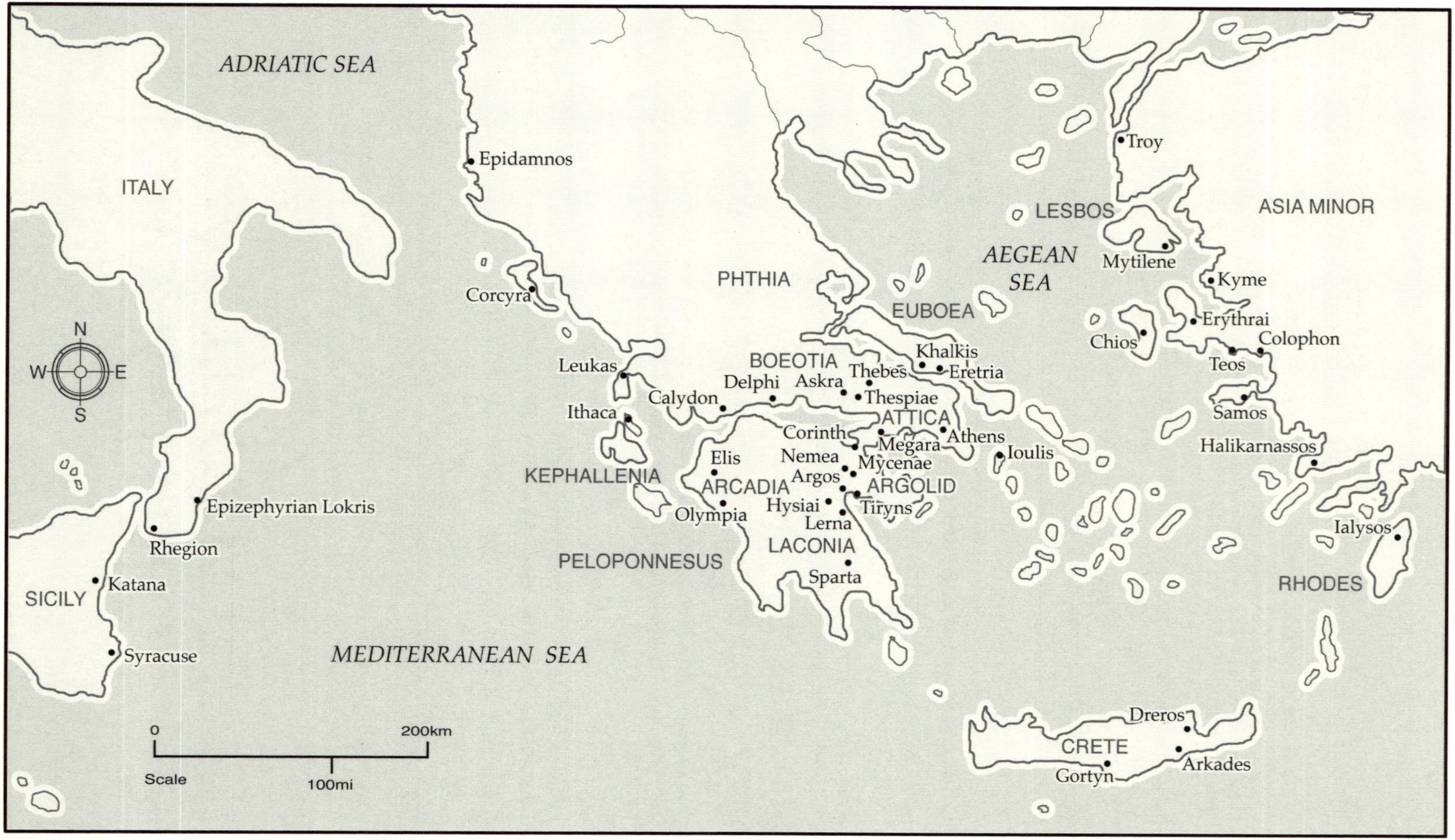
ADRIATIC SEA
ITALY
Epidamnos
Corcyra
Leukas
Ithaca
KEPHALLENIA
Calydon
Delphi
PHTHIA
BOEOTIA
Askra
Thebes
Thespiae
Khalkis
Eretria
EUBOEA
AEGEAN SEA
LESBOS
Troy
Mytilene
ASIA MINOR
Kyme
Erythrai
Chios
Colophon
Teos
Samos
Halikarnassos
Ialysos
RHODES
ATTICA
Corinth
Megara
Athens
Ioulis
Elis
Nemea
Mycenae
Argos
ARGOLID
ARCADIA
Hysiai
Tiryns
Olympia
Lerna
LACONIA
Sparta
PELOPONNESUS
N
W
E
S
Epizephyrian Lokris
Rhegion
Katana
SICILY
Syracuse
MEDITERRANEAN SEA
0
200km
Scale
100mi
Dreros
CRETE
Arkades
Gortyn

CHAPTER ONE

Law, Justice, and Legislation in Early Greece

1. Introduction

In his *Works and Days*, the seventh-century[1] poet Hesiod railed against what he perceived as the grave miscarriage of justice in his central Greek hamlet of Askra. As part of his exposition, he sets out the myth of the devolution of man through five ages, each more degraded than the preceding one. His own age of iron, the fifth and final, would come to an end when, among a host of other problems,

> there will be no joy for the oath-keeper, neither for the just (*dikaiou*) nor good, but rather men will praise the doer of evil deeds and his outrageous behavior; there will be no justice (*dikê*) at hand, nor reverent shame. And the dastard will injure the better man, speaking against him with crooked pronouncements (*skoliois muthoisin*), and he will swear an oath on them.[2]

Some form of the Greek word typically taken as equivalent to the word justice, *dike* (δίκη), appears twice in these five lines, once in its adjectival form, "the just" (for whom there will be no joy), and once in a substantive form, as Hesiod tells us there will be no justice present. It is clear from the context of the passage that Hesiod considered the future lack of justice to go hand in hand with the departure of reverent shame, *aidôs*, the prevalence of "outrage," *hubris*, and the swearing of false oaths.[3] Hence with false testimony and *hubris* ruling the day, justice and reverence would be driven out, and there would be no protection against evil.[4]

To underscore his point, Hesiod moves directly from this general description to an admonitory fable which even the *basileis*,[5] the chieftains of

Thespiae,[6] could appreciate: the tale of the hawk and the nightingale.[7] The raptor of the story explains to his captured prey, who cries pitifully from the pain of her captor's talons, that she is now at his mercy: he is the stronger and thus has the power to do with her as he pleases. He may make a meal of her or set her free, but the decision is entirely his, and her protests are futile. There is no retribution for the hawk, who in Hesiod's version ends the fable with the arrogant proclamation that only a fool resists the strong, for then the weaker will suffer pain as well as shame.[8]

Hesiod has plainly connected the perpetration of merciless injustice to the position of the *basileis*, and he continues by associating both of these issues more specifically still, narrowing his focus from the end of ages in an atmosphere of wickedness and lawlessness to his particular quarrel with his brother Perses. As is well known, Hesiod had apparently lost a dispute over his and Perses' patrimony, largely—Hesiod suspects—because his brother suborned the less than incorruptible *basileis* of Thespiae in their adjudication of the dispute.[9] Hesiod warns his brother that the outrageous behavior of the mighty (a nexus already established around hawk-*basileis*) will ultimately crush its practitioner, no matter how temporarily prosperous.[10]

As we will have occasion to note later, Hesiod's view of the *basileis* and justice is not so uniformly dire throughout his extant corpus. But until the last twenty-five years or so, modern scholars who confronted the problem of justice and the appearance of written law in early Greece focused on Hesiod's less flattering portrait, and accepted in the main the reality of a "system" that promised violence to anything resembling fair play at the hands of those who rampantly abused their power. Moreover, Hesiod—while offering the most extensive contemporary statement on these matters—was not alone in his assessment. A variety of later ancient authorities suggested that, in the absence of written law, the potential was great for the abusive exercise of judicial power by those who were responsible for "remembering" the customs of the community upon which settlement of disputes was based.

THE CENTRAL ARGUMENT of the present study is that that the appearance of written law in the ancient Greek *polis* arose from the inadequacy of existing custom as a structure of authority to regulate elite competition within what had previously been a functional legal culture. Rapid social, economic, and political change, combined with emergent literacy, compelled Greek elites to supplement communally informed dispute resolution, based on received and accepted custom, with statutory laws that primarily addressed issues of greatest concern to the elite members of the *poleis* that adopted such statutes.

A curious chronological divide separated the introduction of alphabetic writing to the Greek world (ca. 800) from the appearance of the first written Greek laws (ca. 660). This more than century-long delay invites attention because the Greeks had employed writing for a variety of uses aside from law and had learned the technology from the Phoenicians, who themselves belonged to a well-established Near Eastern tradition of written law. For much of the twentieth century, scholars typically explained this delay as a product of class conflict. In their view, the elites who controlled the emerging *poleis* dispensed justice from memory and therefore resisted writing down laws as it might undermine their ability to settle disputes, presumably to their own advantage. By following such practices, they enriched their households and maintained their grip on the social, political, and economic reins of their communities. Only when the yeomanry became indispensable to the defense of the state as hoplite soldiers, so the argument goes, did the nonelites agitate for written law as a guarantor of their judicial rights and a protection against elite abuse.

Over the last twenty years or so, scholars have begun to challenge this view. While my own work has been informed by some of these criticisms, I argue that any understanding of Greek law in its seventh- and sixth-century context must rely largely on evidence from the Archaic period. The Athenian literary tradition after 400 dominates the Classical sources that speak about early law. Dependence on these sources has in many respects reproduced fourth-century Athenian attitudes, which had come to recognize written law as the only legitimate source of legal authority. I instead focus attention on the surviving literature of eighth- through early sixth-century Greece, as well as the epigraphic evidence of early legislative activity. This evidence is less contaminated by later theorizing about the relationship of justice to written law, though it is certainly not without its own complications. I employ a legal anthropological approach to the surviving poetry attributed to the epic poets Homer and Hesiod. By identifying and analyzing the trouble cases that appear in this literature, I argue that the Greek world prior to written law had a functional and consistent, if not altogether complex, legal culture. That legal culture featured meaningful participation of the wider community in the settling of disputes on the basis of assumptions about approved and disapproved behaviors, which forces us to examine more closely the indications in our evidence of judicial abuse by the elites: can these be taken at face value, or are there other considerations lurking behind the complaints some Greek authors leveled at those responsible for the administration of justice? Furthermore, the communal and competitive nature of Greek legal culture rendered it highly unlikely that elites could have systematically corrupted the judicial process toward their own ends and provokes us to wonder why some Greeks eagerly sought out their decisions if those judgments were indeed so routinely crooked. Epic song itself was a source of legitimacy or sanction for certain behaviors, both reflecting the values of the society at large and at the same time reinforcing them, and these values would have often determined the ways in which disputants pursued their quarrels and how, if it came to third-party arbitration, those quarrels would be regulated or resolved. In a society where change had moved relatively slowly, the epic tradition had the capacity to keep pace with the evolving assumptions and mores of the community.

One of the keys in interpreting the rise of written law is to appreciate the relationship between traditional modalities of creating legitimate authority, the special challenges introduced by the limited spread of literacy, and the actual content of early written laws, all within the context of the rapid social and economic changes taking place in Greece from the late eighth century through the beginning of the sixth. Even if there had been appalling *systematic* judicial abuse prior to the writing of law, it is unclear that many Greeks of this period would have seen written law as the answer to this problem. The ability to read and comprehend lengthy texts was still significantly restricted, and our evidence as late as the end of the sixth century suggests that high-level literacy remained a limited skill: in other words, a written law that replaced traditional precepts but that few could read would merely have replaced one type of elite power with another or at least emphasized different abilities belonging to the same elite group. Furthermore, certain voices within the Greek literary tradition relate details—and the existing epigraphic evidence provides reasons to credit them—that suggest a somewhat "conservative" purpose in the work of some of the early lawgivers. Writing, rather than being employed to achieve social leveling, instead aimed at creating legitimacy and authority for certain laws. This was necessary for two reasons. First, with the writing down of the epic traditions, and the diffusion of increasingly canonical and fossilized versions of those traditions, epic songs became increasingly irrelevant to the reality around them, a dynamic exacerbated by the significant socioeconomic and demographic changes taking place in the Greek world. Second, the vast majority of what we find in surviving early laws, as well as later literary accounts of the content of other laws, suggests that the "writing up," or drafting, of laws occupied the attention of early legislators far more than their "writing down," or recording. That is to say, much of early written law concerns issues that had arisen rather recently as a result of the *polis* and related pressures, issues that did not impinge significantly upon the Homeric world. Monumental inscription imparted to such new laws the legitimate authority that could not be found for them in the epic tradition and that could reinforce the legitimacy of new provisions regarding, clarifying, or emending older customs as the now increasingly static epics grew further out of touch with the realities of the Greek world-experience and as those older and accepted customs now impinged upon the members of the community in a new set of socioeconomic and political realities.

I argue that the evidence of the seventh- and sixth-century legislation suggests that written laws emerged first and foremost as a response to aristocratic or elite concerns about their own number. A definition is in order. By "elite," I follow Sara Forsdyke's very useful characterization: those who possessed political privilege "based on the claim to some combination of wealth, good birth, divine favor, and excellence (*aretê*) in some socially recognized attainment, whether prowess in battle, political skill, or some other cultural practice."[11] (As Forsdyke states, such elites exercised a monopoly on public office in Archaic Greece.) The laws issued under their leadership covered, among other things, inheritance, adoption, and marriage. In and of themselves, these areas of the law are by no means of interest solely to elites, but the paramount focus of much early legislation was in controlling the allocation of property, even in some cases preserving a current, disproportionate distribution or equilibrium of the ownership of land and other wealth. In addition, we find laws restricting both the iteration (or, if one prefers, ensuring the rotation) of magistracies and the ostentatious display of wealth at funerals. What these laws indicate, I argue, is an attempt by elites to prevent the concentration of various social, political, and economic resources in the hands of too narrow a circle of the elite, such that one group of families, or even one individual household, might come to dominate the public life of the community; whether they succeeded (and often they did not) is another matter. These considerations ultimately lead us to the conclusion that written law emerges in early Greece, not as a result of a deeply dysfunctional legal culture, popular agitation, the expression of communal control over the *polis*, or a range of other variously suggested explanations. Rather, we should understand the appearance of written law as a means by which elites attempted to regulate their own competition for prominence and sought to invest those statutes with authority by giving them monumental, written form.

The availability of established, written rules to which all could refer was only later, and to some degree quite accidentally, a victory for a wider segment of the community in many Greek *poleis*. Indeed, as has also become clear, writing for public purposes may have been as much an instrument of power and legitimization as an instrument for greater judicial and political parity. In the early days of written law, the elites of various Greek *poleis* were responding to radical social and economic changes that heightened tensions among the elites themselves and fueled the agonistic impulses within aristocratic culture to new and dangerous dimensions in many Archaic *poleis*. The writing down of laws was an attempt at stabilization, undertaken by those who possessed authority within the *polis*.

2—Perspectives on Early Greek Law and Justice, Ancient and Modern

For Greeks living in the fifth century—whether Herodotus, a technically traitorous Spartan king, or a captivated Athenian audience—among the many things that set Hellenic culture apart from the world of the *barbaroi* was the special place occupied in it by the law. The exiled Spartan monarch Demaratos, as counselor to the Persian king Xerxes, could explain to his host and benefactor what made his erstwhile countrymen such formidable foes. "They are the most gallant men on earth," he explained of the Spartans, "for they are free—but not altogether so. They have as the despot over them Law, and they fear him much more than your men fear you."[12] This "quintessentially Greek idea that the Law was above all men"[13] only stands out in greater relief when, predictably, the bemused Great King politely dismissed Demaratos and took no heed of the Spartan's warning, ignorant of its true import.[14]

Employing Sparta as an example speaks directly to several aspects of the problematic relationship between written law and society in the Greek world down to the time of Herodotus. As is well known, Sparta's central "constitutional" document, the Great Rhetra, was probably preserved in writing; as for the vast majority of their more quotidian enactments, the Spartans notoriously chose to leave those unwritten.[15] But the words Herodotus placed in the mouth of a Spartan would have rung no less true for his Athenian audience ca. 440–430.[16] The Athenians—in this as in so many other ways—had traveled down a quite different path, having fixed in writing an increasing number of their laws at least since the time of Drakon's legislation of ca. 621.[17] Still, even for the more statute-friendly Athenians, "the law" in the fifth century was by no means strictly written law: tragedians and politicians alike continued to explore and proclaim the force of "unwritten law" at Athens until the very end of the fifth century.[18] That statute and custom could coexist was never doubted[19] until specific circumstances at the very end of the century awakened the Athenians to the malleability and abusive potential of unwritten law in the hands of clever and ill-intentioned people.[20]

With the fourth century, Greek political and moral philosophy began to grow into its maturity, with Plato as its avatar. While recently scholars have mitigated the picture of economic and social upheaval once thought characteristic of the fourth century,[21] it was nevertheless an age of political and constitutional stress in the Greek world. Submerged in an atmosphere of ideological tension and competing claims over the past at Athens[22] and civil war and revolution elsewhere in Greece, serious thinkers turned their attention as never before to the essential structures of political life, and accordingly their attention fell upon the law and its origins. It was a question of frequent importance for Plato and Aristotle, to whom we will have occasion to return often in what follows. For the time being, we may note an intersection of two of the former's ruminations.

The first of our passages from Plato is the rather famous scene from *Phaedrus*, where the founder of the Academy imagines the following interaction between the Egyptian god Thoth and an Egyptian pharaoh, Thamus:

> When they came to the letters, "This invention, O king," said Thoth, "will make the Egyptians wiser and will improve their memories; for it is an elixir of memory and wisdom that I have discovered." But he (the king) replied, "Most ingenious Thoth, one man has the ability to beget arts, but the ability to judge of their usefulness or harmfulness to their users belongs to another; and now you, who are the father of letters, have been led by your affection to ascribe to them a power the opposite of that which they really possess. For this invention will produce forgetfulness in the minds of those who learn to use it, because they will not practice their memory. Their trust in writing, produced by external characters which are no part of themselves, will discourage the use of their own memory within them."[23]

The other excerpt, less picturesque, comes from *Laws*:

> Let no one persuade us, friends, that a *polis* could change its laws more quickly and easily by another way than through the governance of those holding power; neither at present has such happened nor could it happen hereafter.[24]

In these separate passages, Plato has concerned himself with transformations of different sorts. The first demonstrates Plato's theoretical reticence regarding the consequences for the human intellect and human society in learning the art of writing. In the modern, highly literate West, the idea that literacy could be deleterious is counterintuitive. On the other hand, the philosopher's observation in the *Laws* touches upon a more restricted and obvious notion: states change laws, or have their laws changed for them, most expeditiously under the auspices and approval of those who exercise authority within the political community. Whatever reactions the modern reader may have to either sentiment, neither would have struck Plato's fourth-century audience as particularly shocking or perverse; the propositions were, if less transparent in the case of the first passage, more or less readily acceptable, laying the groundwork for the wider arguments toward which Plato built in each of these dialogues.

In an earlier age, however, these concepts—along with the ideas of the sovereignty of law expressed in the mouths of Herodotean characters—would not have been so apparent to the Greeks. The Archaic age of Greece was witness to far-reaching and fundamental changes in the societies of the Aegean world, southern Italy, and Sicily, changes that touched on nearly every sphere of the cultural and political experience of contemporary Greeks. Demographics, politics, economics, religious life, intellectual activity, social hierarchies—all were transformed in these critical centuries. A watershed event during this period—arguably *the* watershed event—was the introduction of alphabetic writing into Greece. From a few preliminary and experimental characters scratched on potsherds, through the rough-hewn and inelegant, albeit poignant, verses preserved as graffiti on pottery,[25] to the transcription and composition of epic and "lyric" verses and the employment of writing for the public recording of laws, the Greeks gradually expanded the uses and refined the employment of this new tool for which later Greeks, such as Plato, might express reservation.[26]

Indeed, over the course of the seventh and early sixth centuries, many Greek communities began to commit to written form perhaps some older, orally preserved customs but more often new rules governing hitherto nonexistent issues.[27] This step was neither a natural nor an obvious one; for whatever inspiration may have come from the Near East (and the Greeks were certainly willing to credit all sorts of things to Near Eastern and Egyptian influence, rightly and wrongly), their traditions about lawgivers placed them all squarely in a Greek context,[28] and what survives of early written law in the Greek world betrays little apparent influence from the East.[29]

In the modern West, of course, law and justice—despite the performative vestiges preserved in oral witness testimony and certain types of punishment[30]—are largely based on literate modes of thought and communication: an established body of written statutes, the admissibility of documents (including written testimony), the referral to recorded previous decisions (precedent), the primacy of a written instrument over hearsay, reputation, and so forth. All of these literate modes of reaching legal truth are rooted, often quite explicitly, in a legal order or system.[31] From this perspective, it is easy to understand as progressive or evolutionary the transition from dispute settlement based on spoken argument and openly influenced by a wide range of extrinsic factors, to the adjudication of conflict with at least some reference to a body of written norms or rules. Though scholars have increasingly come to eschew approaches that speak consciously of progress or evolution, there remains a tacit understanding in much of the general literature on the Greek world that the Greeks—by writing down certain badly needed and newly developed rules—moved from a "primitive," "tribal," or "fragmentary" (even "irrational") system of justice to one which is somehow more advanced, more organized, more rational.

For the Greeks in any given Archaic community at moments of legislation, such distinctions were not, of course, recognized. They were not consciously evolving their society—real people, in real communities, sought to address problems that the revolutionary conditions of the Archaic age had produced; who perceived these problems, and why, remains to be discussed later. For the time being, we may note that the eighth through sixth centuries were an age of great political and social ferment. The writing down of "judicial" customs, as well as expansions of the rule base in a given community, was just one of the responses to the ruptures created in the social fabric. The members of the community who turned to the strategy of writing laws, at some level had come to believe that the traditional means of settling conflict within communities could no longer adequately address such ruptures. The settlement of disputes and the administration of justice appear as important concerns in the literary evidence that either predates or is contemporary with the movement toward legislation in the emerging *polis* as both institution and citizen struggled to define their mutual relationship in this type of community.

The approach employed in this study represents a more thorough attempt than previously has been undertaken to situate the appearance of written law in the legal culture of early Greece and, as a result, achieves a fuller and more nuanced set of conclusions; it nevertheless owes a good deal of intellectual inspiration to the work of Walter Eder. Two and a half decades ago, Eder advanced his "unconventional hypothesis" that the Twelve Tables of Rome and Solon's code for Athens were attempts by the ruling aristocracies of those two cities to secure their preeminent position in the face of popular agitation and social instability.[32] Working independently, Michael Gagarin expressed serious doubts about the interpretation that written laws were a response to democratic demands for legal reform against an aristocratic judicial monopoly.[33] These suggestions have not been exhaustively pursued to date. Other scholars have acknowledged in certain cases the possibility of a more conservative purpose behind the writing of laws, but such notices have generally been asides or sub-arguments in studies dedicated to some other aspect of law in Archaic Greece.[34]

As for Eder's study, it examined the aforementioned particular cases of Archaic Rome and Archaic Athens but not the general appearance of the earliest written laws in Archaic Greece. Furthermore, his argument provides opportunities to pursue avenues he left unexplored. The first of these involves an attempt to place his hypothesis on grounds other than the potentially circular basis of his otherwise stimulating paper: there is, after all, the use of problematic evidence from the Twelve Tables to fill in the blanks of early Athenian law, and then general observations about Greek law are adduced in support of observations about the Twelve Tables. In addition, the question of the involvement of Greek elites in encouraging written legislation is one deserving of consideration in its own right, and the great differences between the Greek world ca. 600 and Rome in the fifth century are probably sufficient to cloud rather than to clarify the issue.

Eder characterized his hypothesis as unconventional because he sought to challenge the prevailing wisdom that the nonelite citizens of Archaic *poleis* demanded laws be written down to curb the abuses of the leaders of a given Greek city-state. As a result of the Hesiodic evidence and the testimony presented by later authors, modern scholars before Eder typically interpreted the writing down of laws as an essentially reformist act. With the forms of the laws fixed, the elites presumably found their discretionary judicial power seriously circumscribed, as they were no longer able to "remember" the laws or determine legal truth however they liked. The previously powerless elements in society, through the agency of various military and economic changes, were in a position to agitate for change and did so. Among their demands, the traditional body of interpretation held, was that the tool of writing be used to protect the community against the arbitrary, crooked justice that Hesiod so eloquently deplored. The elite becomes rather a passive party in the process, dragged kicking and screaming the entire way as their judicial power and privilege crumbled; before Eder, modern scholarship largely denied an active or constructive role to those people best positioned to effect change in the laws and administration of justice in early Greece.

The pioneering modern commentators on early Greek law very much took Hesiod at his word in their reconstructions of how and why the Greeks came to write law, and they saw that development as one largely directed against perceived judicial abuse by the elites and as having taken place in a context of class tension if not outright struggle. Sir Henry Sumner Maine, in his *Ancient Law*,[35] attempted to locate the origins of Greek legal concepts in the nature of *themistes* pronounced by Zeus in the *Iliad*, an effort that clearly violated the tripartite classification for modern law that had been worked out by thinkers such as Bentham and Austin.[36] Law was, at that stage, scarcely even a body of custom but remained, in Maine's famous turn of phrase, "in the air." There was no prescriptive law; only a definitive statement after the fact, pronounced with regard to a particular case by a kingly judge directly "inspired" at the moment of judgment.[37]

However, Maine believed that the world of Homer was one in which the sacredness of kingship was on the wane and individual kings gave way to a usurpation of their authority by the aristocratic chiefs (i.e., the *basileis*). This particular change Maine saw as a universal development among European Archaic societies, as oligarchies assumed the functions of government and kept only the names—if even that—of the older, monarchical institutions.[38] While Maine was careful not to overstate the role that elite abuse of judicial power might have played in the appearance of written law, he did cite as a secondary factor the popularity written laws would enjoy, due to the "protection which they afforded against the frauds of the privileged oligarchy."[39]

Continental scholarship of the ensuing half century proved less cautious than Maine. Fustel sought to couch the rise of law and other civic institutions in terms of the evolution of primitive religious thought, with its emphases on prescriptive rules and attendant sanctions for the breach of same.[40] Just as society issued from the family, so did its laws, meaning that for a long time "justice" could not help but be highly personal and therefore given to what appears to modern eyes as inequity. A generation later, German scholars at the turn of the twentieth century tended to view the entire question of Greek judicial elaboration and legislation purely in terms of class struggle and the redress of aristocratic abuse. The wealthy families now ruled as they pleased[41] and supported their position through their familial connections and a superiority of military training and equipment that only the elite might afford.[42] Thus Greece entered the age of class warfare in the seventh century, as the disfranchised majority sought to wrest its social and political rights from an elite regime that in most states was becoming increasingly irrelevant in the face of broad-reaching economic metamorphosis. Within this interpretative framework, among the very first of those rights to which the downtrodden *demos* turned its attention was the administration of justice.[43]

The strongest expression yet of the notion that written law served as a kind of democratizing palliative appeared in America in 1930 with Robert Bonner and Gertrude Smith's study on the administration of justice from the Dark Age to the twilight of the Classical period.[44] In many ways a synthesis of their earlier scholarship, these volumes represent the most significant and influential treatment of Greek legal history since Maine himself, and many of their findings have retained force into recent decades. The authors perceived the appearance of written law in Greece as the result of social, economic, and political grievances put forth by the nonelite, who demanded the codification of law in order to ensure themselves and their rights against the manipulation of justice by the aristocracy.[45] Taken together, these earlier interpretations amount to a "democratizing" model for the appearance of written Greek law. Despite important challenges to this model, it continues to exercise significant influence on our understanding of early Greek legislation.

On different grounds, some recent interpretations have sought to reaffirm the importance of the *demos* in the evolution of Greek legal thinking in the Archaic period, in what one might characterize as a "public" model. Michael Gagarin, in *Early Greek Law*, argued for the essentially open, public, and deliberative nature of Greek adjudication before the advent of written law, obviating any claims of a judicial monopoly that elites might have exploited. Recently, Gagarin has advanced more vigorously his theory of the essentially public nature of Greek adjudication before written law (with which I agree) and argues that the decision to commit laws to writing was essentially continuous with this dynamic (with which I do not agree). According to Gagarin, the earliest written laws, through their enactment clauses, betray the essentially communal authorship and authorization of these statutes, and the physical forms of the laws indicate a more widespread ability to read them than other scholars have assumed for the last three decades.[46] Thus, he also contends that the appearance of written law had no specific class interest but rather relates to the growing sense of community and governance and the desire to make law more accessible to the community at large.

Zinon Papakonstantinou has recently stressed the importance of recognizing the multiple and coexisting "legal narratives" operating in the disputes, legislation, and adjudication of Archaic Greece. While he studiously avoids the direct question of why the Greeks first wrote down laws, Papakonstantinou clearly imagines legal processes before written law as rooted in norms widely recognized and accepted, adjudicated in a public forum, but nevertheless still very much in the "grip" of the aristocracy. He views Hesiod as an "example of the pluralism of archaic Greek law . . . [and] of alternative legal narratives," through which individuals might try "to advance their own interests" in a presumably open conceptual field of law and justice.[47] He argues for law as a vehicle for social reform though not as the product of class struggle and characterizes a more communal and public interpretation of lawmaking in early Greece as "preferable to agonistic views regarding the control of legislative power in archaic Greece."[48] Thus, for Papakonstantinou as for Gagarin, law, written or otherwise, belonged to the community at large, and he further argues that the adjudication of written law, like customs, could serve as a site of social contestation. On different grounds, Winfried Schmitz has advanced the thesis that the earliest written laws of Greece arose from and reflected the values of the peasants (*Bauern*), rooted as these were in the neighborhood and village societies of the eighth and seventh centuries.[49] These views of written Greek law as a phenomenon very much in the hands of the wider community are at odds with the present argument, and I believe there are numerous grounds for challenging their interpretations. I will reserve engaging the points of disagreement for appropriate sections of the text that follows.

Despite the prevalence of democratizing or public models, in their various forms, there have been alternative interpretations. Written law, another line of thinking goes, did not arise from the demand for equitable judicial administration but rather created the notion of law as something constant and consistently applied. In the 1940s, George Calhoun argued that writing made possible the discernment of changes over time in legal decisions and that, with the writing of laws, further changes must have been made "consciously and intentionally."[50] Subsequent generations have produced studies that attempt to understand the subtle and complex relationship that existed between custom and written law on the one hand, and literacy and orality on the other. Carol Thomas has argued that the writing down of laws allowed for the perception of judicial inequity in the early Greek *polis*, but that no such general temperament could have existed beforehand among the *demos*.[51] Jesper Svenbro has called for a reexamination of our understanding of written texts and of the act of reading in early Greece, including the ways in which a wider public would have received written laws and to whom such laws may, or may not, have been accessible.[52]

In the last half century, some scholars have emphasized understanding the emergence of written law within the context of writing and memory, among them Eric Havelock and Rosalind Thomas.[53] These pursuits have generally stressed a more organic process underlying the development of written law, where public documents tended to serve either as *aides-memoire* for public officials or where the monumental written text was meant as much to overawe as to inform; in either event, the concept of justice continued to be caught up very much in mentalities deeply rooted in older traditions and assumptions.[54] As a result, older but influential arguments regarding the connection between "literate" modes of thought and "rational" endeavors, such as the regularization of tradition and custom through written law, may be called into question as having at their base a serious conceptual difficulty.[55] Scholars have also begun to question the entire enterprise of searching for a relationship among literacy, law, and democracy altogether. James Whitley has very forcefully argued for something of a disconnect between our evidence for the prevalence of legal inscriptions and our evidence for the extent of literacy in any given region of the Archaic Greek world.[56]

Other, also largely Anglophone, studies have called into question the political or constitutional intentions of Greece's earliest attested lawgiver, Zaleukos.[57] Eder scrutinized the introduction of written law as a concession to popular demands for legislation, preferring to see an aristocratic response to preserve power *against* the growing demands for change by relatively lower elements of society.[58] Sara Forsdyke, in her examination of Archaic law as part of her study of exile and ostracism in the Archaic period, understands written law and other public institutions not, like Eder, as an elite defense against popular demands but rather as an attempt by elites to stabilize their own potentially violent rivalries with one another.[59] While her main concern is the development of Athenian responses to elite competition and its potential for violence, she sets her examination in the context of other Archaic *poleis* for which we have evidence of destabilizing intra-elite competition: as was the case, for example, at Mytilene, the inclusion of nonelite elements was designed initially to buttress the incumbent aristocratic faction, not necessarily to empower the nonelites themselves.[60]

While these different, anthropologically inspired approaches have informed the inquiry in Britain and North America, there has developed principally in German scholarship (Eder withstanding) an emphasis on interpreting the emergence of written law in Greece in normativist terms (see further, Chapter 3.1 below). Hans Julius Wolff argued that out of principles of self-help in the pre-*polis* community evolved formal procedures for judicial litigation and the establishment of written law.[61] Wolff's influence is particularly noticeable in the important work of Eberhard Ruschenbusch, one of the more prolific scholars of the problem of law in Archaic Greece, both in its abstract and its concrete dimensions, as well as in the current work of Gerhard Thür.[62] While all three scholars have contributed greatly to the dialogue regarding the development of Archaic Greek judicial procedures and legislation, an emphasis on institutional explanations and the normative force of law characterizes their work; that is, they have tended to see law as "a form of social control which is exercised by the systematic use of power of which a politically organized society disposes."[63] Their exacting work and collection of primary evidence will forever indebt students of early Greek law, but their normative assumptions regarding the imposition of central political authority do not reflect the situation in early Greece as it is currently discernible from both literary and archaeological evidence. The bicentric, or if one prefers, polyarchic, nature of political power in any Greek community in the eighth and early seventh centuries makes such formalism difficult to imagine; furthermore, the dismissal of the importance of public opinion and its pressure on Greek judicial processes before the writing of laws has led these scholars and those influenced by them (most notably and recently Raphael Sealey[64]) to ignore the importance of the community in settling disputes.

Karl-Joachim Hölkeskamp has of late advanced explanations for the emergence of written law that bridge the roles of the community (particularly as embodied in the emergent authority of the *polis*) and the development of official political and judicial institutions; namely, the *polis* sought to gain centralized control and authority over individuals and their previously semiautonomous households as an exercise in state building.[65] Hölkeskamp's theory, similar to the recent arguments of Gagarin and Papakonstantinou, emphasizes the critically important role of public opinion and pressure, though I disagree with two other features of his approach. First, he seems to employ something of an institutional fallacy; the *polis* was, of course, the collectivity of the politically empowered citizens, but Hölkeskamp arguably leaves underdeveloped the question of principal agency in any given Greek *polis*. The *polis* itself was incapable of writing down laws; we must account more precisely for the individuals (or groups) whose motivations would have led to legislation. Second, by ascribing the appearance of written law to the organs of power in a nascent state, Hölkeskamp also takes a quasi-normativist, coercive approach to understanding the law and its force in the early Greek community.

Other explanations have appeared over the years, but with less impact on the central tendencies of the relevant scholarship. Some have seen the appearance of written law as an outgrowth of the increasing awareness on the part of the Greeks of the wider Mediterranean world. Max Mühl argued over seventy years ago for the influence of Near Eastern legal traditions on the legal development of Greece, and his ideas have been cited by Robert Pounder,[66] who has argued for a connection between Near Eastern and Greek legal inscriptions on the basis of perceived apotropaic preambles in the latter.[67] Trade has also been adduced as a possible explanation for the appearance of Greek law, though this theory boasts only one notable proponent, Ronald Willetts.[68] The drive toward colonization has also enjoyed some favor as a potential explanation for the motive force behind the writing of laws, with the cross-fertilization of ideas among the colonies and colonial populations, the need for the integration of different civic traditions within certain, single foundations, and the freedom from "the restraints of conservatism" at home all advanced as potential causative factors.[69] Such explanations, however, do not account for the appearance of written laws in communities that will have had limited contact with the East, were not commercially active, or, in the case of the Greek homeland around the Aegean basin, obviously were not colonies. As this study makes clear, competition among elites provides the most coherent and comprehensive explanation for the appearance of written law in early Greece.

3—The Organization of the Argument

Having stated at the start of this chapter the fundamental outlines of the argument, I now turn to its organization.

Chapter 2 addresses first the questions surrounding primary sources for pursuing the present argument. The focus in the current study places weight precisely where I argue it belongs: on the Archaic age sources, both literary and epigraphic, that shed the most contemporary light on the nature and expectations of written law. I argue that it is the Homeric and other Archaic sources that can most illuminate the problem; for while writers of the Classical period can perhaps provide precious data about early laws that would otherwise be lost, in their interpretations of the motivations for that law they have great potential to mislead. Can we assume, a priori, that ideas of justice and law and expectations regarding the power of written statutes remained more or less static through three centuries of Greek history from Drakon to Demosthenes? Because our fourth-century sources that bear on law and adjudication and legal theory (insofar as the Greeks can be said to have thought about jurisprudence) are copious, eloquent, and sophisticated, they have the power to tempt us into accepting their interpretations as to the significance of a Solon or the designs of a Zaleukos. More caution than this is necessary. Our fifth- and fourth-century sources are overwhelmingly rooted in an Athenian perspective, of course, and we have this geographical lens to consider. Athenians of this period interpreted the Greek past, as do historical thinkers in any age, through the filter of more recent events and changes. The intellectual and sociopolitical milieu of Drakon and Solon, much less that of Hesiod or of the citizens of Dreros who drafted our oldest preserved legal inscription, was not that of Demosthenes and Aristotle.

We are probably safer, therefore, to mine our Classical sources for the preservation of apparently neutral facts or details but to remain wary of their explications of the same. If we are to understand the Greeks of the Archaic age on their own terms, and not view them through a classical glass darkly, a concentration on the sentiments of Hesiod, Solon, and other Archaic witnesses serves our purposes more appropriately. I also make the case that the epic tradition had long served as a guide for contemporaries in enforcing notions of what constituted approved and disapproved courses of action, how to pursue disputes, and what range of remedies were available to disputants. We may supplement such literary sources with the remains of the earliest laws themselves, placed within the context of the society that we may glean from archaeological remains and our historical evidence. Finally, there is much value in applying certain concepts and questions from anthropology and legal studies to the problem of disputes and their settlement in early Greece, particularly as it existed in the Homeric and Hesiodic contexts, as a means of more fully appreciating the social and cultural dimensions of juridical conflicts in the pre- and early-*polis* community.

Having established a useful interpretive framework for analyzing our early evidence of dispute settlement, in Chapter 3 I turn to a description of the patterns of trouble cases and the assumptions and dynamics that governed them in Homeric and Hesiodic Greece. That examination reveals a remarkably consistent pattern of how various classes of trouble cases were handled in epic society. That consistency, from the sources of trouble to the preferred methods for handling disputes and the range of outcomes, indicates a functional legal culture in the world of the epics; the expectations of disputants and the community involved a range of strategies and assumptions that routinely stopped short of the need for formal settlement by referees who wielded political authority. Indeed, it is not altogether clear in the Archaic community how central was public arbitration under the auspices of the *basileis* or, in those places where it became a prominent feature in the life of the *polis*, why it did so. Questions of the degree to which such mediation was voluntary or even in most cases necessary, compulsory, or open to complete circumvention through extralegal self-help, all bear closely on the issue of presumed aristocratic judicial power and how this was tempered by the weight and influence of public opinion and pressure.

In Chapter 4, I test underlying assumptions of what I have characterized above as the democratizing and public models of early Greek written law. Particularly, I examine those assumptions bearing on the issue of literacy and the accessibility of public inscriptions to the average citizen, as well as notions that popular elements in a Greek *polis* would have expected written law to have been a guarantor of fairer judicial practice and thus would have demanded it. After all, the idea that written law would protect nonelites against systematic miscarriages of justice carries with it a necessary implication: those who had presumably found themselves oppressed in a system based on purely customary dispute settlement (rooted in orally preserved traditions) must have possessed the ability to read inscribed laws in order for such laws to have any more benefit to them. A law that no one but a literate minority—or no one but those in the employ of the dominant elite—could read would be no less susceptible to elite manipulation than the customary justice previously dispensed from "memory." It is important to understand not only who could read in the early Greek community but also with what level of skill and comprehension.

The extent to which aristocratically controlled mediation could have preserved political and social peace within the *polis*, and the shortcomings of such a system in a world of flux with no permanent referents, speaks directly to the problem of how order broke down within the community, particularly among its leading lights. It also helps to elucidate the factors that led the prominent members of the community to establish standards by which they might control the destructive tendencies of their competition for status and power in a changing set of economic, social, and political circumstances, problems which I address in Chapter 5.

Next, Chapters 6 and 7 present an analysis of the sources for the earliest written laws and what I believe they reveal within the framework of the evidence presented in the preceding chapters. I offer an interpretation that the aristocracy played the leading role in the writing of law in the Archaic communities of ancient Greece. It was imperative for them to regulate the affairs of the emergent *polis* on their own terms, before the basis of their power as a group, and their competition for it as individuals, eroded in a changing economic and social environment, but *not* primarily in response to pressures from the hoplite or other potentially disfranchised or disadvantaged groups. Rather, they aimed to address their own anxieties, as I describe them, seeking to clarify and amplify the rule base for realms of life of special concern to them, a process that only secondarily and indirectly benefitted the rest of the community. As traditional, customary ways of handling the agonistic impulses of aristocratic society were breaking down and new problems arose pertaining to the government of the *polis*, some referent was needed to control access to and accumulation of the various social, economic, and political resources necessary for elite competition. Finally, I argue that inscription was a means not only of making permanent such referents but also of investing the laws—whether written down or written up—with the kind of mystifying authority that epic had once enjoyed.

Again, this is a book that asks the question why the Greeks first began to write laws, and the heart of my answer to that particular inquiry resides in the final two chapters. However, I believe that we cannot answer that question in isolation and that it requires us to understand the history of early Greek adjudication from its preliterate origins through the rise of the first written laws; this book is therefore also a history of the origins of Greek jurisprudence. As such, all of the subjects I have outlined above are of a piece. We cannot situate written laws in early Greece, or the impetus behind or authorship of the same, in any sort of context without considering carefully the nature of adjudication preceding them and without attempting to understand what sort of legal culture the Greeks already possessed as they began to inscribe laws and whether there was something dysfunctional about that culture that impelled such a significant alteration in the way Greeks conceptualized and ultimately published certain laws in written form. Nor can we, I believe, frame an analysis of the earliest written law without asking that fundamental legal question, cui bono? For whom do the earliest attested laws provide the greatest perceived benefit, and what cultural, social, and economic changes may have led to early attempts to give laws permanent form? Without first answering those questions, we cannot properly understand what laws the Greeks chose to develop and commit to writing or why they did so.

CHAPTER TWO

Approaches to Early Greek Legal Thought and Practice

Anyone who seeks to engage the problem of early Greek dispute settlement, law, and so on confronts immediately the problem of sources and what they may be able to tell us about the emergence of written law in early Greece. In terms of "contemporary" evidence, one might assemble the epics of Homer, Hesiod, the various fragments assigned to either poet, the remains of "lyric" poets, and the Homeric hymns whose dates likely belong to the years between the middle of the seventh and middle of the sixth centuries. This relatively large storehouse of literary information could prove quite useful in reconstructing early Greek legal thought, though as anyone who has dared wade into the waters of Archaic Greek historiography already knows, virtually nothing about this literature or what it represents is uncontroversial. We have, in addition to these potential literary avenues for our inquiry, a number of legal inscriptions dating to the Archaic period, but these are either often fragmentary or preserved as later copies or redactions of the originals. Nevertheless, they serve as valuable lenses through which to view what problems Greeks of the period felt compelled to address through legislation.

Privileging this information in a way that allows a reconstruction of the atmosphere in which written statutes appear necessitates an approach that combines an appreciation of three separate dynamics. First, it is imperative that we not succumb to the temptation to use too easily the extensive legal material from fourth-century Athens, either to fill in frustrating gaps in our knowledge or to guide our interpretations of what law and dispute meant for Greeks of the Late Geometric and early Archaic ages. Reasonably straightforward historical statements in the pages of an Aristotle, a Demosthenes, or an Aeschines *may* provide details that aid us in determining certain events of their past, what I characterized as neutral statements of fact in the previous chapter. These could include the provisions of an older law or the reported activity of a certain early lawgiver, though even these assertions will often require caution. However, when fourth-century writers make claims regarding the motivations and agendas of early legislators or offer interpretations about the reception or importance of written law three or even two centuries prior, we must be skeptical. Fourth-century Athenian jurisprudence, while less developed than that of Middle and Late Republican Rome, nevertheless represented a complex and sophisticated system that is neither analogous nor compatible with the institutional machinery likely available to the early *polis*. Contemporary observers proceeded first and foremost from what was most familiar, so we may doubt the degree to which they appreciated the historical realities of the Homeric world or periods as recent as the sixth century.[1] Furthermore, recent episodes in Athenian history, such as the reign of the Thirty, combined with ideologically driven debates at Athens regarding constitutional legitimacy to heighten animosity toward aristocratic/oligarchic government and sharpen citizens' appreciation of statutes as the only reliable repository of the rule of law and the supremacy of the *demos*. Considerations such as these necessarily colored the perspectives and accounts of fourth-century writers and render highly suspect their observations regarding the significance of early legislative activity.

Second, it is necessary to appreciate the importance of epic, not only for its potential in helping us understand Greek values and assumptions in the eighth and early seventh centuries, but also for what it can reveal about the nature of Greek legal culture before the dawn of written law. The key to unpacking legal culture from epic comes through the analysis of disputes—their sources, courses, and resolution, or lack thereof. Disputes play a prominent role in this literature, and therefore the epics promise to reveal much about the norms, processes, and sociocultural factors that guided dispute resolution. Epic was didactic: it reproduced and reinforced norms and practices, expressing both implicitly and explicitly what constituted approved and disapproved behavior, as well as the rewards and consequences for each. Because epic constituted a *muthos*, an authoritative statement, it served as a vehicle for reproducing the fundamental norms by which Greeks expected one another to conduct themselves and interact with other members of the community. As such, epic articulated and preserved the rule base of early Greek society. Furthermore, since epic had the capacity to change incrementally over time, its relevance and role as *muthos* could keep pace with gradual transformations in the society that produced it and that in turn influenced it. Thus, in the case of Homer we possess a literary record that can illuminate generally Greek culture and society during the Late Geometric period and into the opening stages of the Archaic. Additionally, Hesiod provides us, especially in his *Works and Days*, with an individual perspective of one who has recently suffered disappointment at the hands of his community's juridical practices.

Finally, in order to extract the shape of Archaic Greek law from the sources of that time, we must deploy a coherent methodology, one that will allow us to see Greek legal culture in its entirety rather than through the lens of a few well-known cases. This method, I argue, can be derived from anthropology and legal studies. Students of early Greek adjudication have turned to anthropological insights before, but the results, I would suggest, are incomplete. Many analyses have focused on the most spectacular instances of dispute in the literature, those that have proven difficult to resolve and have resorted to public and formal means of resolution. While such litigation can prove instructive in understanding aspects of a legal system, commentators in legal anthropology and legal studies now recognize that such a narrow focus will distort the resultant picture.

What I propose here is an approach best understood as trouble-case processualism. This method seeks to examine all the various disputes, or trouble cases, we find in a community, great and small, and the various considerations and strategies the disputants entertain in pursuing, regulating, or resolving their problems. Such an examination reveals more quotidian sources of dispute, the informal means through which neighbors resolve problems short of violence or formal arbitration, and the larger system of communication among members of a legal community, communication of which formal dispute resolution plays only a part. In taking a more holistic approach to all the various processes to which trouble cases give rise, including the norms and social assumptions that inform them, we can describe a legal culture and the degree to which it functions or not.

For the early Greeks, it is clear that the vast majority of disputes possessed a highly public dimension, with outcomes negotiated either in direct view, and with the input, of the larger community, or at the very least with an eye to its reaction to the disputants' competing claims and actions in pursuing their conflict. This participation of the wider community in the process of dispute resolution and regulation in early Greece is fundamental to understanding the juridical assumptions and practices of the Late Geometric and early Archaic periods. If the folk, the *laos* or *laoi*, engaged routinely and consistently in the processes of dispute resolution and regulation, and had a significant impact on the maintenance of communal peace, then the implications are great for our analysis of the legal culture that preceded and ultimately produced the earliest written laws.

1—The Problem of Athenian Historiography for Early Greek Law

The largest extant collection of ancient prose reflections, observations, and opinions on Greek law is found in fourth-century Athenian literature, in the form of histories, forensic speeches, and political philosophy. These sources have been extraordinarily useful over the past two decades in reconstructing the shape of Athenian law in the Classical period,[2] and the temptation can be overwhelming to use this information to fill in the infuriating gaps in our evidence for the Archaic period. As we shall see, however, reliance on these sources, no matter how alluring, must be avoided: the political and ideological climate at Athens—which necessarily and often explicitly cited the role of (written) law in social maintenance—affected any and all observations emanating from the end of the fifth century onward. Precisely because the late fifth- and fourth-century Athenian sources represent extensive potential evidence for an inquiry into Greek law, some justification is necessary in rejecting the vast majority of it for our present purposes. Later claims about the nature of Drakon's or Solon's laws, about the nature of law generally and its role in society, or about what imparts authority to laws, are inescapably refocused through three critical lenses. First, Athens' own recent constitutional history, and the self-conscious debates that took place among Athenians regarding their constitutional origins, necessarily implicated quasi-historical or even ahistorical arguments and assumed a necessary tension between oligarchic and democratic government. This conceptualization of polity and its underlying class tensions also affected a second contextual difficulty, namely the identification by Athenians of popular government with the rule of law as a part of democratic ideology. Third, while Athenian jurors continued, by means of their votes, to apply their own sense of what was just in the cases they heard, the legislative procedures established at the end of the fifth/beginning of the fourth centuries, along with a permanent and central state archive, betrays that the Athenians were becoming increasingly statute minded and document minded, and this likewise affected their notions of law: by the fourth century when Athenians thought of law, they first and foremost intended *written* law, articulated through what had become a rigorous process of legitimization.[3]

The emergence of conscious and competing political ideologies about the proper form of the Athenian constitution, emerging in the late fifth and continuing into the fourth century, had a potentially significant impact on the ways writers of Athenian history interpreted their past.[4] Proponents of various forms of constitution—extreme oligarchy, moderate oligarchy, hoplite democracy, or radical democracy—began to refer to the past in their contemporary political debates, assigning to famous lawgivers and reformers the authorship of the *patrios politeia*. Of course, the ancestral constitution posited by any particular author or interested political group might bear a striking and suspicious resemblance to whatever he or they conceived as the appropriate way to govern Athens in the late fifth and fourth centuries. Thus, constitutional history only became a concern, and a highly political one at that, in Athens during and after the late fifth century.[5] It is at this point that Solon slowly becomes in Athenian imagination the father of democracy and the author of a constitution: Herodotus had known him primarily as one of the Seven Sages and repeated an entertaining, and chronologically impossible, anecdote about him while mentioning his laws only in passing;[6] Thucydides, inarguably a far more critical historian and a man willing to challenge the Athenians' political myths, says nothing about Solon in his description of earlier Greek history.

With the rise of antidemocratic critiques around the time of the Peloponnesian War, politicians who favored a more limited form of democracy (or its dismantling altogether) began to claim that Solon framed a system that was intended largely to keep control in the hands of the ancient and aristocratic organs of the state, especially the Areopagus.[7] In these debates, more moderate opponents of radical democracy offered up Kleisthenes as responsible for having adjusted that constitution to allow more popular organs of government, but still within acceptable limits. For critics of Athenian democracy, Ephialtes and Pericles became the villains of the piece, as corrupters of the constitution who brought it to its current state.[8] As these debates continued, and pro-democratic voices managed over time to co-opt Solon to their side, even Drakon quite stunningly entered the picture, as the opposition now credited him with a constitution that was supposedly the true and ancestral form of Athenian government. Such debates no doubt influenced orators, Atthidographers, and the author of the Aristotelian *Athenaion Politeia*; the last of these certainly adduced, albeit confusedly, Drakon's supposed constitution, assuming it was not an even later interpolation.[9]

Thus the Athenians' interpretation of their past was couched in a highly politicized debate, in which the icons of Athenian history were called forth to serve the contemporary ideological aims of those invoking them. Recent Athenian history, of course, gave particular urgency to these debates, and cast a long shadow over Athenian notions of the relationships among law, writing, and the form of government. Traumatic political events, both external and internal to Athens, had shaped the Athenian historical experience dating back to the beginning of the Peloponnesian War, events that revolved around strife between democratic and oligarchic interests. Thucydides marked the eruption of such party strife in Epidamnos as the first step in Athens' march to war with Sparta.[10] During the course of the Peloponnesian War, the Athenians had replaced their democracy with an oligarchy of the Four Hundred, and the issue of the laws and their legitimacy were of importance both in bringing the oligarchic coup to pass as well as in rallying resistance to it.[11] Furthermore, the democracy that returned to power in 410 aimed to prevent future arguments based on so-called ancestral laws and constitutions by establishing a board of *anagrapheis* to collect, determine, and redact the laws of the *polis*.[12]

The work of that board was interrupted by a junta whose discredit far surpassed that of the Four Hundred: the Thirty Tyrants, the narrow, oligarchic regime installed with Spartan backing at the end of the war, in 404/3.[13] Part of this new government's brief was "to draw up the ancestral laws (*patrious nomous*), by which they would run the government,"[14] and under cover of restoring the ancestral regime, the Thirty repealed fifth-century laws that had helped ensure democratic power and conducted what would appear to have been a purge of older laws ("the laws of Solon"), presumably based on the degree to which certain of these were not "genuinely" Solonian.[15] Soon, the Thirty turned their attention to the seizure of property, the pursuit of private political grievances, and arrests and murders—judicial and otherwise—which resulted in the deaths of approximately fifteen hundred Athenians, or at least 5 percent of the surviving citizen population.[16]

Understandably, once democracy was restored, Athenians imagined that tensions between oligarchic and democratic elements involved reprisal, exile, and often bloodshed; what made the reconciliation under the restored democracy so remarkable was its uniqueness and, in a sense, the perception of its fragility. Long after the restoration, Athenian litigants continued to raise the specter of the Thirty's brutality in their court speeches,[17] and the memory was far from an abstract one. Though the Athenian democracy enjoyed stability until its overthrow by the Macedonians in 322, ideological struggles and factional violence still gripped the Greek world around them in the fourth century.[18] Xenophon records a number of instances from the first quarter of the period,[19] and Isocrates wrote of a particularly bloody struggle between oligarchic and democratic factions at Argos in 371, an account amplified by Diodorus, who added that a pro-democracy mob murdered some twelve hundred leading citizens of the city.[20] The Demosthenic quotation of the heliast's oath notes that land redistribution (obviously a manifestation of class-driven struggle) was prohibited at Athens.[21]

The constant recollection of the past for present purposes, in an environment where the general perception was one of regular and potentially violent ideological strife, necessarily influenced the Athenian understanding of constitutional and legal history. Whether the fourth century was as economically and socially dire as scholars once thought,[22] what matters for our purposes is that fourth-century Athenians lived in a world where violence often characterized constitutional changes, changes driven by ideological differences between mass and elite. Aristotle provides the most articulate version of this perception, though the evidence from Xenophon and Isocrates indicates that Aristotle's perception was by no means unique. Aristotle famously posited that only a society ruled by the middle, given over neither to the poor many nor to the rich few, could be a truly just or stable one; as he surveyed his contemporary Greek world, however, Aristotle despaired that scarcely any such societies were to be found and that the extreme elements took turns holding power, ruling in their own interests, and—notably—were unlikely to constitute a common or equal government owing to the violence that had established them in power.[23]

Not all fourth-century residents of Athens were quite as pessimistic as Aristotle, and a great many had come to share certain convictions about what made a society as large and as socioeconomically diverse as Athens cohere: namely, the law. Nowhere is this attitude more clearly stated than in Aeschines' first oration (delivered in 346/5):

> I am not unaware, Athenian gentlemen, that the things I am about to say at the outset, you obviously have heard from others before . . . For they all say that there are three *politeiai* among all mankind—tyranny, oligarchy, and democracy. Tyrannies and oligarchies administer according to the whims of those having been set over them, but those *poleis* living under democracies, according to the existing laws. Be certain, my fellow Athenians, that the laws preserve both the persons and the *politeia* of those living under a democracy (*tôn dêmokratoumenôn sômata kai tên politeian hoi nomoi sôzousi*), but suspicion and main force preserve those of tyrants and oligarchs. And indeed, oligarchs and those governing an unequal constitution must guard against those overthrowing the state by the law of force, but for those like you who have a state based on equality and legality, watch must be kept against those either speaking or having lived their lives outside the laws. For then you will be strong, since you will live according to the laws and you will not be overthrown by the lawless.[24]

In their public speeches, whether for court or the assembly, litigants and politicians frequently appealed to the shared, democratic beliefs of their audiences.[25] Here, Aeschines makes two important claims he expects will resonate with his listeners. On the one hand, we find the manifest contrast between governments by the one or few as opposed to the many, consonant with the general conceptualization of that tension which we examined above. On the other hand, the contrast is as much qualitative as it is quantitative for Aeschines and his audience: it is not just *that* the many rule, but rather *how* they do so, under and in accordance with the laws. Aeschines elsewhere underscores this difference by citing the epigram set up to honor those who at Phyle established the democratic resistance to the Thirty, because they were the first to endeavor the overthrow of a government ruling by *adikois thesmois*, unjust ordinances.[26] Athenian laws—the *nomoi*—enjoyed special protection in Athenian procedure, for unlike other types of fraud or false witness, the introduction of a nonexistent law as part of a litigant's argument exposed said litigant to the death penalty.[27]

Even fourth-century critics of Athenian democracy proceeded from its assumptions about law, seeking to invert them in order to demonstrate the invalidity of the rule of the *demos*.[28] To take but one example, Aristotle described the various forms of democracy in the *Politics* in descending order of quality.[29] For Aristotle, a democracy could have constitutional legitimacy, even in the absence of meaningful property qualifications and with mass participation in the offices of state, so long as the laws remained master of the state.[30] The notion of the rule of law was current in Athenian democratic ideology and is one to which several modern authorities have subscribed as characteristic of fourth-century Athenian democracy.[31] This ideology had become so effective and prevalent that Aristotle had to redefine the terms of the debate in order to criticize Athenian democracy; for him, the worst type of democracy was one where the assembly may declare as it wishes through *psêphismata*, even in opposition to the law, *nomos*.[32] That he had Athens in mind is clear from another source, either penned by him or emanating from his school,[33] which describes the eleventh, final, and current form of the Athenian constitution as one in which the *demos* had made itself lord over all affairs through its decrees—not laws—and its decisions in the courts.[34] This type of democracy was in essence a collective tyranny, and thus reasonably worthy of censure as no *politeia* at all.[35] Only by attempting to deny the Athenian democracy its central ideological claim—that law was the true ruler—could Aristotle criticize it, so dominant had the conception become.

We may note finally in this vein Isocrates' observation regarding sycophants who, as Matthew Christ has recently observed, were conceived as abusing the Athenian legal system and therefore undermining claims to Athenian cultural and even moral authority.[36] Whatever the reality of sycophancy in the Athenian courts, sycophants served as a convenient punching bag in the discourse of Athenian legal culture in the fourth century. Because of their alleged disregard of legal propriety, Isocrates held them up as a special type of villain within Athenian society.

Athenians did not, of course, only begin to associate democracy with law in the fourth century. Traditionally, scholars have identified *isonomia* as one of the fundamental ideological supports of Athenian democracy and possibly a watchword of the Kleisthenic revolution of the late sixth century BCE, though Mogens Herman Hansen has built an aggressive case against such an assumption.[37] But whether *isonomia* emerged as a conscious synonym (or precursor) for democracy as early as the late sixth century, certainly by the last third of the fifth century the notion of Athenian political society as based on law had entrenched itself. Herodotus, in the constitutional debate he imagines among the Persians, has Otanes identify democracy with *isonomia*.[38] Thucydides places in the mouth of Pericles the idea that the laws, whether in the form of statutes or as part of the unwritten code, protect the injured at Athens.[39] The force of both tradition as well as statute law can be detected slightly earlier in Sophocles' *Antigone*, since the action revolves around the protagonist's claim that religious custom compels her to bury her traitorous brother, regardless of what the law of the city prescribes.

As we will have occasion to examine in more detail in Chapter 4, the rather porous boundary between written and unwritten law was an ancient one in Greek practice. For our present purposes, we may note the development of Athenian legal practice from what was a general Greek approach to law and legal knowledge toward a specifically Athenian concept of law as something necessarily fixed, written, and closed to abusive interpretation. Rosalind Thomas has marked the fact that many Greek *poleis* employed "remembrancers" of the law, and Athens had officials, *exêgêtai*, as late as the fourth century whose function was to expound upon the law from memory.[40] At Athens, however, the later fifth century witnessed a new inkling that written law was somehow different, even if Pericles could still claim as late as 430/29 that written and unwritten law could coexist. Where does this recognition find its origin? Sarah Humphreys has suggested that this trend was encouraged when, after the reforms of Ephialtes in 462/1, the *demos* began to identify the conscious exercise of their new legislative power with its result, *nomoi*, laws.[41] Thus, in the imagination of Athenians over the last half of the fifth century, law became an expression of the will of the majority, and as a result, something that was more malleable than custom or "the laws of Solon." We might recognize how this identification had reshaped Athenian assumptions, by noting the differences between Sophocles' *Antigone* and the following lines from Euripides' *Suppliants*, performed in the late 420s:

> But when laws have been written down (*gegrammenôn*), both the weak man
> and the rich has equal justice (*dikên isên*),
> and it is allowed for those who are weaker, whoever may hear abuse,
> to say the same things in turn to one who is prosperous,
> and the lesser man would prevail, having the greater right on his side.
> Indeed this is liberty: "who, having some worthy counsel
> for the state, wishes to bring it forward?"
> And wishing to do such things, one man may stand out, and another, not wishing to do them
> may remain silent; what else is more equal in a city?
> And wherever the commons is absolute master of a country,
> it takes delight in the young men living under them;
> but a man ruling as king considers such a thing hostile,
> and those best men whom he considers to be wise,
> he murders, having become afraid for his despotic rule.[42]

The tension between Athens' unwritten and written laws had persisted deep into the fifth century, but by the late 420s the notion of *written* law as the guardian of democracy had gained considerable ground, to judge from Euripides. Changes that had occurred between the performances of *Antigone* and *The Suppliants* reflect, on one view, contemporary juridicopolitical language and current ideological debates in fifth-century Athens.[43]

For Athenians, the conceptual tipping point in favor of written laws once and for all took place in the years between 410 and 399, a period of extraordinary political upheaval at Athens. As already mentioned, this era saw the *demos* authorize the first systematic attempt to collect and publish all current Athenian law, in part as a response to spurious but irrefutable oligarchic rhetoric about the "ancestral" constitution.[44] Over the course of that decade, Nikomakhos and the other *anagrapheis tôn nomôn* were charged with the task of organizing at least some of Athens' existing law.[45] Modern scholarly opinion remains divided over the extent of the collection and republication, as well as its purpose.[46] As for Demosthenes, he claims in citing the law of Diokles that "those laws (*nomous*) that were laid down before the archonship of Eukleides (403/2 BCE) under the democracy, and those that were set down and had been recorded (*anagegrammenoi*) in the archonship of Eukleides, are sovereign (*kyrious*)"[47]; and indeed, as we shall see, the writing of the laws during the last decade of the fifth century seems to have been associated with a general concern for establishing the primacy of written law.

However, the process of committing such laws to writing—whatever it involved exactly—was a great deal more arduous than originally envisioned. If we can put any stock in accusations leveled against Nikomakhos, he was supposed to have completed the work within four months,[48] but ultimately he and the board of *anagrapheis* took six years before being interrupted by the regime of the Thirty. Once the democracy was restored, it took another three years to complete the task. As P.J. Rhodes has suggested, "The *anagrapheis* were given a task whose nature was not at first fully thought out but was gradually clarified as questions came to be asked and answered."[49] Rhodes also posits that as they went about their task, the *anagrapheis* soon realized that some of the laws were obsolete, or portions of some laws were, and thus redacting and reconciling for final drafts necessitated a much longer endeavor than originally envisioned.[50] We can well imagine and sympathize with the plight of the *anagrapheis*: not only were they confronted with more than two centuries of legal material, but they had to determine the legitimacy and relevance of those laws while operating in a climate of ideological debates over the ancestral constitution.[51]

But the difficulty of their labor also helped encourage the conscious notion at Athens of law as a system (whether it actually was one is another question), one whose authority now became invested in its written form.[52] These attitudes had been prefigured to some extent in the fifth century, but there we find them in more embryonic and implicit form. Martin Ostwald recognized that the semantic field of *nomos* had changed in Athens since it began to be used as a word for statute (probably in connection with Kleisthenes' reforms of the late sixth century), and Athenian references prior to 400 suggest a recognition of *nomoi* as something enacted and a subject of comment when the enactment was not duly or legitimately undertaken.[53] Though Noel Robertson has called into question whether notions such as recodification or constitutional reform are appropriate constructs for conceptualizing the legislative activity of 410–399,[54] even his reconstruction entails elements that would have encouraged a reshaping of Athenian legal thought. He believes that one of the principal jobs of the *anagrapheis* was to write the laws on boards meant for temporary display in front of the monument of the eponymous heroes. These older laws, arranged by rubrics, were available for public display and comment, and once the Council of 500 or the Assembly made necessary or desired revisions, the new versions were displayed again on the same boards, whence—Robertson argues—they might be inscribed on stone. More critically, however, the main purpose of the *anagrapheis* was to produce copies of the current laws for the new central state archive at the Metroön, also established in the archonship of Eukleides (403/2).[55] Archiving was scarcely a pointless exercise: take the example of the citizen who, having received advice from the *exêgêtai*, then decided to go to the archive and check for himself the law in question.[56]

Collection, review, revision, archiving—all speak to a new Athenian attitude crystallizing in the late fifth and fourth centuries regarding documents in general and laws in particular. This attitude manifested itself in a variety of ways. We noted above the law of Diokles cited by Demosthenes, with its emphasis on laws that had been recorded and published. Even more explicitly, the decree of Teisamenos, cited by Andokides,[57] marks the advance of the idea that legislative procedures should be rational, cautious, and based on written statute. Under that decree, in addition to the laws of Solon, any new laws as might be necessary were also to be written up on white boards in front of the statues of the eponymous heroes, but now this task fell to officials known as *nomothetai*—law setters—elected by the Council of 500. The process also involved scrutiny by another committee of so-called *nomothetai*, elected by the local *deme* assemblies. After a public review and comment period, ratification followed, and if approved, a permanent copy of the new law was placed under the guardianship of the Areopagus. Crucially, magistrates could apply only those laws that had undergone this ratification process and were thus current (*nomoi keimenoi*).[58] That applied law had to be *written* law by the beginning of the fourth century emerges from a law cited by Andokides two paragraphs later that in no case were magistrates to apply an unwritten law (*agraphôi de nomôi tas arkhas mê khrêsthai*).[59]

Thus, by the beginning of the fourth century, the procedures outlined in the Teisamenos decree had developed into a formal and complex legislative process known as *nomothesia*, through which all new laws had to be vetted.[60] Procedures for challenging the currency of old laws and for indicting those who had proposed unconstitutional laws (the *graphê paranomôn*) also became an important part of the legal landscape of fourth-century Athens.[61] Furthermore, a hitherto insignificant distinction between the terms *nomoi* and *psêphismata* hardened to a bright line between what modern scholars often refer to respectively as laws and decrees, a distinction not really applicable to the fifth century, but now couched within an insistence on written law and a democratic judicial ethos "remarkable for how it define[d] the new boundaries between popular sovereignty and the sovereignty of the law."[62] By the fourth century, the laws, *nomoi*, were held as the general foundations of Athenian government and society, though on occasion a *nomos* might address an individual case; the boards of *nomothetai* were responsible for such statutes, regarded as overriding and permanent.[63] *Psêphismata*, decrees, emerged as the main instrument of

Assembly action, through which they could act on the specific and largely temporary business pertinent to the more quotidian concerns of the *polis*.

FOURTH-CENTURY ATHENIAN LAW, that about which we know the most, is often characterized as amateur and unsystematic, and compared to Roman law or the English common law tradition, that judgment is probably fair enough. But the present study is less concerned with what fourth-century Athenian law actually was than what fourth-century Athenians *thought* it was, and our evidence indicates that they saw it as the foundation of their democracy. For them, laws were an inextricable part of the form and character of government; indeed, what characterized democracy, *their* democracy, was the rule of law, even if a critic such as Aristotle might disagree. From the end of the fifth century onward, they had developed legislative processes which, in addition to elevating the status of law above that of popular decree, also encouraged fourth-century Athenians to think about their laws as part of an overall system more than they ever had before. Finally, in the fourth century, Athenians had come to think of the written aspect of their laws as the guarantor of their democratic society, laws that large courts of citizen jurors—without the aid of a legal expert and by simple majority vote—applied based on their understanding of those laws and their assessment of the relative claims of agonistic litigants arguing before them. An Athenian mentality had emerged that identified a necessary continuum of democracy–*written* law–popular adjudication. Its opposite was oligarchy–*unwritten* law–expert opinion.[64]

Such was the climate in which average citizens, orators, and even political philosophers operated in the fourth century, and thus any assessments they made about law and society will reflect these assumptions: unwritten law is the tool of oligarchs, written law the protector of the *demos*. As the next two chapters demonstrate, such a dichotomy simply did not exist in the rest of Greece nor even at Athens before the end of the fifth century. Thus, when writers working subsequently at Athens give us a bare description of early legislative activity, or preserve for us the text of a law, the information they provide *may* prove useful. Their interpretations, however, most likely will not, colored as they were by contemporary ideologies about democracy and written law.

2—The Moral Authority of Epic

In order to appreciate why written law emerges, it is absolutely crucial to gain a sense of what came before it, of how Greeks went about identifying, justifying, pursuing, and then resolving or regulating actionable disputes. There has been considerable discussion whether one can speak of law in the absence of writing,[65] but the current project is less concerned with semantic debates than with describing what sort of legal culture may have informed Greek thinking about dispute settlement and regulation in the generations preceding the writing of law.[66] Since unwritten law, if such exists, leaves no archaeological trace, our only hope of such a description resides in the epic tradition represented by Homer and Hesiod. To use such sources for understanding early Greek law, we must focus on two aspects of the epic tradition: the moral authority of epic; and its general flexibility until diffusion and transcription in the Archaic period, and thus its continued relevance to and reflection of social assumptions about dispute and order in Late Geometric and early Archaic Greece.

We may run the risk, however, of building facile conclusions on rather flimsy foundations if we merely *assume* that the Homeric and Hesiodic material can be used the way it is employed in the current study. Hence, some cautionary notes are in order. Reliance on Homer, Hesiod, and other surviving literature from the eighth and seventh centuries necessarily raises questions about literacy and orality. As recent research has demonstrated, situating "Homer" or Homeric society in the type of dichotomy suggested by the "strong" Oral Theory rather misses the point.[67] If we accept the general opinion that Homeric epic represents, in great extent, a written version of an oral tradition as it had developed down into the eighth (or seventh, or sixth) century, then it at once becomes obvious that the society which produced Homer and his poems could be neither fully literate nor fully oral: after all, we would know precious little of Homeric epic were it not for the fact that these verses composed-in-performance were at some point textualized. Furthermore, no society that has acquired writing—however literate—entirely lays aside oral methods and rituals of communication, and later Greek cultures, even Athens, preserved the oral and the memorative alongside the literate and archival.[68] As for the Archaic period, we are talking about a Greek world that had acquired writing but scarcely used it for all or even most things the unsuspecting might think they would. Poetry, curses, funerary monuments, graffiti, yes; but, as far as we can tell, until the middle of the seventh century, the Greeks did not employ their literate skills to record (write down) or draft (write up) their laws, their histories, or the important business of those who managed the early *polis*.[69]

Contemporary epigraphic sources will need less defense as the basis for getting at the nature, or at least the content, of (some) early Greek law. When we are dealing with later copies, such as that of Drakon's code re-inscribed in 409/8, or late collations, such as the Gortynian Code, we will need to proceed on a case-by-case basis in evaluating their authenticity or fidelity to earlier originals. Of course, archaic legal inscriptions survive only by accident, and our sample can never be comprehensive or completely representative. Nevertheless, what remains is by no means inconsiderable. Combined with apparently trustworthy literary references to early laws, it provides a significant collection with which to proceed.

The case of Hesiod is more direct and needs less explanation. Robert Lamberton's argument that Hesiod was a poetic persona much like Theognis[70] has not won many adherents. Most scholars still believe that both the historical testimony and the internal details of Hesiod's major works point to a single author and continue to treat the poet of Askra as a historical personage.[71] Accordingly, the operative assumption of the current study is that Hesiod provides us a first-hand account of one man's perceptions of the juridical assumptions and workings of a seventh-century Greek community, although one very much colored by his own personal experiences and disappointments. Similarly, the various lyric poets of the seventh and sixth century may provide useful information, especially those who speak directly to issues of law and justice, social and political upheaval, and exile (though we hear little from these last that helps to illuminate procedure). Caution is certainly necessary: as one important school of thought has it, much of the poetry produced in this period will have employed poetic personae, transformed potentially historical individuals into rhetorical types, and played to certain ideologies of both the poet or poets who have produced our surviving versions and the audiences for whom the poems were performed.[72] Such a position would necessarily make this poetry highly problematic from a historiographical perspective. However, Forsdyke's argument is well taken that "many poems reveal, in their specific details, clear links with the social, economic, and political problems of particular poleis at particular points in time," and I generally subscribe to her view that the preservation of details and terminology so obsolete that they confounded classical authors speaks to the genuinely Archaic context of most of these poems.[73] Several lyric poets appear in the arguments that follow, and as with Hesiod, I will treat specific historiographical issues regarding each source as appropriate.

As for Homer, over the past half century, many important and influential works of scholarship have appeared that proceeded from the position that the preserved epic tradition could serve as a source for understanding that elusive beast one might conveniently, if dangerously, call Homeric society. M.I. Finley's *World of Odysseus* pioneered the model, reading the *Iliad* and *Odyssey* as a sociologist might in order to construct a vision of a Greek community in the tenth or early ninth centuries. Most students who accept Finley's basic premise would now revise his dates downward to the later Geometric period (largely the close of the ninth and first half of the eighth centuries).[74] A small sampling of the names who have approached Greek epic on assumptions similar to Finley's regarding Homer is impressive: Walter Donlan, Victor Davis Hanson, Ian Morris, Kurt Raaflaub, Richard Seaford, and David Tandy are but a few who have produced hallmarks of scholarship using this approach, though some with results more controversial than others. In the realm of early Greek law, in particular, Hans Julius Wolff, Michael Gagarin, Eberhard Ruschenbusch, Eva Cantarella, and Gerhard Thür are among those who also have looked to the epic material as an important potential source.

It is certainly true that the "canonical" versions of these texts only came about with the criticism of Alexandrian scholars in the Hellenistic period; however, the preponderance of Homeric scholarship agrees that the "final" versions of, for example, the *Iliad* and *Odyssey*, were not—in fact, *could* not have been—significantly different from the well-known tradition as it had crystallized by the sixth century BCE.[75] Those Archaic versions—themselves written representations of a theretofore orally preserved tradition—have raised vexing questions regarding their fidelity to the oral tradition, the literacy (or lack thereof) of Homer, and so on. Related to these concerns, of course, is the problem of whether Homer's tales model or reflect for us a predominantly oral or a substantially literate culture.

For more than a hundred years now, scholars have recognized that the epics of Homer represent a great deal more than simply stories, and those who insist on seeing them as nothing more than fictional amalgams with no relation to the world around them are increasingly in the minority.[76] Since the groundbreaking work of Milman Parry and Albert Bates Lord from the 1920s onward, scholars have increasingly concluded that the early epics, as they survive in written form, bear a significant relationship to the oral tradition.[77] In a society that for generations nurtured its sense of self, its values, and its past (which is not to be understood as history) by and through traditions that fossilized at some point in the Archaic period, those traditions provide a window into how early Greeks conceived of community in the transitional generations when Dark Age communities gave way to the formative *poleis*. How to use that window, and what one should seek through it, is of course a difficult question. For example, it is unquestionably a fool's errand to use the epics to reconstruct the Late Bronze Age or even attempt a narrative for the later context of the poems' performances.

On the other hand, as evolving stories that were cherished, reproduced, and modified over time, our versions of the epic tradition afford us the opportunity to determine some sense of what the Greek communities of the eighth and seventh centuries thought important and what types of behaviors society at large sought to encourage and discourage. In other words, they reveal something about moral authority, and hence they provide a way to examine a wide range of values in early Greek society that will have informed the early Greeks' sense of rules and norms, helping us to understand a culture otherwise elusive in traditional historiographical terms.[78]

The epics served as a means of establishing normative authority for the early Greeks, in large part because of their connections to the power of ritual and *muthoi*, especially if we understand the latter as "authoritative speech acts." Particularly salient here is Richard Martin's brilliant work on the power of *muthoi* as "speech act[s] indicating authority, performed at length, usually in public, with a focus on full attention to every detail. The speaker of a *muthos* is one who possesses or lays claim to power, who expects public reaction, and who believes he is issuing a command that will at least be regarded as persuasive due to his position of influence and authority."[79] More significantly for our purposes, Martin showed that the performer saw the entirety of his performance as a *muthos*: the act of epic song in itself served as an authoritative speech act, forceful and persuasive for a public audience.[80]

For the poet, as Martin suggests, the style and the substance of epic, and, for that matter, early lyric, is a vehicle by which he can compete in an attempt to outdo other performers,[81] and therefore one might conclude that any given version of traditional tales will necessarily represent one particular individual's or social group's outlook, the Archaic Greek equivalent of preaching to the choir. In other words, the vision put forth in Homer may only represent, say, the elite point of view. As we shall see in the subsequent chapter, such a view of epic—Homer as the poet of the nobles, Hesiod of the people—is not necessarily apt; while perhaps true in the broadest sense, this perspective oversimplifies what is a much more complex dynamic among the received tradition, the performer, and the audience's expectations about both. The poet could be creative, but he was ultimately working in a medium that did not allow for artistic originality as we think of it.[82] His canvas was the tradition itself, and therefore he was somewhat constrained by the very nature of his creation. So of what, then, if Martin is correct, might a poet have been trying to persuade his audience? Here, I believe, aspects of the oft-pilloried work of Eric Havelock provide a possible way forward.

Introducing Havelock's name is likely to raise some eyebrows, and I should be clear at the outset that by no means do I embrace or accept all of Havelock's arguments regarding the significance of literacy, his observations regarding literate versus oral mindsets, and so on, which many scholars (including me) view as overdrawn at best. One of his suggestions, however, deserves special attention, and happily it is one that does not necessitate the acceptance of some of his more controversial postulates.[83] Havelock argued that the Homeric epics served as something of a "tribal encyclopedia" for Greek society before the return of literacy in the form of the alphabet.[84] Put another way, epic provided the means for encoding in a socially constructive and useful way the received cultural knowledge of Greek society from one generation to the next in an age without writing, the vehicle for preserving important information in a society with no other means of doing so. Oral poetry has the advantage of being memorable, not only because of the narrative themes it employs but also because of the mnemonically friendly structure of meter and verse. Thus, within the powerful and riveting tales of Achaean heroism we find, as the Greeks would have themselves, accounts of mundane existence, implicitly reinforcing the proper methods for such activities as offering sacrifices, calling assemblies, rigging a sail, and so forth. Even the central components of the narrative, Havelock argued, served the purpose of imparting to, or reproducing for, its audience moral and ethical lessons, explicating the rewards of approved behavior and the potential consequences for disapproved behavior, both of which could involve entire communities. By its very nature, epic in its encyclopedic role could, in a traditional society where change was still relatively gradual, mutate from one generation to the next in order to accommodate changes in social attitudes and organization;[85] indeed, the preservation and permutation of such orally preserved "records" were critical to the maintenance of the civilization and the culture.[86] Until the middle of the eighth century onward, when social and economic change throughout the Greek world accelerated to the point of cataclysmic,[87] the tribal encyclopedia transmitted from one generation to the next the received, though elastic, wisdom necessary to participate in the life of the community.

Though Havelock's theories have generally received a warm welcome and exercised considerable influence in other disciplines, his reception in Classical scholarship has often been less than kind. It seems, however, that if one accepts Finley's basic premise of how we may read the epics, then in turn Havelock's notion of the epic as a strategy for preserving and reproducing culturally valuable knowledge would necessarily also have validity. Part of the fault for the rejection of Havelock's ideas lies with Havelock himself. His own explanation of how his tribal encyclopedia will have operated left important issues open to question, and his sense of how this important information would have become encoded could be read one of two ways: we must accept either a deus ex machina or a process that seems suspiciously self-conscious and manipulative given the nature of epic.

Neither solution is at all satisfactory, of course. Havelock himself rejected the notion of tradition transmitted in the ways Parry and Lord envisioned,[88] and thus he effectively excluded himself from much of the future conversation in which the Parry-Lord thesis took center stage. Furthermore—and this seems to me to be of central importance—Havelock never established explicitly enough *why* it should have been the case that this tribal encyclopedia was encoded, or how it will have exercised anything we might recognize as moral authority from one generation to the next. To say simply that they are *muthoi*, and therefore authoritative, runs the risk of circularity: epic is an authoritative speech-act because the poetry is an act of *muthos*, and *muthoi* are authoritative poetic speech-acts.

Ritual provides the answer here. Internal analysis of the poems has demonstrated the constant reference to ritual activity, which both solemnizes the poetry itself and in turn reinforces its authority. Indirect evidence, namely the conditions of performance in Archaic Athens, likewise suggests that epic audiences did not consist primarily of wealthy elites who enjoyed the stories of Achilles and Odysseus over feasts in their own great halls: rather, the recitation of Homeric poetry took place in public contexts connected to religious festivals. Thus, these traditions were not just vessels for an idealized or imagined past woven around the entertaining exploits of heroic characters. These poems were bound up with rituals—sacrifices, marriages, gift exchange—that made up the fabric of society and solemnly communicated those rituals within the community and across generations.[89]

While reconciliation and synthesis are not always fashionable these days in Classical studies,[90] I would submit that the understanding of epic as a source of moral authority really resides at the junction of the various ideas just discussed. Havelock's notion of a tribal encyclopedia fits best with an orally preserved tradition that was transmitted from one generation to the next by the process envisioned by the Parry-Lord thesis, given the subsequent modifications it has undergone. The importance of that tradition, and the necessity of replicating and reiterating its lessons, was strengthened by the fact that the tradition itself was replete with rituals and performed in public, ritual contexts. That the songs were imbued with these valuable lessons underpinned by cultic and ritual associations allowed them to be authoritative in the sense argued by Martin. In the mouth of a particularly skilled *aoidos*, these *muthoi* could take on additional persuasive force.

Social and moral authority *was* bound up in song, precisely because this was the primary way, before the technology of writing, of disseminating publicly information about morals, approved and disapproved behaviors, and rituals, across generations.[91] The wisdom of accumulated social experience had no other conduit that was public in the sense of being shared by the community: again, this idea is neither novel nor altogether controversial.

However, this bare fact—that song was the *only* means of communal wisdom transmission across time—is often lost sight of in current discussions. Are the poems myths, in the sense of traditional tales? Very probably so.[92] Does that also entail that the individual episodes are *just* myths, devoid of value to the historian? Putting aside Finley's famous observations on the subject,[93] I will take a more recent example, with which I disagree: "It is hard to be sure what 'collective importance' to assign to Homer's barracks-room song on the 'adultery of Ares and Aphrodite' (*Od.* 8.265–365), one of the best known myths in the world, unless it is the story's rash sexual humor."[94] I would suggest that such a reading of this particular episode in the Homeric corpus, especially taken out of context, rather misses the point. Is the tale bawdy and amusing? Of course: entertainment is central to epic, as Havelock long ago recognized.[95] Included in this episode, however, are crucially important ideas, especially juridical ones, about the rights of the cuckold and the importance of ransom and sureties for a captured adulterer in gaining his release.

Before leaving this section, a few further comments are in order about my reading of Homer and the consequences of the writing of the epics. I am aware of the debate that has long existed and continues between Analysts, Oral Theorists, and Neoanalysts, but I do not intend to enter that particular debate here.[96] However, even though the Neoanalysts' insistence on a Homer who composed his *Iliad* in writing has been an obstacle to Oral Theorists accepting much of what the other school offers,[97] of late there have been some attempts to emphasize what these two scholarly perspectives generally share.[98] Both Neoanalysts and Oral Theorists agree that behind the epic tradition there existed a rich stock of orally preserved tales and motifs upon which a particular bard might draw. Most Oral Theorists, at least to my knowledge, would now accept that the poet who sang the versions of the *Iliad* and *Odyssey* as we substantially have them was a performer of the first order. Indeed, it has been suggested that recognition by a wealthy patron of the exceptional quality of such a performer may have prompted the effort to capture his performance with the help of new technology, i.e., the Greek alphabet.[99] Further, both schools of thought agree that the epics represent a version of the stock of inherited tales and motifs from oral tradition as it existed at the time the poems were committed to writing (by whatever means that may have occurred). Until such time, however, the nature of those narrative elements would have remained elastic and mutable, capable of being shaped to the expectations and assumptions of poets and audiences.

With the epics' writing, however, their flexibility will have begun to slip away, though it is better to think in terms of that as a process rather than an event. Following Gregory Nagy, I think we should imagine a "relatively most fluid period" that extends to the middle of the eighth century.[100] I am less convinced than he that there remained no written texts of Homer until the middle of the sixth century,[101] but whether one accepts that argument or not, Nagy believes that in the intervening two hundred years the poems became relatively more stable. In other words, the oral tradition could continue to change to reflect the ideals, realities, and needs of Greek communities down to the middle of the eighth century, but from that point forward, either through the existence of written texts or through Nagy's process of diffusion, the form of the poems began to fossilize. Of course, since there was scarcely a book trade at the time and since we can imagine few would have been in possession of all the rolls that might comprise a "full" *Iliad* or *Odyssey*, there was still opportunity for permutation; this no doubt helps to explain the different local versions that we may glean from antiquity. However, in the face of either a fixed transcript or an increasingly familiar and widespread version of how the story "ought" to be told, performances of Homer will have been more and more similar, even before, if Nagy is correct, the formal process of definition began in Athens in the middle of the sixth century. Thus, the written version of the tradition substantially reflects the concerns of Greeks living in the generations shortly before the middle of the eighth century and continued to reflect those concerns into the seventh. The written versions' ability to keep pace with rapid social, economic, and political change was waning, however, and as a result, the role for Homer's verses as *muthoi*, in Martin's sense of the term, declined. Other means of enshrining authority became increasingly necessary.

3—Greek Adjudication in Context: Legal Cultures and Legal Anthropology

Our evidence from Homer, Hesiod, and other early literature thus represents a potential treasure trove for describing the juridical world of the Greeks during the eighth and early seventh centuries and before the subsequent appearance of written law, but it also requires a careful and thoroughgoing approach to unlock what it may tell us. The key to reading this evidence resides in the insights legal studies and legal anthropology offer and in the useful analytical concepts and vocabulary we borrow from them.

The present study owes much to the concept of legal culture, the complex of juridical ideas, behaviors, and processes a society exhibits, and how these in turn influence and are influenced by that society's broader sense of beliefs, values, and attitudes. Legal culture, as a concept, is still in flux in legal studies discussions, though the related debate has produced the elements of a working definition suitable for our purposes. In this section, I turn first to a description of the concept of legal culture and its components, in order to clarify my use of this term as the argument proceeds.

In order to describe early Greek legal culture in its fullness, I promote the application of trouble-case processualism, a method derived from useful and revealing legal anthropological approaches, as opposed to more normativist-formalist methodologies, the limitations of which I explore in more detail in Chapter 3.1. Early Greek justice, with its highly performative character that persisted well into the fourth century,[102] lends itself to an analysis that examines all the available evidence for disputes but at the same time goes beyond a simple case-method study, itself the underpinning of traditional processualism. This method, not only by examining all disputes, but also by seeking the sources of conflict, the attitudes and expectations of disputants, the processes through which they pursue their grievances, and how cultural values determine the course and outcome of disputes, allows us to construct a clearer and more complete picture of Greek legal culture in the eighth and early seventh centuries.

The resistance of ancient historians and classicists to the type of multidisciplinary approach I apply here has slowly eroded over the last few decades, though more integration is still possible, and the responses in Classical scholarship to such efforts have certainly varied over the years. One might compare the generally positive reception of Finley's *World of Odysseus* with the initial hostility toward Havelock's *Preface to Plato*. Few students of Geometric and early Archaic Greece would these days dare shun the use of comparative material and the insights of other disciplines, though some remain wary of the utility of anthropology.[103]

Caution is, of course, crucial. As Ian Morris has argued, anthropological fieldwork among more recent traditional societies has yet to reveal a culture analogous to what our literary and archaeological evidence indicates for the early Greeks.[104] However, the notion that insights from ethnographical fieldwork cannot aid our understanding of early Greek juridical practices—because they derive from cultures somehow too primitive—is not tenable, and privileges certain prejudices about the Greeks as the progenitors of western civilization. Jack Goody has argued for a reevaluation of such concepts as Western (and the West as fundamentally different from Asia and Africa) as fairly late developments of Eurocentric historiography, which itself privileges Western superiority thanks in large part to economic and political domination by Europe in the last few centuries. He further sees the modern invention of Western "Antiquity" and the modern promotion of Greek uniqueness as particular culprits and has himself argued that the developmental divide between the Archaic and the Classical is illusory at best.[105] David Tandy has adroitly noted that "the fact remains that the closest analogies to eighth-century Greek society are non-Western primitive communities: the early Greeks were, until the organization of the *polis*, primitive and not what we call western."[106] While Goody's observations suggest we should temper or recast Tandy's formulation to avoid the appearance of anticipating the inevitable, teleological emergence of Greek civilization (though I doubt this was what Tandy intended), the latter's general point should still stand: whatever the Greeks became, or we want them to have become, we should eschew the assumption that because they were the Greeks, models derived from legal anthropology cannot be instructive, even if those models find their origins in the study of societies that are regarded as primitive. Rather, an approach informed by legal studies and anthropology will prove crucial to any complete examination of the juridical world of early Greece.

STUDIES IN LEGAL THEORY have increasingly stressed the importance of legal culture, drawing no small amount of inspiration from Lawrence Friedman's and Clifford Geertz's work.[107] Friedman initially defined legal culture as a subset of the larger culture around it, namely "those parts of general culture—customs, opinion, ways of doing and thinking—that bend social forces toward or away from the law and in particular ways"; legal culture, in short, "refers to public knowledge of and attitudes and behaviour patterns toward the legal system."[108] Geertz, for his part, argued that to treat the collection of laws as "law" misses the point of the role played by legal phenomena in culture: "[Law] is not a bounded set of norms, rules, principles, values, or whatever from which jural responses to distilled events can be drawn, but part of a distinctive manner of imagining the real."[109] Legal sensibility, the "complex of characterizations and imaginings, stories about events cast in an imagery about principles," is what gives significance to law, meaning that is ultimately negotiated since members of a society engage the law from a pluralism of different legal symbols and interpretations.[110] Because he viewed law as necessarily inseparable from social practices,[111] Geertz was dubious of the enterprise of generalizing about law across societies and sought to privilege local knowledge. He thus argued for "thick description" as a method for analyzing cultural practices and their semiotic content in general, the "piled-up structures of inference and implication," in order to understand the meaning of "social expressions" that do not immediately admit of coherence or intelligibility to an observer of a given culture.[112]

Culture is, however, often a slippery concept, employed in such ways that it becomes all-encompassing, tantamount to a theory-of-everything, a means of explaining that which otherwise resists explanation.[113] The vagueness of the term has given some legal scholars pause regarding the utility of the concept of legal culture as an analytical tool. Roger Cotterrell has suggested that we might replace that concept with "legal ideology" or a "law-and-community" approach, though he concedes that previous legal cultural models might prove more useful for societies that are smaller and possess less differentiated aggregates of social elements than contemporary, highly complex societies.[114] The discomfort with legal culture as an analytical concept also in part arises from a tendency to view culture as monolithic, "organic, unified, and whole,"[115] or marked by an "elegant coherence," to borrow Naomi Mezey's phrase,[116] rather than understanding that we may employ the term as shorthand for the networks of "signifying or symbolic systems"[117] that give meaning to the "internal inconsistencies, conflicts, and contradictions" of the actions, attitudes, and assumptions of the members of a society.[118] Therefore, I employ the concept of legal culture as something that grows from the interdependent "mutuality and endless recycling between formal meaning-making and the signifying practices" in which members of a community engage[119] when events give rise to disagreements that in turn conceivably will or actually do implicate juridical responses. Put another way, properly understood, legal culture can satisfy Geertz's condition that we should look beyond the rules and surface processes. *It will encompass formal rules and also informal norms (taken together, the rule base), but also the rules and norms for the treatment of those who are perceived to break rules and norms; the reasons for which members of a community disagree over the content of these, and if there is disagreement, the degree to which they perceive their grievances as actionable; what the best recourses and strategies are for pursuing their grievances, and the extent to which they do or do not pursue these through formal or informal processes; how the wider values and opinions of the community, as disputants understand these, affect the aforementioned considerations; and, finally, the consequences, if any, that the sources, processes, and outcomes of a dispute have in reshaping the rules and norms of a society and people's attitudes.* Such an analysis also promises to reveal whether a given legal culture is functional or dysfunctional. Its functionality, or lack thereof, rests in its effectiveness in reconciling disagreements about the content of norms and in preserving social stability.[120]

Again, any legal culture has an inherent pluralism: the realm of the sociocultural is not only "a realm of solidarity, identity and cooperation, but also of power, conflict, alienation and isolation; of stable expectations, systems, custom, trust and confidence, but also of unpredictable action, unforeseen change, violence, disruption and discontinuity."[121] Differences among a given community's members are inevitable, in part because of both the descriptive and prescriptive aspects of informal norms. As Robert Ellickson explains, "*Norm* denotes behavior that *is* normal, and behavior that people *should* mimic to avoid being punished."[122] But, he argues, since most people internalize norms as examples of behavior that typically does not result in conflict, "ordinary behavior is rarely regarded as antisocial behavior"; nevertheless, because norms are typically followed through the self-enforcement of the individual, they are decentralized and to a certain degree open to individual interpretation. The prescriptive and descriptive usages of norm "are potentially conflicting because almost everyone laments some features of the status quo."[123] What makes a legal culture cohere, in part, is that self-interested behavior does not necessarily equal antisocial or selfish behavior: norms tend to be welfare-maximizing, since most social transactions take place, in game-theory terms, in "iterated games";[124] the "players" will likely interact again, or interact with others who may have knowledge of previous transactions. Therefore, short-term gains through norm violation or cheating may diminish long-term personal welfare.[125] Even formal legal processes and institutions are "always imposed against a background stream of nonlegal regulation—enforced by gossip, disapproval, ostracism, and violence—which itself produces important collective goods."[126] As a result, informal shaming penalties are often effective precisely because they implicate networks of communication and people's desire to avoid others who are noncooperative types.[127] In a close-knit community, especially, norms will serve to maximize welfare, or, as Eric Posner puts it, to underscore and encourage equilibrium behavior.[128] What constitutes welfare-maximizing or equilibrium behavior will depend on the larger community, itself best conceived not as a structure but the web of understandings its members have regarding social relations.[129]

HOW, THEN, DO WE DETERMINE the outlines of a particular legal culture, or whether it is functional or dysfunctional? We must begin by deliberately and consciously extending the investigation beyond formal rules and formal litigation. While legal anthropology and legal studies increasingly tend to recognize the value of understanding the pluralism of law and its sources within a community, and many students of early Greek law have come to appreciate the performative and public dimensions of Greek adjudication,[130] there remains the more normativist-formalist inheritance of legal scholarship—that is, an understanding of law that focuses on its embodiment in such rules and processes.

Trouble-case processualism that recognizes dispute as one type of communication within a broader network of legal notions and processes, themselves informed by and informing other cultural beliefs and practices, promises more fruitful returns for our analysis of early Greek legal culture. Through this approach, we identify as a trouble case what Karl Llewellyn and E.A. Hoebel long ago described as "the case of doubt, or . . . that in which discipline has failed, or . . . that in which unruly personality is breaking through into new paths of action or leadership, or . . . that in which an ancient institution is being tried against emergent forces."[131] We must supplement the examination, however, with those disputes that Llewellyn and Hoebel would have characterized as "petty rows."[132] In this respect, the approach here owes some debt to Bronsilaw Malinowski, who stressed that law should be understood in terms of its function within a society, as part of a wider social complex that might also include the various reciprocal relationships that bind a society together and bring cohesion to the community as a whole. Malinowski's functionalism often led him to "confuse law with what produced it,"[133] but nevertheless, Malinowski sought to understand laws and disputes as one part of a cultural system, interdependent on other elements that shaped the society and informed the thought world of its members.[134] Malinowski's ideas, adjusted for their conceptual shortcomings, have enjoyed a renaissance among scholars associated with the Laboratoire d'Anthropologie juridique in Paris, especially Raymond Verdier, Etienne Le Roy, and Jean Carbonnier.[135] This school has emphasized "juridicization," that is, law "not so much [as] a distinct set of social relations as the particular status that each different society chooses to give certain social relations"; the process of assigning status arises from the necessity "to regulate those elements of society which are considered necessary to its maintenance."[136] Law is also seen as part of an internormative system: law converses with other fields, informing them and being informed by them.[137] It is this approach that also inheres in much recent thinking on legal cultures and Cotterrell's law-and-community model. Trouble-case processualism engages us in "modified thick description," not only identifying norms, but also the "interpretive battles" over them, and how these play out within juridical processes.[138]

As we will examine in the next chapter, even formal adjudication in early Greece was regularly attended by communal and public participation in the proceedings. We must, therefore, understand the emergence of written law in that context, because such direct and crucial involvement on the part of the community entails several consequences for our understanding of conflict and its adjudication. First, the principles upon which any dispute was resolved—short of accepted, automatic referrals to self-help—were rooted in the shared ranges of ethical values, norms, and expectations of the wider community that binds it together, that is, its rule base. However, various factors will shape the attitudes and responses of its members to a given dispute: the standing of disputants within the community (socioeconomic as well as reputational), the circumstances surrounding a dispute, the idiosyncratic interpretations of circumstances by individuals depending on their own understanding of relevant norms (though these are themselves shaped and reshaped during the process of dispute settlement, as the opinions of others emerge and community members respond to them), and so on. Second, adjudication in early Greece will have fallen much more under the realm of folk wisdom and common custom than an arcane knowledge over which some narrow corporate social interest might gain and exercise exclusive control. Though it will have been the responsibility of certain individuals in any given community to propose potential solutions to resolve a dispute and restore or maintain communal peace, wider public sentiment will have influenced the environment in which they did so. Third, the disputes within the face-to-face communities of early Greece will have implicated important social and political issues, especially when they involved members who played significant leadership roles and their relationships within the community;[139] the resolution or regulation of such disputes will have been of great concern to the community generally.

As we have already discussed, competing claims within a given legal culture may arise from a variety of origins: in the Greek example, the literature leads to an impression that there were, beyond murder, several major sources for trouble that fall into five principal categories, though these might further be classed into two overarching types. On the one hand, disapproved behavior on the behalf of one party in abrogation of the rule base would result in a perceived injury to another party and give rise to a serious dispute needing resolution before recourse to violence, whether sooner or later. On the other hand, genuine differences of opinion over what constituted approved or disapproved behavior might result in competing claims, with both parties believing that their course of action was just, based on their own internalized sense of the rule base.

These two general sources of trouble were by no means mutually exclusive. In fact, some studies in legal anthropology have shown that changes in the wider cultural complex of a society (for example, major alterations in economic organization) may have the effect of obscuring what behaviors are approved or disapproved. Hence, a perpetrator may not perceive his conduct as innovative: inspired by changing social circumstances, he inadvertently goes beyond the realm of acceptable action, causing offense to other members of the community whose own sense of the rule base might likewise be in a state of flux.[140] Otherwise, the rule base may require one action that results in another, which in and of itself gives rise to a dispute, because the reaction implicates or violates other norms. Two famous examples from Attic tragedy present central conflicts of just such an origin: Aeschylus' Orestes must kill his father's murderers, an act that involves him in matricide, while Sophocles' Antigone decides to bow to religious imperatives requiring the burial of her rebellious brother, despite a law prohibiting that honor for traitors.

Therefore, the most effective way to appreciate as fully as possible the rule base and legal culture of the early Greeks is to examine closely *all* the evidence we have for trouble in the early literature, and then determine how these trouble cases illuminate the interacting values, norms, processes, and resolutions that inform the disputing processes of the early Greeks. Studies of contemporary traditional societies may reveal certain patterns of dispute settlement and rudimentary juridical dynamics that bear similarities to what emerges from the Greek literary record. There is, however, inherent peril in finding linkage too readily by using, say, the Nuer example to complete a portrait of Greek justice in the Geometric and early Archaic Ages. Comparative material, however, can be useful in demonstrating the mechanics of conflict and dispute in human society *generally*, and therein resides its potential value. In addition to the trouble-case–processualism method of investigation, anthropological study of trouble cases and their pursuit in prestate societies with bicentric or polyarchic structures of power (and the Greeks of the eighth and even early seventh century fit that description in broad outline)[141] has established not only a vocabulary for describing the juridical phenomena found in such cultures, but also a variety of theoretical approaches for consideration.

Admittedly, the use of written materials can never substitute for firsthand ethnographic observation but obviously must suffice absent any other way to study conflict in this period. Epic will perhaps offer overly dramatized accounts of sources of trouble and their resolution, but exaggeration does not imply unreliability. What we should try to determine, beyond the fantastic narrative elements, is whether the fundamental sense of the norms and the means of addressing breaches thereof exhibits consistency among the various trouble cases we encounter in the literature. Does the literature reveal a functional legal culture?

Part of characterizing any legal culture will entail an analysis of disputes that *do* indeed find their way to formal or semiformal mediation or adjudication. Both of these types of settlement engage a third party to reach a resolution or some satisfactory regulation of an ongoing conflict. For our purposes, a mediator is a third party who assists disputants in hammering out a mutually acceptable solution on their own, while an adjudicator (whether one prefers the term umpire or referee) has the authority to impose a theoretically binding decision, regardless of how satisfactory the disputants find that solution.[142] In addition, it also is necessary to consider trouble cases that involve bilateral negotiation between the parties (that is, bargaining that does not implicate the direct participation of a third party), as well as the resort to self-help in the form of the exercise of private violence when it is not automatically allowed, which might lead to the death or exclusion of an offending party from his original community.[143] If we approach early Greek adjudication from this angle, we may reveal the underlying legal culture that informed the rule base and was informed by it, especially what Greeks considered as necessarily actionable in a wider, public context, and thus the means by which various community pressures operated to force disputants to an accommodation.

Most social groups will rely primarily on talking as the means by which they prevent or resolve disputes.[144] Anthropologists typically characterize as settlement-directed talking that which aims at defusing tension between two or more parties within the community. Settlement-directed talking assumes three principal forms. Those involved, or about to involve themselves, in a dispute may engage in bilateral negotiation, an attempt to forestall imminent disagreement or resolve any hostility before it engenders such animosity that the parties can no longer deal with one another directly without the likelihood of violence or some other, additional disruption to the community. Obvious danger inheres in bilateral negotiation, since parties discussing the source of disagreement between themselves may further aggravate the situation and make more difficult any resolution through other forms of settlement-directed talking. Mediation represents the second major type of dialogue intended to restore equilibrium between disputants and to the wider community. The mediator's role is to help disputants to a solution of their own choosing; he or she does not have the authority to resolve the matter outright. In circumstances that call for the physical separation of the disputants, for whatever reason, the mediator may likewise fulfill the role of a go-between, relaying messages between the parties. This role affords an opportunity for the mediator to have a direct influence on the mind-set of the disputants, as he or she may communicate each side's position in such a way as to mollify rancor and facilitate a solution. Finally, depending on the juridical character of their society, disputants may submit their quarrel to an umpire or referee, an ostensibly neutral third party who has the authority to act as adjudicator and impose a settlement in order to restore equilibrium.[145] In the Greek context, as we will see, adjudicators could take the form of an individual or a group of leaders proposing settlements before the assembled community.

Having established this methodology and working vocabulary for describing the general treatment of disputes, it remains to examine the disagreements described in early Greek literature, including those that implicate formal means of settlement. In these cases, the expectation was that disputants would in fact submit to some form of settlement-directed talking. The pressure to do so came from the wider community, the importance of whose opinion is never far from the surface of the dispute or the considerations of which, positively or negatively, are never far from the minds of the disputants.

CHAPTER THREE

Legal Culture in Greece before Written Law

1—An Overview of Dispute Settlement before Written Law

Since the work of Henry Sumner Maine, the verdict on "aristocratic," preliterate forms of adjudication in ancient cultures has been overwhelmingly negative. Elites who served as the arbiters of the community's disputes, so the argument has traditionally gone, at best handed down decisions that were uninformed or unpredictable and at worst engaged in systematic, self-conscious, and self-serving corruption. By controlling the mechanisms of dispute settlement, elites enhanced their own economic and political interests at the expense of weaker members of the community, promoting their own class and its goals until the community, no longer willing to stand for the arbitrary abuse of juridical power, pushed for changes ranging from how laws were recorded and administered, to even supporting wholesale changes in the nature of the community's government. There are students of early Greek law who question amelioration of popular demands as a principal motivation for the writing of laws, but typically even they proceed from the assumption that orally transmitted precepts and previous judgments summoned from memory were so subject to vagary that they could scarcely constitute a juridical system. At best, inconsistency was the hallmark of "justice" in the Homeric and Hesiodic worlds.

As we have seen, a surface reading of Hesiod surely encouraged this impression and has sustained it through a century and a half of scholarship. But is such an impression justified? With regard to justice in Geometric Greece,

Homer provides the only elaborate description of a formal hearing to resolve a dispute, the famous and oft-discussed trial scene from the Shield of Achilles (below).[1] Among those scholars who accept Homer's description as more or less representative of dispute settlement (with the necessary adjustments for possible epic exaggeration of certain elements), there is little agreement over what the details of the scene can actually reveal about the processes of litigation in early Greece, but, as we will see, the most striking feature is the manifest involvement of communal—one might even say popular—interest in early Greek litigation. The role played by the folk (*laoi* in this instance) is surely crucial to understanding the processes of dispute settlement in early Greece: their appearance around, and influence on, quarrels is not at all restricted to the scene from Achilles' shield. Rather, our sources regularly assume that the members of the community take an active role in the process of dispute settlement, and in some cases describe the popular element as having taken sides (or being expected to do so) in such matters. This participation of the wider community in the regulation and settlement of disputes is fundamental to understanding the juridical environment of the emerging *poleis* of the Geometric and early Archaic periods.

If the folk engaged routinely as a matter of course in the process of regulating the disputes of other community members, and had a significant impact on the ways in which communal stability was maintained, then the implications are great for our analysis of the context that produced Greece's first written laws. Such direct and crucial involvement on the part of the wider community would entail three important consequences regarding conflict within that community and the adjudication of disputes:

1. The principles upon which any dispute was resolved—short of accepted, automatic referrals to *lex talionis*—were organic: though the members of any society are bound together by shared ranges of ethical values and expectations (a rule base), how these values are interpreted and applied may fall anywhere along a spectrum of potential reactions to any given situation. Therefore, the views of the community's members in response to a dispute will be shaped by the social standing of the disputants, the circumstances surrounding the dispute, the personal interpretations of relevant assumptions within the rule base, and other factors.

2. Adjudication in early Greece will have fallen much more within the realm of folk wisdom and common custom than of an arcane knowledge over which some corporate social group might gain and

exercise exclusive control; in other words, the early Greek community will have necessarily been more legally pluralist than previously imagined. Though certain individuals had the responsibility of presiding over proceedings and proposing possible solutions in order to restore social peace, public opinion significantly shaped the environment in which they did so.

3. The disputes within face-to-face communities of early Greece will have possessed a very political aspect, especially those arising among members who provided leadership to the community; the resolution of disputes among such individuals will have been of paramount importance to a wider section of the population. While the ability of the community to enforce resulting *dikai* will have been informal (principally manifested as public pressure on the disputants), for the reasons discussed in Chapter 2.3, it will not have been any less effective: in small, integrated communities, the refusal to abide by communally reached decisions had the real potential to disadvantage one in future agreements and disputes. I will return to this point in the final section of the present chapter.

What needs to be determined is whether or not these features acted in a systematic fashion, if the evidence we have for early Greece suggests a functional legal culture: a consistent sense of what constitutes grounds for action, the expected means by which parties might pursue resolution, and which members of the community participate in resolving disputes and at what level. If so, then there can be little question of the arbitrariness or unpredictability of adjudication prior to the appearance of written law in Greece. Instead, the origins from which disputes arose in the early *polis*, and the way in which members regulated or settled them, occurred in a context of community influence and popular opinion, based on shared assumptions about the rule base. The pressure exerted on disputants to settle their differences through a variety of means, the agonistic character of dispute, the public character of customary "law," and the active participation of community members did not, as a system, lend themselves to manipulation toward either private individual or corporate class interests.

We will first turn to a general discussion of one type of dispute that resulted in acceptable resort to automatic self-help in the Homeric and Hesiodic worlds, namely homicide. But even here, the picture is at once complicated, and allows us to appreciate the shortcomings of normativist-formalist approaches to early Greek law, since it tends to focus exclusively on formal rules or emphasize those cases that have engaged in formal means of resolution. Concentrating our attention on disputes that proved highly intractable obscures the complexities and often-contingent nature of juridical conflict in this period and necessarily yields an incomplete view. Such cases do expose the mechanisms by which community members addressed their most nettlesome disagreements, but ultimately they can only tell us about the most spectacular disputes or strong-willed disputants. The resultant picture is distorted, because it reveals little about more quotidian sources of dispute, the informal means through which neighbors resolve problems short of violence or the threat thereof, formal arbitration, or the larger system of communication among members of a legal community, of which formal dispute resolution plays only a part.

The Homeric and Hesiodic corpora present us with twenty-five clear and relatively well-described examples of dispute, excluding those which took place between supernatural and human characters, concern themselves only with clear-cut cases of homicide, or are of a strictly intercommunity or military nature. These twenty-five disputes fall into five distinct groups: (A) disputes concerning clearly disapproved behavior (i.e., there is no confusion on the part of either party whether or not the behavior was approved), creating grounds for immediate pursuit of the resulting grievance; (B) serious disagreements over courses of action, or over what constitutes approved or disapproved behavior, which may erupt into wider disputes; (C) responses to personal challenges, threats, or other verbal insults; (D) seizure or loss of property leading to a loss of face; and (E) seizure or loss of property leading to a sense of breach of contract, or violation of a previous agreement resulting in same. These categories are by no means mutually exclusive: a dispute that arises from one of these types may quickly encompass one or more of the others, but for purposes of discussion, I treat the trouble cases according to the original issue at stake. As we will see, public pressure and opinion was considered instrumental to the resolution of disputes, in maintaining social equilibrium and alleviating tensions between disputants.

2—Automatic Self-Help and the Limits of a Normativist Approach

The inheritance of normativist legal thinking stands in the way of describing the fullness of early Greek legal culture. To be sure, individual, difficult disputes that resort to formal resolution may indicate certain features of a legal culture, but in isolation they will leave much unclear. Take, for example, the well-known description of a dispute on the Shield of Achilles:

> And the folk were crowded together in the market, and in that place
> A dispute had arisen. Two men quarreled on account of the satisfaction owed
> For a man who had been killed. One professed loudly that all had been paid,
> Declaring to the people, but the other refused to accept anything at all.
> But both were eager to accept a settlement by a Knower (*istor*).
> And the folk shouted their support for each of the two, aiding both sides;
> But at once heralds restrained the folk; and the elders
> Were sitting on smoothed stones in a sacred circle,
> And in their hands they held the scepters of the loud-voiced heralds.
> Among them thereupon they moved swiftly, each in succession
> Pronouncing a judgment,
> And then in the middle lay two talents of gold,
> To be given to him who among them might speak the straightest judgment.[2]

Homer includes this vignette in his portrait of the city at peace depicted on the Shield, despite the obvious contentiousness of the trial he describes. What renders this quarrel part of the landscape of the peaceful community, it would seem, is that the disputants have submitted it to their fellow community members rather than pursue a private feud that might have violent and disruptive results.

Students of the legal history of early Greece have understandably visited much attention on this dispute, generally agreeing that the scene reflects genuinely the typical procedure for the Homeric world (allowing for epic exaggeration of certain elements), but otherwise differing about the significance of many of the details and what they reveal regarding dispute settlement processes. The most complete description of a formal hearing in the early literature, this scene still raises many unanswered questions. Other indications about formal hearings from Hesiod's poems and the Homeric hymns are also oblique at best, and fifth-century dramatic portrayals of judicial procedure, such as Aeschylus' elaborate description of the dispute between Orestes and the Furies in the *Eumenides*, are surely more representative of contemporary Athenian practice and ideal than of generations long passed. Otherwise, our earliest detailed written accounts of actual legal proceedings come from the forensic speeches of fourth-century Attic orators and from the Aristotelian *Athenaion Politeia*. I have already described the dangers of relying too heavily on this later material in general terms, and one might note that the highly formalized regimen governing the selection of jurors and the special political role and legal sovereignty exercised by Athenian popular courts should further warn against the extensive use of this evidence for elucidating earlier juridical practices.

In a seminal article published six decades ago, Hans Julius Wolff rightly questioned evolutionary explanations for the appearance of formal dispute settlement among the Greeks that viewed litigation as having developed in response to the violence arising from the injudicious resort to *lex talionis* and self-help,[3] something the disputants in the Shield scene have apparently managed to avoid. In so doing, however, Wolff took an inherently normative approach by emphasizing the role of centralized authority—judicial magistrates and panels of judges—that heard cases primarily to determine whether or not a "plaintiff" had the right to pursue execution of his complaint against the "defendant." If the procedure issued in a decision favoring the plaintiff, he could then carry out that execution himself (and, indeed, would have to, failing any coercive state authority beyond the magistrates, whose role Wolff imagined as paramount but restricted to deciding the validity of the complaint), without fear of retribution from the defendant's kin or other allies. According to Wolff, the defendant initiated the process, since he sought to protect himself from the private justice of the plaintiff. By involving the magistrate, the defendant prevented the plaintiff from immediate satisfaction, by appeal to what amounted to the government.

Wolff's hypothesis had the virtue of challenging the tidy model that had previously prevailed, a model that masked much of the informality characteristic of early Greek adjudication, and his theory has continued to attract influential adherents, among them Raphael Sealey.[4] Nevertheless, Wolff himself still applied more formalism and institutional prejudice in his interpretation than the evidence warrants. He assumed that mechanisms existed to provide the would-be defendant an opportunity to invoke the protection of the magistrate before falling victim to a private prosecution. While a scattered, homesteader settlement pattern may or may not have characterized the proto-*polis* communities of Greece,[5] Hesiod unequivocally tells us in *Works and Days* that cultivating the goodwill of neighbors was terribly important, since kinsmen, and presumably, any relevant "magistrate," might live at a distance and take longer to arrive should trouble arise.[6] In such an environment, it is difficult to imagine the practical operation of the scheme Wolff envisaged. It seems there would have been little opportunity for a surprised defendant, in the face of a determined act of self-help, to locate the competent magistrate and employ his temporary protection.

His assumption that the pressure of public opinion was not at all sufficient to restrain the violence engendered by the execution of self-help led Wolff to take this more normativist-institutional view of judicial procedure. Because he did not afford any importance to informal, socially determined influences on potential private justice, he necessarily sought evidence for a well-defined set of procedures governed by specifically empowered magistrates. Wolff emphasized, I believe unduly, the proscriptive sanctions against the unrestrained pursuit of self-help and believed that the central authority responsible for enforcing such sanctions would have been adequately powerful to impose the procedures he hypothesized; this approach to the study of early Greek litigation falls squarely within the normativist attitudes that typified both anthropology and Greek legal history through and beyond the Second World War.[7] Though I agree with Wolff's contention that formal litigation did not thus displace self-help—indeed, within limits Athenian citizens could claim rights of self-help even in the fourth century[8]—we may question his interpretation of the means by which litigants pursued their claims in the eighth and seventh centuries.

Criticizing Wolff's framework is one matter but offering an alternative model that will bear scrutiny is another. Nevertheless, it is critical to any discussion of early Greek law to understand the processes by which disputants may or may not have resolved disputes arising out of competing claims, as well as the role played by such settlements in the overall social system of early Greek communities. As Norbert Rouland emphasizes, "What must be analyzed is the role of mediation in the global workings of each society, in particular in relation to other ways of settling disputes."[9]

In this context, it will be useful to consider actions that resulted not in mediation but rather in an automatic exercise of self-help and, quite often, the exile of the offending party, in the Greek context, as well as in many modern-day traditional societies, the most extreme form of exclusion and tantamount to a sentence of social or even physical death.[10] Homicide and society's reaction to it provide the clearest example of an action that leads directly to self-help and typically to exclusion. Gagarin has collected and commented on the various instances of homicide in the Archaic literature,[11] and there is little need to repeat at length his intelligent discussion of this matter; a summary of his findings will suffice. In considering thirty-one instances of homicide, either successfully executed or contemplated, Gagarin concluded that the most common result was for the killer to flee into exile to avoid retribution.[12] Homicides would find no quarter in the community, as there was no bar to the exercise of self-help by the victim's kin (though the victim's kin might accept compensation, as stated by Ajax in the *Iliad*[13]). In Archaic Athenian law, at least from the time of Drakon, there was protection for the killer so long as he remained outside the territory controlled by the *polis* and avoided the frontier markets as well as amphictyonic games and rituals,[14] venues where he would be most likely to encounter the relatives of his victim. Outside of these circumstances, the exaction of revenge against a killer would result in the same liability to punishment by exclusion or exposure to self-help as the perpetrator himself suffered.[15] Whether these provisions originated with Drakon or stem from earlier customary practices is unknowable, though clues from his homicide law and from epic suggest a deeper history for restraints on the exercise of self-help, however ill defined these may have been. Drakon's allowance for revenge at amphictyonic celebrations and frontier markets implies that these would be the only likely places where the killer and his victim's kin might confront one another if the former fled Athens. In this respect, Drakon's provision includes a notion we find in the epic evidence, which betrays a consistent concept that flight equals safety from blood retribution, particularly in the theme of the suppliant murderer at the court of a powerful benefactor.[16]

Implicitly, Greek culture allowed for automatic self-help against a killer who remained in the area. Indeed, the fact that intentional homicide led directly to an understanding that the killer must either (a) flee the community, or (b) consider his life forfeit unless the victim's kin agreed to some other form of compensation, suggests that the assumptions governing this infraction amounted as closely to a formal rule as any the Greeks of this period possessed. Despite the threat of private violence in response, the sanction for such action existed within a wider community, which would neither protect the homicide nor interfere otherwise with the right of self-help belonging to the victim's relatives. A second implication has already been mentioned, but deserves more exploration. The removal of the killer from the community, in the case of Drakon's code and in the instances from epic literature, placed limits on the ability of aggrieved parties to avenge the death of a kinsman. In Drakon's homicide law, this prohibition is explicit;[17] in the stories from epic, the meme of the less-than-unfortunate fate of the exiled homicide, who even enjoyed honor and wealth in his new surroundings, suggests a longer-standing norm that voluntary exclusion from one's family, resources, and identity sufficed as punishment. So long as the killer removed himself from the life of the community and avoided places of possible contact, he was no longer subject to vengeance and might even prosper. The killer had suffered enough through his exile, and no further action against him by the victim's relatives was acceptable.[18]

Limits on revenge against an exiled killer raise the intriguing problem of why such exclusion precluded any further, legitimate punishment. The aforementioned dangers to the outlaw provide part of the explanation: additional action against the excluded killer may have been viewed as gratuitous and overly vindictive. To the killer's family, he was already as good as dead, and they would have been within their rights to pursue blood feud should the original victim's kinsmen pursue the matter through retributive killing. Notions of pollution and its removal may have played a part. The murder of a human being necessitated expiation, a recognition that a death had occurred and someone or something was responsible: the continued presence of the consequent pollution tainted the life of the entire community.[19] Indeed, even in Classical Athens, the Prytaneion sat to "try" animals, inanimate objects, and unknown killers believed responsible for a homicide.[20] Furthermore, though later Athenian law provided a separate court for the trial of unintentional homicide (the Palladion) and allowed for a category of murder that Gagarin labels lawful homicide,[21] the origin of these provisions is unclear and not necessarily of early date. The first explicit reference to any distinction between intentional (*hekôn, ek pronoias*) and unintentional (*akôn, mê ek pronoias*) homicide occurs in Drakon's law.[22] While later sources designate unintentional homicide as the preserve of the Palladion, with the *ephêtai* sitting as judges,[23] Drakon refers only to the *ephêtai* and does not specify a venue.[24] It seems likely that while Drakon articulated a series of provisions responding to the problematic treatment of perpetrators of different types of homicide, he did not create a separate judicial institution to hear the cases arising from it.[25] Concern with identifying, trying, and removing offending individuals or even objects bespeaks a notion that the unresolved killing of a person, in most circumstances, could contaminate the community.[26] Furthermore, the epic and later traditions regarding it reveal that there prevailed an assumption that pollution followed the killer beyond his home territory, necessitating a ritual purification.[27]

However, pollution can provide only part of the explanation for the perceived necessity to drive a killer into exile, as not all acts of homicide necessarily contaminated the community. As early as Drakon, there is the emergence of at least one type of killing that is excused from penalty, beyond the authorization to slay killers if they remained in town or appeared in the prohibited places.[28] Drakon's statute allowed a free man to kill an assailant—at the time of assault—in instances of violent or unjust robbery or seizure.[29] Drakon may also have provided other exceptions, though here we are forced to speculate. The inscription all but breaks off from lines 31 through 34, and again from line 38 forward, that is to say, on either side of the protection extended to homicide in self-defense. Certainly, by the fourth century, Athenian law encompassed a range of homicide offenses that did not allow for exile as punishment or were simply exculpated ipso facto. These categories of justifiable or lawful homicide included deaths that took place in athletic competition, provided the victor did not *intend* to kill his opponent,[30] and any murder of a fellow citizen as the result of confusion during battle, with intent once again crucial, as ignorance of the victim's identity constituted the exculpatory factor.[31] Additionally, lawful homicide could take place in encounters with highwaymen and others who might wish to seize one's person or property without justification,[32] in the apprehension of thieves attempting to steal by night,[33] or in the discovery of another man's adultery with one's female relations.[34] How old these precepts were by the age of the orators is not known, but in at least one case—the permissibility of homicide in personal self-defense—the law quoted is true to the spirit of the old Drakontian provision. The *ephêtai* heard the claims of accused homicides to have killed lawfully in the court of the Delphinion, a temple of ancient significance dedicated to Apollo and Artemis. Again, the date of this court acquiring its brief is hopelessly obscure. We might note, however, the prominence of self-help in the defense of one's property in these legal exceptions, which might in turn speak to a fairly long history for the use of legitimate deadly force in circumstances other than vengeance for a slain kinsman.

Since some killings did not create a sense of pollution strong enough to drive the perpetrator into exile or to automatically entitle the relatives of the victims to exercise of the *lex talionis*, we should ask the following question: why did the community choose to withdraw support or protection from the homicide in many instances yet defend the right of the individual to exercise private, lethal force under other circumstances? Part of the answer resides in the importance of the community and its stability. The man who unjustifiably killed another has not only created the possibility of a greater conflict resulting from blood feud but also represents a potential danger for the future; he may be capable of killing again.[35] He must be removed, whether through exile or through his acceptable death at the hands of his victim's kin. Alternatively, the community is willing to forgive the homicide whose victim is an obvious malefactor: adulterers, bandits, and burglars were also disruptive to social harmony. Furthermore, punishment by death or exile of an athlete or warrior whose offense was truly accidental did not amount to justice. Such individuals might be less than ideal opponents or comrades, but otherwise the hazard they presented to future community stability was minimal. In short, the treatment of intentional, unjustifiable homicide can enlighten us regarding certain assumptions about social stability and regarding the role of the community in its maintenance; but, unlike the violation of many other norms, intentional, unjustifiable homicide did not admit of informal dispute processes. The choices before the killer were typically automatic and stark and backed by the force of communal opinion.

These dynamics, of course, might be applicable in broad outline to almost all human societies. For the Greeks, however, we will see the paramount authority of the community as well in those disputes that admit of no resort to violent self-help whatsoever but rather required various forms of settlement-directed talking. Despite the thoroughness with which scholars have studied the issue of dispute settlement and law in early Greece, attempts to understand the mechanics of adjudication in the Late Geometric and early Archaic ages have nevertheless typically focused on what prove to be exceptional episodes.[36] The trial scene on the Shield of Achilles, the allusions to litigation in Hesiod's *Works and Days*, and the dispute between Menelaos and Antilokhos over their respective finishes in the chariot race, are all examples of disputes that ultimately implicate some formal or semiformal processes in reaching resolution. Concentrating solely on legally actionable conflicts, especially those that require formal arbitration, runs the risk of ignoring the reaction to, and handling of, a broad range of potentially disruptive occurrences.[37] Any picture of a legal culture or system constructed only from its most dramatic and intractable cases decontextualizes formal processes from the overall matrix of social values and discourses from which disputes arise and by which they might find resolution, whether they be great or small. The maintenance of social order, even in complex societies, can and does depend to a large extent on extralegal mechanisms; to ignore these is to ignore the wider reaction of society to potential disruptions of the social order. In short, a picture of dispute regulation and settlement that relies totally or even principally on cases involving formal and semiformal adjudication is likely to mislead.

TO RETURN, THEN, TO THE FRUSTRATING gaps Homer has left us in the trial scene on the Shield of Achilles, at least one feature of dispute settlement need not remain vague from analysis of this passage alone. While many of the specific issues represented by descriptions of dispute are difficult and controversial, the fact of communal—even popular—participation is manifest in the scene and elsewhere in early Greek literature. Our sources regularly assume that the members of the community will take an active role in any formal proceedings, and, as in the trial scene from the Shield of Achilles, that they will take sides or are at least expected to. Short of formal dispute resolution, the disputants often have the reactions of other community members very much in mind as they proceed. For the reader's convenience, I have enumerated the disputes under consideration by the major categories of dispute (***A–E***).

3—Disputes concerning Clearly Disapproved Behavior (A)

Eight occasions of this type of dispute arise in the literature and implicate courses of self-help, though along lines more complex than cases of intentional homicide. In these trouble cases, though violent attempts at redress may result, the response of the wider community necessarily conditions any violence, whether contemplated or undertaken. Of these eight quarrels, two involve retribution for the slaying of a kinsman, while the other six entail the seizure of property but in such a way as to differentiate them from the types of dispute that belong to categories D and E.[38] In these eight cases, the aggrieved parties considered as incumbent upon themselves an active role in gaining satisfaction. Their right to act sprang from the fact that the behavior that precipitated the conflict was clearly disapproved behavior: the transgressor could not or did not persuasively claim a legitimate basis for his actions, a distinction created of course by the communal sense of right and wrong embedded in the rule base. Therefore, the offended party sought satisfaction directly.

A1. Among these examples are three separate instances of cattle theft. A Hesiodic fragment recounts the tale of Melampos, whom Iphiklos apprehended in the act of stealing livestock. Iphiklos bound the would-be thief and took him to Aegina; we may speculate what was to happen to Melampos next, since Aegina's bustling trade[39] made it an ideal place to sell Melampos into slavery. The foiled thief's gift of prophecy ultimately saved him, however: he predicted the imminent collapse of the house in which Iphiklos was staying, thus saving his captor's life. In recognition of Melampos' good turn, Iphiklos released him, avoiding reproach were he to push the matter further.

A2. The grounds for fearing such a reproach may be found in a similar case of thievery and personal seizure as recounted in the *Homeric Hymn to Hermes*. Hermes had stolen and hidden some of Apollo's prize cattle, and when Apollo learned of the theft he "not unjustly seized glorious Hermes on account of the cattle" after his threats failed to persuade the offender.[40] Apollo, despite his right to deal violently with Hermes, nevertheless decided to submit the matter to the third-party arbitration of Zeus as Hermes suggested, perhaps because he recognized the need for the involvement of the community.[41] Though Hermes offered to swear an oath that Apollo's cattle were not in his possession, Zeus saw through his deception and instead bade Hermes to guide Apollo to the cattle.[42] Upon discovering that Hermes had already slaughtered two of them, Apollo attempted to bind him and only desisted when Hermes had handed over as compensation the lyre that so pleased Apollo; at that point the two had settled the quarrel and swore oaths of mutual friendship.[43]

A3. The other "instance" of cattle theft is that imagined by Achilles, when he reminded Agamemnon that he personally had no quarrel with the Trojans, who were not at fault with him, never having driven away his cattle or horses or spoiled the grain in Phthia.[44] Had the Trojans done so, then Achilles would have been at Troy on his own account, pursuing his own grievance. Similarly to Iphiklos and Apollo, for Achilles an appropriate recourse would have been retributive violence against those who had stolen his property. The extent to which individuals could pursue their own solutions in cases of cattle theft was limited, however; Apollo felt the need to refer the dispute to third-party settlement, and both he and Iphiklos released the offender once suitable compensation had been made.

A4. Seizure of property other than livestock or grain created a much knottier problem in Homeric society and engaged the wider community even more directly and extensively in the resolution of the dispute. In the *Hymn to Demeter*, Hades famously seized Persephone. Once Demeter learned of the abduction, her recourse was not violence but rather withdrawal from the community of the gods and the withholding of her vital skills.[45] Demeter's anger led her to avoid the gathering place of the gods (*agora*) and Olympus, staying apart and causing a year of suffering for humankind as she refused to make the grain grow.[46] In so withdrawing, she would have "destroyed the entire race of articulate-speaking men with grievous famine, and robbed those holding their home on Olympus the glorious honor of gifts and sacrifices."[47] Prompted by this crisis, Zeus sent messenger after messenger from among the gods, commanding Demeter to return to them: she refused and persisted in her noncooperation, reiterating her demand that Persephone be returned before she restored fertility to the earth.[48] Having failed in his attempts at persuasion, Zeus imposed himself as a third-party negotiator between Demeter and Hades, bidding the latter to surrender Persephone; he did so, but only after employing the trick that prevented Persephone from leaving his domain forever.[49] Only when Zeus had hammered out a compromise solution did Demeter agree to bring forth once again the fruits of the earth.[50] Thus Zeus, in his aspect as *basileus*, had interceded and handed down a solution acceptable to both parties, which restored harmony to the community by convincing Demeter to end her withdrawal of forms of mutual support and resource sharing.

A5. In other cases of the seizure of relatives or females attached to a particular household, not everyone observed the circumspection of Demeter. The abduction of Helen by Paris from the house of Menelaos constituted the initial casus belli between the Achaeans and Trojans.[51] Paris' fellow Trojans reminded him that he was liable to stoning for the misfortune he brought on the community: Hector upbraided Paris both personally and in the latter's absence for his role in the city's current troubles,[52] and when Paris proposed single combat between himself and Menelaos to settle the issue, Hector underscored to the Achaeans as he conveyed the message that all the fault belonged to his brother.[53] Despite his fault, however, the Trojans rallied around Paris as his support group, implying that his seizure of Helen did not automatically make his life forfeit; by lending their support, the Trojan community could exert tremendous influence on Paris through public opinion.[54] Only under the weight of communal disapproval did Paris, something of a personal coward, decide to challenge Menelaos to the aforementioned single combat in order to settle the issue, a test of strength for Helen and all her possessions.[55]

The various parties believed this single combat could serve as a mechanism for ending the quarrel and thus the war: Paris stressed the importance of ending hostilities regardless of the duel's outcome, a sentiment Hector reiterated when he announced the proposal to both sides, and both Achaeans and Trojans were pleased at the prospect of the immediate end of the dispute.[56] Because of the faithlessness and arrogance of the sons of Priam, Menelaos insisted that the old king of Troy swear an oath to abide by the results.[57] As the superior warrior, Menelaos quickly gained the upper hand, and only the intervention of Aphrodite saved Paris just before the Spartan king delivered the coup-de-grace.[58] Technically, the quarrel remained open, since neither man had finished the other, but Agamemnon pointed to the fact that Menelaos had bested Paris and directed the Trojans to surrender Helen, her wealth, and such additional compensation as was due: failing the death of Paris himself, his brazen violation of Menelaos' honor could only be satisfied by such returns and payments.[59] All the Achaeans shouted their assent[60] and thus as Menelaos' support group in the quarrel, indicated their readiness to support Agamemnon's interpretation and to continue to aid Menelaos' cause.

With the issue still unresolved, and the hosts gathered uneasily opposite one another, Pandaros fired an arrow and hit Menelaos in the thigh.[61] Agamemnon denounced the false treatment at the hands of the Trojans, accusing them of violating their oath and promising they would compensate ("give honor back," *apetisan*) with their heads, their wives, and their children. This breach of faith remained an issue and now implicated the support groups as direct parties to the dispute. The Trojan Antenor urged the return of Helen, particularly with reference to the broken oath, from which point the Trojans fought falsely.[62] Paris refused this advice but declared publicly that he would offer Menelaos rich gifts and Helen's own possessions, but not Helen herself.[63] When the Achaeans received this proposal, it was not Menelaos but Diomedes who refused it, stating that neither treasure nor Helen herself should be accepted, now that "cords of destruction are bound upon the Trojans."[64] The entire Achaean host shouted their approval, and Agamemnon told the Trojan ambassador that Zeus would be witness to their oaths.[65] Through their violation of the agreements and oaths of the previous day, the Trojans rendered the Achaeans as a whole an aggrieved party that extended well beyond Menelaos' quarrel with Paris. The resolution of this broader grievance could be nothing other, in Achaean eyes, than the destruction of Troy.

Contra Gagarin,[66] I believe we may include this whole episode in an analysis of disputes and their settlements in early Greece, as the military setting does not change the basic features here of the type of extended feud that could take place between support groups within a community. Menelaos and Paris both enjoyed kin allegiance as the bedrock of their respective support groups, into which others were drawn through personal or sociopolitical obligations. Paris, the initiator of the trouble, pressed by the opinion of certain members within his group, found himself forced to offer a solution that would expose him and him alone to danger. Menelaos' skill as a warrior, combined with his desire for personal vengeance on Paris,[67] induced him to accept the proposal for single combat. Both support groups then swore oaths and performed sacrifices to the end that there would be no further conflict between them under the aegis of exacting vengeance for the loser of the duel.

Some scholars, incorrectly in my view, have seen in such devices as the trial by combat and the exchange of oaths an indication of recourse to the irrational in Greek dispute settlement.[68] The combat is not a "method of proof," needed to determine who is in the right and who in the wrong.[69] The quarrel here is clearly defined; the facts of the case are not in doubt, as Paris had violated the customs of guest friendship and dishonored Menelaos by stealing his wife. Even the members of Paris' support group, rather than deny his culpability or defend his actions, regularly remind him of his fault in the matter. Indeed, they apply pressure to him most likely because the costs of their continued assistance have become exceptionally high and their cohesion has begun disintegrating.[70] The personal contest between Paris and Menelaos is best understood not as a method of proof but rather as an example of a mechanism for bringing long-standing and costly episodes of intergroup violence to an end.

The use of single combat would no doubt have been rare—this is the only dispute in the surviving literature where it actually comes to pass—and exercised only as a last resort when two conditions necessarily pertained. First, the original disputants would still have to be alive and agreeable to such a resolution. Second, a groundswell of opinion inside at least one and probably both support groups would have to exist, a rough consensus that the utility of pursuing the feud at a corporate level had passed. Paris, the weaker soldier, offered single combat because opinion in Troy had turned against him; Menelaos agreed because of his superior martial prowess and the growing weariness among the Achaeans to continue the fight. With both disputants having assented to a personal test of strength to end the quarrel, all that remained was to cement the arrangement through the exchange of oaths. Due to Pandaros' violation of the truce between support groups, however, the feud transformed into a corporate grievance, no longer resolvable through the single combat of the original disputants. The role of wider opinion was crucial in both phases of the dispute, despite its having originated from a private individual grievance; furthermore, the clarity of the issues involved, and the ready acceptability to the larger community of the various stages through which the dispute passed, suggest that the expectations and assumptions governing the quarrel as it moved from private to corporate were widely held and understood.

A6. Whereas there was no doubt about the impropriety of Paris' actions, the central dispute in the *Odyssey* involved much cloudier issues. So long as Odysseus was presumed to be dead, the suitors who wooed Penelope and devoured the hero's estate in front of the hapless Telemakhos had legitimate grounds for believing their actions justified.[71] Upon Odysseus' arrival in Ithaca, however, he immediately began planning the exercise of self-help against those who had plundered his property and sought the hand of his wife. Athena, who possessed the special knowledge that the poet and his audience do—namely, that Odysseus yet lived—counseled him, "Take thought how you may lay your hands on the shameless suitors, who now for three years have been lording it in your halls, wooing your godlike wife."[72] No countenancing a peaceful resolution here: at various points between Odysseus' arrival and the slaughter of his rivals, the poet provides justification for the resort to violence.[73]

When Odysseus killed Antinoös, the central character among the suitors, and revealed himself to the others, he enumerated the substance of his complaints against them: "You dogs, you reckoned that never would I return homeward from among the people of Troy, as you have ground down my household, have lain beside the women of the household by force, and courted clandestinely the wife of one who yet lives, neither fearing the gods who hold broad heaven, nor any wrath of men to come afterwards."[74] He next pronounced that upon them all "the cords of destruction" were now bound firmly, an echo of Diomedes' proclamation when Paris' second offer to Menelaos was refused.[75] Though the nature of epic poetry was to employ and repeat certain formulae, as Nagy has argued, those formulae do not exist independently of the themes that inform the composition-in-performance.[76] It may be that in the world of the Homeric poet, a statement such as Diomedes' or Odysseus' signaled the intention of an aggrieved party to pursue the dispute through violence and gain satisfaction through the death of the (perceived) offender.[77]

The remaining suitors responded to Odysseus by admitting the validity of his grievances but also impressing upon him that the ringleader, Antinoös, was already deservedly dead in return for the folly and wickedness of his deeds. Eurymakhos took the lead among the remaining suitors and asked Odysseus to spare them so that they could make good the losses to his property as well as provide additional compensation until such time as they had satisfied his honor (*timên*).[78] Odysseus rejected even a hypothetical offer of all present patrimony and future wealth from the suitors and reiterated his intention to kill them all: it was up to them to fight or flee.[79] The other suitors then prepared themselves for the violence which Odysseus, Telemakhos, and Athena—in the guise of Mentor—wrought upon them. The stakes for joining in such a bloody feud are clear, when "Mentor" appears and Agelaos, one of the suitors, threatens that not only will Mentor pay with his own life for taking part, but that the victorious suitors would mix his property with that of the house of Odysseus and not allow Mentor's son to enjoy his patrimony or his wife and daughters to live in the city;[80] the dispute is a zero-sum game for all those who would pursue it to the end. Indeed, only two survive the slaughter. Phemios, the poet who had entertained the suitors during their revels, supplicated himself at Odysseus' knees (*gounoumai*) and asserted his right to live because his participation was "in no way willing"; Telemakhos bade his father not to cut down this guiltless man and requested also that he save the herald Medon, who had raised Telemakhos, provided that the man was not already dead.[81] Once Medon revealed himself from his hiding place, Odysseus smiled at him and bade him remove himself from the slaughter in the hall.[82]

A7. Despite Odysseus' conviction of righteousness in exacting revenge through violence, and Eurymakhos' acknowledgment—sincere or otherwise—of the justice of his complaint against he suitors, the customs of Ithaca did not sanction his violent actions. As the killing ensued, the suitors twice raised the possibility of notifying the people of the community, whom they expected would side with them and help stop Odysseus.[83] Afterwards, Odysseus' father Laertes anticipated that the matter would result in further violence, involving all the Ithacans and possibly men from the nearby island of Kephallenia, even though he himself considered the suitors to have received what they deserved.[84] Eupeithes, the father of Antinoös, further suggested general public outrage at Odysseus' conduct: he addressed some assembled group of people (the antecedent of the pronouns *hoi* and *autoi* is unclear),[85] but the language of the subsequent passage (*agorên, êgerthen, agorêsato*) indicates that his was a public speech intended for a wide audience.[86] Eupeithes preceded his complaint about the slaughter of the suitors by recalling the fact that Odysseus had first led off many brave Achaeans, folk whom he destroyed along with his ships.[87] The language of the passage (*ôlese laous*) suggests an active role on the part of Odysseus in killing the men who accompanied him to Troy and forms a neat rhetorical parallel with the verb employed in the very next line, *ekteine*, to describe his actions against the suitors. Perhaps Eupeithes sought to raise support for his cause among those who, while they had no relation to the suitors, might still be persuaded to take up the cause against Odysseus on account of others whom he had led to their deaths.

Time was of the essence. Eupeithes expected Odysseus and those who had aided him to flee into exile;[88] the very fact of Odysseus' anticipated, automatic flight indicates Eupeithes' sincerity in seeing the slaughter of the suitors as unjustified, with the homicide and his family sure to take the normal, expected course of action. He urged those assembled to prevent the murderers from escaping, lest the Ithacans become objects of shame for failing to avenge their sons and brothers.[89] Halitherses countered Eupeithes by reminding the Ithacans that they themselves were to blame for what happened, since they heeded neither him nor Mentor when warned to stop the foolishness of their sons; he added that the assembled folk should not seek revenge against Odysseus "lest anyone should find a woe drawn upon himself."[90] Nevertheless, and as before, the majority ignored Halitherses, rising up with cries to gather their arms and follow Eupeithes in battle against the house of Odysseus.[91] The killing of the suitors thus constituted an act that transcended behavior to which Odysseus was entitled, and the better part of the community moved against him. Murder was still murder, and however inappropriate the behavior of the suitors, their kin and supporters felt justified in seeking redress. Laertes killed Eupeithes at Athena's urging, whereupon Odysseus and the rest of his party fell upon the others, but the goddess then resolved the conflict by stopping the carnage and holding back all the people (*laon hapanta*).[92] Athena then ordered all present to cease from grievous war; terrified of the goddess, the disputants swore to a truce under her aegis, ending the poem.[93]

A8. It has been suggested that the ending of the *Odyssey* is thus contrived and awkward, bringing complicated and bloody matters to a rather tidy conclusion, a happy ending, as it were: divine intervention allowed the community to avoid further violence, especially among the elite. Alternate endings were still known later in antiquity.[94] One of these endings—the exile of Odysseus—is far more consistent with the general treatment of homicide in the Homeric epics and other evidence from early Greece, and thus we need not take seriously the dea ex machina at the end of the *Odyssey* as reflective of the usual expectations regarding resolution of such a violent dispute. Furthermore, the denouement of Odysseus' standoff with the angry citizens of Ithaca, in the received version of the *Odyssey*, is also inconsistent with the resolution of its closest analog in the epics, the fallout from the murder of Agamemnon by Aigisthos and the latter's slaying by Orestes.[95] While in the case of the suitors, who as we will see could claim some legitimate basis for their action (***B1***), Aigisthos had no justification for his treachery against Agamemnon (in Homer's presentation, at least; Aeschylus is another matter).[96] Thus, Orestes enjoyed praise for the murder of Aigisthos and all of his followers and in the Homeric version of the tale the son of Agamemnon suffered no further repercussion from the incident.[97] Orestes may have rendered the issue moot by killing *all* of Aigisthos' followers (thus no one remained to pursue the resultant grievance); his matricide could be excused, at least in the epic tradition, since his mother's participation in the crime had been as willing as that of Aigisthos.[98]

However, Orestes may have found further sanction for his actions in the very nature of the deed he sought to avenge, which could in no way be excused or justified. The son of Agamemnon's right to vengeance may have been as absolute as the Homeric world could know: Aigisthos had engaged in clearly disapproved behavior, and thus Orestes' right to redress was automatic and unquestioned. Odysseus' dispute with the suitors, on the other hand, had as its antecedent a quarrel of a different kind, which involved sincere differences of opinion over what did and did not constitute approved or disapproved behavior. The literature offers five such quandaries,[99] and that involving the suitors and Odysseus' son Telemakhos provides a useful starting point for a discussion of these.

4—Serious Disagreements over Courses of Action or Approved/Disapproved Behavior (*B*)

B1. The long-suffering Telemakhos, finally emboldened by Athena in the guise of Mentes, resolved to take his dispute with the suitors to the folk of Ithaca. At issue was the suitors' insistence upon consuming Odysseus' property—Telemakhos' patrimony—until such time as Penelope accepted the fact of her widowhood and chose one among them as her new husband. Telemakhos sought to enlist the support of the community in driving the suitors from his home, and in the assembly he tried to harangue the townspeople into action as he ridiculed the behavior of the suitors, clearly expecting that they should concern themselves with the dispute.[100] Antinoös effectively shifted the blame from the suitors to Penelope herself who, he claimed, had deceived them all and was unwilling to make a choice.[101] Telemakhos then engaged the suitors in debate before the assembly, and the substance of each side's position becomes clearer.

The suitors' complaint revolved around the fact that Penelope had for four years kept them waiting; Eurymakhos underscored the "patience" of the suitors, implying that they should not, and would not, be forestalled any longer, and would continue to apply pressure to Telemakhos' resources unless and until he relented.[102] They expected Telemakhos to send his mother back to her father's house so that a wedding feast and dowry could be prepared for her marriage to the man her father would choose for her.[103] Such a demand was not unreasonable for men who, understandably, believed Penelope to be a widow;[104] in fact, Telemakhos had anticipated Eurymakhos' argument in the opening stages of the debate. The son of Odysseus stated that he could not cast his own mother out of his household, and it would be misery for him to have to pay Penelope's father Ikarios a great price, as he must if he sent her back and thereby insulted his grandfather.[105] The dispute then unfolded between two parties with competing claims as to what was appropriate behavior. On the one hand, the suitors have a legitimate basis for complaint: to all appearances, Odysseus would not return, and the reasonable presumption was that he was dead (even Telemakhos frequently supposed as much). On the other hand, Telemakhos cannot offend his grandfather's honor, nor can he shoulder the burden of paying him the satisfaction for such an offense. Furthermore, Telemakhos does not have the physical or political might to expel them by force, and, as we have already seen, the application of violence by Odysseus was not sanctioned or approved by the wider community in any event. Thus, the route of self-help was probably not realistically open to Telemakhos anyway, even had he the temperament or ability to exercise it.[106] His only recourse was to summon the assembly and enlist the support of the community to aid him, principally, I suspect, by rallying public opinion to his side. Such an attempt by an aggrieved party to engage in semiformal and public means of dispute resolution, particularly with a view to currying community favor, is consistent with a pattern we will encounter below with regard to more formal modes of litigation (***D2***, ***D3***, ***E1***, ***E3***, ***E4***).

Telemakhos was unsuccessful, but not because the folk were *unable* to help. Rather, they were unwilling. Athena, in the guise of Mentor, railed at their apathy and inaction, and Nestor suggested to Telemakhos that he must have yielded to the suitors because the people had turned against him.[107] When the suitors began to fear that public opinion might be turning against them, Antinoös urged the clandestine murder of Telemakhos (their first desperate act), "because he [was] himself skilled both in counsel and mind, and the people no longer at all [bore] toward us any favor."[108] Antinoös also counseled immediate action, before Telemakhos could gather the Achaeans in assembly.[109] The importance of maintaining favorable public opinion is manifest, even in a dispute in which the public had previously been unwilling to participate actively or directly.

B2. More obscure is the quarrel that arose between Amphitryon and his father-in-law Elektryon, as related by Hesiod. The description is admittedly thin, but the poet tells us that Amphitryon, "angry about oxen," killed Elektryon and so left his fatherland for Thebes.[110] Beyond this, Hesiod is silent on the cause of the row between the two characters, but as we have already seen in the cases of Melampos and Iphiklos (***A1***) as well as Apollo and Hermes (***A2***), there may have been a general principle that allowed for violent treatment of a cattle thief. Most likely, Amphitryon believed that the cattle were his; it is difficult to understand why else he might be angry about them, so much as to kill his father-in-law. In slaying Elektryon, however, Amphitryon overstepped the bounds of approved behavior, though he may have believed justifiable his resort to self-help against a cattle thief. As a result of the confusion, and the outrage that must have followed, Amphitryon fled to Thebes. Presumably, short of merely seizing the cattle back, some sort of bilateral negotiation or the type of formal litigation we will encounter below, was the appropriate course of action for Amphitryon to undertake.

The other three examples in this category constitute disputes that indeed are defused through successful bilateral negotiation. All three of these cases involve differences of opinion between members of the divine community, potentially serious quarrels over a course of action. Peaceful resolution through face-to-face, bilateral negotiation—particularly given the divine context—may have served a didactic purpose,[111] an example of how to prevent disputes from becoming disruptive to the society as a whole. Even if this was not the case, the interaction between the gods demonstrated a certain give-and-take probably considered necessary for a successful resolution or avoidance of escalation of disputes.

B3. In the first of these disputes, Hera insisted on the destruction of the Trojans after Aphrodite's timely rescue of Paris from the clutches of Menelaos. She had toiled long toward this end, and she protested when Zeus suggested that the gods might consider establishing peace between the Achaean and Trojan hosts after the duel yielded a result in favor of the king of Sparta.[112] Zeus recognized the passion with which Hera sought to destroy the Trojans and therefore decided not to resist her, saying, "Do as you wish, lest this very quarrel between you and me should become a great strife around us both."[113] However, his acquiescence came at a price: some day when it pleased his heart to destroy a people dear to Hera, she must not hinder his anger but allow him to wreak such destruction as he saw fit. The queen of the gods agreed, and Athena then went to provoke the Trojans into breaking the oaths exchanged between the hosts.[114]

B4. Athena and Apollo similarly avoided allowing a disagreement to erupt into a violent confrontation between them. Athena wished to aid the Achaeans in battle as she, like Hera, favored their victory over the Trojans. Apollo, sympathetic to the Trojans, sped to meet her, hoping to restrain her from joining battle on the side of the Achaeans. He persuaded Athena not to enter the fight, reminding her that ultimately the Achaeans would achieve the seizure of Troy, the goal of the goddesses.[115] As a result, Apollo himself did not have to enter the fray on the side of the Trojans and battle his sister directly, preventing the possibility of violence between them through the same type of offer and counteroffer employed by Zeus and Hera.

B5. Finally, Zeus and Poseidon narrowly avoided what might have been a terrible conflict, much to the relief of the former, who told Apollo, "But this (outcome) for both is far more profitable, for me as well as him, that having been wroth he yielded before my hands, since not without sweat indeed would it have been decided."[116] The dispute between them arose from Poseidon's continued aid to the Achaeans while Zeus slept, when the king of the gods had wished him to desist and sent the messenger Iris to tell the god of the sea to cease from the war and return either to the tribes of the gods or to his watery haunts. Zeus expected difficulty from his brother and so told Iris to remind Poseidon that he could not hope to resist his mightier and elder-born brother.[117] Indeed, when Iris delivered the message, Poseidon rejected Zeus' entreaty, bristled at the latter's intimation of force, and stated that Zeus should remain quietly in the portion given to him, namely the sky.[118] Iris, understanding the reception that awaited such a response on Olympus, then assumed the role of a third-party go-between, essentially asking Poseidon if that was *really* what he wanted to have conveyed to Zeus, the elder born whom the Furies ever follow and aid.[119] At this subtle admonition, Poseidon relented, but did insist that there would be wrath (*kholos*) between him and Zeus if the latter should prevent the destruction of Troy.[120]

In all three of these potentially violent quarrels, it is clear that we have attempts at *regulation* through bilateral negotiation, and in two cases the accession of one party to the other's long term goals in exchange for a short term gain was critical: the parties reached no resolution of the underlying tension. Despite Zeus' and Apollo's agreement to allow the ultimate ruin of

Troy, they both endeavored to forestall the result as long as possible. Even without a final resolution, however, engagement in this type of bilateral negotiation was preferable. Communal peace was preserved; indeed, in none of these cases was the life of the community of the gods disrupted. The ability to resolve disagreements before they became generally violent or upsetting to a wider circle was something of an ideal, perhaps, a divine quality mortals hoped, or were supposed, to realize in their own disputes.

5—Disputes Arising from Personal Challenges, Threats, or Other Verbal Insults (C)

C1. Two disputes belonging to this category found their genesis in curses parents put on their children. The first of these involved Phoenix, Achilles' tutor, who related the story of how he came to reside at the court of Peleus.[121] He explained that his own mother had encouraged him, successfully, to seduce his father Amyntor's favorite concubine, whom his father cherished more than he did Phoenix's mother. This Phoenix did and, when discovered by his father, became the target of a curse by Amyntor that Phoenix should never produce children of his own. Such an imprecation constituted a serious insult, and Phoenix had seriously contemplated murdering his father in retaliation. He did not go through with it, "as one of the deathless ones stayed my anger, lest I might be called a parricide amid the Achaeans," instead choosing to leave his father's halls and escape to Phthia.[122]

C2. Another instance of similar type occurred in the circumstances surrounding Meleager's slaughter of the Calydonian boar and the ensuing quarrel with his mother Althaia.[123] In Hesiod's version of this dispute, Meleager son of Oineus had slain the boar and awarded the pelt to Atalanta who, Meleager said, had drawn first blood from the beast.[124] Plexippos, the eldest of Althaia's brothers, claimed that as the senior of Oineus' brothers-in-law he should receive this prize,[125] while a younger brother argued that it was a man named Iphikles, not Atalanta, who had drawn first blood from the Calydonian boar. Gripped in a fit of rage, Meleager slew them both.

Althaia then placed a curse on her son in revenge for her two brothers, though Homer and Hesiod preserved differing details regarding her imprecation. Other lays of the tale recounted that Althaia hoped to doom Meleager to an unsuccessful defense of Calydon when his other uncles arrived to exact vengeance, whereas Homer sang that Althaia called upon Hades, Persephone, and the Furies to bring death upon her son.[126] Further enraged by this indignity, Meleager refused to face the enemies of Calydon when they arrived, even ignoring the gifts offered him to face battle, but rather abided in his chambers with his wife until she beseeched him to take action when attackers battered the walls of their quarters. Only then did he respond to the assault, but in not accepting the gifts previously offered him he had forfeited his right to them.[127]

THE DISPUTES INVOLVING PHOENIX and Meleager reveal a pattern. One recourse for a parent in dealing with a "treacherous" child was to lay a curse upon him. However, the parent would thus have committed to a dispute for which there were no easy remedies. Phoenix never suggested that he would have been wrong to slay his father Amyntor in exchange for the curse that Phoenix remain bereft of children: his only concern was that the voice of the people would forever brand him a parricide. The offense to his honor was severe enough for him to have considered seriously a resort to violence. Rather than live in indignity, or provoke the potential wrath of the community by killing his own father, he withdrew from the household and the town despite the requests of those close to him that he not do so. In the case of Meleager, he withdrew an important resource from communal enjoyment, namely his martial skill, until his own personal safety was at stake. Then and only then did he reluctantly end his sulk and rejoin his abilities to the general efforts of the wider community.

Even household matters such as these rows between parent and child still encompassed the substantial interest of wider sections of the community. Phoenix recalled that many kinsmen and friends beseeched him with prayers to remain in Amyntor's halls, slaughtering many beasts and consuming wine in great amounts and watching him for nine days to prevent his leaving.[128] As for Meleager, the poet tells us that the elders of the Aetolians defending Calydon, Meleager's father, his mother, and his companions all sought to change his mind after he withdrew to his chamber and had decided not to defend Calydon against the Kouretes.[129]

The gravity of the insults to Phoenix and Meleager might normally have been met by violence or at least reciprocal challenge. Only the honor and deference due to parents, backed by the weight of broader opinion, prevented more direct and aggressive responses by the aggrieved parties, the types of responses that characterize the other two disputes of this type in the literature. Taunts and verbal insults, whether they were diminutions of character or challenges to personal strength or virtue, called for direct response. In two different instances, Odysseus found himself so confronted and sought to remedy the slight against him by answering the challenges.

C3. Arriving among the Phaiakians as a stranger, Odysseus was taunted "to his face" by a certain Euryalos, who said to Odysseus that he looked not like a man who knew contests but rather a merchant more concerned with counting the gains of his greed.[130] Following as it did a suggestion by Alkinoös, king of the Phaiakians, that athletic contests marked true excellence among men,[131] Euryalos' remark was nothing less than a slight against the stranger's very manliness, marking the opening of a quarrel. Odysseus had no option but to respond, telling Euryalos that he had not spoken well, but like a man blind with folly, and that even though he had suffered much he would still make trial, for as he told Euryalos, "Your speech is heart-biting, and speaking thus you have provoked me."[132]

Odysseus retrieved his honor and trumped Euryalos' slight, hurling the heaviest discus farther than any of the Phaiakians.[133] Exulting in his victory, he then bade any Phaiakian to "come here and be tested, since you have angered me greatly."[134] Alkinoös dispersed the tension by praising Odysseus' boast of his own superior athletic skill but asked him to remember the Phaiakians for those things in which they excelled beyond all others.[135] After Odysseus had acknowledged that the Phaiakians were indeed the best dancers, Alkinoös ordered that gifts be made over to Odysseus by the *basileis* of Phaiakia and that Euryalos in particular make amends with words and a gift, "since the word he spoke was in no way fitting."[136] Euryalos agreed, offering Odysseus a fine sword, followed by an exchange of blessings between the two men.[137] Thus they had resolved peacefully their quarrel.

C4. Responses to personal challenges and threats need not restrict themselves to the circles of those who considered their honor of paramount importance, that is to say, the elite. Odysseus considered it not at all unfitting for him to rise to the challenges presented him while he posed as a beggar in his own halls. A beggar of Ithaca, known both as Arnaios and Iros, arrived upon the scene and became instantly jealous of the disguised Odysseus' success in begging from the suitors. Picking a quarrel (*neikeiôn*) with Odysseus, Arnaios warned him to leave before their "strife should come to blows"; Odysseus attempted to assuage the man through bilateral negotiation, urging him not to be jealous as there was ample room for them both at this house.[138] Odysseus may have sought to avoid physical confrontation, for fear his prowess would be manifest and the suitors might suspect his true identity; nevertheless, once Arnaios persisted, Odysseus was ready and willing to meet the other man with violence.

Indeed, the suitors goaded the two men on and swore an oath not to intervene on behalf of Arnaios; Odysseus then quickly dispatched Arnaios/Iros, who left the home as agreed before the fight.[139] At one point, Odysseus pondered whether to deal Arnaios/Iros a lethal blow but decided not to, lest the suitors take note of him.[140] The arousal of suspicion over his identity, however, was the limit of his concern; he never contemplated the problem of culpability for the other man's death. Perhaps because Arnaios/Iros had threatened him with physical violence, Odysseus-as-beggar could claim self-defense in the event of the man's death. Such an assumption would be consistent with our analysis of the underlying assumptions regarding homicide in early Greece, but the passage itself admits of little more than speculation on this point.

FROM THESE EXAMPLES, we see that the verbal, personal insult, be it a curse, a questioning of personal worth, or a direct physical threat, called for immediate response unless one were to lose face. The range of actions open to the aggrieved party was delimited by other factors. Phoenix thought to kill his father and refrained mostly because he feared the opinion of the people and the stain of parricide. Whereas he might have slain another man for such an imprecation and thus salved his wounded honor, he had no such recourse with regard to his father. His only option was to withdraw completely from the community. Meleager's dilemma was similar: he could not win back his honor from his mother's curse without exposing himself to the same consequences Phoenix knew he had to avoid. For Meleager, the course of action was not to withdraw physically from the community but to withhold from it a valuable resource, his martial ability.

In Odysseus' case, the two personal challenges faced by him necessitated different strategies for resolution. Euryalos had not threatened personal violence or called upon the gods to debilitate Odysseus; he had, however, called into question the man's character and his worth as a person by accusing him of disreputable occupation. The appropriate response for Odysseus in this instance was to prove the man wrong, but his extended exultation might have constituted, as he himself acknowledged,[141] an insult to his hosts. Alkinoös astutely intervened, asking Odysseus to recognize the excellence of his hosts in other matters and prompting the offending party to apologize and make additional amends. As for Arnaios/Iros, Odysseus could act nearly with impunity, aside from his own self-interest in keeping his identity concealed. Whether this impunity arose from the low social standing of his opposite number or the public threat of personal violence against Odysseus or both, is difficult to gauge; but a claim of lethal force in self-defense would not have been inappropriate.

Before proceeding to our analysis of the other two categories of dispute, we may benefit from a summation of what we have determined thus far. Despite the genesis of a given dispute, the discussion to this point has revealed that most quarrels in Homeric and Hesiodic Greece engaged a very public element. Even disputants who regulated their grievances by private agreement or through the agency of a go-between or mediator (such as Iris or Alkinoös) often did so with a view to keeping their quarrel from becoming generally disruptive to the community. When a dispute did evolve in such a way as to encompass extensive support groups or even the community as a whole, the pressure of public opinion could be instrumental in forcing the parties to a resolution or at least effective regulation of their quarrel.

The reality and importance of this pressure applied even when the disputants did not resort to the type of formal or even semiformal public hearing we will have occasion to examine below. In the disputes we have already examined, the parties reached settlement or regulation through more or less spontaneous arrangements, ranging from successful bilateral negotiation to the trials of strength between Paris and Menelaos and between Odysseus and Arnaios/Iros. Of the seventeen disputes so far considered, especially in those examples with richer detail, the concern of disputants for the opinions and reactions of other members of the community is manifest in a majority of them.

All four of the disputes involving threats and insults engaged wider circles of the community in their resolution, either through the preemptive concern of the community for the aggrieved party's conduct (Phoenix) or the aggrieved party's withdrawal of an important resource from community enjoyment (Meleager). As for the insults to Odysseus, the public dimension is less explicit, though clearly indicated by Alkinoös' insistence on open apologies and by the oath taken by the suitors not to intervene and to abide by the result of the fight between Odysseus and Arnaios/Iros.

The importance of wider public opinion is more evident in the five cases we have examined where the interpretation of the rule base or disputes over courses of action are at issue. In the three cases settled between gods (***B3, B4, B5***), all through bilateral negotiation, there was a concern that the quarrel could result in greater strife involving the entire divine community, and this possibility was persuasive in enticing the parties to negotiate at least a short-term regulation of their dispute. We also noted the demonstrated anxiety over engaging and holding public favor in the dispute between Telemakhos and the suitors before Odysseus' homecoming (***B1***).

For trouble cases where the transgressor clearly and knowingly violated the accepted rule base of the community, we find even clearer evidence for the value of public opinion and participation in the pursuit/regulation/settlement of the dispute. When Odysseus returned to Ithaca, he did not have an automatic right to slaughter the suitors, and the suitors believed their salvation might reside in alerting the people; their suspicion was borne out in the wrath Odysseus' actions inspired among a majority of Ithacans once they had learned of the murders (***A6, A7***). In the quarrel over Helen (***A5***), we have seen how the opinion of one's support group and the wider population of the community might compel a disputant to seek a resolution that at first blush clearly disfavored him; but without continued public support, he had little choice. If the community failed to take sufficient notice of a dispute, an aggrieved party—much like Meleager in response to the insult to him—might force the matter to public attention by withdrawing a valuable resource (such as in the case of Demeter, ***A4***). Outside of homicide, only cattle rustling appears to have created an uncomplicated right to automatic self-help without reference to the community (***A1, A2, A3***): but even then, as we have seen, pursuit of the quarrel became problematic if suitable compensation had been received.

Public opinion played an even greater role, however, in the two remaining categories of dispute. In cases where a seizure of property had taken place, resulting in a loss of status or a sense of dishonor, or creating a sense of breach of contract, the resort to more public forms of settlement and/or regulation prevailed. The involvement of the wider community may be viewed in one of two related ways. The diminution of status or honor was necessarily a public matter, and in order to gain satisfaction for the offense, the aggrieved party sought restitution publicly. Furthermore, whether status was the root issue or merely ancillary, disputes that arose from seizure of property but engaged competitive strategies for resolution forced disputants to appeal to the weight of community opinion to strengthen their respective bargaining positions.

6. Disputes Involving Seizure of Property Leading to Loss of Status or Dishonor (*D*)

D1. Three such disputes appear in the literature,[142] and the first of these is the prelude to the most famous wrangle of all in the Homeric and Hesiodic corpus, that between Agamemnon and Achilles. Their disagreement, of course, actually grew out of another involving dishonor, that between the king of Mycenae and Apollo's priest, Khryses. Agamemnon had been awarded the priest's daughter after a raid by his fellow Achaeans and later had dishonored (*êtimesan*) the priest by refusing to restore her and simultaneously dismissing him.[143] Khryses had made an attempt at bilateral negotiation, offering Agamemnon a large ransom (*apoina*),[144] but Agamemnon rebuked him; before the king of Mycenae's refusal, however, Khryses had attempted to invoke through prayer the help of others among the Achaean host, perhaps anticipating Agamemnon's recalcitrance.[145] Importantly, all the other Achaeans shouted their assent (*alloi . . . pantes epeuphêmêsan Akhaioi*) to Khryses' request, indicating the expected role of the larger public.[146] Such an appeal, as well as the response to it, indicates that the Achaeans as a whole were expected, and tried, to exert a mediating influence on the dispute between king and priest: Agamemnon ignored the input of the community to the peril of all, including himself.[147] As Donna Wilson has argued, Agamemnon's rejection of Khryses' supplication and offer was a departure from the *regular practice otherwise observed* (and observable to the poem's audience), a gratuitous diminution of Khryses' *timê* and, by extension, Apollo's as well.[148] In terms of the legal culture we have been considering, we might additionally note that Agamemnon aggravated the situation by engaging in clearly disapproved behavior.

D2. Identification of Agamemnon's insult as the cause of the subsequent plague pushed the dispute toward resolution, shifting the center of gravity away from the row between Khryses and Agamemnon and opening the way for a new quarrel. Achilles, seeking to end the suffering of the Achaean host, called an assembly (*agorênde kalessato laon Akhilleus*—note the emphasis on public address to the folk) to discuss their plight and prompted the seer Kalkhas to proclaim the truth: the prophet explained that Agamemnon was responsible for Apollo's wrath, and only the return of the priest's daughter could quell the god's anger.[149] Agamemnon realized that relinquishing the priest's daughter and giving *poinê* was the only feasible solution (her return without ransom, accompanied by sacrifices and hymns to Apollo, ended the king's quarrel with Khryses,[150] but necessarily resulted in a loss of *timê* for Agamemnon himself, on top of that which he had already suffered because of the death of the Achaeans to Apollo's plague[151]); however, he immediately demanded that the Achaeans make another prize for him, so that he would not be alone without one.[152] Achilles responded that no such recompense could be made, except in the future, since the booty had already been distributed, and it would be unfitting to recall the spoils from the folk.[153] Agamemnon's angry response riled Achilles, and their dispute began in earnest.

The Great Quarrel, as Donlan characterized it,[154] necessarily involves enormously complex issues. It provides the central narrative tension of much of the *Iliad*, and much of its dramatic power resides, I would argue, in the fact that—for the poet and the audience—both Agamemnon and Achilles at various turns can lay claim to rectitude in their actions but also at various points violate or ignore larger assumptions and values of the society of which they (and the poet and audience) are a part. In other words, what makes the Great Quarrel so compelling for the performance's notional audience is that the operative rule base could legitimate certain premises and actions of the disputants in such a way that the dispute could appear irreducible and irreconcilable. At the same time, the audience will have recognized (or been asked by the performer to consider) the ways in which both Agamemnon and Achilles engage in actions that could be construed as blameworthy. Further complicating any resolution of the dispute, the two antagonists appeal to current social and political ideologies that coexist but do not always cohere: one is what Wilson has identified as a fixed system wherein Agamemnon can claim preeminence on the basis of his position as leader of the largest Achaean host at Troy, and the other is a relatively fluid system, inherently more agonistic and rooted in the constant demonstration and reaffirmation of individual *timê*. It is the latter set of assumptions with which Achilles identifies and to whose values he appeals.[155] At the same time, both men vie for leadership authority by trying to demonstrate (or refuse the other man's) generosity, a hallmark of the Homeric paramount's claim to preeminence.[156]

Achilles at first attempted to shame publicly the king of Mycenae with taunts and insults, a strategy well described by a wide range of anthropological studies and a form of settlement-directed talking.[157] Achilles' ridicule included calling Agamemnon "one wrapped in shamelessness" (*anaideiên epieimene*) and a "dog-face" (*kunôpa*).[158] As Louis Gernet argued from the literature of the Classical period, *aidôs*—the quality that Achilles accused Agamemnon of lacking—was "a feeling of obligation that is repaid to an associate or acquaintance, a feeling that constitutes an 'advance' for a gift freely given . . . [and] emanates from a generosity that does not calculate."[159] More recently, Kevin Crotty has argued that *aidôs* likewise implies the victor's obligations to show restraint in "exercising [his] prerogatives."[160] Such understandings of *aidôs* seem particularly apt in Achilles' shaming of Agamemnon: the latter's lack of restraint in his treatment of Khryses has already forced him to lose face,[161] and now his threat to seize the prize of another in order to satisfy his own *timê* has violated Gernet's characterization of *aidôs* in two ways. On the one hand, Agamemnon exhibited a lack of *aidôs* by forgetting the obligations he himself owed to other leaders of the host, which Achilles also dialed up as part of his public harangue.[162] On the other hand, Agamemnon likewise had affronted the *timê* of the other leaders, thus creating the grounds for other, potential disputes. Achilles ended his shaming of Agamemnon by underscoring that he himself would be dishonored (*atimos*) should he stay and announcing his own intention to have no part of it,[163] thus threatening the withdrawal of a form of mutual support critical to the success of the community.

Here again, as in the cases of Demeter and Meleager above, we see an aggrieved party countenance the potential removal of reciprocal forms of aid upon which the community relied, most likely to create a willingness on the part of the offending party to desist from their behavior. Throughout the epic, the poet acknowledges both Achilles' value as the "best of the

Achaeans" (a distinction, however, that both he and Agamemnon lay claim to on different bases[164]) and the military valor of his men, the Myrmidons; Achilles believed that the success of the expedition against Troy hinged on his participation and thus withdrawing it became, so he thought, the most effective means of resisting Agamemnon. Agamemnon responded, however, with a public shaming of his own, urging Achilles to flee since others would honor (*timêsousi*) the king of Mycenae; he had no need of Achilles, whose valor, Agamemnon proclaimed, was not Achilles' own but given to him by a god. The leader of the host concluded that he held Achilles' anger as unworthy of consideration and declared his intention to take Achilles' prize, Briseis, as compensation for that which he himself had lost.[165] Achilles had, in essence, made the decision for him, since, as Agamemnon put it, "You should know full well how much more powerful I am than you, and also another may fear to declare himself my equal and liken himself to me to my face."[166] It is a claim to domination by the king of Mycenae, one which he will try to make again even in his attempt later to "resolve" the quarrel, as we shall see.

The most famous dispute in all of Greek literature thus erupted in a very public arena. In fact, the presence of the *laos*, or folk, is crucial to the prosecution of the quarrel between Achilles and Agamemnon. As we have already seen, it is to the assembled Achaean host that Khryses appealed; Achilles believed it necessary to have them present before discovering the cause of the suffering among the ships in the Greek camp; and the folk were still present when Achilles and Agamemnon mutually shamed one another.[167] Though Agamemnon had disregarded the wishes of the assembly, this was clearly a mistake, invoking the wrath of Apollo and ultimately resulting in the loss of Khryses' daughter without ransom and damage to Agamemnon's own *timê*. Finally, the importance of the public element played out in the final breakdown between Agamemnon and Achilles. In challenging the leadership and motives of Agamemnon, Achilles clearly committed an additional and serious affront to the king of Mycenae's honor, but it is the public nature of the rebuke that clearly angered him most. When later Odysseus similarly confronted and criticized Agamemnon with only the *basileis* present, Agamemnon accepted the reproof and submitted that he wished someone would utter better counsel than that for which Odysseus reprimanded him.[168]

Having failed in his attempt to shame Agamemnon publicly, Achilles contemplated violence as a means to settle their dispute.[169] His rage stemmed from Agamemnon's public threat to dishonor him through the seizure of Briseis. Two salient points emerge here. First, the importance of the notions of honor and dishonor are central to Achilles' quarrel with Agamemnon, and the former refers explicitly to this fact several times, which Wilson takes as proof of his rejection of the fixed system (which not only gives Agamemnon dominant power but consequently results in what Achilles views as inequitable distribution of *timê*) and his insistence on the values of the fluid system.[170] Achilles has already characterized Agamemnon's intention as one that would render Achilles "without honor" (*atimos*), sworn an oath that one day the Achaeans would long for his participation in battle (that is, a restoration of the support he had withdrawn), and upbraided Agamemnon for not honoring (*ouden etisas*) the best of the Achaeans.[171] On three subsequent occasions, Achilles underscored the affront to his honor as the ultimate basis for his grievance.[172] Second, the seizure (variants of the verb *haireô*) is integral to the dishonor wrought on Achilles, who accused Agamemnon of seeking to "snatch away" that which he had given. That the king of Mycenae had seized Briseis was an acknowledged source of dishonor: when Phoenix, Ajax, and Odysseus arrived to Achilles as the king's ambassadors, the aggrieved hero thrice mentioned Agamemnon's violence by reminding them that the king had seized Briseis, and the fact of the seizure was also part of Achilles' complaint to Thetis.[173]

It was the peculiarly public nature of Achilles' humiliation that impelled him to entertain thoughts of murder, thoughts from which Athena turned him. Indeed, Athena urged Achilles to continue his shaming of Agamemnon, suggesting a hope that such a strategy might not only bring the quarrel to a peaceful resolution but also one very much to Achilles' satisfaction: he would one day receive threefold the "splendid gifts" (*aglaa dôra*) because of Agamemnon's outrageous insult (*hubris*).[174] Others were well aware of the dishonor done to Achilles, and in Homeric society this only heightened his sense of grievance;[175] such public dishonor will have been particularly acute in a shame culture.[176] The talking from which the dispute between Agamemnon and Achilles grew, and which in turn exacerbated it, led to an escalating cycle of offenses to each man's *timê*. In this case, bilateral talking aggravated the situation, and their attempts to shame one another into desisting from the present course of action failed miserably. Still, we should not underestimate the importance of this effort as a potential mechanism for regulating or resolving dispute; when Nestor first imposed himself as a mediator—a position he could assume thanks to his age and prestige—he sought to shame the two men publicly in order to reestablish equilibrium.[177] However, the offense was already too great: after another round of mutual ridicule, Achilles issued a threat of violence should Agamemnon try to make good on his intent to take Briseis. At this, the two men separated; having contended "with violent words" (*antibioisi epeessi*), they had brought their quarrel to the verge of physical confrontation.[178] The assembly now dispersed, and the third person plural of the verb (*lusan*) indicates that Agamemnon and Achilles both dismissed the assembly;[179] with their dispute having moved out of the realm of debate and public shaming, the role of the assembly as witness and mediator was for now at an end.

After the initial quarrel had erupted, and the efforts of the disputants themselves and Nestor as ad hoc mediator had failed, the handling of the conflict moved entirely to the realm of third-party mediation, with various *basileis* playing the role of go-between for Agamemnon and Achilles. The continued, direct interaction of the parties was now undesirable; Achilles had begun to draw his weapon at one point, threatened further violence at another, and indicated his continued rage by dashing the scepter of Pelops to the ground.[180] Agamemnon, rather than go himself, sent proxies to fetch Briseis, with the notion of seizure once more underlined.[181] Achilles yielded from his previous threat of force, perhaps because Agamemnon did not arrive personally but more likely due to the prohibition of self-help in this instance, as indicated by Athena's previous intervention.

The cooling-off period provided by the separation of the two parties created the opportunity for a potential resolution of the quarrel and the restoration of public peace. With Achilles having removed himself, Nestor once again upbraided the Achaean leaders generally for their conduct, though the target of the rebuke was clearly Agamemnon.[182] The king of Mycenae acknowledged forthwith the validity of Nestor's criticism, expressing regret that Zeus had led him into pointless wrangling for the sake of a girl.[183] This exchange foreshadowed the pressure Nestor applied to Agamemnon in book 9, which resulted in the latter's private admission of wrongdoing and his decision to attempt amelioration of the quarrel with Achilles. There, Nestor shamed Agamemnon with a reminder of the evil of loving strife among one's own people and the dishonor the king did to Achilles, an action to which the Achaeans generally, and he specifically, voiced opposition.[184] Nestor then prodded Agamemnon toward ending the quarrel with Achilles in a way most likely to assuage the latter.[185]

The attempt at reconciliation reveals the potential courses of action to resolve such a quarrel, though as we shall see, Agamemnon's offer of compensation was loaded and not likely to assuage Achilles *personally*. The centerpiece of the offer was, of course, the return of Briseis, with whom Agamemnon was willing to swear an oath that he had not shared a bed. The shortest path to resolution, therefore, was to return as *poinê* the object of dispute in original condition, especially if she belonged, as Wilson puts it, not to the sphere of goods but of (familial) persons.[186] However, handing over Briseis alone would have been insufficient; as we have already seen, the central issue bound up with the seizure of the girl was the affront to Achilles' *timê* that it constituted. Agamemnon was thus required also to restore Achilles' honor to close their quarrel; to that end, Agamemnon proposed in addition a rich trove of treasure, the rule of seven cities currently under his control, the pick of twenty Trojan women after the city fell, and a marriage alliance, wherein he would marry off one of his daughters to Achilles with a rich dowry while asking no bride price in return;[187] with regard to this last part of the offer, Agamemnon told his ambassadors, "And if we should return to Achaean Argos, the richest of lands, he can be my son-in-law, and I will honor (*tisô*) him like Orestes himself."[188] By handing over all of this additional compensation, Agamemnon believed that Achilles should accept his attempt at reconciliation. Nestor praised him for the generous restitution he had just described, and his words pleased all those present.[189]

The onus of the dispute would thus appear to shift to Achilles when he rejected Agamemnon's proposal. However, when describing to the other *basileis* the goods he would give to Achilles, Agamemnon had characterized the offer as *apoina*.[190] Therein lay the problem, as Wilson defines it: Agamemnon is, in effect, ransoming the beleaguered Achaean host from Achilles. On the one hand, this signifies that Achilles is, in effect, the victor, and Agamemnon the victim; but it also casts Agamemnon as the father (in itself a claim to a dominant position), and moreover implicates Achilles as outsider/enemy: friends, *philoi*, do not offer *apoina* to one another.[191] What was required was not *apoina*, but *poinê*: the return of Briseis, additional goods, *and* a public apology ("gentle words," *epessi . . . meilikhioisi*); only this can pay back the harm Agamemnon has inflicted on Achilles' *timê*.[192]

Indeed, the embassy of Odysseus, Phoenix, and Ajax judiciously avoids repeating Agamemnon's language, though Achilles sees the offer for what it is: *apoina* that amounts to a "gift attack," allowing Agamemnon to try to deflect the lack of generosity of which Achilles accused him and indeed demonstrate his generosity on a grand scale.[193] Furthermore, Agamemnon had ended his offer to the embassy with a claim to domination, already implicit in his proposal to make Achilles his son-in-law should they return from Troy: "Let him submit to me" (*kai moi hupostêtô*), Agamemnon says, because he is kinglier (*basileuteros*) and elder-born (*progenesteros*).[194] Odysseus had taken the lead in the embassy, recounting the suffering of the Achaean hosts due to Achilles' absence from the fight,[195] and then had set about retailing the many worthy gifts (*axia dôra*)[196] Agamemnon was prepared to present. Despite Odysseus' eloquent attempt to disguise the syntax (and, perhaps, the spirit) of Agamemnon's offer, Achilles nurses his grudge by citing again the offenses to his honor and adding into the bargain the duplicity of Agamemnon and the fact that he already possessed most of what the king of Mycenae offered.[197] Phoenix admitted the validity of Achilles' position on these counts, *were it not* for the generosity Agamemnon now showed;[198] Phoenix then related the salutary tale we examined previously, that of Meleager (**C2**), who turned aside great gifts and continued his anger. Ajax, concluding the embassy, tried to appeal to Achilles' sense of obligation to his comrades (*philotês*) and upbraided him for his stubbornness over a girl when men accepted *poinê* for slain kinsmen.[199] But Achilles would have none of it: though he acknowledged the hardship, he placed the blame on Agamemnon.[200]

Some recent commentators, such as Donlan and Wilson, have emphasized the audience reaction to the language and events of book 9, interpreting Achilles' actions as essentially justified. Agamemnon's own language, *apoina*, is known to the audience but not to Achilles, though he recognizes the offer for what it is and further recognizes the heavy, future obligation he himself would owe Agamemnon as a result of this gift attack. Further, he had every expectation that Agamemnon would "pay him back" rather than "give," thus diminishing Agamemnon's *timê* and restoring Achilles' own. Though Agamemnon promised to swear a public oath, he did not propose to apologize publicly and, as Donlan notes, "the offer appears friendly, but is really hostile." The audience will have recognized this fact as well as Achilles' rejection of that offer, a rejection that does not include the core value of his heroic society, revenge for his loss of honor.[201] I am sympathetic to these arguments, clearly, though I am not certain we can go so far as to say that Achilles' rejection is as justified as these other students have suggested.

While I have included this dispute under "seizure of property leading to loss of status or dishonor" due to the original source of the quarrel, its complexity implicates other types of dispute as well. Obviously, disagreements over what constituted approved or disapproved behavior played a role in exacerbating the Great Quarrel. Here again, Wilson's description of the coexisting systems in Homeric political society seems apt: from Agamemnon's point of view, that of the fixed system, "it was not at all fitting" (*oude eoike*) that he alone, as paramount, should be without a prize,[202] and from that same perspective, Achilles' challenge of his leadership, when Agamemnon was already reeling from his loss of *timê* in the Khryses debacle, was intolerable. Therefore, Agamemnon's actions may have been irregular, but from one ideological position they were not necessarily wrong.

Indeed, as Donlan also recognized, Agamemnon's offer of amends and Achilles' rejection of it doubtless inspired an ambivalent reaction for the audience.[203] On the one hand, the generosity present in that offer could be seen to balance the ledger, especially once the embassy had edited the potentially offensive language (*apoina*) and Achilles took into account, ideally, the obligations to his comrades. Further, I would contest Wilson's characterization of the label employed by the embassy to describe Agamemnon's offer, *dôra*, "gifts," as generic, "not a marked term for compensation."[204] While this is true relative to words such as *apoina* and *poinê*, we must also consider the larger context and what the audience already knew: as we have seen, Athena had promised Achilles not *poinê*, but *dôra*. Achilles, for the purposes of the dramatic dilemma in which he finds himself, must reject the offer on the basis of *one* core value; but this does not mean that the audience necessarily would have approved of such behavior stripped of its narrative importance to the poem. In fact, neither Donlan nor Wilson takes account of the reactions to Achilles' refusal. Agamemnon (for all of his ineptitude at the "game" of generosity[205]) and his course of action appear validated when news of Achilles' rejection of the offer reaches the assembly: Diomedes criticizes Agamemnon for offending Achilles in the first place and for having offended him further with his offer, but also advises that it would be best to ignore from that point forward Achilles, who, apparently impervious to other social obligations, is proud (*agênôr*) and will fight only when he wishes and when a god arouses him.[206] Furthermore, Nestor continued to criticize Achilles for his withdrawal of reciprocal support in his comments to Patroklos,[207] suggesting that the normal expectation was for an aggrieved party to accept an offer such as Agamemnon's, which included the return of the original property in dispute as well as generous additional compensation.[208] Outside of his own (narrow) insistence on one social value, Achilles' refusal to take into account the total web of obligations, values, and expectations has become a cause for censure.[209]

D3. The other principal dispute involving seizure or loss of property creating a sense of dishonor involved Menelaos and Antilokhos over their respective finishes in the chariot race at Patroklos' funeral games.[210] The quarrel arose from Menelaos' accusation that Antilokhos had employed a trick to pass him and thus staked himself to the prize that rightfully belonged to Menelaos. The immediate complaint of Menelaos was that Antilokhos had disgraced him with respect to his *aretê*, having hindered Menelaos' far superior horses.[211] In the face of the public affront to his standing, Menelaos had no choice but to upbraid the youthful Antilokhos, lest the loss of face become permanent. He immediately demanded that the leaders and rulers of the Argives pronounce a settlement between himself and Antilokhos, concerned as he was that public opinion might later range against him were he simply to bully the younger man into submission.[212]

After having asked for a settlement from the others, however, Menelaos then changed his mind and declared he would pronounce a right or straight (*itheia*) settlement himself.[213] Menelaos' proposal amounted to a potential public shaming of Antilokhos, as he challenged the younger man to swear an oath that his trick to hinder Menelaos' chariot was not intentional (*mê . . . hekôn*).[214] The use of guile to surpass Menelaos, in and of itself, did not have any particular shame attached to it; Nestor, after all, had urged his son Antilokhos before the race to employ such tactics.[215] The salient issue was whether Antilokhos *intended* to slight Menelaos, to make the king of Sparta lose face in front of others. Menelaos thus insisted that Antilokhos swear that such was not the case, leaving the latter only two options should he insist on receiving second prize. He could either admit to embarrassing Menelaos on purpose, presumably opening the way for the sort of enmity that existed once Agamemnon had intentionally offended Achilles' *timê*, or he could swear a false oath in front of all the others. To win the race by guile was one thing, to swear a patently false oath, quite another. Antilokhos' only recourse was to yield to Menelaos, which he did by asking forbearance on account of his youth and acknowledging Menelaos as the better man (*areiôn*); in addition, he agreed to return the horse and offered gladly to Menelaos anything from his own possessions for which the king of Sparta might ask.[216] For his part, Menelaos—once Antilokhos had acknowledged him the better man and proffered gifts—agreed to let Antilokhos keep the mare that now technically belonged to himself.[217]

FROM THE ANALYSIS of these well-described disputes, patterns emerge. By definition, offenses to the status of the Homeric man—whether diminution of one's *timê* or *aretê*, or infractions of the sense of *aidôs*—took place in a public setting and demanded a public response. We have already noted the involvement of the Achaean assembly in the disputes between Agamemnon and Khryses and then again between Agamemnon and Achilles. The poet did not envision the role of the folk as passive; the king of Mycenae ignored their input to his cost in both cases, and his refusal of their guidance was cause for later reproof.

Public offense required public rescinding or was still open to redress. Agamemnon offered to swear publicly a great oath that he had not dallied with Briseis, and Odysseus urged Achilles to accept Agamemnon's oath "in the midst of the Argives."[218] The reiteration of Agamemnon's offer to Achilles, conveyed by Odysseus two nights previously, took place in the presence of the assembled warriors when Achilles came from his huts after the death of Patroklos.[219] Menelaos challenged Antilokhos to swear an oath, again a public act witnessed by others, efficacious in causing the latter to yield. Quite apart from the unquantifiable and insoluble problem of the Homeric religious scruples regarding oaths, to forswear one's self obviously in front of the community would have undermined one's future credibility.[220] The oath in each of these disputes addressed the cause of the dishonor from which each erupted, in each case meant to deny full culpability for a past action which, had it taken place with intent, might have made the quarrel more intractable. That intentionality, or lack thereof, might play an exculpatory role in disputes involving honor would be consistent with early Greek notions regarding homicide. Not only did Menelaos expect Antilokhos to state that he did not mean to offend the Spartan king's *aretê*; likewise, Agamemnon deemed it important to claim that he had been blinded by Ate, and thus made the excuse that his actions were not fully his own ("Ate *made* me do it," as it were).[221] Indeed, Achilles signaled the end of the quarrel when he accepted (however brusquely) Agamemnon's explanation, saying that Agamemnon would not have acted toward him in that way were it not the pleasure of Zeus for many of the Achaeans to die.[222]

Finally, all three of these disputes involving dishonor ended not only with the return of the disputed object to the aggrieved party but also with further gifts. Agamemnon returned Khryses' daughter and offered rich sacrifices to Apollo at the priest's temple.[223] Beyond their religious significance, such gifts benefited Khryses materially and honored him as well as the god he served. Furthermore, the pestilence was only raised *after* Khryses prayed to Apollo to lift it;[224] presumably, without his personal request the Achaeans might have suffered indefinitely. We have already noted that Agamemnon, in order to undo the damage to Achilles' honor, was prepared to hand over great gifts to him. Similarly, Antilokhos extended to Menelaos the opportunity to select whatever he wished from the younger man's household, in addition to the return of the mare. With the exception of Khryses, whose gift was meant nominally for Apollo, the would-be recipients of these additional peace offerings exhibited lukewarm reactions at best. Achilles brushed aside the supplementary compensations, telling Agamemnon the choice was his whether he actually delivered them.[225] Menelaos, for his part, did not acknowledge Antilokhos' offer but instead gave the mare back to the younger man as a gift.

Why these gifts were refused is not difficult to determine. The acceptance of additional recompense may have created a reciprocal obligation that neither Achilles nor Menelaos wished to accept. What was crucial was the offer itself, whether accepted or not, as a means of restoring the aggrieved party's honor. Even after Achilles indicated he was not interested in Agamemnon's additional compensation, Odysseus still directed him to allow Agamemnon to "bring forth the gifts in the midst of the assembly, so that all the Achaeans may see them with their eyes, and you may be assuaged in your heart."[226] The public display of the proposed gifts was necessary to amend the public offense. In disputes involving honor, therefore, the public role was central, and public opinion expected to play an active role in resolving them. Status can only exist with an audience to perceive it, and so offenses to it and remedies to restore it play out before the community and with their participation.

7—Seizure or Loss of Property Involving a Sense of "Breach of Contract" (*E*)

Some disputes in the literature do not so explicitly involve potential or realized damage to one party's social standing. Even in instances where a seizure or loss of property has taken place, the more immediate concern may be a sense of "breach of contract" rather than a diminution of honor. An actionable breach of contract may also arise from the violation of a previous understanding or agreement between two or more parties. The Homeric and Hesiodic evidence offers six such cases, and close analysis of these further reveals the same concern for public involvement and opinion we have seen up to this point.

E1. Juridically, the women of Archaic and Classical Greece were considered part of the property of the household to which they belonged; accordingly, when Hephaistos apprehended his wife Aphrodite in flagrante delicto with Ares, the act constituted the type of offense that among mortals was potentially referable to self-help violence by the aggrieved party. The dalliance between Ares and Aphrodite was not public knowledge, so their affair was not a matter of public shame to the cuckolded blacksmith god.[227] Hephaistos himself only learned of it through Helios, who alerted him to what had been taking place.[228] Hephaistos then prepared a clever trap that ensnared Aphrodite and Ares the next time they shared Hephaistos' bed; once successful in his scheme, he summoned the other gods to witness what had transpired. The goddesses stayed away in embarrassment, but the gods arrived and ridiculed Ares and Aphrodite, enmeshed by Hephaistos' guile.[229]

Two consequences resulted from the incident. First, Hephaistos demanded in return for the release of the adulterers that Zeus, as Aphrodite's father, pay back the bride price for her, since she was beautiful but faithless.[230] Second, while the community of the gods agreed that Ares should pay for his transgression,[231] there was also an expectation that Hephaistos' demand could not or would not be met. Poseidon (perhaps as paternal uncle to Ares, since Zeus was already compromised as Aphrodite's father?[232]), came forward to beseech Hephaistos and to promise that Ares, rather than Zeus, would pay what his captor asked and then personally guaranteed the payment when Hephaistos expressed skepticism over Ares' trustworthiness. At this, Hephaistos released Ares and Aphrodite, with the other gods having witnessed Poseidon's pledge.[233]

E2. A Hesiodic fragment provides the clue as to why Poseidon advanced his suggestion to Hephaistos, describing as it does a dispute over the breach of a previous agreement. In the *Catalogue of Women*, the poet relates the tale of Sisyphos and Aithon and their quarrel over the latter's daughter, Mestra.[234] Sisyphos had paid a substantial bride price for Mestra, a large number of cattle,[235] in order to marry the girl off to his son. She managed to escape, however, and returned to her father Aithon, a scam that the two may have run for some time.[236] Sisyphos demanded the return of either the girl or the bride price, but Aithon agreed to neither.[237]

After this abortive attempt by Sisyphos to engage Aithon in bilateral negotiation, they referred their quarrel to a goddess upon whom they both agreed, since "no mortal could judge the case."[238] The divine judge, whose exact identity is unknown, "unerringly arranged a settlement."[239] That settlement, as it turned out, was the statement of a general principle that once payment had been rendered it could not be reclaimed,[240] and thus Sisyphos lost both the girl and the bride price he paid for her.[241] Even had Sisyphos received Mestra back, he had no valid claim to the cattle he had already paid to Aithon.

In the cases of Mestra's escape and Aphrodite's adultery, we find that an aggrieved husband and/or his family could not pursue the return of bride price even if, as Hephaistos poignantly stated, the bride was beautiful but faithless. In the case of the adultery, Hephaistos' only hope of satisfaction (since he cannot slay Ares as a husband might a mortal transgressor) is to hold the god of war captive until kin offered compensation that the offended party considered proportionate to the bride price. Mortal husbands could presumably likewise hold an adulterer apprehended in the act and ransom rather than kill him, as was the case in Classical Athenian law.[242] In Sisyphos' case, the aggrieved party held no bargaining position; he had no captured relative or other tangible leverage, and all he could do was demand back something no longer in his possession. Aithon could thus ignore Sisyphos' attempt to resolve the matter short of litigation, where the authoritative third party stated a generally recognized maxim which, in this particular case at least, favored the defendant, Aithon.

E3. The balance between private negotiation and public action could prove especially fluid in disputes involving the unilateral alteration of a previous agreement. In the land quarrel between Hesiod and his brother Perses, the two men had, according to Hesiod, already divided their land (presumably equally, based on the nature of the complaint). But Perses, allegedly in violation of this agreement, carried off the greater share and then gained ratification for his action by bribing the *basileis* of the town, if we are to believe Hesiod. The poet then offered his brother an opportunity to reopen the question privately, to engage in a bilateral negotiation (or renegotiation, in this instance) which need not involve the *basileis* of Askra.[243]

We turn to other considerations regarding this dispute in the opening section of the next chapter, including the possibility that Perses has lost his patrimony and Hesiod may fear an attempt by his brother to claim yet more property. Whatever the case, Hesiod's difficulty appears not terribly unlike Sisyphos' in important respects. In both cases, the aggrieved party had no leverage to entice the other disputant to indulge in any further, private discussion of the matter. Perses had possession of what Hesiod believed should be his, and for whatever reason, those members of the community responsible for umpiring the case provided a *dikê* that legitimated that possession. One might surmise that Hesiod had actually been the party who forced the issue to adjudication in the first place, for he had nothing to hold over Perses otherwise. His only recourse, once Perses held the disputed land and Hesiod found himself with no bargaining chip, was to involve the wider community. Once this plan of action had failed, Hesiod had little left to himself than to employ his prodigious poetic talents into a public shaming of Perses—bad farmer, bad brother, bad neighbor—in the hopes that exposing him to public ridicule would force him to revisit the question (or discourage any further, formal legal action).[244] In cases involving breach of a previous agreement, it may have been incumbent on the party with no material or community leverage to resort to more formal litigation in a public setting. Without the force of possession of a useful negotiating position, such as that enjoyed by Hephaistos, or the overwhelming favor of public opinion that might compel the other disputant to settle privately, the aggrieved party would have little option but to try to bring the issue before an umpire or umpires.

E4. To bring this discussion full circle: such a dynamic operated in the famous and controversial trial scene portrayed on the Shield of Achilles.[245] Whatever the exact nature of the dispute's origins, it is certain that a misunderstanding was afoot, and there was perhaps a wholesale attempt to renegotiate a previous agreement. At issue was a quarrel between two men over the satisfaction or penalty (*poinê*) owed for a man who had been killed. While one party (for the sake of convenience, the respondent) claimed that he had paid everything, the other (the complainant) claimed either that he had received nothing or would accept nothing.

If the respondent had already paid satisfaction owed for a dead man, then the complainant would have had to go to a third party to gain further redress. In this instance, the complainant will have had no substantial leverage over the respondent; all he really had on his side was the threat of self-help retaliation. If other kinsmen had already accepted some form of *poinê*, however, the complainant would have exposed himself to retribution if he exercised a right to *lex talionis* already waived by others. Further, he could have expected little in the way of a support group of kinsmen to form around him for protection if they had already settled the matter with the killer. Public opinion, while perhaps sympathetic to the complainant's insistence on further satisfaction such as exile, would not have brooked such a disruption to the community as another homicide might have caused, particularly under the circumstances already described.

The role of the public and the importance of community opinion indeed emerge quite clearly in the episode on the Shield of Achilles. In the scene, the folk were crowded together in the marketplace (or simply, place of gathering) and shouted their support for each of the two sides in the quarrel.[246] After the people had expressed their opinions, heralds restrained them, and then each of the elders proposed a solution to the dispute, presumably with some reference to the wishes of the community as stated by those present;[247] it would be rather odd, in fact, that the townsfolk would crowd in and participate so vociferously if they expected their contribution to have little or no impact. That elder who spoke the "straightest" *dikê* would win the prize, two talents of gold. Even at this stage, we can reasonably expect public opinion to have been crucial. It is difficult to see how the matter of which *dikê* was straightest could have been left to the litigants themselves: they began from intractably opposed positions, necessitating the resort to an umpire in the first place. The reactions of the gathered *laos* and the elders themselves to each proposed settlement would surely have conditioned and influenced the minds of the disputants regarding the best solution.[248] Once public opinion had rallied around a particular proposal, continued pursuit of the quarrel and refusal to abide by the solution put the recalcitrant party at risk of becoming a pariah.[249] Hesiod's *Works and Days* may be seen as an attempt to recapture the public opinion which, for reasons unclear from the poem itself, had gone over to Perses at the time the *basileis* reached a decision in his favor.[250] If Hesiod succeeded, he might have reopened the issue in a public forum, assuming that the shift in public opinion were not so great as to cause Perses to capitulate privately.

RESORT TO SOME FORMAL or semiformal procedures probably tended to be the *last* resort in disputes of this type. The remedy of an adjudicator would be the only hope for an aggrieved party who at a private level had nothing on which to bargain effectively; there would be no incentive for a party with the disputed item in his possession, or one who had already resolved the issue with other potential opponents in the community, to enter into bilateral negotiations—publicly or privately—with a complainant. What, then, might compel the party in such a commanding position to submit to the decision of an umpire? The instances under consideration here provide the clues to an answer. On the one hand, there appears to have operated a principle akin to our notion that possession is nine-tenths of the law. In the cases of Sisyphos and Hesiod, the complainants lost at the hands of third parties. The scene from the Shield of Achilles does not bode well for the complainant, either; the respondent had supporters among the townspeople, and so the possibility of further *poinê*—such as exile from the community—seems unlikely. Therefore, in these instances at least, third party arbitration weighed heavily in favor of the respondent; there is little apparent danger of losing to the complainant.

On the other hand, even considering that the complainant's chances may not have been so bleak, there were perhaps other incentives for a respondent in a commanding position to agree to the settlement of an umpire. The community in the early Greek world took a keen interest in disputes between its members.[251] Refusing to allow a matter to be heard by the leaders and the folk of the community, if such a hearing had been requested by a would-be complainant, might have alienated the very balance of public opinion that had allowed a respondent to resist attempts at a settlement through bilateral negotiation.[252] Furthermore, we do not know the mechanisms by which a third party umpire might have been introduced into the equation: Wolff's hypothesis, as we have discussed, presents logistical difficulties, and the analysis of the disputes of Sisyphos and Hesiod, and that on the Shield of Achilles, militate against it. Deduction from this evidence suggests rather that the complainant, not the respondent (Wolff's plaintiff and defendant, respectively), would have been responsible for initiating more formal litigation. For both Hesiod and the disputants on Achilles' shield, there was a defined group to whom litigants *might* refer their quarrels, but as we saw with Hesiod, private amends were still possible. In the case of Sisyphos, the third party may have been someone mutually acceptable to both parties, but in all events the decision to go to litigation in a public forum was voluntary within certain limits—public opinion might be so overwhelming that it forced disputants to submit the quarrel to the community for formal umpiring. But, although there were no institutional means to force disputants to a public forum, a respondent possessed of a number of advantages that compelled a complainant to test the issue in public may have decided to end the matter once and for all by gaining communal recognition of the validity of his position.

E5. There remains the issue, however, of what happened when the complainant and not the respondent enjoyed the upper hand in cases involving a breach of contract and there were few constraints on the aggrieved party. In the *Iliad*, Hera bade Hypnos to cause Zeus to fall asleep so she could work her mischief among the hosts at Troy.[253] Zeus, however, had established an understanding with Hypnos that he must only cast slumber upon the king of gods when Zeus himself specifically requested. Nevertheless, Hera persuaded Hypnos; but when Zeus awoke, filled with rage, he sought out Hypnos so that he could hurl the god of sleep into the sea, never to be seen again. Zeus' terrible power manifested itself in his ability to toss aside other members of the community of gods as he ransacked Olympus in search of Hypnos.[254] However, Hypnos made his escape to the goddess Nyx, whereupon Zeus desisted in his wrath lest he displease the tamer of both gods and men.[255]

E6. One other dispute also conforms to this pattern of protection extended to the target of a powerful or dangerous aggrieved party. While the suitors despoiled the halls of Odysseus and plotted the death of Telemakhos, Penelope upbraided their ringleader, Antinoös. She recalled for him how once Odysseus had helped the suitor's family, when his father Eupeithes sought Odysseus' protection against the wrath of the *demos* of Ithaca. Eupeithes had joined Taphian pirates, who then harassed the Thesprotians, at that time allies of the Ithacans.[256] As a result, Eupeithes had become a fugitive, "fearing the people, for indeed they were exceedingly wroth . . . and wished to kill and snap away the thread of his dear life and devour his great and pleasant means of livelihood."[257] The people of Ithaca had considered his behavior a violation of their friendship agreement with the Thesprotians and feared his action could reflect negatively on all of them. Only the actions of Odysseus, who had offered sanctuary to Eupeithes, "held them back and prevented them, they being quite eager."[258]

These last two disputes call for a few, brief comments. Due to the relative positions of Zeus and Hypnos within the community of the gods, and the overwhelming numbers of the angry *demos* arrayed against Eupeithes, in each instance the aggrieved parties were in a position to pursue their wrath and attempt violent action. Most of the other gods would have been powerless to stop Zeus, and in fact any attempt made by many of the potential third parties would have met further violence from Zeus: the king of the gods was already casting them about the halls of Olympus in his effort to locate Hypnos. Only the intercession of another god respected or feared by Zeus restrained him, and in this respect Hypnos was fortunate to make his escape to Nyx, an awe-inspiring and fearsome presence in Archaic Greek mythology.[259] Likewise, only a man of Odysseus' status and power within Ithaca could restrain the angry mob that sought to tear Eupeithes limb from limb.

The conclusion one might draw from these stories is that when a complainant, or complainants, possessed much greater social or political clout within a community, he/they might resort to a self-help solution if another, weaker party violated a standing agreement. As we have seen, most disputes in the literature—aside from homicide and cattle theft—are not typically referable to self-help, nor do they typically involve such obvious or overwhelming disparities of status and power between the disputants. In certain cases, however, we can imagine that in the absence or failure of a powerful third party to intercede, stronger disputants might resolve the dispute by strong-arming weaker opponents into submission, or worse. The only option for the lesser party in such circumstances was to appeal to someone else in the community possessed of the wherewithal to offer protection. I would not suggest however, with Wolff,[260] that the powerful intercessor was a magistrate or enjoyed any necessary, official role within the community; the early *polis* probably had several prominent members who could enhance their prestige, power, and circle of dependents by offering protection to someone against a rival for standing.[261]

8—Conclusions on the Nature of Early Greek Dispute Settlement

As raised in the previous chapter, a legal culture (or, if one prefers, a legal community) is characterized by a consistent sense on the part of its constituent members of what the rules are, what the rules for breaking the rules are, what mechanisms are available for addressing disputes over the rules, and what sanctions may apply for breaches of the rules. In addition, within limits those same members may be able to improvise resolutions that will find their inspiration in the rule base, though such resolutions may not necessarily correspond exactly with "the law," even in societies where sophisticated and formal judicial institutions exist. The preceding survey of trouble cases in the Homeric and Hesiodic literature certainly fits these conditions, as disputants handled various recognizable categories of dispute through a range of consistent strategies and procedures. The thick description resulting from the trouble-case processualism employed here demonstrates that the social world of the epics indeed possessed a functioning legal culture, with the following discernible features.

Disputes arose from a variety of causes, from mundane questions (the division of patrimony or the return of bride price, for example) to the issue of one's standing in the community or even irrecoverable loss of face (for example, the curse upon Phoenix and the disgrace of Achilles, disputes ***C1*** and ***D2***, respectively). When differences occurred, most trouble cases obligated the parties to engage in some form of settlement-directed talking, except in those cases that allowed for automatic self-help (most notably, homicide and cattle theft, within limits). Cases where an unambiguous right to *lex talionis* could clearly and unquestionably be exercised were doubtless fairly rare. Often offending parties went into exile to avoid the consequences, and even Odysseus' retribution against the shameless and arrogant suitors was an act that the majority of Ithacans found distasteful and worthy of punishment (***A7***). Therefore, as we have seen in many cases, it was incumbent upon disputants in early Greek society to make at least some attempt at bilateral negotiation. The purpose of that settlement-directed talking was not to exclude the public dimension, but rather to minimize the disruption to it. Bilateral negotiation always took place with a view to public opinion and concern, as there was no guarantee that more formal and public procedures might not come to bear.

The shortcoming of bilateral negotiation, of course, is that it necessitates face-to-face contact between two parties already at odds with one another. Under such circumstances, disputants might exchange words or engage in actions that exacerbate the situation and make its subsequent resolution or regulation more difficult, as in the row between Achilles and Agamemnon, and possibly as part of the backstory of the dispute between Hesiod and Perses as we know of it (***E3***). When such breakdowns occurred, the Greeks clearly believed in the value of a third-party go-between or mediator (the distinction in Homer is virtually nonexistent; Iris and Nestor, for example, simultaneously fulfilled these roles: ***B5***, ***D2***). Ultimately, the effectiveness of third parties depended much upon their own prestige and rhetorical skills and the mindset of the disputants. Despite Nestor's age, wisdom, and persuasive abilities, he could not bridge the gap between Agamemnon and Achilles. Also, bilateral negotiation might only take place in instances where the aggrieved party had something the other party wanted or needed, as when Hephaistos held Ares captive and could demand some kind of satisfaction in return for his release (***E1***).

Otherwise, the opposite party was in a position to resist requests for further discussion of the matter, as would appear to be true in Hesiod's case: Perses had what he wanted, and Hesiod had nothing further to offer. Without any leverage, the aggrieved party might find it difficult to engage the offending party in any meaningful negotiation, either bilaterally or through a go-between. In some cases, such as those of Achilles, Meleager (***C2***), and Demeter

(***A4***), the aggrieved party might be in possession of a resource valuable to the community as a whole, and then withdraw that resource from the reciprocal enjoyment of the entire community in the hopes that public opinion would turn against the offender and force him to reconsider.

Conversely, the society under consideration here was a face-to-face one, lacking what we would recognize as formal or state judiciary mechanisms such as standing courts, professional jurists, a written body of case law, and the like. Many of the quarrels we have examined erupted in public and therefore might be eligible for immediate public redress. The offending party was put on the spot for his offense, as Antilokhos was for his cheat of Menelaos in the chariot race (***D3***). His choice was to yield or to damage his own public standing by swearing a false oath. Even when the deed took place away from the public eye, an aggrieved party might seek to gather witnesses (as Hephaistos did), make public accusation of the culprits and an appeal for help (as Telemakhos did [***B1***]), or engage in scathing declamation of the offending party, meant for public consumption (as Hesiod did). Such semiformal attempts as these to apply public pressure on a "wrongdoer" might or might not succeed in bringing the two parties closer to resolution of the conflict, but clearly they represent available and acceptable strategies.

When attempts at direct settlement failed, relatively more formal types of litigation existed. I have argued that it would have been the aggrieved party, with nothing to lose, who would have been the individual most likely to press for a public and more formal hearing, wherein the third party will have had powers resembling those more of an adjudicator than a mediator and the decision taken more binding on the parties. The binding force of any ruling rested on enforcement through public opinion. As we have seen, the pressure on a respondent/defendant must have been public, since he will have feared an erosion of the favor that had allowed him to resist bilateral negotiation in the first place. In Hesiod and Homer, when disputants appear before *gerontes*, *istores*, or *basileis*, the community is present, vocal, and expected to take an active role in reaching a settlement. It will have also been the community that had the responsibility for policing that settlement, as both witnesses to the procedure and as those whose opinion will have been alienated if either party failed to abide by the decision of the community.

Of course, not every trouble case was pursued or resolved in exactly the same way, but the causes, strategies, mechanisms, and resolutions consistently fall within certain ranges depending on the sources and nature of the dispute. It is this consistency that is key to a functional legal culture, as no two legal incidents are utterly identical, and community members' sense of justice would likely reject a system that produced the exact same result in every case of similar type. Even in such an advanced system of jurisprudence as the United States possesses—based on statute law, precedent, highly formalized judicial institutions from the courts to prisons, and the contest of similarly educated legal experts—prosecutors and defense attorneys, judges, and juries may take into account a broad range of factors in determining and even negotiating criminal culpability and punishment, civil liability, awarding or adjusting damages, and so on. Even American jurisprudence, with its high degree of professionalism, responds in some degree both in the courtroom and in policy to the weight of public opinion and the sense of justice,[262] however flawed, that exists in wider society.[263]

In Homeric and Hesiodic Greece, the variety of outcomes, informed by an underlying and largely consistent communal perception of the rules and ultimately policed by public opinion, points to a healthy and functional legal culture. That is not, of course, to suggest that the Greeks of that world lived in some type of juridical utopia, as is the unfair characterization offered by those who denigrate the importance of public participation and opinion in favor of a more rigidly institutionalized picture.[264] No community—particularly not one that valued as much as the Greeks did individuality, personal excellence (in the literal sense of exceeding all others), competition, and status—is without its share of mavericks, malcontents, malingerers, and misanthropes, who will place their own interests consistently ahead of the community's wishes.[265] Such individuals pursue their agenda with little care for the general opinion of their neighbors.[266] Further, as Zinon Papakonstantinou has aptly demonstrated, the plurality of legal narratives allowed some individuals to try to "game" the system, however genuinely or cynically they may have done so.[267] In the early Greek community, some doubtless got away with it, too: the figure of Perses, even if Hesiod has exaggerated his faults, would scarcely have been an ideal neighbor, and his behavior had yet to reap negative consequences. Nevertheless, reciprocity was of great importance in early Greece, if not from day to day, then certainly over time.[268] To transform oneself into a pariah within the community by consistently ignoring or flaunting its wishes could harm one's ability to form advantageous connections or enjoy good will in future disputes.[269]

Wider public opinion may not have been decisive in every instance, and there was no guarantee the general consensus would conform to any abstract notion of what was just (Hesiod, for one, did not believe so). Yet, informed by the underlying assumptions of their legal culture, the members of the early Greek community provided a basis for maintaining some level of equilibrium among disputants, preventing every single disagreement from evolving into a violent, zero-sum game that threatened to disrupt the life of the community.

The combination of a lack of fixed statutes on the one hand, and the fact of widespread, popular participation in judicial decisions on the other, meant that even the most formal litigation procedures would have possessed something of the character of folk justice. Each individual case might have a different result, despite whatever similarities existed, but always beneath the surface was the generally well-known opinion of one's neighbors in a small-scale society. The system produced by the legal culture we find in Homer and Hesiod did not lend itself to abuse perpetrated by a corporate, aristocratic interest. Rather, the changes across the Greek world in the eighth and seventh centuries necessitated new means of regulating the types of dispute to which those changes gave rise.

CHAPTER FOUR

Judicial Equality, Literacy, and Written Law

The results of our investigation in the last chapter revealed a functional legal culture in the epic world of the Greeks, one whose basic features are settlement-directed talking with a view to the role public and communal participation played in settling or regulating disputes. In the next chapter, we will examine more fully the relationship between legal and social change, particularly in the context of a society such as that we find in early Greek literature. Before turning to that discussion, however, we must address the lingering notion that written law somehow resulted from systematic elite abuse and related popular dissatisfaction. Expressions for reform or complaints of injustice, I argue, are mostly illusory; there was no compelling reason for nonelites to believe that written law would serve as their ally in the event that they did want reform; the extent of literacy in the seventh and early sixth centuries was not sufficient for written laws, in and of themselves, to serve as a guarantor of judicial equality, and in fact offered scope for abuse and corruption; and the continued importance of "unwritten law" alongside statutes indicates that written law was, for a very long time, considered a supplement to, not a replacement for, traditional norms and procedures.

1—The Problem of Demands for Judicial Equality

The Greeks of the Archaic period, if we are to credit an anecdote in Plutarch, were under no illusions as to what the writing of laws could and could not accomplish if they were intended to restrain the powerful for the purpose of protecting the weak:

> Having come to Athens, Anakharsis knocked at the door of Solon's home and said that he had arrived as a stranger in order to make ties of affection and guest-friendship with him. When Solon responded that it is best to make friendships at home, Anakharsis said, "so why not yourself, being at home, make ties of affection and guest-friendship between us." And thus Solon, wonderfully impressed by the man's quick wit, received him affably and remained with him for some time, already engaged as he was in public affairs and putting together the laws. And so Anakharsis, having learned of Solon's business, laughed at him for thinking that he could check the injustice and greed (*adikias kai pleonexias*) of the citizens with written laws [lit., "with letters," *grammasin*], which were no different from spiders' webs but just like them ensnared the weak and small among those captured, but were burst through by the powerful and wealthy.[1]

Solon went on to explain himself, the story goes, that men kept to their agreements when the laws made clear there was no gain for either side in breaking them.[2] One might infer (though Plutarch did not), that the Greeks believed Solon had attempted to clarify his position by suggesting that written laws were meant as much as a restraint on equal parties as a check on abuse by the powerful of their social and political inferiors.

Nevertheless, the notion that written law meant equal justice, and was therefore one of the principal demands of the "hoplite class" and other disaffected groups in the Archaic *polis*, proved intoxicating for most of the twentieth century.[3] Certainly, a new *communis opinio* has begun to emerge that scarcely believes in the very existence of such a class, much less in its consciousness or concerted action;[4] I will have more to say on this topic at the end of the present section. Nevertheless, our own modern preconceptions of the role (and rule) of law in modern western republics and representative democracies for a long time influenced the perception of the political value and meaning of written law in the distant Greek past. Combined with the reflections of certain fourth-century Greek (mainly Athenian) authors, what has emerged is a kind of "democratizing teleology" for Greek law. The use of the written word to capture the precepts and customs of the community becomes a necessary step on the inexorable march toward Greek "democracy."[5] While this interpretation would find few unqualified, explicit supporters today, the underlying assumptions implicit in this model have continued to inform important and influential scholarship on early Greek law and Greek history, and it continues to manifest itself in general works on ancient Greece as well.[6] Indeed, two very recent studies—those of Gagarin and Papakonstantinou—have attempted in various ways to put the popular or public element at the center of explanations for the appearance of written law, citing the language of enactment clauses, the supposed ease with which legal texts could have been read, or interpreting written law as vehicles for social reform through participation of the wider community in the legislative process.[7]

Specific issue may be taken with the democratizing teleology (and the more recent public model) on any number of points. A complete examination of the evidence for early written law in Greece will repay the effort, as will a critique of the premise that the Archaic Greeks believed the writing of older customs and the publication of new statutes would somehow guarantee equal justice or that such a guarantee was even a desideratum for the historical actors. The idea that the middling and lower orders of society provided the major impetus for written law in Archaic Greece represents the model most at odds with the present argument and thus deserves particular attention. It is perhaps the case that the arguments of Eder (or for that matter, Gagarin's earlier ideas on the subject) have not found as much traction as they should because, in part, they do not sufficiently undermine this democratizing model.[8]

Any claims regarding the democratizing intention behind written law have been (and to my mind, must be) predicated on a variety of presuppositions, some of which bear closely on one another. Some combination of the premises below is crucial to supporting the argument that Greeks sought written law in order to ensure more evenhanded administration of justice. A close examination of these assumptions in the context of evidence predating the fourth century will reveal that it is difficult to make a strong case for any of the eight major premises.

Two of the assumptions in the democratizing teleology regard the extent of the use and application of writing and its relevance to the community as a whole:

1. A significant or substantial proportion of the members of an Archaic Greek community enjoyed a sufficient level of literate skill, thus enabling these citizens to read published laws,[9] or

2. If the knowledge of reading necessary to understand a legal inscription was not enjoyed by a significant proportion of the population, those officials responsible for administering the (now) written laws were somehow more evenhanded and less arbitrary in their interpretations of the law than their predecessors (e.g., Hesiod's *basileis*), had been.[10]

Three other premises have to do with the nature of written laws and whose interests such statutes served:

3. The writing of law was the result of dissatisfaction among a particular segment of the population, namely the *demos* (understood primarily as a hoplite class,[11] but not exclusive of a growing, urban artisan or commercial interest in some places), hence

4. The written laws that the presumably disfranchised members of the *polis* wrested from the elite should, in fact, represent a set of concerns reflective of previous opportunities for aristocratic abuse under the purely customary-oral judicial arrangement,[12] and

5. We should not, therefore, necessarily expect to find any laws that aim at the preservation of corporate aristocratic preeminence and privilege, nor should the laws overwhelmingly concern themselves with matters of greater interest to the wealthy and powerful member of the elite as opposed to those of the "average" citizen.[13]

Finally, the democratizing teleology rests on assumptions regarding the interaction of elite and commoner within the community and how law would or could best serve their interests, as individuals, as members of a particular self-identifying group, and as citizens within an Archaic *polis*. For example,

6. The yeoman peasantry or the merchants and artisans necessarily believed that written law would end the abuses of justice which occurred through the judicial expression of elite power,[14] and therefore agitated for the writing of the laws of their community in order to serve their own matrix of individual and class interests;[15]

7. The aristocrats were resistant to such action, because it was potentially erosive of their judicial power over other members of the *polis*,[16] and because they saw no value in having written law as a referent for the disputes that occurred in the community generally or among members of the elite;

8. Both of these assumptions rest on one final postulate, that such systematic rapaciousness existed and that both the elites and commoners were sufficiently aware of this abuse to create and nurture animosity and contention;[17] only then would there have been grounds for agitation for written law on the one hand and the acute need felt for resisting it on the other.

To begin with the last set of assumptions (numbers 6 through 8): as we have seen, Hesiod certainly suggests that some form of abuse went on in Thespiae (which by this point had some influence over Askra), perpetrated at the hands of the *basileis*.[18] Whatever "gift-devouring" means exactly as an epithet attached to them, it is clear that Hesiod, at very best, uses it formulaically and neutrally; it is certainly no compliment. Further excavation of Hesiod's precise attitudes is in order.

One striking feature of Hesiod's diatribe against injustice, so often used as the touchstone of arguments for aristocratic malfeasance,[19] is that the *basileis* are incidental to his argument with/diatribe against Perses and, even if guilty of Hesiod's accusations against them, represent an atypical example of the administration of Greek justice in early Greek literature.[20] Aside from the tale of the hawk and nightingale, very little else in Hesiod's surviving corpus indicates the type of abuse outlined in assumption number eight. Rather, Hesiod directs the thrust of his complaints at his brother Perses who, like Hesiod, was the son of an immigrant[21] and presumably, given the content of Hesiod's warnings to him, a farmer of similar social and economic standing. The *basileis* enter the complaint only insofar as they have settled, or will settle, in favor of Perses; for many modern observers, Hesiod suspected (the possibility of) a bribe—thus his *basilêes dôrophagoi*.[22] Perhaps for Hesiod, only their acceptance of gifts could explain what *he* considered a miscarriage of justice, or might ultimately lead to one, either outcome at his expense.

But should we accept prima facie the equation of the epic *dôron* with the modern notion of a bribe, explicitly intended to subvert the normal workings of a judicial procedure? Was bribery as we understand it what Hesiod intends here? Certainly, there are other indications that in the early *polis*, the gift may have been part of the expected judicial process. In the trial scene from the Shield of Achilles (Hom., *Il.* 18.497–508; Chapter 3.7 above, dispute ***E4***), we found our two litigants engaged in a dispute both having apparently contributed to a handsome prize to be awarded to the judge who spoke the straightest judgment.[23] Homer's verb for the awarding of the prize (*domen*, to give) comes from the same root as the noun (*dôron*) that serves Hesiod's formulation of gift-devouring. Homer's passage suggests nothing amiss or unacceptable about the fact of the gift to the judges—all of this is, after all, taking place in the city at peace. As for Hesiod, he never explicitly accuses the *basileis* of accepting bribes from one side or the other in any dispute, or of acting prejudicially for that reason. The sense remains general that the gifts are simply the payment that the *basileis* receive for rendering judgments, and the appellation may therefore represent a standard honorary epithet.[24] Elsewhere, in the *Theogony*, Hesiod offers a positive view of the *basileus*, wherein the chief-as-judge likewise receives a gift (*dosis*), this time from the Muses.[25]

The only rapacity attested directly by Hesiod in his dispute with Perses is that which his brother has exhibited in unjustly, as far as Hesiod is concerned, obtaining more than his fair share of the patrimony, and possibly his attempt to gain yet more. There may have been at work in the background the emergence of a new socioeconomic and political relationship between the elites at Thespiae and the villages in its orbit, a relationship about which Hesiod and his fellow farmers were none too happy;[26] but in *Works and Days*, the most Hesiod implies about their misconduct is that the *basileis* appear to be guilty of being bad judges, perhaps for a price—yet nothing is suggestive of them acting as a sort of robber-baron class, seizing the lands or possessions of fellow citizens and then ratifying their actions through an inherently corrupt judicial procedure.[27] The dispute, whether already past or incipient, between Hesiod and Perses is between two yeomen,[28] with Hesiod vehemently and eloquently venting his disappointment with the result toward all the involved parties, or (if he is indeed anticipating a hearing) trying to shame the parties involved into doing what he considers the right thing.[29] The *basileis* at Thespiae are not *directly* responsible for the poet's problems nor does he accuse them of being so.

The very same author additionally provides clues that, whatever anger or frustration he feels toward the *basileis*, his emotions are the result of personal and recent circumstances. In his *Theogony*, Hesiod offers a far different assessment of the *basileus*, a man who possesses many of the same talents and divine favors as the bard who can delight the community with epic poetry. With honeyed words flowing from his tongue, the *basileus* as mouthpiece of the Muses will provide straight judgments (*itheiêisi dikêisin*) and end even a great dispute (*mega neikos*).[30] He not only brings the disputes of contesting parties to a satisfactory resolution, but, just as an epic bard might, also makes the rival claimants forget their differences altogether.[31] The context in which Hesiod has placed this highly favorable portrayal of the *basileus* offers nothing to suggest that the poet was being ironic; his praise of the Muses' ability to inspire the sweet words of the *basileus* precedes immediately his invocation to them to speak through him the details of his subject, the genealogy of the gods.[32] There is no necessary reason to doubt the poet's sincerity here.[33]

Furthermore, he provides his audience no clues to help it gain his meaning should such a *basileus* be unfamiliar to their experience. While one supposes that the portrait in the *Theogony* could have been meant to highlight the misbehavior of the elite at Thespiae vis-à-vis the manner in which a "true" *basileus* should act, Hesiod also states he won a bronze tripod at Khalkis in Euboea for his poetry, and thus asserting a purely local audience for all of his verse is not tenable.[34] In addition, we would have to assume *Theogony* to be the later of the two works, though West has argued forcefully and convincingly that the reverse is most likely the case, followed and supported by the even more thorough and technical arguments of Janko.[35] Finally, Hesiod's *basileus* in *Theogony* is one with which his notional listener will be familiar, whereas he goes to great lengths to justify his outrage at the conduct of Thespiae's *basileis*. In so doing, he emphasizes the miscarriage of *dikê* and the danger it poses to the entire community.[36] Are the real targets of such imprecations the *basileis* themselves, or the community as a whole, which needs to be persuaded that the *basileis* are witting accomplices to the ultimate ruin of the entire town? As I argued in Chapter 3.7, Hesiod may have been trying to persuade Perses to revisit their dispute (if the latter had hijacked more than his share of the patrimony and was still in possession of it) or to impugn his brother's reputation and sway communal opinion to his own side (in anticipation of further judicial action).[37] The energy Hesiod pours into his vituperation in the *Works and Days*, as opposed to the concision and familiarity with which he describes the *basileus* in *Theogony*, indicates that Hesiod has put the greater effort into declaiming the misdeeds of the aristocratic judges who dispensed *dikai* for the Askrans, because it was the more difficult case to make.

As Hesiod was an eyewitness to the early Archaic *polis* and its development, he represents in many ways the best source we have for ascertaining the degree, if any, of systematic judicial abuse by the elites. The internal evidence from Hesiod suggests that the *basileis* who have "wronged" him constitute an exception (or even that Hesiod's particular perception of them has changed due to his own wrangle with Perses), an interpretation that would not only explain the praise of the *basileis* in the *Theogony* but also the vehement passion that a genuinely surprised and outraged Hesiod musters in the *Works and Days*. Hesiod's disgust with the *basileis* grows not from the fact that he expects such behavior—if that were the case, one wonders how or why he agreed to have them hear a dispute with Perses in the first place.[38] Rather, he anticipated justice, *dikê* (i.e., a settlement agreeable to him), but instead received an outrage, *hubris* (a settlement favorable to his brother). I suggest it was this reversal of expectation that occasioned Hesiod's heartfelt tirade, aimed primarily at Perses and only secondarily at the elites of his village.

There are obvious counters to the preceding view of Thespiae's *basileis* as Hesiod's highly personalized and negative view of them, counters which involve famous episodes from epic that turn on the abuse perpetrated by the elite. In the *Iliad*, the commoner Thersites criticizes the conduct of the siege of Troy by the *basileis*.[39] Odysseus rewards him for his trouble by seizing Agamemnon's scepter, wading through the assembled folk, and beating Thersites to a pulp. Elite abuse, pure and simple.

Or is it? The scene has occasioned much scholarly comment, often couched in terms of class struggle and assuming a univocal reading of the episode.[40] For both poet and audience, the reception of the events narrated was undoubtedly a great deal more nuanced and complex; I have no intention of peeling that particular onion here, beyond stating that I incline to the view shared by Peter Rose and W.G. Thalmann that the *Iliad* in general—and the Thersites episode in particular—cannot be read as an instrument for enforcing the ideology of the dominant class.[41] Nor can we see simply in Thersites the mouthpiece of an unmediated, antiaristocratic perspective, and Thalmann argues that Thersites should be seen, at least in part, as a comic figure whose outsider and imposter status (in his parody of Achilles' speech in book 1) allows him to serve as both butt of the joke and the vehicle for breaking the tension that has accumulated in the narrative through various crises of leadership.[42]

Again, while acknowledging the multiplicity of voices and perspectives that both poet and audience may have perceived, for our purposes the issue of Thersites' criticism may be considered in the context of the political tension that had mounted within the Achaean camp since the confrontation between Achilles and Agamemnon. As Thalmann aptly noted, the elites of Homer's world justify their position, their honors, and the produce they receive from their communities by their own role, even obligation, in defense of the community's interest; as a group, the ruling class "protects society from external violence and exercises violence in the socially legitimate setting of the battlefield."[43] However, that justification, and the very legitimacy of elite claims on its basis, had been called into question. Violence, or its potential, had already manifested itself *within* the community twice, once when Achilles nearly assaulted Agamemnon, and again when Odysseus had used the scepter of Agamemnon to force the Achaeans away from their stampede for the ships.[44] As Rose has asked, was this the same scepter, emblematic of the authority of the *themistes* from Zeus and invested in the king, that Achilles had dashed to the ground in his quarrel with Agamemnon (a point, as Rose also states, Homer had finessed)?[45] If so, what does this perhaps say about Agamemnon's legitimacy at this point in the narrative, especially when the line of communication from Zeus to the king to the people had failed, being used for deception and thus contradicting the ruling ideology?[46]

Under a more nuanced reading then, Thersites' complaint could represent not an assault on the prevailing order as it normally operates but instead a comment on the subverted order as it has developed since the quarrel erupted between Agamemnon and Achilles, from the point of view of (at least one of) the characters. Certainly, the poem's audience may have perceived a more general indictment of the prevailing elite ideology, being capable as it was of succumbing to its own latent violence and devolving into such disruptions as those that had unfolded up to the point of Thersites' speech. Nevertheless, two further observations are perhaps pertinent here. First and foremost, Thersites directed his complaint against Agamemnon's greed for military spoil and the bickering of the elites *among themselves*, as well as against the resultant damage these squabbles had done to the collective effort. Nowhere does

Thersites claim any direct mistreatment of the common soldier at the hands of their elite chieftains. His own abuse at the hands of Odysseus was the result of his complaint, not its basis, and perhaps not altogether warranted: Achilles, though for his own selfish reasons, had made similar arguments and indicted the host for tolerating Agamemnon's incompetence and cupidity.[47]

The expectation that the people should not tolerate, and had the power to check, misconduct by the elite finds a possible parallel in an episode that might otherwise serve a second objection. As we have seen in the previous chapter (3.4, dispute ***B1***), in the *Odyssey* Telemakhos, despairing at the wasting of his household by the *basileis* of Ithaca, calls an assembly of the townspeople to ask for their aid against his mother's aristocratic suitors. The convocation of the people causes confusion for and comment by Aigyptios, who notes that the assembly had not been called since Odysseus' departure, and one classic interpretation takes this as an indication of aristocratic neglect of popular assemblies after the weakening or disappearance of kingship in Dark Age Greece.[48] Such an argument assumes that only *basileis* might call the assembly, and with a corporate aristocracy in control of the community there would be no compelling reason for one of them to summon, or appeal to, the *demos*. Thus the popular element in early Greek political life eroded, leaving the aristocracy firmly in power.

Is such an interpretation of this episode justified on the basis of its own details? First, the language of Aigyptios' observation does not necessitate that we believe only an important man could call the assembly: "But now who (*tis*) summoned us here? Upon whom (*tina*) has a need fallen, either among the young men or those who are older? Has he heard report of the army returning, which he could tell us with certainty, since indeed he would have heard it first? Or will he disclose some other public matter (*dêmion allo*) and speak (*agoreuei*) on it?"[49] Anyone (*tis*) could have called the assembly: in fact, whoever had been the first to hear of the return of Odysseus' contingents. Second, Athena, in the guise of Mentor, extols action against the aristocratic suitors, saying that the fault lies not with these men but with the community that stands idly by;[50] hardly do we have a sense here that the *demos* should passively accept whatever the handful of local elites might mete out. Third, and related to this last point, one of the suitors—Leiokritos—is able to persuade the assembly to break up with a few brief words, pointing out to the people that the dispute here concerns members of the elite, and hence each man at the assembly returned to his own home, save the suitors, who continued their revelry at Odysseus'.[51] It is a private, not a public, matter. Finally, we may again note Antinoös' acknowledgment that the people in assembly could by force drive the suitors from the homestead of Odysseus.[52]

Later evidence from Archaic Greek literature likewise gives little indication of aristocratic abuse so systematic that litigants should expect crooked judgments from the *polis* elite in their roles as judges. In the Homeric *Hymn to Hermes*, both parties expected and obtained an acceptable settlement under the auspices of Zeus' judgment.[53] Also, the lyric and elegiac poets of the Archaic age provide no strong reason to believe that the misapplication of justice was a persistent or even commonplace issue, except perhaps in its use as a political weapon by the elites against one another.[54] To make such an assertion is not to argue from silence. The poets of the Archaic period often exhibit a concern for the political and social issues of their day, and still others clearly make the hoplite soldier and his importance to the community their primary topic.[55] Despite the fragmentary nature of any single poet's surviving works, taken together the literary remains of this period constitute a considerable body of evidence. Given the large (and somewhat random) sampling that the chances of survival have allowed us, the scarcity of the theme of judicial abuse or its importance to the hoplite citizen-soldier is telling.

The direct literary evidence we can gather from the Archaic period, then, offers one explicit example of a member of an early Greek community who found himself a victim of (what he perceived as) consistent judicial abuse. It is therefore not surprising that our testimony offers no indication (outside of one notable exception) that this same member of the early Greek *polis* was distrustful of the *dikai* he might obtain from the local *basileis* or that he became tremulous at the thought of the local elite settling his disputes. This episode of perceived judicial misconduct, immortalized by Hesiod, loses some of its force when considered in the context of perceptions about the Archaic judge. Hesiod elsewhere, and Homer, both create the impression that the role of the *basileus* within the judicial forms of the early Greek *polis* made them not only respected and trusted figures within those communities but also a positive force for order and stability. The disappointment and anger of one disaffected poet still arguing eloquently across the ages should not blind us to the broader attitudes of the Archaic Greeks. Endemic, systematic judicial abuse as a cover for more general forms of elite misconduct did not characterize the relationship between the majority of community members and their aristocratic judges in the earlier Archaic period. The eighth assumption of the democratizing telos does not hold.

Events at Athens near the end of the seventh century, however, constitute a potentially fatal counter example to the argument so far. Athens was on the brink of civil war in the later seventh century, and the tensions precipitated the election (appointment?) of Solon as archon, *diallaktês*, and *nomothetês* in 594/3[56] to bring stability to the *polis*.[57] The ancient accounts create the impression that certain individuals in the community were exploiting a position of landed wealth and sociopolitical power to expand their estates as well as their influence.[58] They achieved their ends through the dispossession of others, by way of burdensome rents and debt slavery, the control of the supply of staple foods, and concomitant price-fixing.[59] If and when the complaints of the dispossessed reached the aristocratic judges, the latter must have upheld the actions of those who plundered their less fortunate fellow citizens. At this early date, it is probable that the majority if not all of those engaged in whatever social and economic abuse existed were *Eupatridai* (the seventh-century hereditary class of officeholders at Athens) and that their victims by and large were not.[60] In this scenario, Solon's actions to ameliorate the tension, including his writing of laws, constitute a redress of aristocratic malfeasance of *polis* government in the face of popular discontent and threats of violence.[61]

All the same, Solon's codification of Athenian law was only one part of his program of reform, and not even the most crucial at the time of his legislation; he mentions the writing of *thesmoi* as but one of several things he thought he had accomplished.[62] A number of important suspicions have been raised regarding just how extensive or, for that matter, historical, a Solonian codification or reform program was,[63] or just how progressive any such program would have been.[64] Even then, the achievement for which tradition remembered him above all was the *seisachtheia*—the shaking off of burdens—which included, perhaps, the end of extortionate rents, debt bondage, and the price-fixing made possible by the excessive sale of grain to export markets (though Edward Harris has made a compelling argument that the *seisachtheia* actually referred to Solon's attempt to end payment of protection money to local lords).[65] There is nothing in Solon's surviving poetry or in Herodotus' fifth-century account that compels the reader to believe that Solon considered the writing of his laws a singularly important act within the context of his reforms as a whole. The *seisachtheia* and the avoidance of *stasis* were paramount. For the primacy of the written form of Solon's laws, one does not find evidence until much later (the fourth century). To Athenians living at the inception of the sixth century, Solon's legal activity was significant, perhaps, but not primary.[66] There is no contemporary evidence that forces us to believe, or even really *implies*, that the writing of their laws was an aim of the downtrodden Athenians or that the elite opposed the notion of written law in general.

We can look instead to the legislative activity in Athens a generation before Solon to understand why written laws would not likely have been a popular demand or an object of aristocratic opposition. As far as the evidence suggests, Drakon's "law code" of ca. 621 was neither a positive response to public agitation nor met with intransigence by the governing elite.[67] His actions, especially in drafting a law on homicide, may have addressed the lingering aftermath and associated violence resulting from Kylon's attempt at tyranny in 632 and the subsequent execution of his followers in violation of promises of sanctuary by the partisans of the archon Megakles.[68] Even without this specific issue and its ramifications (Gagarin is skeptical of overdrawing the relationship with Drakon's laws),[69] we might well imagine from the many other echoes in our sources that Athens' political culture was stressed in the last quarter of the seventh century (Gagarin assumes general stability because of the growth of the Athenian population, but on what basis is unclear;[70] see Chapter 5.4 for further discussion). The Areopagus council itself may have commissioned Drakon to author the new laws or at the very least alter and transcribe older, presumably orally preserved customs.[71]

Whatever the ultimate fullness of their compass beyond homicide, Drakon's laws did nothing to alleviate social and economic tensions within Athens. Judging from the urgency of the situation by the time of Solon, if Drakon's laws had included any provisions directly and exclusively relevant to nonelites or their relationship to the governing aristocracy, those laws had only led to the further subjection of society's commoner elements to elite abuse. Tracey Rihll has recently envisioned a process whereby the commoners, through a variety of factors, would have been weighed down by Drakon's solution to the problem of increasing "pressure on *convenient* and *appropriate* land" (original emphasis) in seventh-century Attica.[72] Though the argument is quite clever and stimulating—and would help bolster the present argument regarding the years between Drakon and Solon—it assumes Drakon was responsible for a wide range of legislative acts, including an elaborate land reform scheme and regulatory statutes to govern it. Ancient sources do indicate that Drakon's "code" went beyond his homicide law,[73] but we have only scattered, incidental, and not altogether reliable testimony as to what these other Drakontian laws might have concerned, including notices ranging from laws on theft to sacrilege to idleness,[74] and perhaps even a law on tyranny.[75]

The reconstruction in question faces a second hurdle. Aristotle declares that Drakon made laws for the existing constitution, and that there was nothing particularly noteworthy about these, save the severity of their prescribed punishments.[76] The Aristotelian *Athenaion Politeia* attributes to Drakon, on the other hand, a *politeia,* but its outlines are exactly those ascribed in the same source to Solon.[77] There seems here to be, at best, a transposition of Solonian realities into the Drakontian era,[78] and scholars widely regard the "constitution of Drakon" as a fourth-century invention in service to the debate over ancestral constitutions. Of course, though Drakon almost surely did not frame a constitution as such, that does not preclude the possibility that he composed laws regarding land tenure in Attica. It is curious, however, that among the various scraps of evidence we find not a hint of Drakon having done so, and it is even odder still that he would not have been in some way remembered for contributing greatly to the crisis that Solon then attempted to resolve. Whether Rihll is correct or not, we can confidently say that Drakon wrote *some* laws and that over the next twenty-some years, social and economic tensions in Athens apparently worsened. Given these observations, it is difficult to see how nonelites at Athens could have possibly viewed the writing of law as a necessary step on the road to improving their social, economic, and political conditions.[79] And indeed, no source before the fourth century suggests they ever did make such a connection.

Indeed, forces other than popular interests instigated the earliest written legislation in places other than Athens. The ancient traditions regarding the nature of Zaleukos' legislation suggest that the measures contained therein sought to strengthen the position of the elite at Epizephyrian Lokris. Zaleukos' background and his laws have generated controversy among ancient authorities and modern scholars alike.[80] As with Drakon, we do not possess any direct evidence that Zaleukos explicitly sought to increase aristocratic power at the expense of social and political inferiors, though he most likely legislated in the interests of the elite.[81] Whether he did this with any reference to the rest of the community, positively or negatively, is impossible to know. An aristocratic impetus behind Zaleukos' legislation would, however, be consistent with what may be safely surmised of the initiative behind Drakon's "code."[82] It is worth bearing in mind that, among the various traditions about even Solon, we hear that he protected the interests of the elite and that he left the Areopagus in a role of oversight of the constitution.[83] Nothing in the early literary tradition compels us to believe that elites in various Greek *poleis* resisted the writing of law or that they had any special motivation for doing so. Therefore, the notion that Greek elites viewed written law as a threat to their judicial and political supremacy, which in turn protected their social and economic power, is a proposition with which we may justifiably dispense.[84] Assumption seven of the democratic telos model appears untenable.

IF THE ARGUMENTS REGARDING the implicit weaknesses of assumptions seven and eight are at all accepted, assumption number six is at once fraught with obvious difficulties. That an insurgent hoplite class (a notion, as we have already seen, with its own problems) and/or a nascent urban commercial/industrial sector viewed written law as a necessary step toward equality before the law, and thus the general improvement in their social, economic, and political status, is an argument that finds no support in the ancient evidence prior to the fourth century. In Athens, for which we have the most (not to say the best) evidence, even if the conditions of the middling and poorer sectors of society had not deteriorated in the generation between Drakon and Solon, it seems safe to say that they had not improved. As a result, Athens found itself on the verge of civil war. The equation that the writing of law equaled judicial, and thus political and economic, emancipation would be a very curious one for the nonelites of Athens to make when considered in this context; Drakon's written laws, whatever subjects they embraced, had done nothing to help the humbler elements of society. The idea that such elements demanded written law is not offered by the ancient sources—though Aristotle's suggestions in the *Politics*[85] have inspired some scholars to posit it—but rather arises from modern theories regarding the hoplite revolution.

As is well known, the traditional formulation of the theory of the hoplite revolution, in its barest and simplest terms, argues for a cascade of social and political changes attendant upon the introduction of hoplite armor and tactics. As an interpretative model, the theory of the hoplite revolution has something of its own august history extending well over a century now.[86] The new equipment and formation—which by necessity spread throughout the Greek world as a matter of survival once the first few *poleis* adopted it—made it possible for the newly armed and well-organized yeoman farmers to resist the intimidation or outright violence that had previously enabled warrior-aristocrats to dominate society. Thus empowered, it was only a matter of time before the men serving in the hoplite phalanx and responsible for the defense of the *polis* would begin to agitate for redress of their political and socioeconomic grievances. Their dominant military monopoly having eroded, the elites had no choice but to make concessions in order to bring the class of the hoplite citizen-soldiers (property owners themselves) into fuller civic participation and assuage their demands, among which were changes in the administration of justice and an end to the arbitrary nature of settlements based on orally preserved custom. Thus, the mobilization of the yeomanry as a hoplite army becomes a sine qua non for the transition to written law.

It makes for an attractively tidy model and has continued to exercise considerable influence as a framework for understanding political change in early Greece.[87] But the hoplite revolution has also come under no small amount of noteworthy criticism of late.[88] If Frank Frost is correct in characterizing the hoplite revolution as "among the great non-events in history"[89] and we should discard the model altogether, with it would necessarily fall whatever support remains for assumption number six. Whether one rejects the model or not, we may also note that the relationship between the appearance of hoplite tactics and written law (much like that between legal inscriptions and levels of literacy) is by no means clear:[90] for example, hoplite armies may have come relatively late to Crete (later seventh/early sixth century), well after—according to our epigraphic evidence—a burgeoning tradition of written statutes had taken root there. Indeed, one of the greatest difficulties in seeing the hoplite revolution as a spur to written law is one of timing. Whereas the dates of the earliest law codes are relatively secure (mid-seventh century for Zaleukos and Kharondas, 621 for Drakon at Athens, late seventh or early sixth century for the earliest version of the Gortyn Code), the chronology of both the introduction and the progress of hoplite warfare is substantially more uncertain.[91] One may reasonably doubt the extent to which hoplite warfare was widespread or deep-rooted in the Greek world by the middle to late seventh century. The hoplite revolution, by virtue of chronology alone, cannot constitute a necessary causal factor in the appearance of the earliest written Greek law.

Assumptions six, seven, and eight listed above are thus unsupportable on the basis of the Archaic evidence. There is no indication that nonelite segments of Archaic communities viewed written law as a means of effecting a change in their social, political, and judicial standing. Accordingly, we cannot assume they agitated for written statutes. Furthermore, even if such agitation *did* take place and the literary record has simply not preserved it, there is no reason to hold that the elites of Archaic *poleis* resisted such demands. The earliest laws, as I will argue in Chapter 6, rather reflect a number of particularly elite concerns and needs. For the time being, it is enough to note that the evidence in the cases of Zaleukos and Drakon indicates no small amount of aristocratic initiative in the process of writing laws, and there seems no compelling reason to believe that the ruling elites of those *poleis,* at least, considered either the writing up or writing down of certain precepts a threat to their power within the community. The presumed systematic, rapacious abuse, mostly perpetrated directly by members of the elite against weaker parties, also did not exist in such a way as to provide the spur to written law. The testimony of Hesiod suggests that the poet was angry with the *basileis* for upholding the theft, as he saw it, committed by his brother with regard to their inheritance. Other passages from the Hesiodic corpus, as we have seen, indicate that even this degree of malfeasance on the part of the *basileis*—if we may even consider it such—was unusual. Even if the deck were stacked against successful social criticism,[92] it still seems odd that Hesiod remains the only surviving voice that speaks directly to the problem of judicial corruption. Finally, with respect to Solonian Athens, the ancient tradition admittedly did hold that certain citizens oppressed in some way their weaker counterparts. Nevertheless, it appears that economic issues were at the heart of the friction, the remedies to which did not include a demand for a written body of law.

2—Literacy in the Greek World and the Appearance of Written Law

Having concentrated thus far on the case for the appearance of written law as the result of popular agitation against elite abuse and resistance to reform, we turn now to the problem of the accessibility of written law to the wider Archaic Greek community. Literacy lies at the very heart of the first two assumptions presented in the previous section. The notion that written law protected against arbitrary adjudication of disputes carries with it a necessary implication: those who had found themselves oppressed before the advent of written legislation must have possessed the ability to read written laws in order for such laws to have any more benefit to them than "unwritten" ones. A law which no one but a literate minority could read would be no less susceptible to elite manipulation than the customary justice previously dispensed from "memory." It is important to understand not only who could read in the early Greek *poleis,* but to what extent.

The issue of ancient literacy has been a hot topic over the past five decades, and studies on the problem have yet to produce what might be termed a working consensus. William Harris has argued that the answer to the question, "How literate were ancients?" is a resounding "not very."[93] The difficulty in tackling the problem of the extent of literacy is twofold. First, there is little agreement as to what the word literacy does or should mean, even in modern contexts.[94] Second, to speak of literate skill in antiquity, one must define variables. Are we dealing with urban or rural literacy, or both? The ability to read only, or also to write? If only the ability to read, then at what level: graffiti on pots, simple inscriptions, detailed decrees, or sophisticated literature? Are we speaking of the literate skills of the upper echelons of a society (whatever metric one chooses to use), or the entire community? Finally, for what place and for what time does one seek to determine the degree of literate skill?

I begin by acknowledging that the level of literacy is not the only criterion that played a role in the publication of law. The public display of laws, especially on the walls of temples and sanctuaries, could have intended a number of symbolic effects designed to express or foster a sense of solidarity among the community of citizens,[95] even one sanctioned by the gods.[96] As I will also discuss in Chapter 7, the very presence of written laws, in monumental, public, sometimes even sacred contexts, could also serve as a useful tool for elites to bear down on their social peers and political rivals.[97]

In the current context, of course, I am most concerned with the notion that written laws would necessarily be *accessible* to all members of the community and the degree to which such laws may therefore have guarded against the (supposed) domination of adjudication by the elite. The two very recent studies by Gagarin and Papakonstantinou both argue for a high degree of communal involvement in the passage of written laws in the Archaic period, in large part on the basis of the enactment clauses that authorize the statutes.[98] It is true that some Archaic statutes do mention authorities such as the *polis* or the *damioi*; the earliest surviving legal inscription, from Dreros on Crete, includes references to both. The problem, of course, is that we have no means of knowing how large a segment of a community in a seventh-century *polis* was considered to constitute the *demos* and hence count as citizenry. For whatever the notice is worth, Aristotle warned that what was called a (properly constituted) *politeia* in earlier ages was typically that in name only and rather frequently a cover for oligarchies and even monarchies; as Gagarin himself acknowledges, the *poleis* associated with early legislation were more often oligarchies than democracies.[99] Additionally, as we will see in Chapter 6.2, it is clear that laws could also explicitly consign some free individuals to second-class citizen status.

Gagarin, and to a lesser extent Papakonstantinou (who finesses the issue by suggesting that basic literate skills did exist but that it may not have mattered in any case), has additionally argued for a much higher degree of literacy than many scholars, including the present author, accept for seventh and sixth century Greece.[100] He supports his position by citing the marks used by the masons to divide words, the size of the letters, and so on. However, in my estimation he asserts this wider-spread ability to read far more than he demonstrates it. One of the early texts he discusses at length, a Chian law of ca. 575,[101] does not strike one as especially easy to read, as the letters are rotated ninety degrees on three sides of a freestanding stele. The fact that much shorter epigrams on irregular surfaces (such as pots) sometimes appear in this vertical fashion does not, in my opinion, dispel the objection. Furthermore, this interpretation ignores a fifth century law of Teos, considered below, that strongly suggests that theretofore many Teans could not read laws for themselves, at least not proficiently, and now imposed penalties on officials who did not do so to the best of their ability.

To what degree might have nonelites read and understood for themselves publicly inscribed laws ca. 650–550, such that they could have perceived written law as a guardian against elite judicial abuse? Certainly a substantial proportion of the population must have possessed the ability to comprehend a public inscription on their own in order to consider the publication of laws as a means to redress class-based judicial abuse. More recent scholarship on the problem suggests otherwise. Further considerations have altered the earlier opinions that the spread of literacy through the Greek world was rapid and thorough.[102] Harris has rightly indicated the paucity of surviving written materials from the first 250 years after the development of Greek alphabetic writing, which most likely took place in the first half of the eighth century.[103] Though this fact could represent something of an accident, in that any writing committed to perishable media will have long since vanished, the precursory and amateur nature of those examples that do survive indicate a fairly shallow experience of writing in Archaic Greece.[104] An examination of Homeric and Hesiodic verse betrays nothing that compels the modern reader to assume that reading and writing played an important role in the daily lives of Greeks during this period.[105] Harris has argued persuasively that there is no archaeological, epigraphical, or literary evidence that connotes thoroughgoing scribal skill before the year 600 and nothing that indicates widespread readership until the end of the sixth century.[106]

The limitations on literate skill and the tools of writing as late as ca. 600 can be seen in the Greek graffiti left at the Egyptian site of Abu Simbel in the first decade of the sixth century.[107] There were seven, perhaps eight, writers involved in the surviving epigraphy, all of them mercenaries serving the Egyptian pharaoh Psammetikhos II.[108] Of these authors, only one has executed a text of any length that betrays an expert familiarity with letter forms and grammatical skill:[109] it was written by, or on behalf of, Arkhon, son of Amoibikhos, and Peleqos, son of Eudamos (though one modern commentator has suggested that Peleqos is the "axe" with which Arkhon carved the inscription and the original "Oudamos" is a Homeric pun),[110] and runs to thirty-six words composed in five lines.[111] Beyond this more extensive graffito, the remainder is laconic or amateur at best. The second most explicit tag is boustrophedon (as opposed to the rest, which the writers rendered left to right) and provides the author's name and origin (Anaxanor of Ialysos), along with the explanation that he served as a mercenary for Psammetikhos.[112]

Anaxanor's compatriots provide less information still. One graffito furnishes a proper name identified as the possible author, and the missing part of this epigraph clearly includes at least one other name, explaining both the ΚΑΙ at the beginning of what survives as well as the plural form of "wrote."[113] It is not unreasonable to presume that one mercenary here has recorded both his name and that of one or more comrades, perhaps because the others could not. Notably, the "literate" man among them misspelled the verb, omitting the *psi* from ΕΓΡΑ[Ψ]ΑΝ.[114] A different scrawl similarly identifies the author, though this time with a singular verb, and provides his place of origin.[115] The lettering of this graffito is quite poor, as is that of two other inscriptions that include only the name of the writer along with one other identifier: Elesibios of Teos in one case, Python son of Amoibikhos in the other.[116] One other example, the original of which had been lost by the time of A. Bernand and O. Masson's study, also apparently exhibited amateurish writing, and the author may have misspelled his own name along with that of the pharaoh.[117]

We should like to know more of the social origins or standing of the men specifically attested and anything at all of those included in Krithis' inscription. Bernand and Masson believed the men were not rank-and-file soldiers but at the very least commanders.[118] Their supposition is plausible enough, as they appear to be signatories to the lengthier text of Arkhon and Peleqos, and they may have represented what was presumably a larger company of mercenaries. By the same token, these men may have signed, not because of their rank, but rather because they possessed the requisite skills—however limited in some instances—to write at all. Any theory as to why Krithis (or one of the lost names from his graffito) would then have written on behalf of comrades would necessarily be pure conjecture. Whether we are dealing with mercenary commanders recording their names in that capacity or those men capable of writing on behalf of the group, the conclusion is the same: only a very small number of people among that company could write expertly, and a great many not at all. Alone among the graffiti does Arkhon's and Peleqos' text demonstrate truly well-executed letters and a real command of written Greek. The Krithis graffito exhibits a neat hand, but the inscription itself is short and formulaic; the rest are rough and amateur.

Despite its exiguousness, the sample is useful. Those men who attached their place of origin haled from various places in Asia Minor and its environs (Ialysos, Teos, and Colophon). As for the rest, we cannot know their home *polis*, though they may have been second- or third-generation descendants of Greeks who had settled in Naukratis in Lower Egypt;[119] it is perhaps simpler to accept that some men chose to include ethnics and/or patronymics and some did not, without any particularly compelling reason. The sample is in any event geographically random, though the writers' origins—insofar as we know them—cluster in the eastern Greek world, long presumed to have been relatively advanced ca. 600. However, only two of the graffiti suggest their authors approached a mastery of letterforms.[120] Anaxanor's turn is not poor, but pales in comparison to that of Arkhon and Peleqos. The rest, except for "Krithis," are clearly struggling; three can muster only their own names in conjunction with those of their home *poleis* or their fathers, and the letters are crude. An ability to write one's own name and little else should not surprise, as it is consistent with the most common use of script in the early history of

Greek alphabetic writing—applying one's name to mark personal property.[121] Harris seems quite right in suggesting that as late as 575, writing in the Greek world was "still something of a novel toy."[122]

Novelty is apparent in the majority of contemporary applications of alphabetic writing at this time. Even at Athens, where the amount of surviving written material from the seventh and sixth centuries is exceptionally large,[123] the bulk indicates very restricted literacy of the type necessary to comprehend lengthier or more complex texts. In addition to the frequent marking of property (identification of dedications which were typically quite formulaic),[124] the finds from the sanctuary of Zeus on Mount Hymettos are illuminating. Numerous potsherds from this site bear a proper name along with ΕΓΡΑΦΣΕ ("so-and-so wrote [this]"), still others represent abecedaria, most of them dedicated in the later seventh century.[125] Even in and around Athens, where examples of seventh- and sixth-century writing proliferate relative to other sites, the vast majority of what survives is simplistic. Early, lengthier inscriptions from throughout the Greek world, such as the Nestor Cup, the Dipylon Vase, and the Corinthian perfume flask from Kyme, constitute exceptions within a massive body of much simpler writings. The supposed elegance of such exceptions should not obscure the fact that most Greeks in the seventh and early sixth centuries were incapable of short epigrams beyond personal names with patronymics or ethnics, or at most formulaic dedications to the gods.[126]

Limited writing ability does not necessarily entail a commensurate inability to read, of course, but the evidence suggests that reading proficiency was not much more extensive during the early centuries of Greek legislation. Direct testimony on reading ability prior to ca. 575 is nonexistent, but later indications demonstrate restricted literacy well into the Classical period. Until 575, it is rare to find inscriptions on Attic black-figure pottery at all.[127] With the roughly contemporaneous appearance of the Françoise Vase, however, we have suddenly an object exhibiting no fewer than 129 separate examples of writing, mostly personal names.[128] Such a profusion of script represents not the literate skill of either purchaser or producer, but the opposite: aside from personal names, we find "superfluous labels," betraying a "novelty to be exhibited."[129] Afterward, other black-figure ware demonstrates—albeit less dramatically—similar written content. The majority of surviving pieces still bear no writing at all, and those that do sometimes offer up nonsense.[130] Writing may have enjoyed prestige in the black-figure and red-figure markets, but apparently the purchasers either failed to realize or to care that their pots in fact said nothing.[131] In the fifth century, as Attic literacy increased, there was a doubtlessly related decrease in nonsensical inscriptions on pots: craftsmen were perhaps less likely to commit mistakes (or to have to resort to chicanery), and customers became less tolerant of them as formal education, especially for the elite, was on the rise.[132]

As Svenbro has cogently argued, we must also be careful not to forget or underestimate the oral component in Archaic Greek reading.[133] The Archaic writer expected the reader to give voice to the text so he could *hear* what he was reading: the nature of ancient texts made silent reading difficult at best.[134] Reading aloud a text, such as a funerary inscription, transformed it into a more easily understood speech act for the benefit of both the reader and those bystanders unable to read and vocalize the text for themselves.[135] If this is true of funerary monuments, it would be equally so for legal inscriptions, typically lengthier and substantially more complicated.

That reading ability remained rather limited even at Athens at the dawn of the Classical period is suggested by an anecdote in Plutarch's *Life of Aristeides*. Shortly before an ostracism vote in which Aristeides was a candidate, an "unlettered and rude man from the countryside" approached the politician and offered him his potsherd, asking him to write Aristeides' name on it. Aristeides bemusedly asked his fellow citizen what "this man Aristeides" had done to deserve his vote: the man replied he did not even know Aristeides, but he knew he was tired of constantly hearing him referred to as "The Just." Aristeides, without further comment, wrote his own name on the potsherd ballot, an action that for Plutarch was an illustration of Aristeides' character.[136] Had Aristeides so chosen, he might have written anything on the ballot and his fellow citizen would have been none the wiser: only the politician's moral rectitude prevented him from taking advantage of the man's illiteracy. While such moralizing tidbits in Plutarch always deserve some suspicion, this particular story bears some conviction: the story would be an odd one for Plutarch to invent, and it squares well with contemporary evidence about the nature of ostracism ballots in the early fifth century.[137] His compatriot's inability to read in no way surprised Aristeides, and if it is true that Athenians enjoyed comparatively high rates of literacy in the Greek world,[138] then the tale reveals that as late as the early fifth century we should not assume widespread ability to read and write in the Greek world.

The story of Timoxenos, who intended to betray the Greeks at Potidaia in 479, provides yet another example of restricted literacy as late as the early fifth century.[139] The would-be turncoat and his Persian contact passed messages by way of communiqués wrapped around arrows deliberately shot in the vicinity of one another. One of these missiles went astray and fell into the hands of the Potidaians, who took the letter to their generals; the generals, in turn, read the message and identified Timoxenos and his plans. As Svenbro states, it may be that the citizens simply showed deference in taking the message to their leaders, but it seems "more likely that they handed the written message over to [the generals] because only the leaders could read."[140]

Finally, an inscription from Teos dating to around 470 prescribes both divine imprecations and severe civil penalties for any official "who does not read out the writing on the stele to the best of his memory or power."[141] It is clear that the reading out of public documents had been entrusted to particular magistrates. It is likewise apparent upon consideration that a good number of citizens in Teos would not have been able to read for themselves, hence making an incorrect reading—be it deliberate or otherwise—a matter for concern. The establishment of such a statute intimates as well malpractice with regard to this magisterial function, a problem sufficiently worthy of addressing in explicit terms. I shall return to this point below.

In sum, reading ability in Archaic Greece, or the lack thereof, would appear to have paralleled the unevenness and shallowness of writing skill. It is therefore invalid to assume that a significant or substantial proportion of the residents of an Archaic Greek *polis*, even Athens, enjoyed sufficient literate skill to enable widespread effective reading of published laws.[142] What then of the second assumption of the model? Could or would the citizens of Archaic Greek *poleis* assume that the officials administering written law were more evenhanded and less arbitrary than any *basileis* settling disputes based on memory and custom? The answer, unsurprisingly, is no.

3—Memory, Malfeasance, and Elite Adjudication under Written Law

As we have already seen in the previous chapter and the opening section of the present one, the customary system of dispute settlement revealed in the surviving works of Homer and Hesiod was not nearly as unjust, nor the elite custodians of that system as rapacious, as has often been assumed. As far as any abuses which did exist, there is a good deal of evidence to suggest that the writing of laws was not thought to be a guarantee against corruption. The aforementioned law from Teos provides an example of how far the citizens of any given *polis* might be able to trust the officials responsible for the reading out and interpretation of public decrees. This Tean law, by its very existence, implies that magistrates so entrusted at least occasionally did not execute the duties of their office to the best of their ability. The citizens of Teos, as enough of them gained literate skills ca. 470, ultimately legislated against the misuse of power by those upon whom they previously depended to read inscribed pronouncements for them and who held the related offices because of their hitherto prized ability to read complex documents.[143] Even as late as 470, Teans in general still found themselves largely dependent on individuals, often regular magistrates, who possessed a special knowledge of the laws—in this case, the ability to read them.[144] Their skills distinguished them from the rest of the community and provided scope for abuse of written laws and thus the judicial system as a whole. Even if such officials did not incline toward exploiting their rare talents, they could continue to manifest their power and influence well into the fifth century, as at Halikarnassos.[145]

We may extend such a pattern back into the Archaic period as well, after the appearance of the first written laws. Scribes in Archaic Greek communities wielded peculiar and daunting power. Maiandrios, the *grammatistes* of the Samian tyrant Polykrates (fl. ca. 535—522), was noteworthy for the wealth he amassed and the important role he played in the tyrant's government.[146] At Elis, the law explicitly placed the *grapheus* under special protection, so vital was the office to the community.[147] One may further consider the status and influence of Spensithios, serving as scribe in the small Cretan community of Arkades.[148] Around 500, Spensithios' special talents had allowed him to secure his vital position as *poinikastas*, scribe, for life, as well as to pass the office on to his sons.[149] In a small, apparently insignificant community such as Spensithios', the rarity of his talent placed him in a privileged situation and led his fellow citizens to believe the only secure transmission of the office and its requisite skills was to hand it over to his family in perpetuity. In larger *poleis*, enough men were literate that the community could avoid dependence on one individual and his family. In one case, at Erythrai, the citizens believed it imperative to establish strict limits on the influence and power of those who held the important position of scribe. There, after the magistracy of Khalkhides, a *grammateus* could no longer hold another office simultaneously, serve as scribe to the same office more than once (the office of the treasurer is mentioned explicitly), or to serve more than one magistrate at a time.[150] Later, the Erythraians prohibited members of the college of *heleorountes* or their scribes from holding those offices again for another ten years.[151] Where possible, then, communities tried to submit scribes to their authority, or at least control the scope of their power; when this was not practical, a man such as Spensithios might accrue exceptional authority and privileges to himself and his family.[152] The advent of written laws and their interpretation only accomplished the replacement of one type of elite functionary—the *basileus*—with another, also of elite background.

Beyond their ability to read and write, scribes held additional official functions that afforded them exceptional power in their communities. Magistrates responsible for remembering the laws are often difficult to distinguish from those who served as scribes. Spensithios and his descendants were not just to act forever as scribe (*poinikazen*), but also to serve as remembrancer (*mnamoneuwen*),[153] and one may wonder how many other such officials were doubly responsible in this manner. The title of scribe in any number of *poleis* bears resemblance to Spensithios' (*poinikastas*):[154] for example, at Teos, *phoinikographeon*.[155] Two Hellenistic inscriptions[156] refer to the scribal official as *phoinikographosi*, but the inclusion of *phoiniko-*, Phoenician, to indicate writing, along with the evidence from Teos, suggests strongly the title was much older.

In some cases, the duties of scribes had probably grown out of those held by individuals responsible for remembering and announcing public business to the early Greek community before the employment of writing for such business. Françoise Ruzé has detected a continuity between the skilled scribes of the Archaic period and the Homeric *demiourgoi*, "plus précisément" with respect to heralds (*kerykes*).[157] More persuasively, Rosalind Thomas has analyzed the persistence at Athens into Classical times of what must have been an office of the preliterate, Archaic *polis*, the *mnamones/mnemones*, or remembrancers,[158] and officials with titles otherwise related to memory continue to be attested elsewhere around the Greek world well after the introduction of writing. Seventh-century Tiryns had an official known as the *hieromnemon*, as does fifth-century Argos; given the early occurrence at nearby Tiryns and the title of sacred remembrancer, it seems safe to assume the Argive office enjoyed roots stretching back well before the 400s.[159] *Mnemones*, to judge by the Great Code, were important officials at Gortyn.[160] Halikarnassos also employed officials with the same title,[161] as did Nemea, as revealed in a pair of fourth-century inscriptions.[162] As was the case at Argos, we may well imagine that the Nemean office likewise had deeper historical roots. Since many of the magistrates whose titles can be associated with memory are clearly connected with the secretarial functions of writing after its introduction in many *poleis*, the remembrancer must have fulfilled his duties not only by dint of memory—the traditional means—but also used writing to help remember those facts for which he was responsible.[163]

Thus, in a world where literacy was only slowly making itself and its consequences felt, those whose duty it was to preserve previous actions and decisions of the community did so with the tools at their disposal: their memory *and* the records that writing and an increasingly literate mentality made available to them.[164] Whether an official's title emphasized his scribal duties (e.g., *poinikastas*) or the role of memory or knowledge (e.g., *mnemon*, *gnomon*), such functionaries lived in or even between two worlds. Such men employed their literate skills as a supplement to the general functions of memory required for the discharge of their magisterial duties to the *polis*. Written laws did not displace or wholly succeed unwritten law, but rather existed alongside them, and often the interpretation of both rested in the hands of individuals who belonged to a group no less exclusive or juridically powerful than the *basileis* of Homer and Hesiod.

When it comes to laws, a comparison of such officials with the Hesiodic *basileus* of the *Theogony* may be particularly apt. Evidence for the singing of laws promulgated initially in writing suggests a possible continuity with Hesiod's *basileus*, and serves to underscore the twilight between literacy and orality in which scribes and remembrancers operated. Athenaios, citing the third-century biographer Hermippos of Smyrna, relates that Athenians sang the laws of Kharondas at wine parties.[165] This would make of Kharondas a *nomoidos*, a law-singer,[166] and it was typically assumed that Kharondas originally composed his laws in verse.[167] Clement of Alexandria believed that the famous seventh-century poet and musician Terpander sang the laws at Sparta,[168] a state renowned for its unwritten laws.[169] In Crete, according to Aelian, the youth were to learn the laws to melodies (*manthanein ekeleuon tous nomous meta tinos melôidias*), in order to remember them better and thus make more effective use of them.[170] Plutarch claimed that Solon had originally attempted to put his laws in verse rather than prose;[171] given that Solon used verse for a variety of political purposes,[172] the suggestion is quite plausible.

Indeed, the assumption that law must be written in order to be law, in the sense of a binding rule, does not apply to the Greek world before the end of the fifth century. Even at Athens, where rates of literacy were probably considerably higher than in most of the Greek world by the middle of the fifth century,[173] the notion of unwritten law existed alongside that of the city's statutes, and both placed obligations on citizens. From his thorough examination of Sophocles' *Antigone* and Euripides' *Suppliants*, Giovanni Cerra concludes that the debates presented in those tragedies—and the evolving viewpoint from one to the other regarding written law—reflect contemporary juridical and political language.[174] The notion of unwritten laws and their validity remained powerful until the opening of the Peloponnesian War, when Pericles in his famous Funeral Oration cited laws both written and unwritten as protectors of the injured.[175] Athenians may not have even *begun* to identify equality and justice with written law until after the reforms of Ephialtes, when the *demos* won its legislative power and citizens started to imagine the *nomoi* they passed as an expression of that power.[176] If so, that process took another two generations to unfold, as evidenced by Pericles' proclamation and the fact that we do not have an explicit statement of written laws arming lesser citizens with rights until the late 420s.[177] As we have seen, when the Athenians decided finally in 403 to illegalize the application of unwritten law, they did so less because of any philosophical qualms, but rather due to recent historical events.[178] Only then and, so far as we know, only at Athens, had the citizens come to perceive that written law must completely displace unwritten custom as a presumed guarantor of judicial equality.

In the Archaic age, then, written law did not—nor was it intended to—displace unwritten custom; rather, it supplemented it. In Chapter 6, we will examine the extant evidence of the earliest written laws, which reveals that a great deal of their content aimed at establishing and giving authority to new rules, not giving written form to old ones. For the time being, we may note that in the seventh and sixth centuries, there was no question for the Greeks of one legal system or ethic overthrowing an aristocratically controlled ancien régime in the sphere of law and justice: suspicion about the potential abuse of custom, of so-called ancestral laws that remained unwritten, did not arise until much later. It is thus difficult to sustain a view that most nonelite Greeks living in Archaic *poleis* believed they could place greater trust in, or gain more benefit from, the application of written laws to the administration of justice. The introduction of written laws was so gradual that it existed for generations alongside oral judicial practices in many Greek communities. In one famous instance, at Sparta, the *polis* conducted its business with few written statutes at all.[179]

The limitations on popular literacy, the presence of officials with roots in a preliterate past (and powerful talents when it came to reading and writing), and the lack of stigma attached to unwritten laws well into the Classical period, all suggest that there was little abstract sense that if the Greeks perceived systematic judicial abuse, written law would solve the problem. Moreover, in two particular examples for which we have comparatively detailed evidence, the administration of justice after written law remained securely in the hands of elite functionaries of the Archaic *polis*: Gortyn and Athens.

At Gortyn, the principal magistrates were the *kosmoi*, and from the seventh century onward they were primarily responsible for the administration of justice. Though they appear to have been supplemented by further officials called *dikastai* by the fifth century,[180] one scholar has suggested that the *dikastai* are in fact simply the *kosmoi* when they are exercising their judicial duties and prerogatives.[181] Perhaps this would have been to distinguish their judicial functions from other responsibilities, but there is no certainty. However, there can be little doubt as to the social standing of those men who served as *kosmoi*. As late as the fourth century, only members of "certain clans" could hold the office, which in the Cretan context signified a group possessing hereditary privileges.[182] Thus, the elite, maintaining control of the important judicial offices of the *polis*, were in a position to continue dominating the administration of justice and the enactment of legislation at Gortyn, even with the existence of codified law.

Athenians believed Drakon and Solon had both promulgated codes, though the extent of each of these codifications is a subject demanding caution. While scholars largely accept as authentic the surviving republication of Drakon's homicide provisions,[183] there is little agreement as to what else his legislation might have covered. While Solon was alleged to have replaced all of Drakon's laws save those concerning homicide, the attribution to Drakon of a constitution was, as we have seen, a fourth-century fiction inspired by the political arguments of the day.[184] That Solon deserves credit as an active lawgiver is beyond doubt; the Athenian taste for assigning to him all laws of remote and uncertain origin, however, complicates our picture. While the substance of their overall legislation remains unclear, both Drakon and Solon left the administration of justice in the hands of elites. The former's surviving law on homicide provided that the *ephêtai* were to sit as judges, a statement that has caused difficulty since antiquity: Plutarch tried desperately to reconcile this with the fact that he knew the Areopagus sat as the homicide court of Athens.[185] Modern scholars have attempted a variety of ingenious explanations, though that advanced by Robert Wallace is the most elegant and does the least violence to the evidence: the *ephêtai* were members of the Areopagus Council.[186]

Likewise, Solon left the reins of the *polis* in the hands of the Areopagus. Aristotle explains that, while Solon was often blamed for degrading other elements of the population in favor of the popular jury courts, in fact the rise in the fortunes of the *demos* was "rather the result of a mishap" than from Solon's intentions, since he had appointed all the offices from the notable and wealthy.[187] The point is repeated in the Aristotelian *Athenaion Politeia*,[188] and seconded by Plutarch, who appears to have been working from a source other than Aristotle.[189] Such testimony deserves skepticism, of course: by the fourth century, when Aristotle and (presumably) Plutarch's sources were written, Solon had long been a favorite topic for political propagandists at Athens. However, those who favored democracy had successfully co-opted him by the middle of the century, so Aristotle provides us with the more sober (and unpopular) version of the historical Solon.

To empower the Areopagus as Solon did was not commensurate with any supposed popular interest at Athens. Aristotle refers to that body as the oligarchic element in the *polis*, and further states that, with regard to the officials of the community and the council as well, Solon merely refrained from destroying existing institutions.[190] Solon himself claimed to have given the Athenians the best laws they would accept, and Plutarch said the lawgiver suited his laws to the situation, not the situation to the laws.[191] Among other things, this would have meant leaving the composition of the Areopagus unchanged: if Solon indeed changed the criteria for the selection of archons by creating a new property qualification and shifting eligibility from birth to wealth, the Areopagus would still have comprised former archons and represented the most politically successful of Athens' most prominent citizens.[192] The Areopagus will have retained its elite character well after Solon's reforms, and the ancient sources report that the council was to serve as a guardian of the constitution and could serve as one of the anchors to "keep the people silent."[193] Enjoying prerogatives that allowed it to intervene in any proceeding that threatened to undermine the state, the Areopagus' judicial and political influence remained paramount after Solon's reforms.[194]

LITTLE EVIDENCE EXISTS TO SUPPORT the assumptions outlined at the beginning of this chapter and that we have so far had occasion to examine (1–3, 6–8). In the previous chapter, we saw how the surviving epic material indicates a functional legal culture in the Greece of Homer and Hesiod: that legal culture rested on communal participation and a common sense of the rule base, itself given authority and reinforced through song. In that context we can more easily understand the ancient reports that early lawgivers, such as Kharondas and Solon, sought to versify their laws. As we saw in Chapter 2, song represented an authoritative utterance, and for the Greeks—long after they first thought to commit some laws to writing—unwritten custom, stored up in memory, continued to play a vital role in their judicial practices. We may therefore doubt that widespread, systematic abuse existed, Hesiod's screed against the *basileis* in *Works and Days* notwithstanding; the legal culture of the Greek world at the horizon of written law militates against the corporate monopolization of justice and interpretation of custom in the narrow interests of a circle of individuals, among whom judicial and political power was an object of intense competition anyway. Thus, popular agitation regarding the regulation and settlement of disputes by elites is unlikely.

Furthermore, the extent of literacy when Greeks first began to write laws was insufficient to make justice based on statutes more accessible to a significant portion of the citizenry. Written law in and of itself could not and did not render the adjudication of disputes necessarily more equitable than it would have been previously, and we have seen that the restriction of literate skill provided scope for a type of judicial abuse impossible prior to the advent of statutes. Again, memory remained prominent in the legal procedures of the Archaic *poleis*, and those whose memory mattered enjoyed considerable political and judicial power; as far as our evidence informs us, that power belonged to the elites of their respective communities. Their reliance on memory now enjoyed greater influence through their additional ability to read documents, honestly or otherwise, that many others could not.

Our examination also militates against the notion that nonelites in the seventh century believed written law would change the basic nature of justice in their favor: indeed, events after Drakon, to judge from the ancient tradition, might well have persuaded Athenians of the opposite. As for the elites themselves, much of the surviving literary evidence indicates that they were not resistant to written law and in fact played an active part in bringing it about in the cases of Zaleukos, Drakon, and Solon. Consequently, as we shall see in Chapter 6, measures that redress political or judicial complaints of nonelites are absent among the earliest surviving Greek laws, while the majority concern matters that could and did cause dispute and alarm among the great and powerful and the resultant violence that threatened the community as a whole. First, however, we must consider the impact on elites of the socioeconomic and political transformations taking place in early Greece in the late eighth through the seventh centuries.

CHAPTER FIVE

Elites and the World of the Emerging *Polis*

The "canonical" version of Homer's *Odyssey* ends, as we have already discussed at some length,[1] with the rather awkward scene of Athena restraining the members of Odysseus' household and the adherents of the slain suitors from a wholesale slaughter of one another. Divine intervention alone allowed the community to avoid extreme violence, especially among its elites. Among others, Richard Seaford has hypothesized that Homer's lay of the tale is a self-conscious and deliberate attempt to provide the *aristoi* with a mirror in which they might see themselves and their values represented.[2] It is a Homeric device to provide for his audience a salutary moral lesson (as things ought to be) as well as a convenient "happy ending," as the antagonists avert the peril that spoke to the darkest fears of a community's leading lights: devastating reciprocal murder arising from spiraling, violent competition among the elites.

Be that as it may, one still puzzles over Homer's mention of the incident at all: considerable agreement now exists that one version of the *Odyssey* concluded with the reunion of Odysseus and Penelope in their bedchamber.[3] Other ancient witnesses attest to a further variant, wherein Odysseus and his entire household retreat into exile.[4] As we have seen, this last course of action will have conformed more closely to the general expectations regarding homicide elsewhere in the epics, and in the extant version some at Ithaca recognized it as a distinct possibility.[5] The *Odyssey* as we have it allows violence to break out before Athena intercedes, and but for her intervention a bloodbath that annihilated the community would have ensued, a scenario surely not lost on the imaginations of Homer's eighth- and seventh-century listeners.

The multiple endings of the *Odyssey* reflect the changing world of that time, and the horrific implications of the violence that only the dea ex machina can stop speak to the potential dangers the elite faced as a result of that change. The variations are echoes of a series of possible realities created by the upheavals that attended the transition from the Dark Age to the world of the emerging *poleis*. The eighth and early seventh centuries were a period of rapid transformations in the Greek world—demographic, economic, political, and social—altering the lives of Greek communities. All-encompassing and dramatic change did much to confuse the networks of social relationships and the ways in which people communicated about them. As a result, the rule base of many Greek communities in this age of transition would have proved inadequate for addressing new tensions that arose from the realignment of important social and economic relations and incapable in the short term of guiding responses to wholly novel problems created by that realignment. The prevailing legal culture inherited from the world of the epics was no longer sufficient.

These changes, and their impact on the rule base, will have profoundly affected elites of the eighth and early seventh centuries and created new circumstances in which the realities of their competition offered new challenges, with stakes higher than before. Homer, of course, paints a vivid portrait of an aristocratic culture deeply rooted in agonistic impulses, pursuing zero-sum games in their competition for status and demonstration generally of their *aretê*. For many generations, that competition had been, like much else in the Greek world in the Dark Age, largely parochial. Furthermore, important ties of ritual and reciprocal behavior had governed elite agonism and social relationships. Before the *polis*, the elites of small communities circulated wealth in what was principally, if not solely, a gift-exchange economy, where every economic transaction was necessarily a social one as well: Karl Polanyi's embedded economy. Reciprocity and redistribution informed elite relations with the wider community as well.

Significant population growth, beginning at the end of the ninth century, had profound effects on the physical and socioeconomic landscapes of the Greek world. Existing communities grew; new ones appeared. Increases in population coincided with a substantial increase in long-distance trade within the Aegean basin, with other peoples beyond, and with and through the colonies Greeks founded beyond their homeland. Wealth-as-commodity began to displace wealth as a means of formulating and maintaining social relationships; it *disembedded* the economy and further altered older perceptions of the land. Land itself came to be seen as a commodity, something one could acquire, accumulate, and exploit economically, largely independent of the types of social relationships that once informed its use.

As available productive land grew scarcer, elites especially sought to gain as much as they could, both as a symbol in their ongoing competition with one another for status and also as a source of wealth for that contest. The more land one could gain, the more power one might possess, with necessary consequences for failure to do so; this shift in land use and economic patterns not only intensified economic competition among elite households, but also changed the nature of their reciprocal and redistributive relationships with lesser households on whose support they relied.

Demographic expansion also meant increased competition among communities for land and access to resources. War was one response; another was for the growing villages and proto-*poleis* to join together into larger communities. *Synoikismos*, "the bringing together of *oikoi*," was a process that strained rule bases even further. While many of the customs and norms of various Greek villages will have been largely consistent, they will not necessarily have been identical. Differences regarding marriage, inheritance, and funeral customs doubtless existed, and while these differences could have been minor, they still would require some sort of reconciliation. Additionally, the prominent household or households of an absorbed community found themselves no longer in competition only with one another, but also with the elites of other constituent villages that had participated in a *synoikismos*.

How to share power and prestige, while still competing earnestly for it, indeed proved one of the great challenges for the elite as the protostates of Greece matured into Archaic *poleis*. Questions of definition were important: who qualified as an *aristos* was a concern for the elites of the early *polis*. Competition and conflict continued to characterize relationships among the elite, and for all that the early *polis* may have been an aristocratic state, we can no more speak of class solidarity among them than we can identify a class-motivated demand for written law. Indeed, of prime concern to elites was the problem of someone, either from the *aristoi* or forced to the margins of elite culture, achieving a position of political superiority over his social peers: the tyrant. Such an individual effectively "won" what was supposed to be an ongoing competition for status and power, ending that competition and putting himself in a position to disgrace, exile, or even eliminate his former rivals. Meeting these new challenges would require new rules, and those rules would take the shape of written law.

1—Legal Cultures and Social Change:
The Geometric Household and Homeric Reciprocity

As we have already seen, Greeks in the worlds of Homer and Hesiod possessed a coherent and effective legal culture through which they addressed disputes, or potential disputes, usually avoiding personal physical violence or other serious disruption to the life of the community. The ability of the small-scale communities of Geometric Greece to handle conflict—often without resort to formal means of dispute settlement—combined with the substantial role played by public opinion in defusing, regulating, and policing the scope of disputes to maintain equilibrium in a society given to contentiousness. Overall, these elements obviated the need for Greeks to change their juridical practices in any meaningfully self-conscious way for a long time. Understanding of the rules, and the rules for breaking the rules, allowed members of late Geometric communities to protect the general peace and stability of the pre-*polis* community without having to employ written law for at least a century after their acquisition of writing. Through the eighth century, the strategies we discerned in Homer's and Hesiod's poetry must have proved more or less adequate for governing the conduct of disputes generally and for dealing more especially with tensions arising from certain categories of behavior. By the middle of the seventh century, however, some Greek communities began to commit rules to writing. I have argued that popular literacy and popular demands for written law cannot explain this phenomenon. Rather, the specific challenges and strains that the elites of the eighth and seventh century faced as a result of the development of the *polis* seems the more likely impetus behind this significant change in the legal and juridical practices of the Greeks.

Anthropologists have recognized for at least two generations the relationship between technological and moral changes in a society and the resultant alterations in its rule base and the adjudication of the same. In most modern societies, there exist organs for the express purpose of framing new, legally enforceable rules as needs arise, a "municipal" system of law. Communities without recognized or formal legislative organs tend to experience changes in the law more slowly than changes in the behaviors it might govern.[6] As a result, serious discrepancies can and do occur between problems arising on an increasingly frequent basis within the community and the existing mechanisms for handling such problems.[7]

This divide between behavior practiced and behavior governed allows for several consequences. First, disagreements may result from incidents against which there was no existing particular stigma but which have become offensive to certain members of the community. Second, and following from the first, the scope increases for disputes to arise and subsequently remain unresolved, as confusion over what might or might not constitute approved behavior encourages further misunderstandings and places disputants outside of traditional sanctions and procedures for resolution. Third, in a society reciprocal by nature, as Greece was in the late Geometric and early Archaic

Ages,[8] the potential for tit-for-tat bickering and retaliation may further aggravate any dispute that continues unresolved or unregulated: indeed, this is precisely what we found in the Homeric and Hesiodic literature when initial steps at resolution failed. Fourth, precisely because there is no central, recognized authority or institution that may formally and self-consciously attempt to alter the rule base to accommodate new categories or sources of dispute, the potential for broader, more troublesome, and persistent conflict increases.

As we have seen, the Greeks during the ages of Homer and Hesiod overcame these problems to a great extent through the attendant pressure of public opinion, itself formed by a knowledge of—and ability to abide by—certain commonly held notions of what was acceptable and what was not. But in a society experiencing rapid social, economic, and political changes, what then of the ability of public opinion to crystallize around approbation or opprobrium for certain actions? If the problems afflicting a society grow out of the challenges of confronting a new set of realities, ones for which traditional values hold few ready answers, the wider community will be just as confused about what is appropriate as were the individuals whose behaviors led to dispute in the first place. The interface between the community and its laws is a thoroughgoing one, involving a wide cross section of its members.[9]

Such interdependence between public knowledge of the rule base of a society and the outcome of dispute is quite common in societies that have what Rouland has characterized as a communal system of law.[10] In such a system, the individual community tends to be characterized by bicentric or polyarchic political authority, and reciprocal rights and obligations define most, if not all, of the community's social, economic, and political commerce. In effect, the diffusion of political and judicial authority renders all disputes—between individuals belonging to the same community but to different domestic units—power struggles between more or less equally matched, autonomous juridical units.[11] Arrangements like this are typical of stateless societies or societies where something like the state is just beginning to emerge.[12] And, however sophisticated the internal organization of any Greek hero's household in the *Iliad* or the *Odyssey*, the world portrayed in those poems, and the nature of the disputes found there, point to a pronounced lack of real state organization.[13] To the degree that centralized institutions appear in the poems, only the merest beginnings of them are discernible,[14] and the power of the Homeric *basileis* was entirely personal and charismatic, resting not on any institutional bases but on their ability to persuade and cajole.[15] Only one clear example of public finance appears in the epics,[16] and there is no palpable sense of magistracies or of the rights or duties of a community member as such;[17] of all the various societies depicted in the epics, only the fantastic land of Scherie has something of an urban hub and a more defined state organization.[18] This is not to say that there are no *poleis* in the world of the epics: on the contrary, as a number of commentators have noted, the conception of the *polis* as a communal space undermines Finley's claim that "neither poem has any trace of a *polis* in its political sense."[19] Kurt Raaflaub is surely correct to emphasize that Homer's use of *demos* is consistent, that assemblies are not without influence and power, and that there is a recognizable public sphere.[20] However, none of that necessarily makes the communities Homer describes states, and indeed, many of the "ideas intrinsic to *polis* formation"—the rotation of executive power, the idea of conformity of that power to law, and so on[21]—remain absent entirely from the epics.

Though the primitivist-modernist debate in the study of early Greece has doubtless been overdrawn, members of powerful households acting to some degree in accord with wider public sentiment while pursuing their competitive rivalries does not constitute a state. As they appear in the epics, leading *oikoi*, the relations among them, and the interactions among these relationships and the public sphere, seem to amount to what the legal anthropologist S. Falk Moore has described as "semi-autonomous social fields."[22] In a less complex society with more bicentric or polyarchic arrangements of political authority, the autonomy of the separate social fields will be greater than it is in modern societies or legal systems; nevertheless, these distinct social fields are still subject to certain external influences. Disputes between such semiautonomous fields, in the Homeric context, had to be resolved by some form of compromise if they were not to lead to outright violence: there was no central legal and political authority capable of enforcing a unilateral resolution. Adjudicators, whether more formally constituted judges or knowers (such as on the Shield of Achilles or Agamemnon) or spontaneous go-betweens (as when Alkinoös intercedes in the quarrel between Odysseus and Euryalos),[23] make suggestions for compromise, but ultimately it is up to the actors of the separate juridical units to accept these and to comply with their terms. In Homeric and Hesiodic Greece, public pressure was often the external constraint that encouraged parties toward a resolution and its observance. Even the most powerful of individuals, such as Agamemnon or even Zeus, could not defuse judicially oriented tension by fiat.[24]

Legal cultures that rely on processes so "informal" to the perspective of the citizen of a modern state may appear to produce few solutions or binding decisions at all. Indeed, for much of the twentieth century, legal scholars and anthropologists often regarded other systems as broken if they allowed for conflict and dispute to the same degree as Homeric society.[25] The very presence of dispute indicates something pathologically wrong with a culture, as if the law were not doing what it is supposed to do. Such a view, even were it accurate, ignores that the rule base, much less formal law, will always be to some degree out of phase with the daily existence of its members and the problems that might arise from it. Once established, a norm/rule—whether the gnomic utterance of a poet or a law enshrined in stone—will immediately begin its slide toward obsolescence, for no society is completely static. In a slowly changing culture, the severity of this lack of phase will typically be less; in a rapidly changing culture, more. The challenge for any community's legal culture or system in defining and maintaining its rule base is not whether there is conflict at all but whether the mechanisms for managing conflict increasingly fail, leading to serious social and political disruption and threatening the society as a whole. It is then that new solutions may be required to handle new problems and the lack of phase.

Indeed, legal change often arises from "social indignation or social catastrophe,"[26] and there can be little doubt that the various changes taking place in Greece ca. 725 to 600 produced plenty of both. The remainder of this chapter addresses those changes that transformed the Greek world during this period and how the reorganization of so many facets of Greek life impacted especially those individuals who enjoyed positions of leadership and privilege, the elite.

THE HOMERIC EPICS DESCRIBE RICHLY the values, actions, and assumptions of the most economically and socially powerful members of Greek communities in the final generation or two of the Geometric period. Though it is unclear when exactly they began to think of themselves as an aristocracy or elite, we may think of them as such for the sake of descriptive convenience.[27] As mentioned at the outset of the present study, I follow Forsdyke in conceiving of this elite as those individuals whose political privilege was grounded in the claim to a combination of wealth, birth, divine favor, and virtue[28] and whose same privilege in turn allowed them to monopolize the levers of magisterial authority and dominate the economic production of the early *poleis* to the benefit of their *oikoi* and those of their sociopolitical allies. In the premonetary, largely stateless world of the epics, the individual household (*oikos*) was the basis of political and economic activity and served as the foundation of whatever wider networks of cooperation may have existed.[29] The means by which the various important households maintained their strength and position depended almost entirely upon reciprocal relations (amicable or hostile): through these, households obtained everything from intangibles such as political support to essentials such as weapons or luxury goods.[30] The employment of various items in reciprocal relations, in the Homeric instance, exhibits the properties of gift exchange rather than commodity exchange,[31] not at all unusual for a society where power is polyarchic and based on a basic kinship unit such as the household. The members of an important household used such gift exchange and other reciprocal obligations to establish relationships with members otherwise entirely outside the ties of their own community (in the form of guest-friendship or marriage), with the members of other semiautonomous households of roughly the same standing within the same community (possibly through marriage and in associated two-way exchanges of goods, or even with regard to the demands of vendetta), and with individuals within the community whose households could offer the powerful *oikos* primarily loyalty in return, thus making of them followers.[32]

Ties formed outside the community altogether or with other powerful households typically took the form of some sort of guest-friendship (*xeniê*) or through the exchange of gifts (*hedna*) associated with marriage. The former was by definition a relationship between households of different communities and was heritable from one generation to the next. Mechanically, guest-friendship operated along the following lines, as is well known: at some point, participant A offered some kindness to participant B while the latter sojourned in A's community. Most often, the cornerstone of A's generosity would have been hospitality, including lodging for B, perhaps B's companions, and meals for him (them) besides. Upon B's departure, A cemented the *xeniê* with gifts, or *xeineia*. This act of generosity would then create an obligation on B's part to offer similar hospitality should A ever visit him or his land, and so on in a continuing cycle of reciprocity. This exchange, of course, did not close the relationship: B would strive to demonstrate greater generosity, thus obligating A for the future. As Tandy puts it, "A balance is never reached whereby no further obligations exist. Something is always owed, in one or another direction."[33] A and B were now *xeinoi*. Homer presents numerous examples of such exchanges and the attendant obligations. Though the epics tend to stress the foreign connections thus established, we can surmise the establishment as well of such reciprocal obligations among households within the same community, broadly conceived. In the *Odyssey*, Penelope scolds Antinoös for not properly observing the obligations owed by his family to the house of Odysseus,[34] and Hesiod underscores the absolute necessity of honoring one's own reciprocal obligations with other members of the community and of choosing carefully those with whom to enter such relationships.[35]

Though Homer and Hesiod do not distinguish terminologically such intracommunal ties, their presence is unmistakable, and technicalities governing them do not appear fundamentally different from those governing *xeniê*. The lack of semantic separation in Homer may in part result from powerful households interacting with one another in more or less the same fashion, whether they belong to the same or different communities. Homeric society's lack of a true state and the semiautonomy of *oikoi* perhaps rendered geographical proximity a minor factor in the means of establishment of reciprocal relations between prominent households.

Marriage constituted another primary way of creating and maintaining ties between households, particularly those possessed of greater wealth and significance. The evidence for endogamy among poorer households is difficult, though the practice seems to have become common by the later Archaic age. On the other hand, the prevalence of—and status accorded to—the exogamous marriage in the Homeric epic suggests a marker by which elites defined themselves even in the Geometric period. To marry outside the family was to advertise the possession of wealth that might be detached from the household without undermining its status or prestige. Homer called the wealth exchanged in the form of wedding gifts *hedna*, and they could travel in either direction in a marriage, though always involving only the immediate families of the bride and groom.[36] Though many of the marriages Homer describes occur between elite households of separate communities—a situation not unfamiliar from the sixth and early fifth centuries[37]—there is no particular reason to believe similar arrangements did not exist between the semiautonomous households of a single community. Precisely because the most attractive son-in-law was the hero from abroad,[38] we might infer that such unions were not altogether common or readily available. The marriages between great families of two different communities were noteworthy—both to Homer and the sources that record them from later periods—due to their relative rarity. Of course, one did not have to resort to foreign marriages to demonstrate the wealth and standing of the *oikos* through exogamy.

The attraction, however, of a foreign marriage was surely two-fold. First, as scholars have noted, the obligations and ties created by gifts of *hedna* were not substantially different from those created by *xeineia*.[39] Thus, the in-laws could expect the same quality of aid in battle from their new kin as a guest-friend might provide. Naturally, this aspect of the relationship would have been present in marriage ties between households of the same community as well. What differentiated the foreign marriage was perhaps the second reason for its attraction, namely that a household could execute it without creating intracommunal ties that might later prove troublesome. Further, it did not involve a transfer of wealth in the form of *hedna* to a household of the same community, thereby potentially strengthening it at the expense of one's own *oikos*. In contracting a foreign marriage, one might avoid the embarrassing consequences of one's kin by marriage falling into hostile reciprocity with another household of the same community, with which a feud might not be desirable.

Exchanges of gifts in Homeric Greece, whether associated with bonds of guest-friendship or marriage, were the primary means of binding wealthy and powerful households in peaceful relations and bonds of mutual obligation. Of course, relations among such households were by no means always placid. The competitive ethos was already alive and well by the time our version of Homer had developed, and the ability of the individual *oikos* to compete effectively in reciprocal displays of generosity and in acts of hostility will have depended greatly on what Walter Donlan has called "established social position."[40] Defining the established social position of any particular individual defeats all attempts at precision, because preeminence or dominance depended on "a complex of inheritance, remote divine sanction, age, personal wealth, and numbers of followers."[41] While members of the group may recognize in certain others excellence at a given skill (Achilles for his martial prowess, Nestor for his wise counsel, and so forth), there is no hierarchy as would be typical of a ranked society, and all those with established social position are roughly equals. The leadership positions of Agamemnon among the Achaeans or Hector among the Trojans (or, for that matter, Zeus among the gods) did not guarantee the obedience of their respective followers. Maintaining a position of leadership in a society more egalitarian than ranked was a constant process of negotiating one's established social position among a group of men and their households who might lay claim to it.[42]

A preeminent man who possessed such established social position headed an *oikos* that typically comprised the following: himself, a wife and children, including adult sons and their wives, and, in the cases of particularly strong households and with the proper inducements, adult daughters and their husbands. In addition, the wealthy *oikos* would possess some unfree persons as a household staff, but their loyalty could prove dubious[43] (as was clearly the case in the house of Odysseus and presumably so in the instance of Agamemnon's murder). Occasionally, we encounter the *therapôn*, a free, nonkin individual whom the *oikos* has received more or less as one of its own (as Peleus received Phoenix and Patroklos, exiled from their own lands). Most critical, however, was the ability to attract followers (usually *hetairoi* or *philoi*), especially for *oikoi* with few sons. Followers allowed the ambitious man to augment his manpower from among the *laoi* or *demos* and at the same time to keep his rivals from doing the same.[44] In a society of such powerful, semiautonomous households whose connections reached throughout the community, and where paramountcy was an achieved status based on a complex of qualities that all rivals for it possessed in some measure, it was potentially always open season in the competition for chief authority. Homer offers many examples of the tenuousness of the head man's position, and it is clear that Homer and Hesiod both easily imagined communities where it was altogether more accurate to conceive of *basileis* in the plural rather than the singular, none institutionally more powerful than the others.

We may discern the most important elements of one's established social position. Though age might be stressed for certain courses of action in particular circumstances, such as Nestor and Phoenix employing their experience when counseling reconciliation, or Antilokhos deferring to Menelaos' seniority, it was not a prerequisite for standing: Achilles and Hector are both young men in comparison to many of the warriors at Troy, and the suitors at Ithaca are portrayed as relatively young. In none of these cases does their relative youth prevent these men from assuming positions of importance. The glory of one's ancestors and the perceived favor of the gods are nearly invariably attached to men who also possess wealth and power, who are already *basileis*: "position exists on an almost totally undifferentiated continuum, in that all who hold position are *basileis* and share more or less equally, the descriptive nomenclature of position."[45] The qualities of such men become essentially circular justifications for their wealth and power: X has standing because the gods favor him and he is of good parentage, and because he has divine favor and good parentage, X should have standing. However, the variables that may fluctuate among men of roughly equal position are those that differing levels of wealth will affect directly, namely, the ability to give well and create obligations, the ability to marry well and attract followers through these mechanisms, and, finally, the ability to distribute wealth without expectation of material return but rather in exchange for loyalty and military service from the recipients of that wealth. It is this wealth, as it moves through a series of reciprocal obligations, that will determine the individual, semiautonomous household's exercise of wider social and political authority.

Alternatively, one might argue that it was the Homeric *basileus*' ability that guaranteed him the attraction of followers, since it was through his charisma and skill as a raider (and possibly trader, as circumstances might warrant) that the important individual maintained a following. Indeed, Tandy has concluded that in the world of the epics, wealth followed status, an important distinction since he argues that one of the principal changes of the eighth century is that status began to follow wealth.[46] Though it appears that the means by which leading Greeks obtained wealth changed significantly in the eighth century (see the subsequent section)—and therefore led to significant changes in the definition and acquisition of elite status—I doubt the relationship he posits between wealth and status in Homeric society. The passages Tandy cites to support his argument that wealth followed status,[47] I would argue, read much like the other types of justification for one's privileged social and economic standing within Donlan's criteria for established social position. Status and wealth appear to be two sides of the same coin for the prominent Homeric man: each is a sine qua non for the other. *Aretê* manifests itself in someone precisely because he has wealth and power, the same sort of circular support for vaunted position in a mainly egalitarian society as provided by claims of divine favor and good parentage. The root issue, the common denominator, remains the acquisition of material goods with which to reward followers as well as undertake other acts of generosity and display that allow the man of standing to maintain his position. In other words, his ability to acquire further wealth helps the important individual support a following of men who have only their services to offer in return and thereby exalt his own position of authority.

Wealth remains the primary ingredient: the ways in which powerful households established relationships with one another, as well as maintained their own competitive viability, depended mostly on the redistribution and recirculation of wealth in a primarily gift-exchange economy, itself embedded in a protostate, polyarchic community.[48] That community, most typically, comprised a settlement of a variable number of economically self-sustaining, politically and juridically semiautonomous units, each consisting of the family, its attendants, and such followers as it could attract. Such communities, however, arguably developed in a relatively thinly settled landscape with low rates of population growth and limited contact with the world beyond the Aegean, at least when compared to the Mycenaean era that preceded this period and the Archaic age that followed. The world described in the Homeric epics stands at the threshold of a series of profound demographic and economic changes that would render unstable, at least in their current form, the polyarchic power arrangements and reciprocal relations that prevailed in Homeric society. In short, the socioeconomic system of the Homeric epics was becoming unembedded,[49] and the means for establishing and maintaining social and political equilibrium would necessarily be affected. Furthermore, these developments allowed for the crystallization of a different type of political organization, in which elites had to redefine their relationships with the wider community and with one another.

2—Demographics, *Oikoi*, and the Disembedded Economy

For decades, scholars interpreted the available archaeological evidence for post-Mycenaean Greece as indicative of dramatic depopulation between 1200 and 1125, followed by a prolonged period of depressed population and ending only with a substantial *increase* in population beginning near the end of the ninth century.[50] During the past twenty years or so, some students of the Dark Age have mounted a determined challenge against this picture, arguing that numbers of settlements and burial practices may distort the situation on the ground. For example, Nicholas Purcell has noted that the apparent paucity of Dark Age settlements is possibly an illusion, owing to the fact that many sites from this period may yet remain undiscovered.[51] Ian Morris has also argued against the severity of depopulation that A.M. Snodgrass posited (in the range of 80 to 90%) and has therefore also cautioned against seeing a massive increase during the later phases of the Geometric period (while still admitting some expansion).[52] Robin Osborne has likewise expressed doubts over interpreting the concentrations of burials or settlement sites to support dramatic increases in population in the ninth and eighth centuries, preferring to see steady population growth dating well back into the tenth century and thus negating the need for positing a population explosion in the eighth.[53]

Unquestionably, relying on settlement density and numbers of graves per generation has its dangers, and we will never attain certainty regarding population figures for the Greek world from the Mycenaean collapse to the end of the Geometric. However, one might answer Purcell's observation by noting that we have likely not discovered all Bronze Age sites, either. While I am sympathetic in some respects to Osborne's argument, it is also the case that a small population, increasing at a relatively steady rate of growth from one generation to the next, will nevertheless reach a point where that iterated increase will result in substantial increases in the overall numbers. The dramatic burial evidence for growth in places such as Attica (perhaps as high as 4.4% per annum) and the Argolid (with similar increases) for the century from 825 to 725, even if somewhat distorted by changes in burial practice, seem difficult to explain on that basis alone. It is surely correct that these figures are too high, but even cautious estimates point to accelerating demographic expansion in the eighth century. Furthermore, the grave evidence does not exist in isolation: changes in diet, the digging of new wells, dispersal and new community foundations within Greece, and the colonial movement out of it, all point to significant increases in the Greek population during that period.[54]

One might further explain the sustainability of dramatic growth, once it had begun, through social factors as well. Those households that could produce (and provide for) more children would have an advantageous position compared to others, vis-à-vis manpower. Not only did adult sons strengthen an *oikos*, but the wealthier and numerically stronger household might also be able to attract additional male resources in the form of potential sons-in-law looking to enhance their fortune. A small number of sons was clearly a cause for regret and anxiety in Homer. Once certain households could produce a surfeit of manpower, there would have been attendant pressure on rival *oikoi* to keep pace. In addition, the evidence for internal colonization in Attica, Boeotia, and the Argolid intimates that there was plenty of land available, so long as one had the hands available to claim it and work it.[55] In other words, the pressures of sociopolitical and socioeconomic competition doubtless combined with nutritional factors to drive population growth once it had begun.

Demographic changes on this scale could not help but profoundly affect the economy and politics of the protostate, small-scale, polyarchic communities described above. An examination of the political developments will await the next section of this chapter. As for alterations to the socioeconomic landscape, the increase in population had wide-ranging consequences, including an increase in long-distance trade, the emergence of greater economic specialization within and between communities, and greater accumulation of wealth. Last but not least, alongside the gift-exchange economy that had characterized much of the Dark Age, commodity exchange (or, if one prefers, market exchange) appeared and then waxed as an important means of moving and acquiring wealth.

Tandy has recently argued that "the driving force in the transformation that shook the Aegean [in the eighth century] was the introduction of markets into the economic realities of Greek communities."[56] The reasons for this are manifold but the two most important were the rapid development of overseas trading networks (including colonies as centers of production and exchange) that served Greek economic interests and the development of specialization of production (and the concomitant rise in the availability of exchangeable goods), which increased population densities supported.[57] Together, these factors, along with the goods created for and the wealth created through trade, helped make commodity exchange an important component of the economies of Greek communities in the opening decades of the Archaic age. The increase in wealth and its changing nature marked a shift away from an embedded economy, based on networks of reciprocity and redistribution, toward a disembedded one, increasingly rooted in commodity or market exchange.[58]

As households could now accumulate wealth outside the nexus of social *and* economic relationships that typified the Homeric world, a number of disruptive trends emerged. Wealth passed from potential communal enjoyment and became unobligated with respect to the community at large: instead of circulating by way of gift exchange or redistribution, among either *oikoi* of roughly equal standing or the various lesser households attached or allied to a particular *oikos*, such dissemination and re-collection no longer needed to take place for the prominent *oikos* to acquire wealth and status, and thus power, within the community. In this sense, wealth could and did become a private commodity, and its transfer and any relationships established (or, if the transactors chose, *not* established) by its movement could be negotiated.[59] Because wealth was disembedded, the norms that governed its movement no longer necessarily depended on older networks of communication or symbols,[60] or, by extension, traditional checks of communal opinion. The rule base did not, and could not, have immediate or obvious answers for difficulties created by this type of wealth.[61]

A dramatic transformation of the ties between the powerful *oikos* and its followers attended this shift in the nature of wealth upon which standing and influence had been established and maintained. Tandy has described lucidly the resulting trauma:

> Previously, smaller households could depend upon the "spokes"[62] of the redistributive system to provide help in hard times; now the smaller households are forced to use the "spokes" to acquire all nonsubsistence and some subsistence goods. Since the center is able to control the negotiations, the peripheral person or household becomes indebted. In a redistributive system, thanks to the social "safety net," a person owes only so much as he has or can give; after the introduction of private ownership, in this system of limited markets, as in *any* disembedded system, a person can owe *more* than he has or can give.[63]

In addition, sources of wealth once not thought of as commodities increasingly were conceived as such. For example, land became an alienable source of wealth and thus transferable and capable of acquisition at the expense of someone else. Once Greeks began to view land as an acquirable commodity, certain of them treated it as an object of elite competition, a valuable wealth resource. As land grew scarcer due to population increase, competition only heightened conflicts over land use, as the elites used "rich bottomland for grazing their herds, which served mostly a display function, at a time when the population had increased sufficiently to force people to seek out more land for growing grains."[64]

There is one further ramification of this development that Tandy does not notice: the powerful *oikos* at the center of a reciprocal/redistributive system of wealth had become disembedded from traditional networks of social obligations but so too had the households upon whose loyalty the *oikos* at the center had depended. The prominent household found its following among the general populace of the community, exchanging socially and economically obligated wealth in return for loyalty. With the economic transformation of the eighth and early seventh centuries, however, the allegiance that lesser households might exchange also became increasingly unobligated. The heads of such households, detached now from the complex of reciprocal relationships and attendant norms and practices, could now negotiate the best terms for their support. Any negotiable relationship is, of course, renegotiable: as the constraints on such renegotiations weakened, the relative standing of powerful *oikoi* with respect to manpower will have become increasingly fluid and unstable. The fact of augmented competition for supporters itself stood to some degree outside the capacity of the rule base to regulate it: social disruption and rapid innovation renders older norms obsolete at an alarming rate but often not before new ones develop that have gained wide enough acceptance to replace them.

3—PUTTING TOGETHER THE *POLIS*: *SYNOIKISMOS* AND THE ELITE

The demographic and economic pressures described above led to the territorial expansion of many communities[65] as growing populations required more land for their sustenance and elites sought to acquire more land as a means of producing wealth and engaging in competitive display; additionally, new foundations appeared as a result of the internal colonization of open territory. A countryside once characterized by intermittent contact at most among small hamlets isolated by distance, was transformed in the course of a century.[66] Now, Greek communities grew closer together and competed for the same resources, particularly in relatively fertile regions such as Attica, Boeotia, the Argolid, and the southern Peloponnesus. The members of these burgeoning settlements could not avoid cooperating or, failing that, going to war.

The Greeks themselves believed that the first interstate wars occurred roughly in the heart of the century of great transformation, some time around 725. According to tradition, conflict erupted between Corinth and Megara,[67] followed shortly thereafter by the so-called war of the Lelantine Plain on the island of Euboea, pitting Khalkis against Eretria.[68] Archaeology provides some corroboration for the latter, though the sequence of events is beyond the proof or disproof of the data. The Corinthians, Megarians, and Euboeans were among the most active Greeks in establishing trade routes and colonies in the eighth century,[69] both Euboea and the Corinthiad experienced growth similar to that described above, and the two regions possessed less arable land than places such as Attica and Laconia. It is surely no accident that the communities of these regions suffered early the pressures created by the transformations of the age and fell into conflict over resources.

Alongside warfare and the seizure of contested resources by main force was the trend toward *synoikismos*, the integration of smaller, previously autonomous settlements—whatever their internal composition in terms of population, distribution of wealth, prosperity, and so forth—into the beginnings of a single *polis*. The coalescence was typically slow and even haphazard, and *synoikismos* was probably usually more of a process than an event. Though the literary tradition of the Greeks recalled *synoikismos* as a usually peaceful phenomenon, obviously the process was not necessarily mutually exclusive with armed conflict. Four examples of *synoikismos* traditions illustrate its dynamics and foreshadow the attendant problems in governing the resultant community, those of Athens, Argos, Sparta, and Corinth.

The Athenian *synoikismos* is the best described in the literary sources, although this is to some degree its own difficulty.[70] The recorded tradition is almost entirely legendary and centers on the heroic figure of Theseus, into whom the Athenians consolidated the credit for many of their past achievements, real or imagined.[71] Though the details of the literary descriptions will always prove nettlesome, the Athenians believed their *polis* had once consisted of independent communities scattered across Attica, and archaeological evidence and later literary tradition support such a development.[72] During the process of *synoikismos* of the plain, local leading families of previously autonomous settlements managed, ultimately, to develop and establish the organs and institutions of the early Athenian *polis*.[73] Thus, what had once been parochial elites in the Athenian plain slowly transformed themselves into a regional aristocracy that dominated the political life of Athens into the sixth century but whose internal tensions were manifesting themselves in violence by the last third of the seventh.[74]

At Argos, we have little in the way of literary sources to understand the process of *polis* consolidation, but the archaeological record there is instructive. Argos was the only town in the Argolid to develop into a true *polis*,[75] and the *synoikismos* of its immediate environs may have begun as early as 900 and proceeded over the next several generations.[76] While residents progressively abandoned the surrounding settlements at this time in preference for the Argive acropolis, the Larisa, the lands associated with them remained important to at least some of the elites, as they continued to bury their dead there in rich graves,[77] analogous to a similar trend in Attica.[78] Following the initial *synoikismos* that produced the *asty* at Argos itself, further consolidation of the Argive plain took place beginning in the eighth century. Older towns that shared cultural affinities with the Argives, such as Tiryns, Mycenae, and Lerna, were incorporated to varying degrees under the political suzerainty of Argos, with religious observance playing an important, but not necessarily principal, role. The construction of the massive Argive Heraion, built five miles from the center of Argos, had a distinct political purpose as well.[79] An extraurban temple, it sat among the towns inhabited more or less continuously since Mycenaean times, three miles from Mycenae and six from Tiryns. The choice of location was significant, as well, since there is no evidence for long-standing religious activity at the site. Taken together with roads and bridges that date to the eighth century, there was an obvious concerted effort to tighten the political and economic organization of the Argolid around the Heraion. François De Polignac, who stresses the religious origins of the *polis*, likewise acknowledges that the temple was an expression of Argive sovereignty, namely that it was highly visible from virtually every approach to the plain and could be seen easily from Mycenae and Tiryns.[80] As Hera was a goddess primarily associated in the region with Argos, the political implications of the temple commanding the entire plain are clear.

Settlements that appeared in the Argolid during the eighth century were the result of the increasing population and prosperity of Argos[81] and would have necessarily fallen under its domination. Villages whose cultural or religious traditions made assimilation difficult or impossible for their inhabitants became an object of hostility, and we know of one case, Asine, where the Argives chose destruction over incorporation.[82] In general, though, the continuation of rich burials and other observances largely associated with elites, such as hero cult, at the secondary towns of the Argive *polis* suggests that local aristocrats with local interests were incorporated into the leadership structure rather than having been displaced.

Sparta presents a more difficult picture. The problems of reconstructing early Spartan history are notorious, complicated by the fact that the vast majority of our information comes from external observers and by the fact that the Spartans *themselves* constantly reinvented their past to claim its continuity with the circumstances of the present.[83] The surviving tradition does, however, preserve some familiar elements. Though it would be fruitless to try to pinpoint the origins of certain Spartan institutions based on the literary tradition alone, certain peculiarities in the archaeological record and in later Spartan government perhaps betray a *synoikismos* that stopped somewhere short of the completeness of those at Athens and Argos.[84] Classical writers were aware that distinct villages actually comprised Sparta in their own day,[85] and a Hellenistic wall enclosed four of these: Pitana, Mesoa, Limnai, and Kynosoura.[86] The first two may have formed an early part of the *synoikismos*, while the latter two may have joined in the process more or less simultaneously; the final synthesis came some time afterward.[87]

Exceptionally in the Greek world, the Spartans retained kingship and were unique in their establishment of a dual monarchy along parallel hereditary lines, the Agid and Eurypontid. The former had its royal cemetery on the acropolis near Pitana, while the latter buried their dead in the eastern portion of the *polis*, near Limnai and Kynosoura.[88] When the two pairs of villages underwent *synoikismos*, it would seem they struck a compromise to retain the "kings" of each as part of the leadership structure. Furthermore, the Gerousia council absorbed the kings as ex officio members, probably at an early date.[89] Aside from their responsibilities of war leadership, the official privileges and functions of Spartan kings did not differ significantly from other members of the Gerousia,[90] and Finley believed that the Spartan kingship had no Homeric roots at all but was, rather, a product of developments in the Archaic period.[91] In other words, the executive authority of the state resided in the hands of what was originally an aristocratic council, and the inclusion of multiple elites may reflect an attempt to incorporate the leading families of the four villages.[92]

One other peculiar feature of Spartan government merits notice here as it may further illuminate the concern of integrating of local authority and power into a collective, aristocratic arrangement. The ephors of Sparta numbered five, one for each of the constituent villages of the *polis* after the incorporation of Amyklai in the middle of the eighth century. Scholars have suggested that this is no coincidence and that the ephors originated as representatives of the local interests of the five *obai*.[93] Their function as overseers of the Great Rhetra and their ability to discipline kings (but not members of the Gerousia) may have served as an early safeguard of elite control against the potential centralization of power in the hands of one man and his *oikos* once the *synoikismos* had begun. If so, we have another governmental institution of the early *polis* reflective of the challenges of establishing political equilibrium and cooperation.

Finally, at Corinth, the circumstances of *polis* development are exceptionally unclear and scholars have divided over the question of whether a *synoikismos* ever took place and, if so, at what time.[94] The possibility of tension between aristocrats at the center and periphery is suggested by seventh-century events, as we will see in the next section, and such friction may represent an echo of the incorporation of several local elites into a single political entity. Greek sources also express confusion regarding the origins of Corinth's political organization, based on eight tribes and districts. One source posits that the replacement of the three traditional Dorian tribes was the work of an early Corinthian king and the putative author of its *synoikismos*, one Aletes.[95] Aletes and his achievements may be as historical as Theseus; one tradition at least remembered a Corinthian *synoikismos* and political reorganization at the end of the Dark Age. Another late and scarcely more reliable source refers to eight tribes established possibly after the fall of the Kypselid tyranny, a terminus post quem of ca. 580.[96] The passage is difficult, to be sure,[97] and the language admits of interpretations that would place the institution of the eight tribes anywhere from the eighth to the fourth century.[98] We need not resolve the question of an exact date but rather note the confusion it created even in antiquity. The reorganization of Corinth had apparently been a process of trial and error and was so obscure that even the ancients were reluctant to hazard many guesses about it. By the end of the eighth century, however, one segment of the Corinthian aristocracy had secured domination over the *polis*' institutions and established itself as a narrow ruling clique at the expense of other members of the elite.[99]

In sum, the precise details of *synoikismoi* at the birth of the *poleis* will, in all likelihood, forever remain beyond our comprehension, but what the scattered literary clues and the results of archaeological investigation indicate is a phenomenon wherein local elites confronted the difficulty of integrating their communities and maintaining their own prominence and competitive standing within a larger and expanding polity. While a given *synoikismos* most readily took place among communities with more or less common cultural traditions, the distinct towns and villages that joined together varied in their observance of certain ritual practices and norms that governed them, especially at a time when major social and economic changes were afoot and traditional relationships were breaking down; marriage, to take just one custom, was already undergoing significant changes,[100] and intermarriage was of course just one important component of elite power relations.

How were the influential men of these new polities to wield the power of its emerging institutions, and how would they compete for it? Who qualified to compete, and what would their responsibilities be, to other elites and the rest of the community? The answers to these questions would not be automatic: many of these problems were new, and beyond the capacities of an increasingly static epic tradition to keep pace or the traditional rule base to provide guidance. Furthermore, in this potentially volatile environment of political, economic, and social change, the specter of internal political violence haunted the early *polis*. Failure to address effectively these issues had consequences that were already becoming clear before the earliest attempts at written law, among them, the possibility that a head of one household might attain a position of unsurpassed political supremacy, establishing himself as a tyrant.

4—Cohesion or Conflict? Exclusion, Inclusion, and Tyranny

The Homeric aristocrat, as we have seen, did not require much definition: a man was good because he had *aretê*, and because a man had *aretê* he was good. With some notable exceptions that prove the rule,[101] the archaeological record of the Dark Age betrays significant but by no means huge gulfs in wealth between the leading members and the rest of the community. Only with the century of rapid transformation that we have been describing do we begin to detect a series of behaviors indicating a conscious sense of elite status, activities that sought to affirm social and economic position. Among these pursuits were the great and relatively luxurious feasts held by and for the wealthy,[102] the increased burial of expensive and important objects with certain deceased individuals,[103] the construction of monumental temples that may have served (among other purposes) as focal points for elite competition in both construction and in display through dedications,[104] and the rapid spread of hero cults and hero worship, often associated with certain families or individual *oikoi*.[105] David Tandy, among others, has deemed the Homeric epics the deliberate and self-conscious attempt by elites to define identity and the meaning of *aretê* necessary for status as an *aristos* or *kalokagathos*, though in my view incorrectly.[106] The archaeological evidence, as well as literary testimony, suggests that elite competition intensified and demanded ever greater resources—politically and economically—if one were to maintain one's standing and the right to continue to compete for prestige and power.

Manifestations of a conscious separation from the rest of the community have frequently been taken to represent the emergence of an elite possessed of class solidarity strong enough to encourage corporate political and social action. Together, strategies of display constitute "tools of exclusion,"[107] designed to advertise superiority for those who had the resources and status to participate and to shut out those who did not. There is a clear obverse, however: strategies of exclusion are at the same time capable of defining inclusion, of determining who *should* belong to a particular group as much as who should *not*. In an ever-changing atmosphere such as the one described in the two previous sections, the importance of defining and redefining who might hold positions of preeminence or leadership was considerable. The means by which one might become wealthy had changed, of course, as a result of the economic transformations taking place, and there are forceful and persuasive arguments that it was largely men of already substantial wealth who engaged in long-distance trade,[108] despite the prior Homeric disdain for it.[109] As Donlan has demonstrated, while upward mobility may have been rare at this time, there was an awareness of the possibility of it.[110] A contest emerged between those who saw the source of their standing as more traditional and those who either augmented their resources or gained them through more unorthodox endeavors. Indeed, as fragmentary as is the historical record for the seventh and early sixth centuries, it provides numerous examples of disharmony and struggle among the wealthiest and most prestigious members of the elite over questions of political and social power.

NO SPECTER HAUNTED the imagination of the Archaic aristocracy and later political thinkers quite like tyranny.[111] Generally, attempts to establish tyranny involved the head of one aristocratic *oikos* and his supporters seeking to gain singular political supremacy over the other prominent members of the community. As Forsdyke has ably demonstrated, early tyrannies at Mytilene, Megara, Samos, and Corinth were the result of intraelite competition and typically represented the narrowing of the ruling elite until one man held power; though nonelites may have lent their support to one side or another (as in Mytilene), the emergence of tyranny was the triumph of one aristocratic faction over another (or others), and successful tyrants co-opted at least some significant portion of their fellow elites.[112] Though not every *polis* fell under the rule of a tyrant in the Archaic period, the phenomenon prevailed widely enough and in many cases predated our evidence for laws regarding the sharing of political office among the elite. Even in the seventh century, many *poleis* were still developing their institutions, and the parameters that defined magisterial power within an emerging state remained hazy.[113] Competition for power persisted among those with the means to do so, and as the consequences of losing became more serious (i.e., possible exclusion from the elite culture that allowed one to compete at all and/or physical exile from the community altogether), that competition became increasingly desperate and prone to eruptions of violence and even revolution.

Internal strife is a common theme in the establishment of the Archaic tyrannies. At Argos, tyranny arrived in the person of Pheidon.[114] Later Greeks associated his tyranny, and the subsequent Argive domination of the Peloponnesus, with his introduction of hoplite warfare among the Greeks. As we have already had occasion to discuss (Chapter 4.1), the whole question of a hoplite revolution is suspect, and just what Pheidon was doing differently from his aristocratic peers is therefore unclear. That he introduced some sort of military innovation that gave him substantial advantages, however, finds support in the events that followed his ascension to tyrannical power at Argos. Argive power crushed the Spartans ca. 669 at Hysiai; Greek historians believed that Pheidon extended his control across the Peloponnesus to the shrine at Olympia and that he dominated the island of Aegina as well.

This string of victories assumes added importance when we place the association between tyrants and hoplites within its internal political context. Both the ancient Greeks themselves and many modern scholars have thought that the most effective route to tyranny was for an aristocrat to gain the support of a wider segment of the nonelite population, who could serve as a potentially overwhelming fighting force against other *aristoi* and their supporters in the *polis*.[115] If this were the case, Pheidon provided something of an archetype, and his actions served as a blueprint for other tyrants, many of whom also were thought to have been elite men who armed and organized their own supporters and bowed other preeminent men in their communities to their personal authority to an extent not known before. Perhaps this accounts for Pheidon's reputation as both *basileus* and tyrant in the Greek tradition; once he had squelched competition within his home *polis*, Pheidon then turned the tactics that had served him so well domestically against his neighbors in southern Greece.

Such an interpretation need not rest on notions of a hoplite revolution, nor does it preclude the idea that the struggle for power was essentially a contest that took place among elites. Forsdyke's nuanced interpretation of intraelite competition allows for the role of nonelites in determining the outcome of such strife, be they prosperous individuals who could afford hoplite armor and aligned themselves with a particular aristocratic faction or poorer individuals who threw their support behind one or another contestant because of promised redress of economic grievances or a general concern for the survival of the community. Thus, there is nothing particularly outrageous or incredible about the ancient tradition that Pheidon may have been able to mobilize certain nonelite elements at Argos in his power struggles with fellow elites.

Pheidon's reported end is also instructive. The tradition reports that he met his death fighting in Corinth, a *polis* not subject to his suzerainty, warring on behalf of one side in an internal conflict for control of the polity.[116] A precise date for Pheidon's intervention and death at Corinth is unknowable on the present evidence, but it would have fallen between his stunning victories of the 660s and Kypselos' establishment of tyranny at Corinth ca. 658.[117] Perhaps

Pheidon died in the struggle that ultimately vaulted Kypselos to power; but whatever the case, there existed a common climate of internal strife within the more prosperous communities of the Greek world, which in the Corinthian example manifested itself as a rejection of the domination of a particular segment of the elite, the Bacchiadai.[118] Exactly how this "clan" of some two hundred elites managed previously to gain such a preeminent position is unclear, but the remarkable success of the Corinthian colonial movement in the late eighth century suggests the answer. Members of the Bacchiadai supposedly led the colonial expeditions to Syracuse and Corcyra,[119] and it may be that their commercial pursuits allowed them to out-compete their fellow Corinthian *aristoi* and ultimately exclude them altogether from competition for office and honors. In any event, the century or so of stable, uninterrupted control by the Bacchiads from ca. 750–650 suggests that the majority of elites and nonelites regarded as satisfactory their stewardship of the *polis*.[120]

Ancient accounts suggest some sociopolitical displacement of non-Bacchiad elites. According to Herodotus, Kypselos' father, Eëtion, was an aristocrat who had not been afforded the honor due him,[121] suggesting he belonged to that portion of the elite forced to the margins of status and power by the Bacchiadai. Furthermore, Eëtion hailed from Petra, perhaps an outlying village (*deme*) of the Corinthian *polis*.[122] According to the tradition, Kypselos was a threat to the people of "beetling Corinth"—the acropolis and commercially bustling agora controlled by the Bacchiadai—perhaps indicating that his father may have been part of a rural aristocracy whose wealth derived more from land than did that of the mercantile Bacchiads.[123] Alternatively, Corinth's fortunes may recently have declined, as the Megarian Orsippos had, shortly after 700, reclaimed territory previously seized from Megara;[124] Thucydides records a naval battle between Corinth and her colony Corcyra, usually dated to the first third of the seventh century, though he mentions neither the reasons nor the outcome.[125] Meanwhile, the adventuring of Pheidon would have done nothing to increase Corinthian power. This downturn in Corinthian fortunes perhaps prompted a challenge to the ruling Bacchiadai, possibly from a narrow circle within their ranks.[126] Whatever the case, as the Kypselids did not engage in extensive land redistribution[127] and appear to have continued Bacchiad commercial and colonial policies, we may rule out widely divergent class interests as a motivating factor: this was one segment of the elite displacing another in the competition for power.[128]

Violence among the elites characterized the establishment of tyranny at Megara as well. There, Theagenes catapulted himself to power through the slaughter of livestock and the seizure of some of the property of the "rich,"[129] though this act should probably be seen as Theagenes striking at the holdings of his own elite rivals. We may doubt the extent to which the motivation here was class rather than a struggle for pre-eminence among parties of the elite.[130] The relationship of the Megarian tyrant with the author of an abortive attempt at tyranny at Athens, the aristocrat and Olympic victor Kylon, confirms Theagenes' own elite status; the latter was the former's father-in-law.[131]

Kylon's own failed attempt at tyranny in Athens ca. 632 offers several insights into the rough and tumble world of aristocratic politics in the seventh century.[132] His participation in the Olympic games indicates Kylon's membership among the *aristoi*, and thus he found himself a part of the intensified competition for power and status typical of his time. Precisely what justification he offered for his coup is unknown, but the sources speak to him gathering enough supporters to seize the Acropolis, with an expectation that sympathizers would come into the city from the countryside.[133] Not only did the reinforcements fail to materialize, but a group of Athenians, both elite and humble, gathered under the leadership of Megakles, a member of one of Athens' most powerful *oikoi* and at the time one of the archons.[134] Under a guarantee of safe conduct, Kylon and his band quit the Acropolis and abandoned the coup, but Megakles' men broke the truce and killed many of the Kylonians after their surrender.[135] Kylon and his brother escaped into exile, and a generation later Megakles' descendants (he was by then dead) fell under a curse for the treachery of his followers and for a time left the city.[136]

The Kylonian conspiracy reveals two different aristocratic interests with followers drawn from the common elements of Athenian society.[137] Passions ran hot enough for one side to disregard promises of sanctuary and slaughter the other nearly wholesale. But the story did not end there. Despite the absence of the prime antagonists, according to one account, tensions continued to run high at Athens between their supporters and other sympathetic parties for another generation.[138]

Another seventh-century episode of tyranny amidst intense and violent intraelite competition occurred at Mytilene on the island of Lesbos, spanning two decades divided by the turn of the sixth century. Contemporary testimony about events there survives principally in the fragmentary poetry of the Mytilenean aristocrat Alcaeus, and his rhetoric and attitudes shed further light on the elite tensions that roiled the *polis*. Aristotle preserves some of the backstory, at least as it was known by his time. For a while, until about the middle of the seventh century, a group known as the Penthilidai held sway at Mytilene, maintaining their political monopoly through the use of force.[139] Their self-conscious claim to heroic descent confirms their elite status; furthermore, they remained important on the local political scene until the end of the seventh century. At some point, after other elites under the leadership of men named Smerdis and Megakles had established themselves as viable rivals to the Penthilidai, another named Melankhros seized sole power.[140] Another tyrant followed, namely Myrsilos, about whom Alcaeus tried to warn his fellow Mytileneans and against whom he plotted, leading to his first exile.[141] Strabo's later account, probably based on an earlier authority on Alcaeus, associates these two tyrannies with a period of civil unrest among rival aristocratic groups; indeed, from this source we learn that Alcaeus allegedly called the poems in which he railed against Melankhros, Myrsilos, and an aristocratic lineage called the Kleanaktidai, his *Stasiotika*, the "Affairs of the Civil Wars."[142]

Alcaeus actively participated in these struggles and in conspiracies to bring himself and his friends into power. At one point, his "party" aligned itself with Pittakos and his followers, swearing an oath to kill Myrsilos or die in the attempt, an alliance that that had perhaps been responsible ca. 612–609 for displacing Melankhros and his supporters from preeminence.[143] Pittakos, however, abandoned this coalition and joined forces with Myrsilos until the latter's death.[144] The demise of Myrsilos was for Alcaeus a cause for great celebration worthy of high drunkenness[145] and allowed for the poet's return from his first exile. His joy did not last: Pittakos secured a position as *aisymnetes* over Mytilene,[146] and it was not long before Alcaeus contemplated that Ares might once more set the city to strife.[147] Pittakos himself was clearly a man of status who had a substantial group of followers and allies, Alcaeus's accusations of low birth and unseemly appearance and behavior notwithstanding.[148] Even before his alliance with Alcaeus' family, Pittakos had been a distinguished war leader and married into the old aristocracy of the *polis*.[149]

What emerges from Alcaeus' poetry is a more detailed, if fragmentary, firsthand account of the trends in elite political struggle. Because of his testimony, we may construct a clearer, if partisan, picture of the internal politics of one particular polity, and that picture is one of confusion and upheaval among the leading families of Mytilene. In its broad strokes it corresponds well with the scantier notices regarding other communities undergoing episodes of tyranny and unrest. Were there an Alcaeus for Corinth, Athens, or Megara, we would surely find that contests for power in those *poleis* developed along similar lines, with struggles shifting the balance among ambitious, elite individuals and their *oikoi*. Because such struggles continued to be zero-sum games that often physically excluded certain rivals from political and social competition—Alcaeus rued his removal from the city, its councils, and the agora[150]—disappointments and resentments were bound to be fierce. One may wonder, for Alcaeus at least, if *tyrant* simply did not become a convenient term of abuse for a rival who established political domination at the expense of Alcaeus' own *oikos* and its associates.

DURING THE EIGHTH and seventh centuries, dramatic changes across the Greek world disembedded the economy from the social relationships that had characterized Greek communities for generations. Increases in people, wealth, and the fluidity of the ties that once held the community together created difficult and dynamic times for those who lived in that world; the effects of that transformation were nothing short of "catastrophic."[151]

The emerging *poleis* of this period, in all of its aspects, created situations for which the older legal culture and the rule base that informed it had few ready answers. *Synoikismos* brought together populations whose values and practices may have been consistent and mutually intelligible but not identical at a time when relationships within the constituent, smaller communities were breaking down. In this environment, new methods of claiming and augmenting elite status were devised to complement the long-standing competitive ethos among the *aristoi*, but as the seventh century continued, the competition for the necessary resources of elite agonism—up to and including political supremacy—could become increasingly violent. Moreover, because the avenues to competing for status were themselves mostly innovative and appeared in the period under discussion, there could be no proper or traditional way to handle and resolve the conflicts that arose from them. Consequences ranged from confusion and insecurity to violence and civil strife, the latter with some frequency.

This last observation returns us to where we began this chapter, with a consideration of what compels major changes in the judicial practices and assumptions of a society. Traumatic changes in the social, political, and economic systems of the society are frequently responsible, creating as they do a lack of phase between the accepted rule base and individual behavior. Innovative actions are not clearly approved or disapproved, in many instances: they simply *are*, but that does not mean that the behaviors in question will not create serious offenses and grievances that prove difficult to resolve. Unresolved tensions may lead to a level of dispute that the community finds unmanageable and dangerously disruptive.

To move, then, from the abstract to the concrete with respect to Archaic Greece: that traumatic changes took place is clear. They affected Greek society in virtually all aspects, but as we have seen, these changes presented special challenges to the elite, altering the ways in which they had traditionally defined and maintained their positions and confounding the rule base through which they interacted with one another and with the community at large. Clarifying the rule base and establishing new components of it through writing responded especially to aristocratic anxieties and concerns, as the elites sought ways to ensure competitive balance, limit violence amongst themselves, and define relationships anew within the context of the *polis*.

CHAPTER SIX

Aristocratic Anxieties and the Writing of Laws

1—Rituals, Reciprocity, and the Elites

In an engaging 1994 monograph, Richard Seaford argued for the importance of the inextricable relationship between the reciprocal ties that bound the households of the early Greek world on the one hand and ritual on the other. It was reciprocity that informed all the guises under which ritual appeared, and it was ritual that structured those fundamental relationships examined in the second section of Chapter 5. Furthermore,

> in the creation and maintenance of relations between those united neither by kinship nor by citizenship ritual may operate either by bringing them together in an expression of shared emotion and identity, or like supplication in Homer, as a means of controlling relations *between* individuals and groups [original emphasis]. Such relations are . . . often mediated by the giving or exchange of gifts, according to a generally accepted code of reciprocity, which may easily coexist, in the absence of judicial authority, with a similar, generally agreed code of hostile reciprocity more or less regulating violence between hostile groups.[1]

One may then ask, what happens to rituals when the obligations imposed by reciprocal relations are no longer clear, owing to a rapidly changing set of social, economic, and political factors? If the "generally agreed codes" for reciprocal behaviors—both peaceful and violent—deteriorate, the rituals they inform will soon experience sympathetic reverberations. Those daily actions that gave meaning to a broad range of political, social, and economic relationships become increasingly irrelevant and unable to govern the life of the community in any meaningful way. Such circumstances necessitate a redefinition of the rule base, and in particularly disquieting situations there may exist an impulse to make the supposedly "new and improved" rule base more stable and reliable than the shifting reality around it, by whatever means available. In addition, such new or improvised rules will necessarily generate elsewhere than the traditional modes of reinforcing and transmitting authority, as epic became increasingly canonized and far less malleable to the changing realities of society.

While the transformations of the early Archaic period will have affected virtually everyone in the Greek world, elites would have found themselves and their relationships with each other profoundly challenged by the changes taking place. As we saw in Chapter 5.3, the growth of population and the influx of wealth impacted the basic political organization of many communities in the Greek world. The *polis* was in part a response to the inadequacies of the essentially bicentric, household-based, and semiautonomous nature of the community in the Middle and Late Geometric period. On the one hand, this development undermined the traditional underpinnings of Homeric elite power. A number of scholars have effectively argued in recent years, to my mind rightly, that the economic gulf between elites and nonelite *landowners* was substantial but not enormous,[2] and we should probably imagine that early *poleis* were, at least as far as self-sufficient farmers were concerned, more egalitarian than the literature of the late nineteenth and much of the twentieth century assumed; indeed, such nonelite, self-sufficient farmers could perhaps play crucial roles in encouraging the elites toward compromise amongst themselves, especially when their competition threatened to damage the community as a whole.[3] Further, as I suggested in the previous chapter, the breaking of older systems of economic exchange based on reciprocal ties had not only the effect of liberating the elite from the obligations such ties had imposed but will have also made possible negotiation by self-sufficient farmers for their support in contests for power and prestige among the elite.

On the other hand, whatever role the *demos* may have played in early *poleis* (and it is entirely plausible to conceive of the *demos* in the earliest *poleis* as exclusive of those who were economically dependent), it is abundantly clear that these communities were guided by men of wealth and status, competing for power and honor through the emerging institutions of the protostate, in Lin Foxhall's evocative phrase, "like rivals on the playground taking turns."[4] They necessarily had to define new means of relating to one another, as the exercise of power shifted from a semiautonomous chieftainship model of organization as embodied in the *basileis* to a new political rubric in which the elite (ideally) acted in a more cooperative fashion while at the same time still angling to outdo one another. How was power to be shared under the emerging arrangements? How was one man, or one household, to be prevented from dominating the entire community through the monopolization of magisterial office? Not only had these relatively novel issues assumed fundamental importance in defining the power relations of the emergent *polis*, but they reshaped necessarily the motivations and methods by which the elites competed for power, in turn creating separate crises calling for new solutions in and of themselves.

In addition, the nature of wealth and the basis of economic power had been completely transformed in some communities and had altered the dynamics of prestige and status to some degree in many others. The rise and importance of trade reshaped relations between communities, but it also had a profound effect within them as well. We have already traced how the new means of acquiring wealth and status created something of an identity crisis within existing elites. Though in a few cases, such as Corinth, commerce may have ushered in an aristocratic element quite unlike the Homeric elite, in most communities it was more likely the case that trade benefited those who had already possessed the necessary resources to engage in such ventures. Some men and their households grew quite prosperous, while the yeoman peasantry continued, much like Hesiod, to concern themselves with the management of more modest but apparently quite sufficient farmsteads. The greatest losers in the world of the emergent *polis* were members of the elite who had not kept pace with their fellow *kaloikagathoi* and became increasingly unable to participate in the two principal prestige- and power-building strategies open to them: reciprocity and competitive display. As a consequence, the rituals bound up with reciprocity and display (or generosity in general)—marriage, funeral cult, largesse, the attraction of personal followers—increasingly failed to inform elite behavior as the distribution of competitive resources changed. These aspects of community life would need to be redefined and delineated if serious political and social upheaval were to be avoided.

It now remains to test the hypothesis that elites sought to write laws in order to establish more clearly the rules for their interaction with one another and with the larger political community of the *polis*. Any popular demand for such a codification of the rule base in the various communities of Greece beginning in the middle of the seventh century is difficult to locate and will have been mediated in any event through the agency of the elites who held power. Further, in Chapter 3, our study of the nature of Homeric and Hesiodic legal culture, before the writing of laws, revealed the general consistency of judicial procedure and its public character; further, the nature of "law" before its commitment to writing was such that it was very much embedded in the traditions of the community and affected by the climate of public opinion and therefore not easily subject to the manipulation of a particular group in order to serve its narrower interests. Justice was negotiable, contingent, and dependent to a great extent on the wider discourse of relationships within a community, but of course, in the context of elite competition, therein lies part of the problem for the political life of the community. That same justice was also dependent on a commonly held set of notions among the members of that community, values and assumptions conditioned by life in a prestate society with a small population and a largely local economy and underscored by a generations-old tradition of authoritative pronouncement, represented by epic. The bicentric, pre-*polis* community underwent radical changes, as considered in Chapter 5, resulting in state formation and the *polis*, and particularly impacting the political and economic elite and their semiautonomous households. It was this same elite, I argue, that was responsible for the writing of laws in the early *poleis* of Greece, not (contra Eder) in order to wield a tool of political repression, or consciously to preserve their own position as a social and political class. Rather, elites recognized the danger presented to themselves individually by the inherent instability of the changing sociopolitical world of the early *polis*, especially when that instability involved increasingly violent and desperate contention among and with their peers in an ever more fluid society.

Elites attempted to stabilize their communities by reestablishing or revising some customary rules which might still prove useful in thwarting violence and unrest by making them more prominent and permanent: in this way, confusions over what was or was not accepted behavior would be removed as a source of tension and escalations of reciprocal violence. In addition, they would need to define new laws within the broader discourse of the community's rule base, in order to clarify and regulate new behaviors for which the traditional, inherited rule base offered no guidance: when written, these were statutes in the truest sense of the word. If these hypotheses are accurate, the earliest written laws should betray a preoccupation with those institutions and practices, social, economic, and political, of greatest concern to the elite, particularly as those institutions impacted their effectiveness to govern and maintain stability. Indeed, the earliest surviving laws demonstrate just such a dynamic. While there are a number of categories of written law that betray aristocratic bias, three invite particular attention due to the frequency and wide geographical distribution they exhibit: transfer of property through marriage, inheritance, and adoption; reciprocal violence and the related issue of funerary cult; and office holding and misconduct of office.[5]

2—The Movement of Property in the Early *Polis*

Of the laws that survive either epigraphically or in later literary testimony, those that concern themselves with the movement of landed property—either through marriage (and the associated dowry), inheritance, or adoption—figure quite prominently,[6] and as we will see in this section, the hallmark of those laws was an attempt to preserve existing patterns of wealth distribution, often by legislating to keep patrimonial inheritances in established lines of patrilineal succession. The need for such explicit measures arose from a variety of causes. Population growth, naturally, played an important role in the necessity for defining who should hold property and how they might receive it. As the landed resources of a given community shrank in proportion to the numbers of people dependent on them, new pressures inevitably came into being. At the same time, unobligated wealth circulating within a disembedded economy—independent of significant population growth—might be employed for the purpose of expanding the private holdings of certain *oikoi*, further narrowing access to land in general and providing successful households with a significant and (potentially ultimately decisive) competitive advantage. Furthermore, the marriage and adoption customs of various smaller hamlets will have differed as these settlements fused into the larger *polis*. Some standardization and regularization became necessary, especially as marriage in particular but also adoption touched on the especially important issues of the transfer and inheritance of property, the sine qua non of aristocratic competition in the Archaic age, the source of wealth for competitive display and the attraction of followers.

Before pursuing an examination of more detailed (and in some cases epigraphically preserved) statutes touching on these matters, attention should be drawn to two general laws believed to have been promulgated in the earliest phases of written legislation in Greece. Aristotle in the *Politics* reports the legislative activities of, among others, Pheidon of Corinth, and Philolaos, a Corinthian exile who took up residence at Thebes, where he became a lawgiver (*nomothetes*).[7] In both cases, the legislators sought to fix the current number of households by law and—at least in the instance of Pheidon of Corinth—to freeze the size of the individual holdings in their present condition as well as the number of citizens. Again, while we must necessarily be suspicious of fourth-century interpretations of Archaic legislative activity, the substance of the laws in Aristotle's report has been widely accepted as reflective of some historical fact, and Pheidon's activity is usually placed during the period of Bacchiad rule at Corinth.[8] As for Philolaos, Aristotle explicitly calls him a Bacchiad who left Corinth when his lover, the Olympic victor

Diokles, could not abide the erotic feelings his own mother exhibited for him and therefore quit the city.[9] The Olympic victor lists suggest a possible date for Diokles of 728, which would accord with the period of Bacchiad supremacy at Corinth as well.

We have, then, reports of legislative activity on the part of two members of the Bacchiad clan, the aristocratic government of the Archaic age par excellence. The analysis of these statutes reveals a similarity of purpose: the stabilization of the landholding status quo in Corinth and Thebes.[10] Pheidon of Corinth established the current landholding situation at Corinth as a legal mandate, although the size of the plots (*kleroi*) was unequal; Philolaos, meanwhile, may have been legislating in reaction to the concentration of more and more land into the hands of fewer *oikoi*, which absorbed vacant plots when the owners had died without heir.[11] In both instances we have an essentially conservative act, aimed at stabilizing the pattern of landholding and curbing the tendency toward concentration of landed wealth, which could occur not only through lack of inheritance but also through the movement of property, by sale, marriage, and dowry.[12] The inequalities of the existing pattern of ownership were apparently immaterial to Pheidon, if it ever occurred to him that they were problematic at all, and in all likelihood his laws formalized a situation in which those already without land (or without much) had little prospect of gaining enough to win the attendant political rights.[13] Likewise, Philolaos legislated to *require* the childless landowner to adopt an heir so that his property would not be left vacant and possibly absorbed into the possessions of another *oikos*.

Concentration of wealth was far more likely to raise anxieties among the elite than among the *demos* at large in the eighth and early seventh centuries, inasmuch as great differences of wealth among the elite would have, as suggested in the previous chapter, placed certain members of the leading group at a competitive political and social disadvantage. In the case of Corinth, colonization provided an outlet for surplus population and the opportunity to go elsewhere for those formally shut out of large-scale landowning or political participation—that is to say, the ambitious and/or discontented members of the nouveaux riches and the *demos* generally. Thebes in this period is more obscure, but it seems likely that the possibility of intestate *oikoi* of substance was more apt to cause concern to the elite than smaller parcels such as that belonging to the contemporary Boeotian peasant Hesiod. Indeed, Hesiod—if his view on this matter may be taken as typical of the nonelite element in his society—had a rather ambivalent attitude towards the entire question of heirs.[14]

Any one *oikos* or group of kindred *oikoi* accumulating substantial properties would have positioned them well to absorb future defunct households as these became available through intestacy, marriage, failure and/or debt (as may have been the case with Perses), and so on. This ability to absorb additional landed property and its resources would, necessarily, grant the heads of such households a considerable advantage in the various arenas of elite competition, an inherently destabilizing dynamic. We may also consider that Pheidon of Corinth might have hoped to formalize the situation as it presently stood, wherein the Bacchiadai had achieved a position of competitive superiority through the acquisition of land—a scarce enough resource in the Corinthia—and now sought to prevent potential rivals from doing the same. In any event, the question of resources used as the basis for elite competition would appear to be at the root of this early legislation as it is reported.

Instructive in this regard as well is a law from Elis attributed to Oxylos, the legendary Dorian king supposed to have conquered the area.[15] While we may safely dispense with Oxylos' historical involvement in lawgiving, the law itself is generally accepted as a genuine sixth-century statute, at a time when Elis was ruled by an aristocracy.[16] The thrust of the law forbade the sale of *prôtoi klêroi*—first farms—or the use of a certain portion of one's estate for the purpose of securing loans. Once again, we have what would seem to be a pressing concern over the possibility of too much land concentrating in the hands of few through pressure to sell or through foreclosure on land standing as surety for debt. Likewise, at Gortyn, a law from the Great Code also prohibited the purchase of land from a son while the father yet lived or his securing a debt against it.[17]

Similarly, adoption in Archaic Gortyn[18] on the island of Crete would appear to have been primarily a concern for the privileged-citizen classes, and again we find the preservation of the property-holding status quo as paramount. For an adoption to be recognized as valid at Gortyn, the adoptive father had to make a public proclamation to the citizens in the place of assembly[19] and further offer a sacrificial victim and a measure (*prokoos*) of wine to his *hetaireia.*[20] In the Gortynian context this distinction was particularly significant. Only the aristocratic ruling class of Gortyn belonged to and participated in the *hetaireiai*, which served a variety of social and political functions, including the recognition of legitimate heirs to the political and economic rights of the father.[21] All other free persons within Gortynian society were excluded from rights of political participation and designated as *apetairoi,* that is to say, those away from *hetaireiai.* While the precise position and function of the *apetairoi* remains controversial and beyond the scope of the present argument,[22] what is pertinent for our purposes is the manifest devaluation of these citizens vis-à-vis those who did participate in the *hetaireiai*, those citizens labeled free, the *eleutheroi*. Rape committed by an *eleutheros* against another free person carried a fine of 1,200 obols, whereas the associated penalty for the rape of a member of the *apetairos* class was an order of magnitude less: 120 obols. By way of comparison, the disparity between this last fine and that for raping a slave was much smaller, as the latter offense netted the perpetrator an assessment of 30 obols.[23] Similar scales of valuation inhered in the fines for adultery,[24] and the threshold for evidence needed to secure a judgment against an *eleutheros* was substantially higher than that for *apetairoi*.[25]

The concern over property and its succession to adopted children also figures prominently in early Cretan law, and careful provisions were promulgated regarding both the priority of inheritance where adopted heirs were involved, as well as their formal denunciation by their adoptive father. The Great Code of Gortyn preserves the regulations pertaining to the adopted heir's rights to the *oikos*, and it is clear that while the adopted son enjoyed the citizen privileges of his (new) father, he remained at a serious disadvantage relative to any brothers who happened to be biological sons.[26] The adopted son appears only to have succeeded to full usufruct of the patrimony in the event that no acknowledged children (*gnesia tekna*)—that is, legitimate—survived besides. In the event that other, biological, sons were present, the adopted son was to receive from these brothers just as any sisters were, which is to say one part (*mian moiran*) for every two portions (*duo moirans*) enjoyed by the biological sons.[27] Moreover, if the adopted son were the only succeeding male but heiresses were present, then he was not to enjoy this double portion normally reserved for sons but rather only an equal share (*wiswomoiran*) with his sisters.[28] The distinction between biological and adoptive sons appears to be quite old at Gortyn, as it occurs in an earlier text,[29] dating to approximately 550 and perhaps an earlier version of the provision enshrined in the Code.

Furthermore, if the adopted son alone remained, but was unwilling to fulfill the obligations "towards gods and men" imposed on him by its possession, then the property was to revert immediately to the adoptive parents' kinsmen (*epiballontes*).[30] Gortynian law also made provision for the denunciation of the adopted heir during the adoptive parent's lifetime, as a simple procedure could nullify the adoption before the assembled citizens in the *agora*. The adoptive parent renounced the adoption from "the stone from which proclamations are made" and deposited 10 staters (120 obols) with the court, whereupon the *mnamon* for the *kosmos ksenios* would pay this money to the erstwhile adoptee.[31] The procedure probably involved the magistrate responsible for persons outside the aristocratic tribal structure of Gortyn, the *kosmos ksenios*, through his scribe, the *mnamon*, because the renunciation of the adopted son placed him in a position where he could not now inherit, was outside of an aristocratic *oikos*, and thus made of him an *apetairos*.[32] The 10 staters given to him through the court were presumably meant to ease his transition into his new life and status.

The precarious position of the adopted heir reflects an obsession within Gortyn to preserve property within the male line of the *oikos*,[33] insofar as that might prove possible, and within the clan at all costs. This particular obsession not only manifests itself in the degree to which an adopted son found himself hedged around by a number of restrictions and perils but also in the provisions made for the succession to property failing even an adoptive heir. Adoptive heirs most likely suffered as a result of their having come from outside the *oikos* lineage proper and the fact that they had not hailed from among the *epiballontes* of the adopter. Contra Willetts,[34] any number of notices within the code militate against assuming a close blood affinity between adopter and adoptee. The laws clearly stated that the adopting parent could choose anyone he wished as adoptive son,[35] and the granting of such latitude in itself indicates a desire to make certain that the present head of the *oikos* would incline to choose someone (anyone?) to perpetuate his holding, related or not.

The explicit and definitive rights granted to the decedent's *epiballontes* in the event of no heir at all certainly suggest that this last consideration was the driving force behind the law, rather than the granting of exceptional individual discretion to the *eleutheros*. When the *eleutheros* at the head of an *oikos* died without heir or heiress in the next generation, the order of succession to his property was clear and wide ranging: extending to any surviving male grandchildren or great-grandchildren within the decedent's own line, then through successive generations to the grandchildren of the dead man's brothers, and, failing these, the grandchildren of the deceased's sisters.[36] If no direct descendants remained from the *oikos* of the decedent's father—in other words, if there were no *epiballontes* (commonly translated as kinsmen) to assume possession of the property[37]—then the land went to the serfs or other household personnel associated with the holding.[38] Indeed, these last individuals were to inherit before the property would pass through sale into the holdings of another *oikos*, a situation which apparently could only occur if the *epiballontes* named earlier in the inscription (and one assumes there could be several surviving relations among those described as eligible to succeed) had taken possession but had failed to agree on the division of the property among themselves.[39]

Taken together, these statutes reveal the concern for preserving the stability of property ownership within the family at Gortyn, and preventing the easy acquisition by, and resultant concentration of, the lands of *eleutheroi* in the hands of a few. In this context, the suspicion toward, and handicaps placed upon, the fully legitimized and legally recognized—but adoptive—heir become intelligible: preservation within the biological family was preferable, and this fact alone would explain the ease with which a father could disinherit an adoptee, presumably in favor of natural sons who had survived into adulthood and could inherit instead of adoptees who were encouraged principally as a safeguard against the intestate *oikos*.[40] The adoptee was ultimately an outsider, and perhaps as such his trustworthiness was questionable; the power of the head of the *oikos* to select an heir from whatever source he chose speaks to the possibility that the adoptee could be drawn from the classes outside the privileged class of the *eleutheroi*, as does the apparent reversion of many disinherited adoptees to the status of *apetairoi*.

We might surmise that the *oikos*-holder reduced to adopting an outside heir probably sought to avoid making a choice from among other houses of *eleutheroi*, a prospect that carried with it the danger of making of one's heir someone who might be all too glad to align himself and his new resources with his birth family after the death of the adoptive father, to the detriment of the latter's kinsmen. Whatever the case, the adoption of an outsider reveals itself as an altogether undesirable, if sometimes unavoidable, alternative at Gortyn, as evidenced by the restrictions and diminutions suffered by the adoptive heir in the presence of biological children. Nevertheless, the Gortynian aristocracy clearly considered adoption preferable to the prospect of landed wealth moving too easily within the society from one lineage to another: it was more desirable that even household servants enjoy a property than that it should be sold.

Although Gortyn provides us with our fullest evidence regarding adoption as a means of securing regular inheritance within the line of an existing *oikos*, the ruling elements of other Archaic *poleis* also saw fit to legislate regarding inheritance generally. Solon reportedly promulgated laws against the possession of property beyond a certain limit (to what effect we may wonder), and other communities in pre-Classical Greece attempted similar safeguards against the concentration of wealth.[41] At Lokris, Aristotle reports, a man could not sell his land unless he could demonstrate some great misfortune,[42] and the repeal of an old statute at Leukas that had preserved the "ancient allotments" led to radical democracy there.[43] These last two laws, one presumes, would have likely been accompanied by measures enforcing the childless to adopt an heir or other contingencies, such as at Gortyn, to ensure the preservation of *oikoi* within the same family lineages. Only in this way could authors of laws against the sale or reallotment of land have hoped to succeed.

Indeed, it is most difficult to try to examine individually issues such as adoption, inheritance, or the transfer of property generally, since the laws of

Archaic Greece exhibit a fair degree of overlap with regard to these various juridical problems. Inheritance laws typically addressed, therefore, what happened in a patriarchal society to property when the dead man who owned it did not have an obvious heir—a son or sons—and as we have seen, several communities promulgated constitutional protections for the stability of landholding by prohibiting certain types of transfer or abandonment of property. By requiring other actions before an impasse was reached, inheritance measures thus purposed to prevent a property crisis, wherein the possessions of a decedent could become objects of intrigue, envy, or even open conflict among other members of the community.

As with any laws, however, we may presume that such measures were not fully or automatically effective at all times in preventing the types of scenarios they were designed to check. Details needed negotiation in the law and its adjudication, particularly in a society with an emphasis on procedure. Failing an obvious heir, to whom might the property fall next, especially if the general tenor of the community's norms was to keep possessions within a particular patrilineal succession? Clearly, the elites at Gortyn deemed it necessary to define such issues carefully. Confusion over who constituted the circuit of the individual *oikos*—and who might therefore succeed to its associated possessions—may have inspired an attempt at Katana in Sicily to define the composition of the household. Aristotle relates that Kharondas, the famous lawgiver associated with that *polis*, referred to those who comprised the household as *homosipuoi*, those who eat together.[44] Given that Aristotle's primary interest in Kharondas at various points in the *Politics* is in the latter's legislative activity,[45] it is likely that Aristotle understood this provision to have come from among the various laws Kharondas supposedly promulgated in seeking to delimit the family as those who shared in the same *oikos*. If we accept Adcock's position that the tales of early lawgivers provide a primary tradition of credible though sparse biographical and factual details (such as the substance of certain laws) and consider as well both the preoccupation with family/inheritance/property law that Aristotle suggests for the early lawgivers and the similar concern over the *oikos* and its property demonstrated by the Gortyn Code,[46] it would be reasonable to accept Diodorus at least on the point that Kharondas busied himself over the problem of inheritance.[47] Such a law would be consistent with the law regarding heiresses likewise ascribed to him, as well as those attributed to Philolaos of Thebes and Pheidon of Corinth: all sought to preserve the continuity of the *oikos* and thus assure the relative stability of the overall pattern of landholding in their communities.

Kharondas' preoccupation with the preservation of the *oikos* and current patterns of landholding, as reflected in Diodorus' account, becomes even clearer when we examine the rest of the notice. The lawgiver of Katana is said to have provided that orphans should have the following protections: the next of kin on the father's side would manage the property, while the mother's relatives would rear the child or children.[48] Diodorus offers the following interpretation: Kharondas showed particular ingenuity with this law, since the distaff kin would have no reason to plot against the life of the orphan(s), as they stood to inherit nothing were the child, or children, to die. On the other hand, the patrilineal relatives would steward the property well, as they would take possession of the *oikos* in the event that the orphan(s) died through disease or certain other happenstance.[49] The language of the passage also suggests that this measure was part of a larger set of laws that also included a law of allotment (*klêronomia*), stipulating that the mother's side would have no share in the property of the orphaned children in the event of their deaths while in guardianship. Whether this is a general prohibition on matrilineal succession, or the practice was predicated on the existence of surviving patrilineal relatives, is impossible to discern from the available testimony. There is a parallel for the law Diodorus cites, giving his report some credit. The Great Code of Gortyn also provided specifically,[50] just as did the reported law of Kharondas, that an heiress (a woman without a father or a brother by the same father) was to be raised by her mother's relatives while her father's kinsmen administered the property. Based on this evidence, it would appear that Kharondas, similarly to the anonymous provisions from Gortyn, took care that an individual *oikos* and its heir would survive in sufficient condition to preserve the household as a distinct possession, unlikely to be absorbed into the holdings of others, even those of close relatives.

Diodorus also reports that Kharondas set laws regulating heiresses and their property, though, of course, thinking of the two as distinct legal entities is misleading; as Sealey has noted for Athens, any number of restrictions hedged around the heiress and limited her "ownership" of property to the point that, as *epikleros* (upon the allotment), she was inseparable from it.[51] While Diodorus' explanation as to how the law had evolved to its contemporary state is anecdotal and most probably spurious, the details of the statute—that the heiress was to be assigned to her next of kin for marriage and that if he refused to take her must then provide her dowry[52]—reflects similar Archaic measures around the Greek world and probably preserves at least the outlines of the older law. For example, Solon directed a law toward the purpose of ensuring that an heiress could not choose a husband at will but had to select from among her paternal kinsmen.[53] At Gortyn the position of the heiress is more complex,[54] insofar as she may have had more discretion than counterparts in Katana or Athens so long as certain preconditions prevailed. First, the heiress was to marry her father's oldest brother, and if more than one daughter and more than one brother of the decedent survived, these were to marry in descending order of their age.[55] Failing the presence of living paternal uncles, the oldest of the woman's surviving parallel cousins became the next eligible groom, once again in descending age until the suitable candidate was found (in the order of all the sons of the eldest uncle, then all the sons of the second uncle, and so on).[56]

In the event that no parallel cousins either survived or were willing to marry the heiress, she was allowed some latitude in her choice, but only after further litigation encompassed by the Gortyn Code. If a groom-elect in his majority (*dromeus*) refused the marriage, then the woman's *kadestai* were to bring the matter to court, whereupon a judge statutorily ordered the marriage to take place within two months.[57] Again, the relatives responsible for bringing the action are the woman's *kadestai*, probably her kin on her mother's side, as distinct from her patrilineal relatives, the *epiballontes*.[58] These last must have supported, for whatever reason, the recalcitrant husband-to-be, for he would scarcely have been in a position to refuse at all had they wanted to see her (and necessarily her property) remain within the agnatic line. Despite this legal mechanism, the law still envisages grooms-elect successfully resisting such marriages: "And should he not marry her as is written, holding all the properties [she will marry] from the *epiballontes*, should there be another."[59] The preceding provisions indicate that another (*allos*) would be the next parallel cousin in succession as already prescribed.

If, on the other hand, the heiress were to reject a groom-elect from among the *epiballontes*, either for his minority or other unspecified reasons, the law penalized her for this decision by allowing her to keep her dwelling but to forfeit as much as half of her property to the spurned, prospective groom.[60] A problem of language arises here, but in the context of the other provisions, the way out is clear. Following those lines that provide for the division of the estate exclusive of the physical dwelling,[61] we hear that she is to give property to "the same man,"[62] with the intervening stipulation that allowed for the marriage of the heiress to whomever of her tribesmen had asked to marry her.[63] Therefore, the pronoun (*iôi*) could indicate either the erstwhile groom-to-be or the new suitor, but a number of considerations militate in favor of the former. First, we have already seen the lengths to which the Gortynians went to keep property within the circle of *epiballontes*. Second, if an heiress were not of marriageable age, her father's brothers were to administer her property while she took a half share of the produce,[64] suggesting that the other half was employable at their discretion. Therefore, we seem to have an underlying principle that half of the property belonged among the *epiballontes*. Finally, the code envisages the possibility that the heiress might not discover any takers among her kinsmen and provides in that event for her *kadestai* to make a proclamation throughout the tribe, "Does not anyone want to marry her?" If no one came forward, then the heiress was to marry whomever she could,[65] or—at this last resort—whomever she wished, though even then only within her tribe.[66] If the other half of her property were to devolve automatically to the man she married, it is difficult to understand such a profound (and apparently not altogether infrequent) lack of interest in marrying the heiress. At Gortyn, if an heiress could not find a match among her paternal kinsmen, the *epiballontes*, they would end up with half of her inheritance.

Lastly, it is worth mentioning in this context a few rules regarding dowry. Plutarch states that Solon enacted a law forbidding dowries in all marriages save those which occurred between an heiress and her kinsman, the bride otherwise bringing with her only three changes of dress and inexpensive household goods.[67] On Crete, we find attempts to regulate the "wife's property"—namely, those goods that she had brought with her to the marriage.[68] In the event of a divorce, the wife was to retain her own property, plus half of any of the produce (*karpos*) that her property had yielded during the marriage, as well as half of any of the goods she had manufactured, which the authors of the statute imagined principally as textiles.[69] A widow might remarry, but she was to have only her own property, plus whatever the husband might have given her in accordance with the law, three *eleutheroi* having witnessed the bequest.[70] The remainder of the patrimony went to the children; any attempt on the part of the widow to gain anything additionally from her dead husband's property—now legally belonging to his children—was actionable, that it is to say, "it would be for trial" (*endikon êmên*).[71] If the husband died leaving the wife childless, the same conditions applied concerning both the amount of property to which she was entitled and the resultant court action should she attempt to acquire more.[72] The decedent's belongings, houses, and land reverted to the relatives of his patriarchal line as described above.

In addition, the Great Code of Gortyn provided detailed measures concerning the husband's rights over the wife's property. Gortynian law forbade a husband from selling or pledging the property of his wife, or a son that of his mother (for whatever reason, though one presumes the primary concern was sureties for loans).[73] Abrogation of this rule carried a stiff penalty: the mother or wife would retain control of her property, while the perpetrator had to pay double the value of the pledged or sold property to the man with whom he transacted.[74] Further, the law severely restricted the husband's control over the wife's property in the event of her death. If a wife died childless, then her property as well as half of the *karpos* from that property and her labor reverted to her *epiballontes*, her paternal kin; the husband retained control over her property only if they had children.[75] Even here, however, the law barred him from offering these resources as security for a loan or other types of pledges, unless the children were of age and had consented to such.[76] If he violated this measure, then similar penalties applied as in the case of securing loans or pledges on the dowry of a living wife; in this instance, the property would fall under the control of the children (again, presumably administered by their *kadestai* were they not of age) and the husband had to pay double restitution to the person with whom he had contracted the loan or pledge.[77] Finally, if the widower remarried, the mother's property automatically fell under the administration of the children (or the *kadestai* if the children were minors).[78]

THESE STATUTES REGARDING the control of property exhibit a common concern: the preservation and stability of the patterns of resource-ownership, particularly within the male line of a family. As we have seen, the husband's discretion over his wife's dowry was severely circumscribed, and his abuse of its supervision, at Gortyn at least, could issue in forfeiture of his rights to that property and other penalties besides. A woman's property could always revert in the last instance to her *epiballontes*—her kinsmen through her father—and we have examined at length the care taken by several *poleis* throughout the Greek world to ensure that heiresses be married to kinsmen through her father's side. The primary motivation for such rules was to preserve patterns of landholding and resource distribution. As we have seen, at Athens Solon forbade the transfer of property in marriages that did not take place between kin, and the reports about Kharondas indicate that he instituted steep disincentives for the man who chose not to marry an heiress from among his father's agnatic kin.

Taken together with the laws regarding adoption, inheritance, and sale or alienation of property, the overall effect of such legislation was to conserve the distribution of wealth and resources and to prevent the easy movement of property and the destabilization of social and political arrangements within the community as a result. One can imagine that these laws will have been of interest to any landowner in an early Greek community, but there can be no question whose interests such laws will have served first and foremost: those who already enjoyed access to those resources and who sought to prevent others from using the alienation of land or the easy movement of property through marriage as a strategy to increase their holdings for the purpose of out-competing fellow elites. It remains, of course, possible that there was reaction here to calls for the redistribution of land and that early lawgivers could have seen two advantages to the prohibition on various forms of reallotment of the original or ancestral *klêroi*:[79] on the one hand, such laws might discourage these demands by ensuring the present pattern of landholding through the authority of statute; on the other hand, the legal preservation of an economic balance of power within the community was perhaps meant to stabilize and strengthen that stratum of the community which, so long as it remained united, could resist such demands.

However, we must consider such reactionary motives within the broader context of a concern expressed in the foregoing statutes regarding the movement of property generally in this society. The rapid and no doubt alarming trend created by the new wealth and its disembedded nature as discussed in the previous chapter had engendered a situation whereby fortunes could rise and fall more easily than ever before, and the political and social costs of falling behind were quite serious. It was not reaction to popular discontent that informed the efforts to regulate movement of property, but rather the accumulation of disproportionate wealth by individual *oikoi*—through marriage, purchase of intestate land, or the other means we have discussed. The primary reason for such anxiety was, of course, the desire to maintain competitive ability among the "best" households.

3—Retributive Murder, Funerary Cult, and Ostentation

The concern over competition, and the employment of excess wealth in its pursuit, is nowhere better exemplified than in the laws concerning reciprocal violence and funerary ostentation. As we have already seen, the consequences of aristocratic competition for political power and social clout were potentially very serious, extending to cyclical factional bloodshed and putsches aiming at, and sometimes succeeding in, establishing tyrannies. Any attempt to stabilize the emergent *polis* and regularize the means by which its most influential members were to hold and exercise power necessitated the elimination of violence and the propagandistic public funeral as tools for political competition.

Literary and archaeological evidence allows us to envision the following scene from Athens in the late seventh century. An individual from one of the community's powerful families has just died, and his kin set about mourning their loss and commemorating the departed. They lay out the corpse at home, either indoors or out, in the *prothesis*. After the female relatives of the deceased complete a ritual bathing and clothing of the dead man, they place him on a bed, the *klinê*, and there he may remain for an indeterminate period of time, but certainly longer than a single day: the *prothesis* traditionally had no set limit.[80] It is during the *prothesis* when mourners from the family, as well as professionals hired for the occasion, perform ritual lamentations. These are sometimes spontaneous, though mourners employ prepared cries also, as those left behind rue their loss and its impact on their lives.[81] After the lament, the family transports the body from its place of *prothesis* toward its final resting place in the procession called the *ekphora*: at least in the case of a wealthier funeral, a horse-drawn hearse carries the corpse to its burial site, surrounded by the cortege of mourners. The attendees—large numbers of men and women—carry ample supplies of food and bring along animals intended for sacrifice and along their route stop regularly, particularly at intersections, to attract a maximum amount of attention.[82] Once the procession arrives at the cemetery, the mourners deal with the remains. Though inhumation and cremation are both known at Athens, from the early seventh century until the early sixth, primary cremation—that is, the burning of the body inside the grave itself—predominates among the wealthy.[83] The dead man's kin then slaughter the sacrificial beast(s) and share the yield from it among those present at the gravesite, while certain relatives of the deceased pay their final respects with speeches in praise of the dead.

Such a sight would not have been at all unfamiliar at Athens, until Solon sought to regulate the commemoration of the wealthy and powerful dead as part of his legislation ca. 594. Scholars have for some time recognized that Solon's funerary legislation in the early sixth century purposed to rein in potentially disruptive tributes to Athens' aristocratic dead.[84] More recently, alternative but less convincing interpretations have appeared, perceiving the lawgiver's precepts as an expression of a general trend to "push away death."[85] While there can be little doubt that Greek societies were concerned with limiting the pollution associated with death, there seems to have been little horror or fear attached to the corpse qua corpse in Greek thought,[86] and interpretations that focus on miasma as the inspiration for funerary laws tend to ignore the fact that the living did not seem to have been in any terrible hurry to dispose of the dead. Rather, the surviving laws indicate that it was the *funerals,* not death itself, that were potentially dangerous to the political, social, and psychological stability of the community, so much so that Solon felt compelled to restrict them. As we have already noted, a climate of political violence and disturbance characterized the end of the seventh century at Athens (and elsewhere in the Greek world).[87] The extravagant funeral could serve as a vehicle to remind the kin of the deceased and the members of the *polis* generally of the injury to the victim of such a political murder; it might also have been an occasion to announce the intentions of his aggrieved *oikos* to exact justice from the deceased's killers.[88]

Drakon's homicide legislation of 621[89] appears to represent an attempt to regularize and control the possibly endless cycle of murder and revenge, such as might arise in the aftermath of a failed putsch and the slaughter of a would-be tyrant's followers, as had occurred in 632.[90] In the surviving law, we find that Drakon moved to control the exercise of *lex talionis* that appears to have operated prior to his legislation, as he stipulates that all those who have killed previously (*hoi de proteron ktenantes*) were to be bound by his law (*en toide toi thesmoi enekhesthon*).[91] The legislation of 621 may have done nothing more than require an aggrieved party to gain state sanction for a retaliatory killing: the kinsmen of a victim had to make a proclamation in the *agora* against the killer, while the prosecution fell to a wide circle of kinsmen and phratry members.[92] The "fifty-one" (most likely the *ephêtai* mentioned earlier and subsequently in lines 17 and 35–36 of the inscription) were responsible for conviction, and in that event the homicide became an *atimos* and thus beyond the public or private protections of the community or the claims of his kin to reciprocal violence. In such a case, it would be in the best interest of the offender to withdraw from the community (precisely the scenario envisioned by the law for either the original killer or one who would exact revenge against him; the killer is encouraged to stay away from frontier markets, games, and Amphictyonic sacrifices, where he might accidentally encounter his victim's relations and thus was subject to being killed or arrested himself).[93] As long as the killer remained outside Athens and the arenas prohibited by the law, anyone who engaged in retaliatory murder against him would now face the same penalties. Removing the offender before the shedding of further blood, prohibiting the automatic exercise of self-help, and defining the mechanisms by which the will of the community might be expressed could represent means for formalizing the potentially decisive pressure of public opinion[94] we examined in Chapter 3. It is also perhaps noteworthy in this respect that while kinsmen had to make the proclamation, phratry members were also to participate in the prosecution; could this have been meant to draw more of the community into the decision, or even to discourage frivolous actions by requiring the support of those outside the circle of kinsmen? The evidence does not admit us to go beyond speculation on this point but, whatever the case, tensions remained in the body politic of Athens after Drakon's legislation, and in trying to stabilize the community a generation later, Solon apparently felt compelled to retain Drakon's homicide law and additionally to restrict certain funerary practices that may have played a role in exacerbating those tensions.

We should like to know a great deal more about homicide law from the rest of the Greek world in this era, but the notices are thin. Gortynian law is of no help, as the Great Code, for all its comprehensiveness, remarkably does not treat the issue of homicide. The lawgiver Androdamas of Rhegion, Aristotle tells us, framed laws regarding heiresses and laws regarding murder, but adds—rather unhelpfully at this remove—there was nothing peculiar about his legislation.[95] Whether we are to infer from this that his homicide regulations resembled Athenian ones with which Aristotle might have been most familiar is impossible to say.[96] A sixth-century inscription from Sicily preserves another homicide law, perhaps even one of Kharondas.[97] Aside from the securely attested words for murder (*phon-*) and death ([*th*]*anatos*), the text is too fragmentary to permit legal analysis.

Predictably, then, the regulation of murder was not strictly an Athenian problem, and other Archaic legislators beyond Drakon tried to effect regulations regarding it. Several factors no doubt motivated removing the treatment of homicide from the realm of private, traditional redress to more formal procedures. As we noticed in Chapter 3, the ideal Homeric/early Archaic age community was one in which the consequences of murder were contained and submitted to the wider community for its adjudication, as in the trial depicted on the Shield of Achilles. However, the emotional responses to insults to one's honor and/or an impulse for revenge could easily override more peaceful considerations, raising the specter of wholesale slaughter engulfing an entire community. In this context, it is worth noting Aristotle's report of a very old and, as he saw it, savage law from Kyme in Aeolis.[98] According to Aristotle, the provision for the trial of murder stated that, so long as the prosecutor on the charge could produce a certain number of his own relatives to serve witness, then the accused was declared guilty on the charge. Such measures regarding homicide (*ta phonika nomos*)[99] found their root in customary rules of kin assistance and were not likely to lead to satisfactory resolutions: at least on Aristotle's account, this Kymean law seems little more than a barely rationalized substitute for household-on-household violence.

We cannot, of course, consider homicide legislation in a vacuum. A funeral followed the death of a member of the community, and here also existed the potential for disrupting social and political stability, especially if the slain man was from an important household and had died as a result of violent rivalry. Thus, Solon and other early legislators sought to regulate funerary practice; at Athens, especially, we can imagine the urgency ca. 600: in an atmosphere crackling with the electricity of impending civil war, there remained in the background the hostility resulting from the massacre of the Kylonians. In addition to the potential for advertising murder and vendetta, the pre-Solonian elite funeral at Athens was an important and central aspect of the circumstances surrounding the demise of the deceased. Before Solon's legislation, funerals provided the important family and their supporters with an opportunity to demonstrate the power and largesse of the dead man as well as that of the kin he left behind, regardless of how he may have expired. Furthermore, the aristocratic funeral gave the friends and relatives of the deceased a venue for praising the living as well as the dead and likewise a chance to decry their enemies. The centrality of, and the critical role played by, the funeral as an advertisement of political and social influence is further demonstrated by the transformation of aristocratic commemoration after Solon had outlawed the ostentatious funeral. Once the law required elites to shift their energies away from funerary rites, they showcased their efforts and resources through a new type of commemorative and competitive display of reverence for the important dead, the ostentatious grave marker.

Solon's legislation gives us a sense of what he found troublesome in elite funerals at Athens. Plutarch provides the most complete description of his funerary laws. The ancient biographer tells us that Solon forbade the tearing of one's flesh while mourning, the use of rehearsed laments, and the bewailing of anyone besides the deceased at the gravesite.[100] Furthermore, Solon did not permit the sacrifice of an ox to the dead or the placing of more than three cloaks with the body; he also prohibited approaching the graves of others except at the time of burial,[101] and presumably Plutarch means that one was permitted to approach only the grave of the person presently to be buried. In addition, general legislation applying to public appearances of women, who predominated in funerals,[102] would have applied by extension to the *ekphora*; Solon banned the wearing of more than three garments by women when in public, nor were they to carry more than an obol's worth of food and drink.[103]

In examining what would appear to be a late fifth-century, Athenian-inspired law from Ioulis,[104] we find that such expense restrictions surely do not indicate an attempt at sumptuary law. This particular measure places a cap on funeral equipment of 100 drachmas, well beyond the means of average citizens.[105] One recent commentator has suggested that the law of Ioulis has political overtones but then makes the rather puzzling assertion that while the regulations may have grown out of attempts to combat aristocratic ostentation in funerary practice, the ultimate purpose of the law had been to preserve the good order of the *polis*.[106] This would suggest that the two were unconnected, which I do not believe to have been the case. Limiting expenditure in funerals to a cap still beyond the means of most citizens need not have been intended, of course, to control the expenditure of resources on the dead in general. Such a ceiling could have a purpose more political than economic, in restraining the expenditure of those families for whom wealth was not a concern and who could turn a funeral into a public spectacle not in harmony with the desired *kosmos* of the city.

Demosthenes provides more specific information about certain aspects of Solon's funerary legislation. In *Against Makartatos*, the speaker directs a clerk to read out the text of a Solonian law:[107] from this citation we learn that the lawgiver restricted the participation of women under the age of 60 in the *prothesis* and the *ekphora* to those who were within the degree of children of cousins to the deceased. Clues indicate that Solon's concern extended to all relatives, since the speaker notes the lawgiver's earnestness with respect to relatives and does so in the masculine gender, in this case apparently encompassing both men and women, as the law that follows explicitly refers to the latter. The nature of the case seems to have dictated the speaker's emphasis on female participation, since he was engaged in a dispute over the estate of a certain Hagnias, between parties making claims through different female relatives. It does not seem unreasonable to infer from this passage that Solon sought to restrict participation in the *prothesis* and *ekphora* to the circle of fairly close relatives, both male and female. Other specifics emerge from the text of the Solonian law quoted in Demosthenes: the family was to lay out the corpse indoors and carry it out on the following day before sunrise, the men leading the way and the women following.

Finally, we hear from Cicero who, drawing on Demetrios of Phaleron, confirms that Solon legislated against the tearing of cheeks by women and the wearing of more than three garments while mourning. He adds that the lawgiver made no provisions with respect to graves themselves, aside from prohibiting their damage or destruction, and stating that the remains of one person might not replace those of another.[108]

Three sets of concerns emerge from our evidence regarding Solon's funeral legislation. The first has to do with the defacing of grave markers and the disturbing of deposited remains. It may be that Drakon's legislation of a generation before had frustrated the desires of some to pursue vendettas among the living, and perhaps such individuals had sought their vengeance upon the monuments of their dead rivals. This is only speculation, and it may be that in this case Solon was not responding to a specific problem, although Plutarch informs us of the exhuming of dead members of the family of Megakles, the author of the Kylonian massacre, and the subsequent removal of their remains from Attica.[109] The same author also states that Solon made it illegal to speak ill of the dead in public,[110] and it may well be that he wished to ensure piety and respect for the dead in political speech. However, the restriction on defaming the dead appears to have had a specific purpose within the context of early sixth-century Athens; I return to this point shortly.

Second, the lawgiver took aim at conspicuous display of resources during the funeral. The check on the raiment of both the living in the *ekphora* and the dead inside the grave indicates prior extravagance. Indeed, the prohibition on the sacrifice of oxen to the dead could only have directly affected households of more than middling economic means. The restriction to relatives within the degree of cousins' children also constituted a limit on expenditure for elite funerals: it put an end to the traditional practice of hiring professional mourners,[111] a measure that would make sense given Solon's prohibition on the singing of prepared or rehearsed laments.

But more important than disrespect for the dead or the limits on expenditure, and I would argue central to his program of funerary reform, was Solon's attempt to eliminate public spectacle from the Athenian funeral. This concern is the common thread that runs through all of his attested laws with respect to funerals. The restriction to one day for the *prothesis*, now held indoors without fail and limited to kin, clearly sought to privatize what had previously been a much more public affair.[112] Solon's concern to limit the *prothesis* indicates that previously it could have lasted much longer, in full view of passersby who would witness the striking scene of numerous mourners and musicians bewailing the dead in prepared laments.

The *ekphora*, judging from the practices Solon sought to curtail, would have been no less dazzling in the late seventh century. In full light of day, the funeral procession would trail through the city, its ranks swelled by perhaps scores of relatives, mourners and musicians, friends and associates, noisily proclaiming their grief as blood streamed down the torn cheeks of richly clad women. Stopping at every intersection, the cortege of the *ekphora* would attract great attention to itself, and thus to the deceased and his family.

Finally, at the gravesite, the spectacular flames of a primary cremation[113] would be followed by the slaughter of an ox or oxen. Beyond its cultic and religious significance, this sacrifice also represented an opportunity for the dead man's family to demonstrate its largesse to a wider segment of the community. The meat from a single ox (the largely undesirable portions having been offered to the gods) would have fed a great many people: certainly enough for the family, friends, and professional mourners, but also anyone who had joined the procession as it made its way to the cemetery with an ox (or oxen) in tow. To the large group assembled at the gravesite, the members of the deceased's family would deliver speeches in praise not only of the commemorated dead, but also of the surviving important men of the family, and no doubt of the glory of previously buried generations. It is easy to imagine, as well, that the important family took advantage of the opportunity to decry the family's rivals, living and dead.[114]

Those aspects of the elite funeral that heightened its spectacle particularly concerned Solon; by turning the burial of the important dead into a public event, the members of an aristocratic family could have advertised the greatness of their household, showcasing their wealth and influence, and used an emotionally charged setting to proclaim their own importance and at the same time slander their enemies. Solon recognized the destabilizing elements involved in such commemorations and tried to eliminate them from prevailing practice. No longer would the funeral be a place for the elite to display their wealth and power, proclaim the merits or deficiencies of anyone other than the deceased, or to distribute largesse (and attach additional followers to themselves) in the form of communal meals following the sacrifice. Solon apparently worried about the effect of such spectacles on the body politic, and with good reason. Less than half a century later, Peisistratos could use public spectacle as a means of seizing power, however briefly, for the second time.[115]

Competitive commemoration of the elite dead had become an integral part of aristocratic politics at Athens, so much so that Solon's legislation effectively redirected elite efforts in this regard; he did not, nor could he, stamp out this practice, but only the expression it took. The transformation and refocusing of commemoration around the time of Solon demonstrates clearly this fact. Previous to Solon's legislation, graves and their markers were fairly simple. The typical grave in Attica took the form of a mound, with a larger and more elaborate one measuring anywhere from 6 to 10 meters in diameter and 1 meter in height.[116] Such a tumulus would contain several generations of burials and was frequently associated with offering ditches. The latter have produced animal bones,[117] and it appears these were the tombs of the elite, where the family commemorated not only the recently deceased member but also its ancestors, several generations of whom lay inside. Markers for such tombs, however, were relatively humble: a simple limestone stele mounted in a limestone block, accompanied by a ceramic vessel (often a krater or amphora) for libations to the dead.[118] Overall, the physical monument was unassuming, because the funeral itself was the focus for the resources of the living.

A significant shift occurs in the archaeological record ca. 600, however, and indicates that the energies Athenian elites once dedicated to the funeral, they now redirected to monuments, as a result no doubt of Solon's laws. Further, the expense and execution of the new competitive display, based on the grave monument itself, provides an idea of the type of expense and spectacle previously committed to the funeral before Solon's restriction of funerary ostentation. The prevalence of large, round burial mounds gave way to elaborate grave stelai.[119] Large, marble grave markers now predominate, topped with cavetto capitals and sphinxes carved in the round, and quite expensive in their production: even the earliest phase of this type of monument, dubbed Ia by Gisela Richter and dating from ca. 600 to 575, offers examples of sphinxes measuring up to 55.5 cm tall, 47 cm wide, and 11 to 17 cm thick.[120] The workmanship of the pieces is typically impressive. The sphinx and capital sat atop the stele proper, which probably measured up to four times the height of the sphinx itself.[121]

In the following phase, Ib (ca. 575–550), Athenian elites employed increasingly elaborate grave monuments. Among the surviving examples, the trend is toward even larger and more finely carved sphinxes, as well as the evolution of the capitals.[122] Still of the cavetto type, the capitals now exhibit carved figures as well as decorative elements such as palmettes, lotuses, and volutes. One capital depicts a status symbol of the commemorated, the deceased's mounted squire, which presumably stood above a stele portrait of the deceased himself, as is the case on several extant examples.[123] For phase Ic (ca. 550–525), most of the evidence survives in fragmentary stelai and capitals.[124] One restored monument—sphinx, capital, and stele—surpasses 4.2 m in height.[125]

I would suggest that the sudden shift in Attic grave marker types around the time of Solon is no coincidence, nor is their increasing size, elaboration, and expense over the first three-quarters of the sixth century an accident;[126] the trend speaks to the type of ephemeral displays that had previously characterized the commemoration of the elite dead. Once Solon had removed public spectacle from the aristocratic funeral and therefore ended its utility as a means of political and social competition, elite families after Solon's legislation now directed their resources toward grave markers in commemorating the important dead. These monuments, typically bearing inscriptions naming the deceased and those who buried him, still signaled to passersby the power and wealth of the deceased's family.[127] That aristocrats continued to put substantial resources toward the commemoration of their dead signifies the centrality to elite culture of memorializing the dead prior to and subsequent to Solon's legislation. Before Solon, the ritual of the spectacular funeral not only honored the deceased but provided the opportunity for the aristocratic family to demonstrate their own greatness while attacking their rivals in front of large and emotionally charged audiences. Solon recognized the danger of these festivities to the precarious equilibrium among the groups who wielded power in Athens and sought to eliminate them from prevailing practice.

Once again, then, we find measures promulgated to regulate competition among the elites. In his attempt to restrict potentially volatile displays of aristocratic power and friction, Solon aimed to sublimate particularly emotional and, in some circumstances, perhaps hostile expressions to quieter forms of competition. While one leading scholar has interpreted this turn of events as a victory of the *polis* in asserting state authority over the actions of even its most prominent citizens,[128] I believe that there is a danger of engaging in an institutional fallacy. Citizens constituted the *polis*, and some of the individuals among them were responsible for the actions that curtailed aristocratic competition and its worst impulses and consequences. Was the regulation and containment of violent elite competition beneficial to the community at large? Doubtless it was, and we may well imagine that the wider body of nonelite citizens countenanced measures that promoted stability with no small amount of approval and relief. But ultimately, it was the leading citizens who were most responsible for drafting those measures and enforcing them in the Archaic *polis*. How they went about doing so, and how they shared that responsibility, was therefore also a major concern of early legislative activity.

4—Political Office and Magisterial Misconduct

Limitation on the exercise of political power through magisterial offices that developed in the Archaic period represented an important focus of early Greek law. The exact origins of official positions within the governing structures of early Greek *poleis* will probably always remain obscure. But, it appears to be the case that elites, known formally or informally as *basileis*, *aristoi*, or some other aristocratic designation, supervised the *polis* from its beginnings. Such men acted as judges and commanded whatever military force the community mustered; they wielded power and influence in an environment accentuated by competition among themselves for the material and political resources of the *polis*; and, by the seventh century, the worst of all possible worlds for the aristocracy was the emergence from their number of a single individual who might dominate the political life of the community as a tyrant.[129]

With defined offices came defined competencies and responsibilities, and many laws betray a concern with constraining individuals from possessing too much power or abusing what powers they legitimately held. At Athens, as is well known, civil, religious, and military authority was attached to three discrete magistracies, ostensibly preventing their concentration in the hands of a single member of the office-holding elite. Other *poleis* also offer examples of magisterial regulation, principally with regard to duration and iteration of tenure, the extent of power inherent in any particular magistracy, and penalties and procedures for abuse of mandate or dereliction of duty. Such attempts will have been directed primarily by elites toward their peers, whose prolonged and uncomfortably effective service (or, alternatively, their inability or unwillingness to execute their duties) could corrode the management of their political relationships with one another and with the wider community.

The earliest surviving legal inscription from the Greek world—from Dreros in Crete—dates from the middle of the seventh century (perhaps as early as 660)[130] and addresses specifically the problem of iteration of tenure in the office of *kosmos*,[131] a principal official at Dreros.[132] An outgoing *kosmos* was not to hold that position officially or—of greater concern to those who drafted the law—continue to perform one of the chief duties of the *kosmos*, the dispensation of judgments in disputes, for ten years. If he did act as a judge while out of office, he was subject to a fine equal to twice the amount of the decision he had rendered and was automatically disqualified for life from serving again as *kosmos*, possibly losing his citizen rights altogether.[133]

Pierre Demargne and Henri van Effenterre believed this law's designers intended it as a device to prevent tyranny, particularly given its proscription against iteration of the office within ten years.[134] The question of tyranny aside, it seems such a law could simply be aimed at assuring the regular sharing of the office among the Drerian elite and preventing its domination by one *oikos* (or a small group of sympathetic *oikoi*), since it would have been difficult for a single family to provide enough eligible individuals to hold the office through a cycle of ten years.[135] Michael Gagarin once posited that the law was directed against (or at least inspired by) the attempt of one particular *kosmos* to use the power of his office to thwart Dreros' established government; he further inferred that the *kosmos*' judicial role was his most important and that a *kosmos* might have used his role and reputation for personal enrichment outside of office.[136] More recently, however, Gagarin has argued that the writing of the Drerian law is a manifestation of the will of the *polis* (whatever that meant at Dreros ca. 660), since the rule against iteration was otherwise of interest only to a few and that "current and potential *kosmoi* could easily follow the rule if it were communicated to them orally, and if someone were going to violate the rule, it seems unlikely that a written version would be a more powerful deterrent than an oral version."[137]

In my opinion, on this matter Gagarin was closer to the truth two decades ago than in his most recent study. His latest interpretation of the Drerian law rests on three fundamental assumptions that do not bear scrutiny. First, he presumes that the law modified "an earlier situation in which there was no restriction or perhaps a different time limit on repeating as *kosmos*."[138] I do not share his confidence that the magistracy had existed long enough for understood or accepted rules about it to have developed at all. Arguments against a much deeper history for the office would be, admittedly, as speculative as the assumption in favor of it. However, the only relatively secure date we have for the origins of an annual magistracy elsewhere in the Greek world, at Athens, puts the beginnings of that office ca. 683. The gaps in the record for Athens prevent any reconstruction regarding rules (or lack thereof) on iteration, though at least as late as the early 650s it was still possible for the same man (Miltiades) to serve twice within a six-year period; and as late as the 580s, one man (Damasias) could hold on to the office for two consecutive one-year terms and then some, necessitating his removal from office by force though not resulting in memories of him as a tyrant.[139] Dreros is not Athens, of course, but the latter example should encourage caution about the nature of early magisterial offices and any "constitutional rules" regarding the same.

A second assumption reveals itself in Gagarin's statement that I have quoted above, namely that potential *kosmoi* could follow orally transmitted rules. Fair enough, but *would* they? The mere fact of the establishment of the law suggests that at least some of those who had held or might hold the office did not follow whatever orally transmitted (or broadly understood) rules might have existed, and our general examination of the context of seventh-century changes militates against them doing so. Even if Gagarin were correct that the main impetus behind the law was the Drerian nonelite flexing its political muscle, it would be odd indeed that the citizens would select this particular issue were it not demonstrably problematic or perceived as such. Restricting iteration is one matter; outlawing continued arrogation of the authority of the *kosmos* after his term of office is quite another, and it seems more likely that this problem was one that would not have been notional or imaginary but rather based on past experience of at least one *kosmos* having behaved in such a manner.

Finally, we must ask who benefited from this measure. It is certainly true that the community at large would have suffered at large from unrestrained aristocratic competition for power and influence, and therefore they may have sought to regulate the destructive impulses of their elite leaders. If such was the principal motivation for this Drerian law, then that state of affairs, it seems to me, would vitiate Gagarin's assumption that those eligible for the *kosmos*-ship exercised self-discipline in this matter. If such violent (or at least questionable) competition did not exist, then we must ask why "the *polis*" would have thought it necessary to enact this legislation or how the citizens thought it self-serving in the first place. As Gagarin himself has argued elsewhere, Herodotus' story of Deiokes records one Greek meme about the origin of kingship and lawgiving, that the decisions of one particular nobleman were so wise and popular that everyone preferred his decisions to all others.[140] One would indeed presume that any given former *kosmos* of Dreros could have only continued to act in an unofficial judicial capacity in the event that many citizens preferred his rulings to those of his successors in office: why then would nonelites have sought to curtail such a man's ability to offer settlements they found preferable to those handed down by his sociopolitical peers? Further, there is the internal evidence of the law itself: while the enactment clause of the law indicates that "the polis has decided" (*had' ewade poli*), we have already noted that we cannot baldly assume that this term was all that inclusive (Chapter 4.2, above). Indeed, the end of the law suggests that the major role of those outside the office-holding elite (if, in fact, that is how we should understand the *damioi* and the "twenty of the *polis*"[141]) was as witnesses to the agreement, perhaps in the event that members of the office-holding class disputed the new arrangement.

It seems rather that the most sensible interpretation is that this written law aimed to establish a new rule where no clear norm or practice existed before and that it determined to prevent the domination of this office or the informal arrogation of its powers by a given aristocrat after his term as *kosmos* ended. It is entirely possible that the community at large appreciated the fact that the law would eliminate judicial confusion, but the primary beneficiaries of the law will have surely been those individuals who wanted to ensure the rotation of the office and its influence among themselves. Whatever prompted the measure—the prevention of tyranny, the curtailment of a single family's power, or the discouragement of resource accumulation by an aristocratic individual through his role as a magistrate—the implication is clear. The primary concern was to keep some members (or one) of the elite from distancing himself from the collective, probably represented by the "twenty of the *polis*" sitting, however informally, as an aristocratic council. Elsewhere in Archaic Crete, the *polis* of Gortyn sought to prevent frequent iteration of important offices among the elite, though we do not have the pertinent penalties for violation.[142] The purpose appears the same as at Dreros: limiting the scope for ambitious misuse of magisterial authority to gain political advantages at the expense of other members of the elite.

Evidence is otherwise spotty for the penalties imposed on magistrates for abuse of power or dereliction of duty, but it provides glimpses into political dispositions at several *poleis*. A pair of inscriptions from Arcadia, perhaps Pheneos, describes a sacral infraction involving the obligatory dedication to Demeter Thesmophoros of "colorful raiment" worn by a woman and the punishment to fall upon the magistrate who allowed it to happen.[143] A local official, the demiurge, was liable to a fine of 30 drachmas for failing to prevent the offense and for having neglected his supervisory responsibilities.[144]

Furthermore, should he refuse or fail to pay the fine, he fell under the charge of *asebeia* and its associated stain for ten years,[145] presumably preventing him from serving in public office during that time.

Also from the Peloponnesus, at Olympia, there is a group of inscriptions that probably dates to the first half of the sixth century and further demonstrates the concern to define and delimit magisterial power.[146] Of special interest is a law that names a certain official who is guaranteed protection and security, and offers other insights regarding the sanctions for violating this safeguard for the designated individual and his descendants. If anyone were to curse him, that man was to be exiled. Beyond this general statement, however, are provisions regarding the responsibilities of those in charge of the affairs of the *polis*. If the man in the highest office—*to megiston telos*—or the *basileis* did not impose the penalties for any infractions of this measure, they were to pay a fine of ten minae, dedicated to Olympian Zeus and payable to the *hellanodikai*, who were responsible for imposing the penalty. The demiurges were to impose "other penalties." In the event that these penalties were neglected or ignored, the *hellanodikai* and/or the demiurges were to pay double when they rendered their accounts.[147]

Of similar intent is a series of measures preserved from seventh-century Tiryns that regulates the activities of officials known as *platiwoinoi*, *hiaromnemones*, *platiwoinarkhoi*, and *epignomones*.[148] The exact roles of these officials are obscured by the quality of the text and the etymology of the titles, but what does emerge from the inscription is an attempt at oversight. As Osborne has noted, the "penalties . . . are the very opposite of imaginative—fines all around."[149] The hierarchy among the various officials is not entirely clear, but perhaps that is the point. Aside from the (probably) supervisory role the *platiwoinarkhoi* played vis-à-vis the *platiwoinoi* (as the etymology would suggest), there is no means of determining what relationship either of these offices enjoyed with that of the *hiaromnemon*, whose title suggests the types of sacred remembrancers we encountered in Chapter 4 and who perhaps served a significant secretarial role, or the *epignomon* (possibly a judge, as a "knower about [things]"). Aside from the language of the inscription, which indicates a single *hiaromnemon* and only one *epignomon* at any given time, but multiple *platiwoinoi* and *platiwoinarkhoi*, little else on the stone allows for certitude.

A few features nevertheless deserve highlighting. As early as the seventh century in Tiryns, we may note the emergence of a system of checks and balances—however unimaginative—as an attempt by the drafters of the law to impose disincentives for the shirking of responsibilities and the attempt to ignore resultant fines. There was apparently little opportunity to escape punishment once an official was found guilty. The *hiaromnemon* was in charge of collecting the fine owed by a *platiwoinarkhos* (or several of them), either for his own negligence or for his refusal to exact the thirty *medimnoi* owed by an errant *platiwoinos*. Furthermore, the *hiaromnemon* was to exact the penalty wherever the people (*damoi*) had decided to hold the court. After a difficult lacuna in the text, on the other hand, we learn that the *epignomon* had the power to impose a fine on the "mob" (*oqlos*) if they did not provide the penalty to the *platiwoinarkhoi*, presumably from their own resources (*woikothen*, from the household). Whether this refers to the same problem addressed in the rest of the inscription or the text had turned in the interim to another matter, is impossible to say. However, we may infer that the reference to the "people" deciding where to hold the court should not necessarily indicate popular political or judicial power. They may have played a role in the conviction of certain officials, but the fines and penalties were levied and enforced by aristocratic office holders. We may likewise note the distinction between the *damoi*, who have some form of judicial influence, and the *oqlos*, who are more passive and liable to pay off some sort of penalty to the *platiwoinarkhoi*. The explicit distinction between the *damoi* and the *oqlos* should caution against reading the former label too inclusively when it appears in Archaic legal inscriptions.

The overall impression provided by the laws on office holding in early Greece is that authors of statutes sought to define and regulate the ability of individuals from among the elite to hold and wield power. Of greatest concern were the limitation of tenure in office, a set of severe disincentives for the abuse or neglect of one's official duties, and the means for enforcing penalties for abrogation of the rules. While we should not underestimate the long-term effect such measures had for ensuring the general welfare and political stability of the *polis* and its citizens, the motivation for drafting such laws surely was the same as for the other measures we have examined in this chapter: constraining the ability of any one member (or one family) of the elite to put himself in a position wherein he might out-compete his peers and establish a position of supremacy. As with the laws we have examined elsewhere in this chapter, the aim of the measures regarding office holding was to circumscribe the concentration of another important resource of aristocratic competition, in this case magisterial authority and power.

In Chapter 4.1, I suggested eight criteria that must prove valid if we are to accept any democratizing or public impulse for the appearance of written law in early Greece. Having examined preserved statutes from the Archaic age, I wish to return now to those criteria that I left aside in that earlier chapter: the writing of law was the result of dissatisfaction among a particular segment of the population, namely the *demos* (understood primarily to be the hoplite class, but not exclusive of a growing artisan urban interest), hence the written laws that the lower orders of the *polis* wrested from the elite should in fact represent a set of concerns reflective of previous opportunities for aristocratic abuse under the purely customary-oral arrangement, and we should not, therefore, necessarily expect to find any laws that aim at the preservation of corporate aristocratic preeminence and privilege, nor should the laws overwhelmingly concern themselves with matters of greater interest to the wealthy and powerful than the average citizen. The measures we have reviewed in this chapter disprove the last of the preceding criteria. What the surviving evidence indicates is a preoccupation with rules designed to discourage the accumulation of resources into the hands of a circle of households (or an individual household) within the preeminent elite and the destructive competition that such accumulation might engender. With regard to property holding, this concern manifested itself through attempts to preserve the existing number of *oikoi*, to prevent the abandonment of *oikoi* whose property might then devolve to the control of another elite *oikos*, and to make extremely difficult the passage of property outside the patrilineal succession of a family.

In the case of Athens, we have seen how Solon attempted to limit the expense and public display that characterized the aristocratic funeral. The centrality of the funeral to the competition of the elite at Athens has been demonstrated above, and Solon—empowered by the elite as well as the commoners of Athens to make laws—believed it necessary to restrict this form of elite display and *agôn*. I have suggested that the funeral had become a symbol, if not a constant reminder, of the elite strife and bloodshed that had haunted Athens since the Kylonian conspiracy of 632. Establishing equilibrium among the elite will have been a prerequisite in Solon's mind for stabilizing Athens. As I have argued in Chapter 4.3, we should be very careful about ascribing too much populist sentiment to a man who left the wealthy in charge and the Areopagus in a transcendent position above the constitution.

The elites of the early Greek *poleis* also attempted, as we have seen, to limit the degree to which any one of their number might exercise power through the emergent magistracies of the *polis*. This is a concern primarily for those elites who held or hoped to hold magisterial power, and only secondarily will the nonelites have considered this problem to be of importance. Sole rule by a member of the aristocracy was not necessarily a cause for lament among the nonelites of a *polis* that fell under the sway of a tyrant. Indeed, despite the self-conscious disdain professed for tyranny in later sources, more than one Classical author found himself trying to reconcile the "evil" of tyranny with a general and persistent sense of tyrants as "civic-minded" and "populist." Therefore, the rules regarding limitations on magisterial power should not be construed as serving the conscious interests of the nonelites searching for some sort of constitutional safeguards. Furthermore, the other rules we have examined were even less reflective of what we might imagine as the concerns of the *demos* in the early Archaic period. Restrictions on the easy movement of property, especially its accumulation, the prohibitions on the marriage of daughters outside patrilineal descent groups, the legal prescription on the numbers of *oikoi* within a community, all of these discouraged upward social and economic mobility, and sought to preserve for the elite their wealth where they believed it belonged: in their hands, roughly distributed so that no one of them would gain potentially insurmountable competitive advantages.

As for presumptions of popular dissatisfaction, we cannot deny that some people were unhappy. We might return briefly to our friend Hesiod in seventh-century Askra and recall his heartfelt rant against the injustice perpetrated in his hometown and nearby Thespiae. Solon refers to the disquiet caused by economic hardship at the turn of the sixth century in Athens. These sources, however, are rhetorical and meant to serve particular agendas. They are, for that reason alone, difficult to take completely at face value. What complicates them further is the preponderance of evidence we have amassed against the notion that written laws could have been the response to democratic agitation or popular discontent. The earliest written laws of Greece were written by elites, aimed at addressing their anxieties over sharing power and preeminence in a new social and political creation, and were not meant to salve the wounds of injustice that some Greeks, such as Hesiod, may have occasionally felt. Some of the measures enacted in early *poleis* may have benefitted nonelites as well, but it is difficult to identify any trend in Archaic Greek law that suggests this happened at the expense of elite power or influence. We may simply recall Plato's remonstrance, "let no one persuade us, friends, that a *polis* could change its laws more quickly and more easily by another way than through the governance of those holding power; neither at the present has such happened nor could it happen hereafter."[150] As the preceding study has shown, it was the elites of the early *polis*, for reasons of their own choosing, who decided to take the step of writing down their communities' first statutes.

CHAPTER SEVEN

Conclusion

Writing and Authority

Roger Cotterrell, one of the leading thinkers in current legal studies, has stressed approaching the study of law from the perspective of its relationship to the community, especially in understanding "law's role in fostering the kind of highly developed trusting relationships that are fundamental to a society at ease with itself in conditions of rapid change and increasing cultural and social diversity."[1] Were we to change "diversity" for "complexity," the last part of his statement could apply easily to the Greek world in the eighth and early seventh centuries.

The rapid changes that occurred during the period had profound consequences for the traditional legal culture reflected in the epics and the hymns. In particular, these transformations shook the elites. Conflict and competition among a community's leading figures had, of course, characterized the Homeric world. What is so remarkable, as trouble-case processual analysis of Homer's surviving texts and other early literature reveals, is how rarely disputes led to open violence, even when highly contentious issues were involved. Greek literature nearly begins with regicide: the deeply and justifiably offended Achilles was moments away from murdering Agamemnon, but he did not. Athena, visible only to Achilles in this scene, dissuades him from violence, but her reasons are those that Achilles could have internally worked out for himself. Agamemnon's public shaming of Achilles should meet with public shaming in return, not with bronze; the former's offense was unwarranted, and as a result, he would eventually have to pay back honor in greater measure to the son of Peleus. This course of action was consistent with other disputes we examined in Chapter 3, and Achilles acted as others who believed their grievance was so great they could not participate in the society until they received satisfaction for it, such as Meleager or Demeter: they withdrew a valuable good or service from communal enjoyment to apply pressure to the offending party.

Even in the most extreme and convoluted disputes, settlement-directed talking with a view to the welfare of the community, not violence, was the expectation. Homer's "city at peace" on the Shield of Achilles shows disputants engaged in peaceful resolution of their quarrel, with communal participation, over something as potentially combustive as blood price for a dead man. Homeric legal culture implicated the community in other ways, as we have seen. Even if the disputants' anger distorted their own sense of the norms and their rights of claiming satisfaction, their ability to pursue a grievance depended in many cases on the willingness of a support group to aid them. Violence, to judge from the epics, was something the Greeks of the Homeric world imagined as directed largely against other communities, not an internal feature of communal life, and those who did introduce violence through intentional murder were expected to flee or die. Overall, there was a functional legal culture among Homer's Greeks, rooted in long-standing norms and the importance of public participation in dispute.

However, Odysseus' actions at the end of the *Odyssey*, and the awareness of other possibilities resulting from them, betray the breaking down of that legal culture as the Homeric world ended and the world of the *polis* replaced it. Here we find unfettered violence, as when the son of Laertes gave no thought to the claims of the suitors. As we have seen, the suitors may have acted arrogantly, but in the web of communications about social relations and the norms of Ithaca, they had a valid claim for wooing Penelope and pressuring Telemakhos, as demonstrated by the Ithacans' indifference to Telemakhos' pleas and the suitors' urgent belief that the community would rally to their side if news of Odysseus' butchery in the halls could reach the folk. Odysseus paid no heed to the expectations of the community, nor did he exhibit any concern for the reaction of the support groups of his victims. When the suitors offered generous restitution for the offense to his honor and his wealth, obviously believing the offer would save them, Odysseus rejected it. For all of these reasons, Odysseus and his household should have fled into exile, as the father of Antinoös expected they would. Instead, Odysseus chose to stand his ground, despite the fact that his doing so would most likely lead to the virtual annihilation of the community's elite and many of their supporters. Only divine intervention, again in the person of Athena but this time visible to all, awkwardly and artificially stops the impending slaughter.

Acute competition and violence among the elite was abetted by the fundamental changes taking place, all of them in the context of the developing *polis*. These transformations profoundly affected the relations of elite households with one another and the wider community. Many *poleis* were the result of separate communities joining together through *synoikismos*, a process that entailed its own challenges regarding the reconciliation of different norms, practices, and traditions. Furthermore, it widened the stage on which previously local, village elites would now have to compete but also cooperate in the embryonic political structures of the *polis*. Their competition required new strategies and resources: land was now a commodity, wealth in general had increased, and the disembedding of the economy also meant that the attraction of followers would proceed along different lines than before. The inherited rule base from the world of the epics provided no obvious guidance for many of the problems that arose in the late eighth and early seventh centuries, and the innovative and improvised behaviors that resulted led to tensions and conflicts that would have found, at best, incomplete answers in older norms. Already by the second quarter of the seventh century, the competition for power and prestige had issued in struggles that could turn violent and potentially end with the worst of all possible outcomes for an agonistic elite: the rule of a tyrant. So daunting was the prospect of tyranny that, according to the tradition, Athenians under the leadership of the archon Megakles in 632 violated even promises of safe-conduct based on religious sanctuary. If communities ultimately find their validity, viability, and stability in "mutual interpersonal trust,"[2] there was apparently little of it among the elites of Greece's seventh-century *poleis*.

The traditional repository of moral authority had been the epic tradition itself: as *muthoi*, epic lays embodied authoritative speech acts, all the more for that they served as a "tribal encyclopedia," preserving and transmitting received wisdom across the generations and serving as a model for social relations and behaviors. Until its commitment to writing, beginning in the eighth century, the epic tradition had the inherent ability to mutate with circumstances, maintaining its relevance to its performers and audiences; and, before the transformations of that century, the changes with which the epics had to keep pace remained gradual in the vast majority of the Greek world. The advent of writing, however, initiated the slow fossilization and diffusion of the "canonical" epics, a process already largely complete by the early seventh century, even if the final product did not formally appear until the middle of the sixth. The great transformation of the eighth and early seventh centuries involved changes so dramatic that the usual processes of epic reinvention may not have been able to keep pace in any event. But the fixation of previously oral and elastic narrative traditions rendered impossible the use of epic as a tribal encyclopedia. As Greek society continued to develop and undergo many fundamental alterations, moving forward ever more rapidly, the epics now increasingly stood still.

If writing had been part of the problem, calcifying the stories through which Greeks had previously transmitted and reinforced their social norms and ideals, it also suggested part of the solution. Written law did not arise, I have argued, out of class conflict; insofar as our sources speak of socioeconomic grievances motivating written law, they do so in the terms of and perspectives from the fourth century. There is no reason to believe, based on the current state of our knowledge, that sufficient literacy prevailed to encourage the belief that written laws would secure judicial fairness or consistency; indeed, there is evidence to suggest that limited literacy led to specialist expertise that allowed scope for abuse. A theory of class conflict also assumes some sense of solidarity among the elites, and the evidence for the seventh century suggests that, if anything, the aristocrats of the early *poleis* enjoyed even less cultural and political solidarity than the leading figures of Homer had.[3] There existed no unified perception of elite interest, either for the commoners to assail or the elites themselves to protect through written law.[4]

Rather, the elites of the seventh century *poleis* used writing as a means in part to clarify old norms that were under stress, even more to draft new rules, and to invest the whole with authority. Procedure remained largely oral,[5] but the new realities of *polis* society required more than traditional norms could provide in informing judicial processes. The vast majority of the surviving Archaic laws are substantive rather than procedural, and they address elite concerns: despite the disparateness of subject material, they exhibit measures to prevent the concentration of competitive resources—economic, social, and political—which in turn could lead to unfair advantages for one segment of the aristocracy against the other, even one *oikos* against the rest.

Part of the challenge in regulating these issues was their novelty: in many cases, they were beyond the scope of anything the epics reveal as problematic or even existent in Homer's world. The offices of the *polis* may have grown out of the informal structures of leadership authority that previously prevailed, but they had changed beyond recognition. Rules regarding how often a man or his relatives could serve as *kosmos* at Dreros, or the fines owed for magisterial misconduct, or primitive checks and balances among officials, were new because the problems they addressed were relatively so themselves. Laws also treated new dimensions of older issues. The commoditization of land and other wealth made possible their accumulation through inheritance, adoption, and marriage, and across the Greek world we see attempts to stabilize the distribution of wealth and/or prevent its easy passage from the control of one *oikos* to another through these practices. Increased wealth was capable of deployment in conspicuous fashion as a way of advertising greatness and attracting followers, and one of the particularly dangerous arenas for this competition was the elite funeral. To judge from our evidence, families had begun to use the funeral procession as a means to celebrate their past, denounce their rivals, and engage in spectacular displays of wealth. These practices took on new and potentially menacing connotations in an environment of intensified and frequently violent elite competition, an atmosphere so unstable that, at Athens, clarification was even required for the treatment of intentional homicide, the one largely invariant norm in Homer that was for all intents and purposes a formal rule.

As Hölkeskamp has argued, the earliest laws of Greece responded to perceived problems that required formal address through statutes,[6] and, unlike the law codes of the Near East, Greek laws do represent legislative acts, not ideal statements of divinely inspired royal justice.[7] However, he locates the responsibility for this with the *polis*, arguing that written law was the device by which it sought to assert its supremacy over individual households and citizens. The problem, however, is that the *polis* of itself does nothing; human actors were responsible for the legislative acts we find in the record, and those human actors will have been those who exercised leadership and wielded power in the early *polis*. Occasional references in the laws to the *demos* or its equivalent, such as at Dreros and Tiryns, should not mislead. As we have had occasion to remark throughout, few scholars today would advocate plainly the theory that class conflict or a popular perception of systematic judicial abuse led the hoplite class or other nonelites to demand written law. After all, who belonged to the *demos* in many Archaic *poleis* was a matter of definition, and the evidence for participatory government before the end of the sixth century is fragmentary and obscure.[8] And though the democratizing model is no longer fashionable, we have seen that its influence is still discernible in the scholarly literature, particularly in the public model of legislation that inheres in the recent analyses of Gagarin, Papakonstantinou, and Schmitz. We return, then, to the question of agency and the maxim from Plato's *Laws* we have noted twice previously: the *polis* changed its laws most quickly and easily through the agency of those holding power,[9] and in the seventh century, those holding power were the elites.

Why, then, did the elites ruling the *poleis* turn to writing as a way of drafting new rules, of writing up the law? Part of the answer resides in the power of monumental, public texts in Greek usage generally. Writing was one means of constructing power in antiquity, though there was great diversity in the exercise of this strategy among the cultures of the ancient world.[10] In the Greek context, in both the Archaic and Classical periods, we do not see writing employed in the service of establishing religious authority as it did in other civilizations, and even in Classical Athens, texts remained peripheral to judicial procedure in all but the most specialized cases.[11] Greeks did, however, exploit the power of writing through public display, using the monumental inscription to impress the beholder through the commitment of its content to stone, as "the continuing existence of the stone meant the validity of that decision."[12] In the Archaic period, the legal inscription not only claimed its power through its monumentality and permanence, but also, because its content was inaccessible to many, it possessed almost magical qualities;[13] and, as was often the case elsewhere in the ancient world, the fact that something was written down was as important as what it said.[14]

The response to a legal inscription by its audience, however, does not solve what suggested to Greece's first legislators why they should use writing to craft new laws. After all, the Greeks had possessed the technology for a century. Our sources about early lawgivers and legal activity indicate that attempts to bring stability to elite competition, and by extension, the early *polis*, was a process of trial and error. A tradition persisted that early laws were sung, as we saw in Chapter 4.2: the *nomôidoi* of Asia Minor, the singing of Kharondas' *nomoi* in Athenian symposia, Solon's contemplation of setting his own *nomoi* to music. The reports to this effect have met with understandable skepticism since, as Gagarin has rightly noted, the surviving written laws from Archaic Greece are "prosaic in the extreme."[15] However, I would argue that the legends here deserve some credence, not only because they are completely out of keeping with later practice, but also because they make perfect sense, given the previous sources of authority. The semantic field embraced by the Greek word *nomos* was wide: it meant law, but also custom, in early usage. Given that moral authority had, for generations, been embodied in song, it is easy to imagine why those who sought to develop new norms would first attempt to set them to music. In this respect, it would perhaps be more accurate that such sung laws were more akin to maxims. However muddled were the later understandings of this transitional phenomenon, the central theme of those stories does not strain credulity; earlier "lawgivers" would have thought to use music as a way to invest their proclamations with authority, because *muthoi* had been set to music.

Poetry proved inadequate, of course, for law. Already by the middle of the seventh century, Greeks cast their new rules in prose, a fact all the more remarkable since sixth-century philosophy and even technical treatises continued to employ poetry as their principal medium, the latter probably for ease of memorization.[16] The reasons for law's precociousness in Greek prose resulted in part from the fact that the difficulties confronting elites of the early *polis* were too complex for verse to capture all that needed to be said on a subject. One might argue the same could be true of sixth-century philosophy. Quite apart from the fact that we have precious little direct evidence for the content of that thought and cannot be certain just how sophisticated it was, we can also see that the stakes were not nearly as high. Shades of interpretation in Anaximander's cosmology were far less dangerous than the political consequences of misconduct and misunderstanding among the elites of an early *polis*. For those portions of the rule base that needed clarification, or even invention, what were needed were rules in the form of substantive laws, not informal norms, not maxims. It was, after all, the inadequacy of traditional social norms that propelled potentially irresolvable conflict.

However, the earlier fixation of poetry in written form likely inspired the move to written laws. Carol Thomas observed a generation ago that written laws did not result from a perceived need for standards, but rather written laws *created* the perception that written standards could exist, and Michael Gagarin has recently reasserted this position.[17] In the main I agree with these conclusions, but I believe we may push this intellectual step back even further. Greeks used writing, when they first acquired it, for a variety of purposes; the recording of poetry was one application. The epic tradition was one of the first beneficiaries (or victims, depending on one's point of view) of the new technology, and by the early seventh century that tradition was already substantially standardized. While Nagy is probably correct that the final canonization of Homer was not complete until the middle of the sixth century, that canonization was the end of a long process that witnessed an increasing stress on getting Homer "right," a notion that in and of itself depends on written versions. True epic, still composed-in-performance, does not concern itself with exactitude of details or fidelity of verbatim replication. For those verses attributed to Homer, their transcription meant their death as living epic, capable of keeping pace with the assumptions and problems of their performers and audiences and serving as a vessel for the inherited wisdom and rule base of generations, their death as *muthoi* in Martin's sense of the term. On the other hand, it also marked the beginning of their long history as a literary classic. An authoritative version began to coalesce, thanks to writing; and if writing could establish the notion of authority for poetry, not as it was but as it "ought to be," it could do the same for the new rules necessitated by *polis* society. Living oral poetry proved unequal to that task; the new rules required a new form, prose, set in stone before all, to underscore their validity.

THE WRITTEN LAWS OF EARLY GREECE constituted a response by the ruling elites of the early *poleis* to the anxieties and challenges created by the transformations of the eighth and early seventh centuries, as they attempted to work out how to compete for power and prestige but at the same time prevent anyone from gaining overwhelming advantages through the accumulation and concentration of resources. That the laws they framed may, in some *poleis,* have failed in their purpose should not blind us to the motivations for those statutes. At Athens, for example, Drakon's written laws on homicide apparently did not check politically motivated violence altogether,[18] nor did Solon's attempts to stabilize the *polis* prevent a decade of extraordinary political confusion, including two years without archons and what appears to have been a short-lived tyranny.[19] Even in functional legal cultures, some laws succeed, some fail, but nearly all laws will have unintended consequences: Solon's legislation against the ostentatious funeral merely refocused the resource expenditure and competitive display of elites toward the funerary monument. The greatest unintended consequence of early Greek legislative activity was the eventual association, in Athens and elsewhere, with written law as the guarantor of the power of the *demos* and the rule of law. That development was nowhere in the minds of the elites who initiated written legislation in the seventh century. They needed new rules to govern realms of social, economic, and political behavior for which older norms offered no obvious answers, and they turned to writing as the means to clarify and lend authority to their statutes.

Notes

Abbreviations

I have generally followed throughout the standard abbreviations employed in *The Oxford Classical Dictionary*, third edition, especially for ancient authors and works. However, for frequently cited works (such as those of Homer or the principal works of Hesiod) I have opted for a shorthand to obviate the need to include "Hom.," or "Hes.," *ad infinitum*.

[Arist.], AthPol. = *Athenaion Politeia*, ascribed to Aristotle
FGH = Jacoby, F., 1954–. *Die Fragmente der griechischen Historiker*. Leiden.
ICret = Guarducci, M., 1935–50. *Inscriptiones Creticae*. Rome.
IE = Engelmann, H., and R. Merkelbach, 1972–. *Inschriften von Erythrai und Klazomenai*. Bonn.
IG = *Inscriptiones Graecae*.
Il. = Homer, *Iliad*.
IvOlympia = Dittenberger, W., and K. Purgold, 1966. *Inschriften von Olympia*. Amsterdam.
Nomima = Van Effenterre, H., and F. Ruzé, 1994–95. *Nomima. Recueil d'inscriptions politiques et juridiques de l'archaisme grec*. Rome.
Od. = Homer, *Odyssey*.
P.-W. = Pauly, A., and G. Wissowa, 1958–63. *Paulys Realencyclopädie der classischen Altertumswissenschaft*. Stuttgart.
Rose = Rose, V., 1886. *Aristotelis qui ferebantur librorum fragmenta*. Leipzig.
SEG = *Supplementum epigraphicum Graecum*.
SIG = Dittenberger, W., 1915–24. *Sylloge Inscriptionum Graecarum*^{3}. Leipzig.
Theog. = Hesiod, *Theogony*.
WD = Hesiod, *Works and Days*.

Chapter 1

1. All dates BCE unless otherwise noted.

2. *WD* 190–94. Translations are my own, unless otherwise noted.

3. For "shame" in Archaic Greek thought, one of the best discussions remains Gernet 1981, though see now also Crotty 1994. For *hubris*, see the recent reflections of Cairns 1996; Adkins 1972, 87–94.

4. *WD* 201.

5. Most typically the word carries connotations of (petty) kingship in the *Iliad*, but in the *Odyssey* and in Hesiod the use of the word is plural and rooted in a local context. Hesiod seems to be thinking more of "chiefs," perhaps the heads of important households in nearby Thespiae (see subsequent note). See the discussions in Finley 2002, 84–86 on the contentious nature of the term *basileus*, referring to either a king or the head of an important house in Homeric epic (in and of itself a telling semantic slippage). Also, see Drews 1983; Morris 1987, 94–96, 201–5, who argues that epic *basileis* represent a governing group over a wider circle of relatively well off but nongoverning peasants; Whitley 1991, 184–86; and Qviller 1981, for the *basileis* as "big men"; Donlan 1985, 292–98; C. Thomas 1976.

6. Debate remains over the exact nature of the relationship between Askra, a town of considerable size (between 15 to 25 acres: Bintliff and Snodgrass 1985, 137) and nearby Thespiae, which Strabo reports as 40 stadia to the southeast of Askra (9.2.25). Tandy 1997, 207–8 posits a more dependent relationship for Askra; A. Edwards 2004, esp. 64–68, 73–77 sees close-knit interaction between the two but not necessarily dependence for Askra. Nevertheless, Edwards argues, Thespiae will have served as the main urban settlement of its district, and it was probably there that Hesiod's squabbles of the marketplace will have occurred.

7. *WD* 202–12.

8. *WD* 210–11.

9. *WD* 35–39. A. Edwards 2004; see Gagarin 1974, 108 on the interpretation of the phrase regarding the dispute between the brothers.

10. *WD* 213–16, a conclusion also reached by A. Edwards 2004, 65–66, who addresses other passages meant for the *basileis*. Contra: Nelson 1998, 77–81.

11. Forsdyke 2005, 12.

12. Hdt. 7.107.4, translated by Grene 1987, 504.

13. Cartledge 2001, 34.

14. Hdt. 7.105. Cf. the description of the savage Cyclopes in Homer, as those who had neither assemblies nor laws (*Od.* 9.112).

15. MacDowell 1986. See also the recent comments of Papakonstantinou 2008, 74–76 regarding the relationship between law and writing at Sparta.

16. For the date of Herodotus' activity at Athens and the character of his public readings and their audience, see most recently R. Thomas 2003, with literature cited.

17. For the date and authenticity of Drakon's legislation, see Sickinger 1999, 14–24; Gagarin 1981a, 19–29; 2008, 93–94; Stroud 1968, 66–71; Cadoux 1948, 92; for an exhaustive study of Drakon's law in the context of Archaic justice and its continued importance in the legal landscape of Athens, see Carawan 1998.

18. Cerra 1979; see as well Chapter 4.3 below.

19. For an excellent overview of the continued role of memory in Athenian political and legal matters, see R. Thomas 1989, 38–82; 1996.

20. See Chapter 2.1 below.

21. For the most recent discussion, see Buckler 2003, although Fuks 1984 is still in many ways quite persuasive regarding the general sense of despair in fourth-century Greece.

22. The loci classici for the assertion of the democratic ideology in the aftermath of the oligarchic revolutions of the late fifth century are Xen. *Hell.* 2.4.40–42; Lys. 12. See Chapter 2.1 below for further examination. For a stimulating discussion of the meaning

of history in Athenian debates over democracy, see Ober 1999, 54–72, 265–73. Wolpert 2002, esp. 119–41 provides a recent and useful examination of political and legal attitudes in Athens in the generation after the end of the Peloponnesian War and the ouster of the Thirty. Fuks 1953, for whatever issues one may take with him on individual points, has demonstrated beyond question the ways in which late fifth- and fourth-century debates shaped Athenian understanding of their legal and constitutional past.

23. Pl. *Phdr.* 274e–75a; adapted from the translation by Harold Fowler 1925.

24. Pl. *Leg.* 711c (μηδεὶς ἡμᾶς πειθέτω, ὦ φίλοι, ἄλλῃ θᾶττον καὶ ῥᾷον μεταβάλλειν ἄν ποτε πόλιν τοὺς νόμους ἢ τῇ τῶν δυναστευόντων ἡγεμονίᾳ, μηδὲ νῦν γε ἄλλῃ γίγνεσθαι μηδ' αὖθίς ποτε γενήσεσθαι).

25. The most famous early examples are, of course, the "Dipylon Vase" from Athens (Jeffery/Johnston 1990, 15–16, 68; Attica no. 1), dated to around 740–730, and the "Nestor Cup" of the last quarter of the eighth century (Jeffery/Johnston 1990, 235–36, 239; Euboic Colonies no. 1).

26. R. Thomas 1992, 52–73 provides an excellent overview of the evolution of the application of writing across Greece through the course of the Archaic age. See also Jeffery/Johnston 1990, 8–21, 426–27, and Heubeck 1979 for the early eighth-century date for the introduction and spread of alphabetic writing to the Greek world, a date favored by most Greek historians. Some Near Eastern scholars have argued for dates of transfer and influence as far back as the Protogeometric period (e.g., Cross 1967; Naveh 1973), but their arguments have not won wide acceptance for the reasons stated in Jeffery/Johnston 1990, 426–27.

27. For a stimulating discussion of how this process may have unfolded in seventh-century Athens, see Sickinger 1999, 8–24, with literature cited.

28. Mühl 1933 originally made the case for a connection most vigorously, but his argument on this point, articulated subsequently by Jeffery 1976, 189 and Boardman 1970, 23, has not won wide acceptance; see Gagarin 1986; 2008, 174–75 for reservations and relevant literature that points out the important distinctions between Near Eastern and early Greek laws. One might further note that in the most recent work by one of the greatest (intellectually responsible) proponents of Near Eastern influence in the Greek world, Burkert 2004 nowhere suggests that the Greeks were inspired toward written law by their neighbors to the east. For the purely Greek context of the Greek lawgiving traditions, see Adcock 1927; Szegedy-Maszak 1978.

29. See the observations of Gagarin 2008, 167–74.

30. Foucault 1977.

31. C. Thomas 1984, 253n18.

32. Eder 1986.

33. Gagarin 1986, 121–26.

34. For example, Humphreys 1988; Camassa 1988, 153–55, where the discussion of the role of the aristocracy as a motive force is restricted to the final two and a half pages of a twenty-five page study; Hölkeskamp 1992b; 1994; 1999, 270–73, where he ascribes the transcription of law to the *polis* as part of an emerging sense of identity and sovereignty. Forsdyke 2005 offers an enlightening discussion of the dynamic at Athens, but her work is not centrally concerned with the problem of Greek legal culture or the appearance of written law.

35. The original appeared in 1861; the present study employs the 1986 Arizona edition, which appeared as part of the "Classics of Anthropology" series.

36. Bentham 1988; Austin 1995.

37. Maine 1986, 4–7.

38. He cites, as examples, the "kings" of Sparta (by which he means the *archêgetai*; cf. Plut. *Lyc.* 6), who became hereditary generals; the "functionary" king archon (*archôn basileus*) at Athens; and the "formal hierophant," the *rex sacrificulus*, of Rome: Maine 1986, 9.

39. Maine 1986, 15–16.

40. Fustel de Coulanges 1980, 178–85 for a summary.

41. Meyer 1954/1893, 3.510–11; Busolt 1893 and 1895, 1.626, 2.254; Beloch 1912, 1.1.213ff.

42. Meyer 1954/1893, 3.279–80 provides a representative analysis.

43. Meyer 1954/1893, 3.509–12, 521–2; Beloch 1912, 1.1.365; Busolt 1895, 2.223.

44. In addition see Bury and Meiggs 1975, 104; and Glotz 1904, 239–43, who make similar arguments.

45. Bonner and Smith 1930, 78ff. This interpretation had been followed with few substantive adjustments until the appearance of Eder's essay. For example, Snodgrass 1980, 83–84, 118–22 implies that the publication of laws such as Drakon's were aimed at a "curtailment of aristocratic privilege" and did so due to the benefits of widespread alphabetic literacy. See further the discussion by Hedrick 1994, 213–15, which treats the "liberal" assumptions in scholarship on the subject. Even Gagarin 1986, 143–46, whose views Whitley 1997, 639n19 has characterized as "divided," has suggested that the purpose of written law was to make law available to all citizens; Gagarin 2008 has recently expressed this synthesis even more forcefully, arguing that a nexus of increased literacy and sense of community helped to propel the development of written law (see subsequent text). Whitley's 1997, 639 remark that "few now believe that written law developed simply in order to curb the arbitrary power of magistrates or lords in aristocratic states" is more wishful thinking than an accurate reflection of the actual tenor of the literature, as belied by his own footnotes; the tendency remains strong, as discussed in Chapter 4.1 below.

46. Gagarin 2008, esp. 39–92. See also my comments in Hawke 2009.

47. Papakonstantinou 2008, esp. 23–48, with quote at 46.

48. Papakonstantinou 2008, 62.

49. Schmitz 2004, esp. 148–258.

50. Calhoun 1944, 22–23.

51. C. Thomas 1977.

52. Svenbro 1976; 1993, 109–23.

53. Havelock 1963; 1978; 1982; R. Thomas 1989; 1992; 1994; 1996.

54. Especially R. Thomas 1989, 15–34; 1992, 15–28, 44–50, who has raised the question of how distinct literacy and orality would have been in the *poleis* of Archaic Greece.

55. The starting points for relating the two developments are Goody and Watt 1963 and Goody 1977. Though the ideas in Havelock 1963; 1978; 1986 are often closely associated with Goody's and Watt's hypotheses (e.g., the comments of Whitley 1997, 638), his conclusions are often far more qualified and reserved than theirs. Scholars who have recently challenged the equation between literacy and rationality include Scribner and Cole 1981, 3–15, 134–60; Street 1984; Bloch 1989; and Halverson 1992. For "irrational" uses of writing in Archaic Greece see Langdon 1976; Svenbro 1989; 1993; R. Thomas 1992, 78–88; Andersen 1989; and Varhelyi 1996. See also, of course, W. Harris 1989, who argues

persuasively against inflated assumptions and estimates regarding the quantity and quality of literacy in Archaic and Classical Greece.

56. Whitley 1997 notes, specifically, the profusion of written law from Crete (where evidence for widespread literacy is troublesome at best; see below), and the lack of legal inscriptions from well-excavated Attica, the region of Greece for which the strongest arguments for higher levels of literacy may be made.

57. Graham 1982, 3.183–95; Link 1992; van Compernolle 1981.

58. Eder 1986.

59. Forsdyke 2005.

60. Forsdyke 2005, 36–77, 99.

61. Wolff 1946. See also Wolff 1980.

62. See the bibliography for the list of Ruschenbusch's and Thür's pertinent publications that have informed the present study. Thür, e.g., 1996, departs somewhat from Wolff and Ruschenbusch, stressing what he perceives as the fundamental importance of oath swearing and oath challenge over that of central political power as a source of legal authority and legitimacy. However, he has essentially replaced the centrality of political agency in society (where Wolff and Ruschenbusch would prefer to see the motive force for legal change) with a presumed centrality of religious authority and scruple, deemphasizing the shaming effect a broken oath would have on public opinion of the man who forswore himself.

63. Radcliffe-Brown and Pound *apud* Rouland 1994, 38.

64. Sealey 1994.

65. Hölkeskamp 1992b; 1994; 1999.

66. Pounder 1984.

67. Mühl 1933; Pounder 1984.

68. Willetts 1967, 9; 1974, 27; 1982, 3.240; Gagarin 1986, 126–27 has effectively dispatched this interpretation, citing the profound lack of trade-oriented laws in the early legal tradition as it survives, even among the more "economically" focused laws of Solon.

69. Bonner and Smith 1930, 1.69.

Chapter 2

1. Fifth-century Athenians had a highly contingent sense of the events of the previous one hundred years and frequently reshaped or misunderstood narratives to suit the present. See Lavelle 1993; 2000; 2005, 5–13; Robertson 1978; Anderson 2003.

2. The most exhaustive survey to date of Classical Athenian law is now Todd 1993, though older treatments such as Harrison 1955; 1968–71; and MacDowell 1978 remain important. In addition to these works, a number of important treatises and articles have appeared on particular issues in late fifth- and fourth-century law, as well as on individual orators and their approaches to Athenian law: Hansen 1974; 1976; 1980; 1999, 161–224; Ostwald 1986; E. Harris 1995; Paulsen 1999; Worthington 2000; Carey 2000, 43–59; Gagarin 2002.

3. See discussion below.

4. Ober 1989; 1998 provides excellent studies, respectively, of the ways in which elite litigants appealed to democratic assumptions and values in the law courts and the articulation of elite criticism of democratic society.

5. For discussions, the classic treatments remain Fuks 1953; Ruschenbusch 1958; Finley 1971; and Ostwald 1986, esp. 343–411. Recent examinations include Wolpert 2002, 35–38; Anderson 2003, 43–47.

6. Hdt. 1.29–33. His only other mention of Solon is a poem he supposedly wrote in praise of the Cyprian tyrant, Philokypros (5.113).

7. It is good to note, however, that the discussions could be earnest, whatever the conscious or unconscious motivations of individual political actors, such as in the crisis that followed (413–411 BCE) the Sicilian disaster. See Ostwald 1986, 343–68, 371ff. On ideologically informed political struggle in fifth- and fourth-century Greece beyond Athens (and Sparta), see Gehrke 1985, esp. 321–24.

8. Fuks 1953; on the generally favorably treatment of Ephialtes in [Arist.] *AthPol.*, see Rhodes 1993, 29–30, 283–85.

9. Fuks 1953, 84–97 is still one of the better discussions, to my mind, of the origins of the "constitution of Drakon"; see also Rhodes 1993, 85–87; Ober 1998, 358; Carawan 1998; Ste. Croix 2004, 273.

10. Thuc. 1.23.6–33.3.

11. The account of the government of the 400: Thuc. 8.67–97. On the relationship between the law and the oligarchy, 8.67.1–2, where he emphasizes that the redrafting of laws was turned to the purpose of installing the oligarchy. Thrasyboulos and Thrasyllos note the subversion of "ancestral" laws by the oligarchy in the context of an ideological struggle at 8.76.1, 6.

12. Ostwald 1986, 407–9, 415–18, 511–12 for discussion.

13. Xen. *Hell.* 2.3.1–4.34 provides the most complete narrative account of the reign of the Thirty. See also the accounts in [Arist.] *AthPol.* 34.2–39.6; Lys. 12. As Wolpert 2002, 15–24 notes, the discrepant descriptions of Xenophon and the *AthPol.* cannot be reconciled in all of their details, but the overall point remains the same: the Thirty established themselves, and ruled, through violence.

14. Xen. *Hell.* 2.3.2.

15. [Arist.] *AthPol.* 35.2; cf. Xen. *Hell.* 2.3.13.

16. For the total number of murders as fifteen hundred: [Arist.] *AthPol.* 35.4; Isoc. 7.67, 20.11; Aeschin. 3.235 (who gives the figure as "more than" fifteen hundred). Strauss 1986, 15–16, 42–44 estimates the total citizen population in 400 BCE to have been as low as twenty thousand. For general discussion of the composition, character, and reign of the Thirty, see Krentz 1982.

17. Wolpert 2002, 58. Oligarchy, of course, ceased to be a viable alternative at Athens thanks to the actions of the Thirty, and the term oligarch became one of political abuse there; Krentz 1982, 18; Ober 1999, 6–10. Nevertheless, litigants found it worthwhile to paint themselves (and their jurors) as defenders of democracy and their opponents as men who had oligarchic pasts (and, by extension, possible oligarchic futures).

18. Gehrke 1985, passim.

19. The murder of a man thought to be the leader of the democratic party at Kyllene in 398/7, with violent reprisals (Xen. *Hell.* 3.2.27–29); the confusion in the cities of Ionia, ca. 396/5 with respect to the form of their government, precipitated by the fall of the oligarchies which Lysander had installed (3.4.7); a recent change of government is suggested in Rhodes, where in 391 the Spartan commander Ekdikos "sailed to Knidos and discovered that the democrats were in charge everywhere" (4.8.22–23), democrats whom Ekdikos hoped to overthrow with the aid of disaffected oligarchs on the island; in the following year, the Athenian Thrasyboulos installed a democracy, presumably by force, at the strategic city of Byzantium (4.8.27); oligarchic and democratic party strife broke out at Mantinea in 385/4, and the expectation of the defeated democratic leaders was that they would be put to death

(5.2.3, 6–7); a similar struggle took place at Thespiae and several other Boiotian towns in the early 370s, also with anticipation of violent reprisal (5.4.46–55); the Athenian Autokles accuses the Spartans that what they called the independence of the Greek cities was really nothing more than the installation of narrow oligarchies who maintained their position by main force (6.3.8); finally, we learn of a pro-Spartan (oligarchic) and pro-Athenian (democratic) party in many cities by the late 370s (6.3.14). Further, there are several, less direct references to the possibility of democratic and oligarchic strife at Corinth (4.4.1–3), Thebes (5.2.25), and at Sparta itself, where a certain disfranchised Spartan, Kinadon, had allegedly hatched a plot to overthrow the Spartan government with the backing of socially and politically disadvantaged elements of Spartan society (3.3.5–11).

20. Isoc. 5.52; Diod. Sic. 15.57–58.

21. [Dem.] 24.149.

22. Fuks 1984 provides a survey of the political, economic, and social disruptions in fourth-century Greece; see also Gehrke 1985; Buckler 2003.

23. *Pol.* 1296a1–38, with his summation of the problem at 28–33.

24. Aeschin. 1.4–5.

25. Ober 1989; Christ 1998; Yunis 2005.

26. Aeschin. 3.190.

27. [Dem.] 26.24; Carey 1996, esp. 34 with n. 7 for discussion.

28. For the general tendency of critics to use the political language already monopolized by democratic discourse, see Ober 1999.

29. *Pol.* 1291b31–1292a41.

30. *Pol.* 1292a1–5.

31. Ostwald 1986; Sealey 1982; 1994, with a summary at 146–48; Wolpert 2002, 38–42.

32. *Pol.* 1292a5–8. For the distinction between *psephismata* (decrees) and *nomoi* (laws), cf. Sealey 1994, 33–35; Hansen 1983, 162–63.

33. Against Aristotelian authorship, see Rhodes 1993, 61–63; for a sustained and convincing argument in favor, see now Ste. Croix 2004, 254–57.

34. [Arist.] *AthPol.* 41.2.

35. Arist. *Pol.* 1292a11–32.

36. Isoc. 15.299–301; Christ 1998, 48–71.

37. Hansen 1999, 81–84. Hansen states the case against *isonomia* ever serving as a particularly cherished notion in democratic Athens, though aside from Herodotus' explicit reference (5.78.1) to *isegoria* as the contrast to tyranny, Hansen's argument is one based on silence and omission, albeit considerable. See the response by Raaflaub 1996, 143–46, with literature cited. For *isonomia* as a foundation of Athenian democracy: Finley 1976, 10; Bleicken 1985, 32, 191, 263, 312; Ober 1996, 51–52 speaks of a "demotic vision" of society based on essentially spontaneous notions of equality; Anderson 2003, 78 suspects that *isonomia* was the most important concept in what he sees, *contra* Ober 1996; 1998, as a deliberate program masterminded by Kleisthenes and his circle, but admits that this cannot be proven.

38. Hdt. 3.80.6.

39. Thuc. 2.37.3.

40. R. Thomas 1989, 62–71; 1996, 19–25.

41. Humphreys 1988.

42. Eur. *Suppl.* 433–46.

43. Cerra 1979, 12, 79–88, 90–91; his study cites other examples and is so thorough that one may be directed there with confidence; cf. also Guthrie 1971, 117–31 for the impact of contemporary philosophical debates about the different natures of written and unwritten law; Ostwald 1986, 148–61.

44. Hansen 1999, 161–63.

45. Lys. 30.2: to record the laws of Solon; *IG* I^3 104.4–7: the *anagrapheis* were to record Drakon's law on homicide and publish it on a stele in front of the Stoa Basileos. *IG* I^3 105, however, concerns judicial powers of the Council of 500, and therefore could not have been a law of Solon, strictly speaking, but by this time it is clear that most laws with any sort of accepted authority were often claimed as laws of Solon, thus leading to the type of confusion necessitating the collection and republication of the laws. Furthermore, a series of inscriptions (*IG* I^3 236–41) deals with a variety of issues from sacrifices to the *dikasteria* and also to overseas citizen colonies, a fifth-century institution.

46. Oliver 1935, 7 and Clinton 1982, esp. 28–34, both have argued that the *anagrapheis* were only to record the laws of Drakon and Solon, and Ostwald 1986, 415–18 suggests that if that had been the entirety of their charge they probably could have completed the task in the originally allotted four months (see discussion below); Harrison 1955; MacDowell 1978, esp. 47; Sealey 1987, 45–46; and Rhodes 1991 all see the recodification as far more inclusive. Robertson 1990 dislikes the notion of a recodification, seeing the work of the *anagrapheis* as essentially one of collection for the purposes of a new central archive.

47. Dem. 24.42. MacDowell 1978, 47 believes the first part of the clause cited by Demosthenes referred only to laws republished by the *anagrapheis* under the democracy of 410–403 BCE.

48. Lys. 30.2–3. The unusual term of four months alleged by Lysias, when most appointments were annual or without fixed term, perhaps reflects that Nikomakhos came into the term in the last third of 410, after the fall of the interim government and the return of democracy; see Sealey 1987, 45–46.

49. Rhodes 1991, 91.

50. Rhodes 1991, 92–94. He also argues that for someone (such as Lysias and the prosecutor for whom he penned the speech) who was not intimately familiar with the existing material and its inherent problems, it might indeed seem that the *anagrapheis* were unnecessarily extending their term and introducing new laws while ignoring the old. See also Robertson 1990, 54, arguing from Lys. 30.19–21 that Nikomakhos and the *anagrapheis* had uncovered so many outdated ritual measures that Lysias could plausibly attempt to censure him for the resulting excessive expenditure, even though that may not have been the case; see Robertson 1990, 66.

51. Ostwald 1986, 343–68. In addition to the contemporary frustrations they may have encountered, the *anagrapheis* also may have been dealing with material (and the traditions regarding it) that will have been shaped in some sense by previous generations of Athenians willfully revising the past; see Lavelle 1993; 2005; Anderson 2003.

52. Sealey 1987, 46: "The work of revising the laws may have made the Athenians think about the nature of the law and their authority."

53. Ostwald 1986, 85–92 with 93: "The social and religious norms of the last half of the fifth century presuppose a society in which the written legislation is so much taken for granted that its standards can be applied to aspects of human life that are not normally regarded as capable of regulation by the acts of a legislature."

54. Robertson 1990.

55. Robertson 1990, 55–56; for the date and discussion of relevant literature, see now Sickinger 1999, 105–8.

56. [Dem.] 47.71.

57. Andok. 1.83–4.

58. Andok. 1.84.

59. Andok. 1.87.

60. See Harrison 1955; MacDowell 1978; Rhodes 1985; Sealey 1987, esp. 36–45; Hansen 1999, 168–77; and Todd 1993, 293–97 for discussions of the nomothetic process. Harrison saw *nomothesia* as a later development, perhaps in the 380s, though in light of subsequent critiques it is difficult to sustain this view.

61. Hansen 1974; 1999, 207–11. See Ostwald 1986, 108–29 on the concepts of *ennomos* and *paranomos*.

62. Ostwald 1986, 523.

63. Todd 1993, 294–97.

64. Robertson 1990, 72–74 makes a compelling case that the prosecutor of Lys. 30 is most likely a conservative who will have opposed the emergent democratic ideology I have suggested in the text: the prosecutor is hostile to the anagraphic process, prefers the "special reports" of the *syngrapheis* who had expert knowledge on ritual, and had to defend himself against the charge that he himself was a member of the 400 (Lys. 30.7–8).

65. See now, for example, Gagarin 2008, 30–36, with literature cited.

66. See Chapter 2.3 below for descriptions of legal culture.

67. J. Foley 1997; 2002.

68. R. Thomas 1989.

69. As Papakonstantinou 2008, 48 has aptly put it, "There is nothing inherently developmental or teleological in the use of writing to record law. Some Greeks willingly wrote down and publicly displayed their laws and decrees and others did not."

70. Lamberton 1988.

71. Most recently, see Tandy and Neale 1996, 5–9; A. Edwards 2004, esp. 19–25; C. Thomas 2005.

72. For example, Nagy 1990a, esp. 52–115; Morris 1996.

73. Forsdyke 2005, 35–36.

74. Though recent arguments suggest, or even explicitly state, that the tradition would have remained flexible enough to reflect some contemporary changes in attitudes and assumptions until the early sixth century; Nagy 1990a, 21–25, 52–81; 1996, 48–55 argues that the tradition would have maintained a certain plasticity during its diffusion in the Archaic period, while van Wees 1999 makes a case for Homeric epic being generally reflective of Greek society in the late seventh and early sixth centuries; see also Wilson 2002, who argues that the *Iliad* constitutes a transitional text, wherein we find competing, contemporary visions of how Homeric society (and in particular, merit and authority in that society) should be modeled.

75. Haslam 1997, with literature cited. See also Powell 1991; 1997; 2002.

76. Morris 1986 offered arguments about the internal consistency of the world presented by Homer that are persuasive to the point of conclusive, answering the criticisms of Snodgrass 1974. See also the work of Donlan 1982; 1985; 1993; Rihll 1986; and Adkins 1971; 1972, esp. 10–21, for further support of the idea that Homeric society is generally consistent, especially when considered alongside the findings of archaeology and political anthropology.

77. Though with important and necessary adjustments to the "strong" Oral Theory: J. Foley 1997.

78. Adkins 1960; 1972; van Wees 1992; Morris 1986; Qviller 1980; Snodgrass 1993.

79. R. Martin 1989, 22, 37, 47–65.

80. This is the implication of R. Martin's argument throughout, though he explicates at 231–39, with a summation at 238: "Homeric poetry is a muthos, specifically an act that we can classify as a feat of memory, the third heroic genre of discourse . . . [T]his is poetry meant to persuade, enacted in public, created by authority."

81. R. Martin 1989, 238.

82. See, among others, Parry 1930; 1932; Lord 1991; 2000; Finnegan 1992; and J. Foley 2002.

83. For a useful overview of Havelock's legacy, both positive and negative, see the recent discussion in Yunis 2003b. Cf. also Bowman and Woolf 1994b, 3–4 about the negative overreaction to the ideas of Havelock and others.

84. Havelock 1963, 36–96.

85. See also Havelock 1978.

86. Havelock 1963, 41–44. With regard to justice in particular, a representative but by no means isolated statement may be found in Havelock 1978, 181, where he argues eloquently that the justice of the *Odyssey* is based on the conservation of mores.

87. Chapter 5.1–2 below.

88. Havelock 1963, 41–44.

89. Seaford 1994.

90. See the comments of Nagy 1996, 6–11.

91. See discussion in Chapter 4.3 below about the traditions of early laws being set to song, which suggests a transition between the authority of poetry and written statute law.

92. Nagy 1996, 119–27.

93. Finley 1975.

94. Powell 2002, 19.

95. Havelock 1978.

96. For interested readers, the Oral Theory grew out of the work of Parry and Lord, who concentrated on what they saw as the epic poets' fundamental building blocks of formula and theme (for a useful reclamation from misuse and misunderstanding of these terms by the unsympathetic, see Nagy 1996, 16–27). Neoanalysts believed that the Parry–Lord thesis made too much a mechanic of Homer, and instead argued for the originality of a poet engaged in such literary devices as foreshadowing and intertextuality. Hallmarks of the Neoanalyst School include Kakridis 1949; 1971; Pestalozzi 1945; Schadewaldt 1959, 1966; and Kullman 1984. Willcock 1997 provides a lucid survey of the development of Neoanalysis. One might note Parry and Lord both assumed that a change in the "way of living" in the society of both poet and audience would prompt innovation within the epic tradition; as J. Foley 1997, 160ff. has noted, however, Parry did not make this argument altogether prominent and helped to prompt a strong reaction against the terms in which he framed his argument. See also, with literature cited, the discussion in Wilson 2002, 1–4.

97. Holoka 1991.

98. Kullmann 1984; Willcock 1997.

99. Powell 1997; 2002, who has revived Wade-Gery's 1952 theory of transcription of a live performance as the most likely means by which a poem so markedly oral in character found its way to the roll.

100. Nagy 1990a, 9–10; 1996, 42.

101. Nagy 1990b, 52–81; 1996, 42, 65–112; in agreement is van Wees 1999. Cf. Powell 2002; Janko 1982.

102. Farenga 2006.

103. For example, Thür 1996, 58: "efforts . . . now being made by David Cohen . . . Michael Gagarin . . . and also by Uwe Wesel [to combine legal history and anthropology] . . . adopt approaches which appear to me to be dangerous. There is in particular a risk in turning to anthropological analysis before all the evidence of the Greek sources is exhausted."

104. Morris 1987, 2.

105. Goody 2006, esp. 26–67.

106. Tandy 1997, 8, with further explanation at 84ff.

107. See especially Friedman 1975; Geertz 1983.

108. Friedman 1975, 15, 193.

109. Geertz 1983, 173.

110. Geertz 1983, 215, 232. See also Papakonstantinou 2008 for the pluralism of "legal narratives" in Archaic Greece.

111. Geertz 1983. See also Sarat and Kearns 1998b, 10.

112. Geertz 2000, 5, 10.

113. Mezey 2001, 35 with n. 2 for important literature; 39. See also MacAulay 1989, 1547.

114. Cotterell 2006, 65–78, 88–93.

115. Coombe 1998, 23.

116. Mezey 2001, 43.

117. Williams 1983, 91.

118. Rosaldo 1998, 28.

119. Mezey 2001, 55.

120. The important point here is stability. The prevalence of conflict or its potential is not necessarily an indication of a weak social regime or a dysfunctional legal culture. What will matter is whether that conflict is sufficiently constrained so as not to encourage instability or even disintegration of the social whole.

121. Cotterell 2006, 15; see also Merry 1988, 873: law entails "plural forms of ordering . . . participating in the same social field."

122. Ellickson 1991, 126.

123. Ellickson 1991, 126–32, with quotes at 126; see also E. Posner 2000, 4, 43–44. M. Harris 1980, 275: "No matter how deviant or unexpected the act, a psychologically intact human being can always appeal to some set of rules someone else will recognize as legitimate, although perhaps misinterpreted or misapplied."

124. Ellickson 1991, 164–76

125. See Bloch and Parry 1989, 23–30 on this dynamic with regard to money exchanges.

126. E. Posner 2000, 4. See also MacAulay 1989, 1546, who notes that rules are only part of a legal system.

127. E. Posner 2000, 91.

128. Ellickson 1991, 55, 156, 177; E. Posner 2000, 43–58. Cotterell 2006, for his "law-and-community" approach, sees "mutual interpersonal trust" and individual responsibility for its maintenance as crucial to the health of a particular legal culture.

129. A. Cohen 1985, 19.

130. Gagarin 1986; Lanni 2006; Farenga 2006; Papakonstantinou 2008, esp. 105–26.

131. Llewelyn and Hoebel 1941, 21.

132. Nader 1965, 16: "Especially relevant are the descriptions of trouble cases before they are found in a recognized court or tribunal. Such descriptions are important if we are to enhance our understanding of the origin of breaches and norms and the reaction of society to breaches of its rules; such 'social dramas' are important as well for an understanding of conflict as a product of culture change, a source of culture change, or as an aspect of a stable social system."

133. Rouland 1994, 37.

134. Malinowski 1926.

135. Verdier 1981 (on his influence, see Motta 1983); Le Roy 1972; 1978; Carbonnier 1971; 1979. See also Ellickson 1991, 150: "Functionalists have been on the right track," with explication at 167–83.

136. Rouland 1994, 127.

137. See especially Carbonnier 1979, 257–64.

138. Mezey 2001, 61.

139. I fundamentally disagree with Schmitz's 2004 characterization of Archaic Greek peasant and elite cultures and values as distinct and separate from one another. The cases studied in the next chapter reveal a society that is bound by a generally common set of assumptions, even if emphases may have differed based on economic standing.

140. Bohannon 1967b, 43–58; 1967a; Demerath and Robertson, eds. 1968; Gulliver 1973; Nader 1965; Reay 1974; Comaroff and Roberts 1981, 216–42; Roberts 1979, 51–53.

141. Chapter 5.1 below.

142. Roberts 1979, 72–78.

143. Anthropologists typically refer to ostracism in order to describe the banishment of an individual wrongdoer, whether in the sense of physical removal from the community or barring him from essential forms of economic cooperation or other reciprocal assistance. I have chosen to employ the word *exile* throughout this study to avoid confusion with the Athenian political practice.

144. Roberts 1979, 69ff.

145. Roberts 1979, 69–78.

Chapter 3

1. *Il.* 18.497–508. Fundamental, older treatments of the trial scene include Wolff 1946, 34–49; Andersen 1976; Hommel 1969; Thür 1970; MacDowell 1978; Ruschenbusch 1982. More recently, see Gagarin 1986, 26–33; 2008, 13–19; Thür 1996, 66–69; Cantarella 2002; Farenga 2006, 117–19; Papakonstantinou 2008, 32–34.

2. *Il.* 18.497–508.

3. Wolff 1946.

4. Sealey 1994, 109ff.

5. In favor: Hanson 1995; against, Foxhall 1997a; 1997b.

6. *WD* 343–45. See Schmitz 2004, 52–60 on the importance of neighbors in the world of Hesiod.

7. Typical of this approach was Weber's 1968, 78, 83 emphasis on the state as the ultimate repository of social order and control: "[The state] has been successful in seeking

to monopolize the legitimate use of physical force as a means of domination within a territory . . . The right to use physical force is ascribed to other institutions only to the extent the state permits it."

8. See, for example, D. Cohen 1995, 127, 135; Phillips 2008. In some cases a jury decision at Athens only cleared the way for a private, self-help execution of a judgment or exculpated an individual who had already pursued redress for an injury that would have qualified for a self-help remedy. I return to a discussion of self-help in Athenian law in the subsequent text.

9. Rouland 1994, 112.

10. Roberts 1979, 65–67; for the perils to the Greek outcast (*atimos*), see Dem. 23.62; Hansen 1976, 55–63, 77–8, 81ff.; Manville 1980. Generally, see Rouland 1994, 271.

11. Gagarin 1981a, 5–10.

12. Gagarin 1981a, 10–12.

13. *Il.* 9.632–33.

14. *IG* I^3 104.26–29; Stroud 1968, 53ff.; Gagarin 1981a, 58–61.

15. Stroud 1968, 56–57, 80ff.; Gagarin 1981a, 60 with n. 84.

16. For example, *Il.* 2.661–70, 15.431–39; *Od.* 14.380–81, 15.271–82; Hes. *Shield* 9–19, 80–85.

17. See n. 14 above.

18. Among the Gamo of the southern Ethiopian highlands, the murderer is expected to flee the community and thus remove himself and his own kin from the possibility of vengeance; he may return if the victim's relatives forgive him; Bureau 1980.

19. R. Parker 1996, esp. 104–44; Gagarin 1981a, 2–4.

20. Dem. 23.76.

21. Gagarin 1978, 112 and n. 7.

22. Stroud 1968, 38; Gagarin 1981a, 66. The notion of intent with regard to other "offenses" does, however, appear earlier. For example, Menelaos challenges Antilokhos to swear that he did not intentionally (μὴ . . . ἑκών) use a trick to pass him in the chariot race and thereby disgrace him (*Il.* 23.585); see discussion of dispute ***D3*** in Chapter 3.6 below.

23. [Arist.] *AthPol.* 57.3; Dem. 47.52–73.

24. The absence of explicit reference cannot be conclusive, of course, given the imperfect condition of the inscription. However, Köhler 1867 and Stroud 1968 have between them confidently restored to near completeness the section of the law where we might expect to find mention of a court, namely lines 15–20. If Gagarin 1981a, 101ff. is correct, that Drakon supplemented and clarified the prevailing situation regarding intentional homicide, then the lawgiver essentially created a new category of crime. The lack of any specific mention of the venue indicates that a separate judicial competence had yet to appear or, at the opposite end of the spectrum, that the locations of hearings for certain types of crime had long been fixed by custom. The Areopagus remained the court for the trial of intentional homicide in the fourth century (Dem. 23.67; [Arist.] *AthPol.* 57.3), and presumably had tried all such cases before the publication of Drakon's statute; Busolt and Swoboda 1926, 2.811; Hignett 1952, 80; and Stroud 1968, 36 all argue that this was the case, though Gagarin 1981a, 125ff. expresses doubts, assuming that the Areopagus and the *ephêtai* represent discrete groups and undertook different functions in pre-Drakontian Athens. Cf. Wallace 1989, 10ff., who argues persuasively that attempts to deny the Areopagus the trial of all homicide before Drakon, and its continued supervision of intentional homicide afterward, are perverse and should be discarded.

25. Wallace 1989, 13–20 makes a compelling case that the *ephêtai* were none other than the members of the Areopagus in their capacity as juror-judges in trials for intentional homicide.

26. Though see Gagarin 1981a, 17–18, 165–67, who argues for the pronounced and conspicuous absence of explicit expressions of pollution in the epics or the remains of Drakon's law. There are, however, implicit suggestions; see the following note and accompanying text.

27. Achilles must go to Lesbos to perform sacrifice and receive purification at the hands of Odysseus, both in atonement for his murder of Thersites (Proclus *Chrest.* 2), and in Photios, *Lex.*, s.v. Τευμήσια, we read that in the *Epigonoi* Kephalos the Athenian traveled to Thebes, where he received expiation from the Kadmeians for the unintentional killing of his wife. Though Odysseus, Telemakhos, Eumaios, and Philoitios do not have to leave Ithaca after their slaughter of the suitors, Odysseus orders his nurse Eurykleia to bring sulfur and fire so that he may cleanse and purge the hall of the pollution resulting from the killings: *Od.* 22.481–84, 493–94.

28. *IG* I[3] 104.30–31, extensively restored by Stroud 1968, 5.

29. *IG* I[3] 104.37–38; Stroud 1968, 56–57.

30. [Arist.] *AthPol.* 57.3 omits the qualification of intent, but Dem. 23.54 claims that the lawgiver responsible for the measure "did not regard the event, but the intention of the agent" (οὐ τὸ συμβὰν ἐσκέψατο, ἀλλὰ τὴν τοῦ δεδρακότος διάνοιαν) in determining an athlete not guilty of the death of another contestant.

31. Dem. 23.55; [Arist.] *AthPol.* 57.3.

32. Sealey 1987, 73 contends that "no satisfactory definition can be offered" for Dem. 23.53 (ἐν ὁδῷ καθελὼν); in this he appears unduly cautious. The phrase, "coming upon someone in the road," must surely refer to the killing of a bandit whose intention it was to seize and/or rob a would-be victim. Further, we find a complementary provision at Dem. 23.60: "If one should be killed straightaway in self-defense while seizing or carrying off another violently or unjustly, there will be no penalty for his having been killed" (καὶ ἐὰν φέροντα ἢ ἄγοντα βίᾳ ἀδίκως εὐθὺς ἀμυνόμενος κτείνῃ, νηποινεὶ τεθνάναι).

33. Dem. 24.113. The aggrieved party could also choose to wound the burglar or remand him to the custody of the Eleven.

34. [Arist.] *AthPol.* 57.3; Dem. 23.55. We get a briefer and more oblique description in the *Athenaion Politeia,* which refers to this provision as an example of a homicide committed "according to the laws, as when catching an adulterer" (κατὰ τοὺς νομούς, ὂιον μοιχὸν λαβών). Demosthenes quotes the text of the law, without attribution, and informs us that unlawful sexual intercourse with another man's wife, mother, daughter, sister, or concubine kept for the purpose of producing offspring, exposed the offender to the aggrieved party's exercise of self-help; cf. Lys. 1.30–31, which confirms Demosthenes' representation of the general outlines of the law. As Rhodes 1993, 645 notes, an Athenian man's women were regarded as analogous to his property, so the right of defense against their "seizure" by lawful homicide belongs to the same broad category of law already indicated by the other statutes allowing the use of lethal force in defense of one's self and property. For further discussion of Athenian adultery law, see D. Cohen 1984; 1991, 100–108; Todd 1993, 276–78; Cantarella 2005, 240–41.

35. See Rouland 1994, 281 on the Plains Indians (Native American), with literature cited.

36. Gagarin 1986, 19–50, in his attempt to construct a picture of dispute settlement, considers a broader variety of disputes than have many other scholars. However, he

still limits his analysis largely to disputes that devolve to resolution by some third party, formally empowered to suggest or impose a settlement.

37. Rouland 1994, 114–56.

38. Retribution: Orestes' vengeance for Agamemnon's murder (*Od.* 1.295–99, 3.306ff.), and the claims of the relatives of suitors slain by Odysseus (*Od.* 24.352ff.). Seizure of property: Achilles' imagining the circumstances under which he might have a personal quarrel with the Trojans (*Il.* 1.150ff.); the dispute between Menelaos and Paris over the seizure of Helen (*Il.* 3.56ff.; 4.104ff.; 6.281ff.; 7.357ff.); Odysseus' quarrel with the suitors, the reasons for which appear throughout the *Odyssey,* though Odysseus explicitly enumerates his grievances at *Od.* 22.35–40; the dispute between Melampos and Iphiklos over the former's attempt to steal the latter's cattle (schol. Apoll. Rhod. *Arg.* 1.118 = Hes. fr. 261 Merkelbach and West); Hades' abduction of Persephone and the resultant grievance of her mother, Demeter (*Hymn. Hom. Cer.* passim); and Hermes' theft of Apollo's cattle (*Hymn. Hom. Merc.* passim).

39. The island supported a population of forty thousand when its own agricultural resources would have sustained four thousand inhabitants at most; Figueira 1986, 18ff.

40. *Hymn. Hom. Merc.* 71ff., 212ff., 316 (οὐκ ἀδίκως ἐπὶ βουσὶν ἐλάζυτο κύδιμον Ἑρμῆν); 255ff.

41. *Hymn. Hom. Merc.* 312 (δὸς δὲ δίκην καὶ δέξο παρὰ Ζηνὶ Κρονίωνι); the assembly of the gods as witness to the dispute before Zeus, 325–26.

42. *Hymn. Hom. Merc.* 332–35; 383; 389–96.

43. *Hymn. Hom. Merc.* 408–9a; 523ff.

44. *Il.* 1.152–56.

45. *Hymn. Hom. Cer.* 75–87.

46. *Hymn. Hom. Cer.* 91–92; 302–9.

47. *Hymn. Hom. Cer.* 310–12 (καί νύ κε πάμπαν ὄλεσσε γένος μερόπων ἀνθρώπων | λιμοῦ ὑπ' ἀργαλέης, γεράων τ' ἐρικυδέα τιμὴν | καὶ θυσιῶν ἤμερσεν Ὀλύμπια δώματ' ἔχοντας).

48. *Hymn. Hom. Cer.* 313–33.

49. *Hymn. Hom, Cer.* 347–74.

50. *Hymn. Hom. Cer.* 441–56.

51. Wilson 2002, 24–27 discusses the Menelaos-Paris-Helen problem with regard to Helen as belonging to the sphere of persons rather than goods, and thus Menelaos can demand *poinê* for her; see also Seaford 2004, 32–33. I will return to this issue in greater length in Chapter 3.6 below.

52. *Il.* 3.56–57, where Hector tells Paris, "But the Trojans are cowards, since otherwise you would already be inside a cloak of stone on account of the evils you have done" (ἀλλὰ μάλα Τρῶες δειδήμονες· ἦ τέ κεν ἤδη | λάϊνον ἕσσο χιτῶνα κακῶν ἕνεχ' ὅσσα ἔοργας). Hector repeats the theme of Paris' culpability, insinuating the Trojans would be better off were his brother dead at *Il.* 6.282–85, and rebukes Paris again at 6.326–29 and 6.523–25 for the troubles he had brought on the entire community.

53. *Il.* 3.86–87.

54. In addition to Hector's repeated shaming of Paris, Antenor also suggests that the Trojans and their allies hand over Helen along with treasure to the sons of Atreus (*Il.* 7.347–51). Only Antimakhos supports Paris unequivocally, hoping for personal gain through gold by opposing the idea of returning Helen (*Il.* 11.123–25).

55. *Il.* 3.67–70.

56. *Il.* 3.71–75, 3.92–94, 3.111–12.

57. *Il.* 3.105–8.

58. *Il.* 3.373–83.

59. *Il.* 3.455–60 (τοῖσι δὲ καὶ μετέειπεν ἄναξ ἀνδρῶν Ἀγαμέμνων· | κέκλυτέ μευ Τρῶες καὶ Δάρδανοι ἠδ' ἐπίκουροι· | νίκη μὲν δὴ φαίνετ' ἀρηϊφίλου Μενελάου, | ὑμεῖς δ' Ἀργείην Ἑλένην καὶ κτήμαθ' ἅμ' αὐτῇ | ἔκδοτε, καὶ τιμὴν ἀποτινέμεν ἥν τιν' ἔοικεν, | ἥ τε καὶ ἐσσομένοισι μετ' ἀνθρώποισι πέληται). Note the emphasis Agamemnon placed on honor, *timê*.

60. *Il.* 3.461.

61. *Il.* 4.104–40.

62. *Il.* 7.351–52 (νῦν δ' ὅρκια πιστὰ | ψευσάμενοι μαχόμεσθα).

63. *Il.* 7.361–64.

64. *Il.* 7.402 (ὡς ἤδη Τρώεσσιν ὀλέθρου πείρατ' ἐφῆπται).

65. *Il.* 7.403–4, 7.411.

66. Gagarin 1986, 29n34.

67. *Il.* 3.351–54.

68. Most notably Armstrong 1950.

69. Thür 1996 believes that disputes in Greece were settled by methods of proof, typically the swearing of oaths by the disputants, though his argument does not preclude other irrational means of deciding cases. He overemphasizes, I believe, the fear of supernatural agency at the expense of considering other very real possibilities, such as the consequences of forswearing one's self in a face-to-face community; see subsequent text.

70. It may be noted that the Achaean host, Menelaos' support group, also tired of the conflict and was ready to abandon the war entirely when Agamemnon, as a test, suggested the possibility of flight (*Il.* 2.139–54).

71. As will become clear in the following argument, Odysseus' slaughter of the suitors qualified as disapproved behavior at the communal level in Ithaca; the dispute between Telemakhos and the suitors, however, engaged sincere differences of opinion over what constituted approved or disapproved behavior, and I will therefore treat that issue separately (dispute ***B1***). See also the discussion in Schmitz 2004, 320–29.

72. *Od.* 13.376–78 (φράζευ ὅπως μνηστῆρσιν ἀναιδέσι χεῖρας ἐφήσεις, | οἳ δή τοι τρίετες μέγαρον κάτα κοιρανέουσι, | μνώμενοι ἀντιθέην ἄλοχον . . .).

73. For example, *Od.* 13.394–96, where Odysseus acknowledges his debt to Athena in helping him avoid the fate of Agamemnon, murdered by his wife's paramour when he returned to Mycenae; *Od.* 14.91–92, where Eumaios the swineherd notes the fact that the suitors have no thought of the wrath of the gods or of pity, and that "they do not wish to woo justly" (οὐκ ἐθέλουσι δικαίως | μνᾶσθαι)—note the importance of intention on the part of the suitors, which the poet stresses in order to justify violence against them.

74. *Od.* 22.15–24; 22.35–40 (ὦ κύνες, οὔ μ' ἔτ' ἐφάσκεθ' ὑπότροπον οἴκαδ' ἱκέσθαι | δήμου ἄπο Τρώων, ὅτι μοι κατεκείρετε οἶκον, | δμῳῇσιν δὲ γυναιξὶ παρευνάζεσθε βιαίως, | αὐτοῦ τε ζώοντος ὑπεμνάασθε γυναῖκα, | οὔτε θεοὺς δείσαντες, οἳ οὐρανὸν εὐρὺν ἔχουσιν, | οὔτε τιν' ἀνθρώπων νέμεσιν κατόπισθεν ἔσεσθαι).

75. *Od.* 22.41 (νῦν ὑμῖν καὶ πᾶσιν ὀλέθρου πείρατ' ἐφῆπται) ; cf. *Il.* 7.402 (ὡς ἤδη Τρώεσσιν ὀλέθρου πείρατ' ἐφῆπται).

76. See now Nagy 1996.

77. This particular formula makes only one other appearance in the epics, when Polydamas tells Hector (*Il.* 12.78–79) "the Achaeans will not stand fast, if indeed the

cords of destruction are bound firmly to them" (αὐτὰρ Ἀχαιοὶ | οὐ μενέουσ' εἰ δὴ σφιν ὀλέθρου πείρατ' ἐφῆπται). However, this pronouncement followed the one already made by the Achaeans themselves, and may only reflect the hopes of the Trojans (note the conditional εἰ δή) that it would be the Achaeans rather than themselves who would suffer ruin.

78. *Od.* 22.45–59. Donlan 1993, 170–71 regards the slaughter of the suitors as justified, "because they corrupt the important social institutions of feasting and hospitality, are automatically to be recognized as evil and therefore deserving of slaughter." In my opinion, as will be clear in the analysis that follows, the situation is not so straightforward as this for the poet and his audience.

79. *Od.* 22.60–67.

80. *Od.* 22.213–23.

81. Phemios' entreaty: *Od.* 22.344–53, with the disavowal of intentionality (ὡς ἐγὼ οὔ τι ἑκών) at 22.351; I return in greater detail to the significance of intentionality in other types of dispute below. Telemakhos states that Phemios was not at fault (ἀναίτιον, 22.356), and covered Medon with this same condition by asking immediately for his life as well.

82. *Od.* 22.367–77.

83. *Od.* 22.77–78. (ἔλθωμεν δ' ἀνὰ ἄστυ, βοὴ δ' ὤκιστα γένοιτο· | τῷ κε τάχ' οὗτος ἀνὴρ νῦν ὕστατα τοξάσσαιτο: "Let us go up to the town, and then could the cry be raised most swiftly; at that, quickly would this man have shot his last.") That the suitors envisioned here the aid of the people becomes clear at *Od.* 22.132–34. (ὦ φίλοι, οὐκ ἂν δή τις ἀν' ὀρσοθύρην ἀναβαίη | καὶ εἴποι λαοῖσι, βοὴ δ' ὤκιστα γένοιτο; | τῷ κε τάχ' οὗτος ἀνὴρ νῦν ὕστατα τοξάσσαιτο: "Friends, will not someone get out the side door and tell the people, and then could the cry be raised most quickly? At that, quickly would this man have shot his last.") Melanthios notes, however, that the passage is covered, and that they will have to find arms and fight for themselves: *Od.* 22.135–41.

84. *Od.* 24.351–55.

85. *Od.* 24.415, 24.420; furthermore, those who spoke after him addressed the assembled crowd as "men of Ithaca" (Ἰθακήσιοι, as uttered by Medon at 24.443 and Halitherses at 24.454), suggesting a general audience of the folk.

86. *Od.* 24.420–25.

87. *Od.* 24.427–28.

88. *Od.* 24.430–31.

89. *Od.* 24.432–35.

90. *Od.* 24.454–62 (462: μὴ ἴομεν, μή πού τις ἐπίσπαστον κακὸν εὕρῃ).

91. *Od.* 24.463–69.

92. *Od.* 24.516–25, 24.528–30.

93. *Od.* 24.546–47.

94. See introduction to Chapter 5 for sources.

95. I concern myself here with the tale as it is known from the epic tradition, rather than the fuller and very possibly embellished Aeschylean version. Orestes' killing of Aigisthos is first mentioned at *Od.* 1.29–30.

96. *Od.* 1.32–37, 39–40, where Zeus ruminates on how the mortals blame the gods for the evils they suffer, when in fact they are victims of their own foolishness, using Aigisthos as his examplar. Later in the narrative, Nestor explained to Telemakhos that had Menelaos been in Greece, not even would Aigisthos have been buried but left rather to be savaged and unmourned (*Od.* 3.255–61); he further refers to Aigisthos as "having

achieved the fearsome act which he had never hoped for in his heart" (*Od.* 3.275), perhaps recalling the imprecation of the gods that Aigisthos' actions were beyond his portion, "those baneful things" in which he had "devised a treacherous device" in plotting the murder of Agamemnon, "pondering dastardly deeds." Aigisthos had acted against all acceptability and morality, and his Homeric epithet was "deceitful" or "crafty" (δολόμητις; *Od.* 1.300, 3.198, 3.250, 3.308, 4.525). Aeschylus (*Ag.* 1577–1611) has Aigisthos expound on the retribution (*dikêphorou*) exacted against Agamemnon for his father's offenses to Thyestes, but that part of the tradition does not appear in Homer.

97. Praise for Orestes: *Od.* 1.298–300, 3.198–203; death of Aigisthos' followers: *Od.* 4.537. The epic tradition betrays no knowledge of judicial consequences for Orestes for the murder of Aigisthos, his followers, or even Klytemnestra, even though the epic tradition knew of the matricide (*Od.* 3.235, 3.310, 9.423–40). The only aftermath the epic poet mentions is the funeral feast celebrated by Orestes over Aigisthos and his own mother, and the treasure that Menelaos then conferred upon him (*Od.* 3.309–12).

98. *Od.* 3.272.

99. The dispute of Telemakhos with the suitors of Penelope (*Od.*, passim); three quarrels between various gods over what constituted an appropriate course of action (*Il.* 4.32ff.; *Il.* 7.17ff; *Il.* 15.158–228); and an argument about oxen so infuriating it moved one party to murderous action (Hes. *Shield* 11–13, 80–82).

100. *Od.* 2.44–77; 2.138–45.

101. *Od.* 2.89–128.

102. Antinoös notes the long interval at *Od.* 2.89–97 and 2.106–7; the comments of Eurymakhos: *Od.* 2.203–7.

103. *Od.* 2.194–97.

104. See also Schmitz 2004, 326–27.

105. *Od.* 2.130–33. It is interesting to note that Telemakhos would have "to give honor back" (*apotinein*) if he were willingly (*hekôn*) to send Penelope out of the house. This connection between intentional insult and the need to satisfy another's honor will be explored below.

106. He referred once in the assembly to the wish that he could defend himself or that the household, without Odysseus, had the strength to ward off the suitors (*Od.* 2.58–62); however, whether he envisaged the kind of violence Odysseus wrought is unclear.

107. Athena's criticism of the assembled citizenry: *Od.* 2.235–41, with further discussion in Chapter 4.1 below. Nestor's observation: *Od.* 3.212–15. I disagree here with Schmitz 2004, 144, who argues that Telemakhos' call to the commons to intervene was inapt and that the folk remained passive and uninterested. He bases his argument principally on the suitor Leiokritos' upbraiding of Athena/Mentor (*Od.* 1.242–56), but it seems just as, if not more likely, that Leiokritos' speech is rhetorical and meant to dissuade the Ithacans from taking action, as he acknowledges the possibility that those who oppose the suitors might be in the majority (1.244–45).

108. *Od.* 16.374–75.

109. *Od.* 16.376–77.

110. Hes. *Shield* 11–13, 80–82.

111. Havelock 1986, 8ff., 75ff.

112. *Il.* 4.25–29, 4.13–19.

113. *Il.* 4.31–38 (4.37–38: ἕρξον ὅπως ἐθέλεις· μὴ τοῦτό γε νεῖκος ὀπίσσω | σοὶ καὶ ἐμοὶ μέγ' ἔρισμα μετ' ἀμφοτέροισι γένηται).

114. *Il.* 4.40–43, 4.54–56, 4.66–72.

115. *Il.* 7.17–32.

116. *Il.* 15.226–28 (ἀλλὰ τόδ' ἠμὲν ἐμοὶ πολὺ κέρδιον ἠδέ οἱ αὐτῷ | ἔπλετο, ὅττι πάροιθε νεμεσσηθεὶς ὑπόειξε | χεῖρας ἐμάς, ἐπεὶ οὔ κεν ἀνιδρωτί γ' ἐτελέσθη).

117. *Il.* 14.258ff., 15.158–66.

118. *Il.* 15.194–99. Poseidon begins his rejection of Zeus' message with a preamble recollecting how the three brothers (himself, Zeus, and Hades) had received their three domains by lots, but that the earth and Olympus were common to them all (*Il.* 15.187–93). The tale appears to be a justification for Poseidon's refusal to recognize Zeus' jurisdiction over his activities among the hosts, as he immediately declares that he would not accede to Zeus' will (*Il.*15.194).

119. *Il.* 15.201–4. The threat was not without force: the Furies secured the moral order of the Homeric family.

120. *Il.* 15.206–17.

121. *Il.* 9.448ff.

122. *Il.* 459–61; *Il.* 464–83.

123. *Il.* 9.527–99; Hes. fr. 25 Merkelbach and West = Berlin papyrus no. 9777; the fifth-century writer Bacchylides (5.94–139 Maehler) provides background information on the tale preserved by Homer and Hesiod.

124. Hes. fr. 25.6–9; Bacchylides 5.125ff. Maehler.

125. The details are scattered across a number of sources from the ancient world, some late, but fit within the context and expectations of the Homeric version of the story. Homer referred to many men killed by Meleager in direct connection with the slaying of the boar (*Il.* 9.546). Other ancient sources that expound on the genesis of Althaia's wrath and Meleager's hard feelings against her (also recorded by Homer, *Il.* 9.555) are Apollodorus 1.8.2–3; Hyginus *Fabulae* 171, 174, 273; Paus. 4.2.5, 8.4.7, 10.31.2; Callimachus *Hymn to Artemis* 220–24; Athen, 14.71.

126. *Il.* 9.565–72; Homer's tale may have differed slightly because the purpose of Phoenix in telling this story to Achilles was perhaps to serve as a *paradeigma* to persuade his younger counterpart of the dangers of cherishing one's wrath over receiving the peace offerings of an offending party. See further Wilson 2002, esp. 96–104.

127. *Il.* 9.555–59.

128. *Il.* 9.464–71 (464–65 for those who tried to persuade him: ἦ μὲν πολλὰ ἔται καὶ ἀνεψιοὶ ἀμφὶς ἐόντες | αὐτοῦ λισσόμενοι κατερήτυον ἐν μεγάροισι).

129. *Il.* 9.574–89.

130. *Od.* 8.158–64. The verb νείκεσε appears at line 158.

131. *Od.* 8.97–103. For the professed scorn toward the merchant profession in the Homeric world, see Tandy 1997.

132. *Od.* 8.166; 8.184–85.

133. *Od.* 8.186–98.

134. *Od.* 8.205.

135. *Od.* 8.202–53.

136. *Od.* 8.382–84; 8.396–97.

137. *Od.* 8.401–15.

138. *Od.* 18.8–19.

139. *Od.* 18.36–104.

140. *Od.* 18.94.

141. *Od.* 8.205–11.

142. The quarrel between Agamemnon and Khryses, priest of Apollo (*Il.* 1.11ff.); the ongoing dispute between Agamemnon and Achilles, which erupts at *Il.* 1.133 but dominates much of the narrative afterward; and Menelaos' disgrace after the award of second prize to Antilokhos in the chariot race (*Il.* 23.423ff.).

143. *Il.* 1.11; the poet reiterates the dishonor done to Khryses at 1.94, when Kalkhas reveals Apollo's wrath as the cause of the Achaeans' suffering.

144. For an excellent discussion of the way in which Homer employs the terms *apoina* and *poinê*, see Wilson 2002. To summarize her complex argument with regard to these labels, *apoina* is equivalent to ransom, that which someone, usually a father (or other paternal figure) offers to the victor in order to win back someone else from a captor, the victim typically belonging to the familial sphere of he who offers *apoina*. *Poinê*, on the other hand, is offered as compensation by a party who acknowledges they have inflicted harm upon another party, a harm that resulted in a diminution of *timê*, honor, of the aggrieved individual. The *poinê*, among other functions, serves to restore the *timê* of the wronged party, at the expense, and in recognition of the loss, of *timê* for he who pays *poinê*. For an interesting but limited parallel, one can look to the Beti, principally of Cameroon and Equatorial Guinea: there a wronged party speaks of "returning the injury" (*vudan*) and offenders are expected to "compensate" (*kun*); Rouland 1994, 274; Verdier 1980, 28–30, with literature cited.

145. *Il.* 1.13, 1.25ff., 1.15–21.

146. *Il.* 1.22–23, 1.376–77.

147. In retribution for his dishonored priest, Apollo sent a plague upon the Achaean camp (*Il.* 1.35–54). Agamemnon did not limit his foolishness to the outrage against Khryses and, by extension, the god he served; ignoring the general will of the Achaeans is a key component of Agamemnon's *atê*. His refusal to consider the wishes of the larger community and the disastrous consequences for the Achaeans as a whole can be viewed as an object lesson in irresponsible behavior by leaders. Cf. *Il.* 5.76–78, 16.603–5.

148. Wilson 2002, 43–48.

149. *Il.* 1.54; *Il.* 1.84–100.

150. *Il.* 1.111–17; 1.389–90; 1.432–74.

151. Wilson 2002, 50.

152. *Il.* 1.118–19; the principal justification for his demand was that he could not be the only one without a prize, "when it be not at all fitting" (ἐπεὶ οὐδὲ ἔοικε). Presumably, this unseemliness arose from his position as leader of the host, as implied by his threat at 1.135–39; if the Achaeans did not provide what he regarded as suitable restitution, he suggested he would seize the prize of Achilles, Odysseus, or Ajax. Only the prize of another *basileus* would satisfy Agamemnon's honor; anything less would constitute a loss of face.

153. *Il.* 1.125–26.

154. Donlan 1993.

155. Wilson 2002, esp. 20–27, 37–39.

156. Donlan 1979; 1993.

157. Roberts 1979, 61ff. with literature cited; Rouland 1994, 260.

158. *Il.* 1.149, 1.159.

159. Gernet 1981, 147–48.

160. Crotty 1994, 33–34n17.

161. Wilson 2002, 50.

162. *Il.* 1.158–60.

163. *Il.* 1.169–71 (νῦν δ' εἶμι Φθίηνδ', ἐπεὶ ἦ πολὺ φέρτερόν ἐστιν | οἴκαδ' ἴμεν σὺν νηυσὶ κορωνίσιν, οὐδέ σ' ὀΐω | ἐνθάδ' ἄτιμος ἐὼν ἄφενος καὶ πλοῦτον ἀφύξειν).

164. Donlan 1993; Wilson 2002, 80–81.

165. *Il.* 1.173–86.

166. *Il.* 1.185–87 (ὄφρ' εὖ εἰδῇς | ὅσσον φέρτερός εἰμι σέθεν, στυγέῃ δὲ καὶ ἄλλος | ἶσον ἐμοὶ φάσθαι καὶ ὁμοιωθήμεναι ἄντην).

167. That the assembly was still present is clear from *Il.* 1.188–90 (Πηλεΐωνι δ' ἄχος γένετ', ἐν δέ οἱ ἦτορ | στήθεσσιν λασίοισι διάνδιχα μερμήριξεν, | ἢ ὅ γε φάσγανον ὀξὺ ἐρυσσάμενος παρὰ μηροῦ | τοὺς μὲν ἀναστήσειεν, ὁ δ' Ἀτρεΐδην ἐναρίζοι).

168. *Il.* 14.82–108; the presence of only the *basileis* in this meeting is suggested at 14.27–28. Hoebel 1940, 50ff. describes how among the Comanche a grievous insult, in a case of adultery, only became a cause for action by the aggrieved party once the adulterer's grandfather made it public knowledge during an open gathering, a stick game, at which the cuckold (already aware of the affair), his wife, and the adulterer were all present, along with other members of the group. The cuckold's response, the killing of the grandfather's favorite horse (first, in fact) as well as a pony belonging to the offending younger man, demonstrates that the former's public disclosure was just as serious an insult as the adultery itself.

169. *Il.* 1.188–205.

170. Wilson 2002, esp. 52–56.

171. *Il.* 1.171; 1.233–44.

172. His complaint to his mother Thetis: *Il.* 1.352–56; his reiteration to Patroklos that Agamemnon took Briseis as if Achilles were a wanderer without honor: 14.58–59; and his rejection of Agamemnon's first overture to mend the rift through the offer of gifts: 9.607–8 (οὔ τί με ταύτης | χρεὼ τιμῆς· φρονέω δὲ τετιμῆσθαι Διὸς αἴσῃ: "I have no need of this 'honor,' since I believe myself to have been honored by the apportionment of Zeus"), which references Achaean reverses that Achilles had requested of Zeus through Thetis.

173. "Snatched away" (ἀφέλεσθε): *Il.* 1.299; seizure as a cause of dishonor: *Il.* 14.58–59 (see preceding note); the rejection of the embassy on the grounds that Agamemnon had seized Briseis (εἵλετο): *Il.* 9.336; 9.344; 9.368; the complaint to Thetis: *Il.* 1.356 (ἑλών).

174. *Il.* 1.197–214.

175. For example, Nestor reminded Agamemnon, "he whom the gods have honored, you have dishonored (*Il.* 9.110–11: ὃν ἀθάνατοί περ ἔτισαν, ἠτίμησας). Poseidon also alluded to the fact that Agamemnon had taken honor from Achilles: 13.113, ἀπητίμησε. The instances could be multiplied; a wider awareness existed of Achilles' loss of *timê.*

176. Dodds 1951, 17: "[Homeric] man's highest good is not the enjoyment of quiet conscience, but the enjoyment of *timê,* public esteem"; Adkins 1960, 49: "the Homeric hero cannot fall back upon his own opinion of himself, for his self only has the value which other people put upon it." More recently, van Wees 1992, esp. 71.

177. *Il.* 1.247–84. The authority of age in considering advice was also asserted by Odysseus over Achilles at 19.218–19; see also van Wees 1992, 75. Wilson 2002, 62–63, 82–87 makes much as well of the paternal role asserted by various figures, including Nestor, though sees his intervention in book 1 as failing because of his inability to recognize the "qualitative difference" in *timê* enjoyed by the "king" in her "fixed-system," the very thing Achilles despises and contests. Nestor's injunction to the parties to cease their strife appears at 1.275–84.

178. *Il.* 1.286–304.

179. *Il.* 1.305.

180. *Il.* 1.294, 1.303, 1.245–46.

181. *Il.* 1.323 (χειρὸς ἑλόντ' ἀγέμεν Βρισηΐδα).

182. *Il.* 2.342.

183. *Il.* 2.370–72, 375–78. See Dodds 1951, 1–27 for the ascription to divine agency for Agamemnon's conduct.

184. Loving strife: *Il.* 9.63–64; the dishonor to Achilles: 9.111; the voicing of opposition: 9.106–9, also acknowledged by Agamemnon at 19.85-86 (πολλάκι δή μοι τοῦτον Ἀχαιοὶ μῦθον ἔειπον, | καί τέ με νεικείεσκον). See also the discussion in Donlan 1979.

185. *Il.* 9.113–14.

186. Wilson 2002, 26–27.

187. *Il.* 9.121–57.

188. *Il.* 9.141–42.

189. *Il.* 9.162–64, 9.173.

190. *Il.* 9.120.

191. Wilson 2002, 74–80.

192. Wilson 2002, 75; Donlan 1993.

193. Donlan 1993.

194. *Il.* 9.160–61.

195. *Il.* 9. 229–48.

196. *Il.* 9.260–61.

197. *Il.* 9.308–429.

198. *Il.* 9.515–18.

199. *Il.* 9.624–43, with the appeal to *philotês* at line 630, and the juxtaposition of *poinê* for slain kin and Achilles' obduracy over Briseis at 632–33 and 636–38, respectively.

200. *Il.* 9.645–48.

201. Donlan 1993, 163.

202. *Il.* 1.119.

203. Donlan 1993, 161–62.

204. Wilson 2002, 74.

205. Donlan 1993.

206. *Il.* 9.697–703.

207. *Il.* 11.664ff.

208. Compare the rejection of Paris' offer, which did not include the return of Helen (***A5***).

209. Griffin 1995, 21 argues that the heroes see Agamemnon's offer as satisfactory.

210. *Il.* 23.423–613.

211. *Aretê: Il.* 23.570–72 (Ἀντίλοχε, πρόσθεν πεπνυμένε ποῖον ἔρεξας. | ᾔσχυνας μὲν ἐμὴν ἀρετὴν, βλάψας δέ μοι ἵππους, | τοὺς σοὺς πρόσθε βαλών, οἵ τοι πολὺ χείρονες ἦσαν). *Aretê* forms part of the same vocabulary as *timê* and *aidôs*, in terms of status and worth as determined by others, and thus Menelaos was accusing Antilokhos with diminishing the former's standing in the community by showing a lack of deference; for a discussion of this vocabulary with literature cited, see van Wees 1992, 69–77.

212. *Il.* 23.573–78.

213. *Il.* 23.579–80.

214. *Il.* 23.580–85.

215. *Il.* 23.306–30.

216. *Il.* 23.587–93.

217. *Il.* 23.602–11.

218. *Il.* 9.131–33; 19.258–66; 19.175–76.

219. *Il.* 19.140–41, 19.40–46.

220. *WD* 343–51, 700–701 speaks to the importance of good opinion among one's neighbors. Hesiod also stresses the importance of having witnesses to agreements: *WD* 370–72. See also Chapter 2.3 about the importance of reputation in game theory.

221. *Il.* 19.86–96, 19.121–38 for Agamemnon's tale of Ate and how he, too, was stricken "blind" by her. Dodds 1951, 2–15 provides an excellent discussion of the role of Ate in Agamemnon's apology and many of its implications for the psychological make-up of Homeric man. I cannot, however, agree with his conclusion (3) that "early Greek justice cared nothing for intent—it was the act that mattered." As the present discussion demonstrates, the question of intent was crucial to both Menelaos and Agamemnon; and as we have already discussed, Odysseus decided to spare Phemios and Medon because their participation in the wasting of his household had not been intentional or willing.

222. *Il.* 19.270–74. Contra, Donlan 1993.

223. *Il.* 1.442–45, 1.458–74.

224. *Il.* 1.451–57.

225. *Il.* 19.146–47.

226. *Il.* 19.172–74 (τὰ δὲ δῶρα ἄναξ ἀνδρῶν Ἀγαμέμνων | οἰσέτω ἐς μέσσην ἀγορήν, ἵνα πάντες Ἀχαιοὶ | ὀφθαλμοῖσιν ἴδωσι, σὺ δὲ φρεσὶ σῇσιν ἰανθῇς).

227. The poet refers to Ares' act as having shamed the bed of lordly Hephaistos (*Od.* 8.269–70), but the notion of a disgrace to honor is notably absent. The concepts of *timê*, *aretê*, and *aidôs* are not connected with this tale, except when the goddesses stay away from the spectacle of the apprehended paramours; see discussion below.

228. *Od.* 8.270–71.

229. *Od.* 8.276–84; 8.296–305; 8.324–27.

230. *Od.* 8.317–20.

231. *Od.* 8.329–32.

232. Hephaistos suggests that he holds Zeus otherwise indirectly responsible for his grief: *Od.* 8.308–11.

233. *Od.* 8.344–60.

234. [Hes.] fr. 43a.31–57.

235. [Hes.] fr. 43a.31–36.

236. Gagarin 1986, 35n49; schol. Lycophron 1393 = Merkelbach and West 1967, fr. 43a.

237. [Hes.] fr. 43a.35–38.

238. [Hes.] fr. 43a.38–39. Why no mortal could resolve the matter is unclear, but there is explicit reference that the disputants turned to and agreed upon the goddess. The resort to a divine adjudicator may have grown out of the inability of the parties to settle on anyone within their own community ostensibly impartial enough to resolve the matter fairly. This is admittedly speculative, but it makes sense within the context of the story.

239. [Hes.] fr. 43a.40 (ἀτρεκέως διέθηκ[ε] δίκην). Gagarin 1986, 35 presumes the goddess to be Athena, though there is no reason to think that she could not be the personification of Dike.

240. [Hes.] fr. 43a.41–43.

241. Thus Gagarin 1986, 35–36, with competing literature cited.

242. D. Cohen 1984; 1991, 100–108; Todd 1993, 276–78; Cantarella 2005, 240–41.

243. *WD* 35–39.

244. See Ellickson 1991, 57–58, 232–33 on the value of "truthful negative gossip" as a form of self-help employed in a rural American community, usually intended to force its object to play by the rules; as Ellickson 1991, 57 notes, "this usually works because only the extreme deviants are immune from the general obsession with neighborliness."

245. *Il.* 18.497–508.

246. *Il.* 18.497–502 (497: λαοὶ δ' εἰν ἀγορῇ ἔσαν ἀθρόοι—note the same concepts of *agora* and *agoreô* used to describe the setting of the disputes between Achilles and Agamemnon.)

247. *Il.* 18.503–6.

248. I agree with Gagarin 1986, 30–31 that public opinion played a determining role, but I would go further than he does. While Gagarin views acceptability to the litigants themselves as a necessary condition for a *dikê* to be the straightest, I argue that this could only be true insofar as the pressure of the community indicated which *dikê* must be accepted by the disputants. For example, the *dikê* handed to Hesiod and Perses was clearly not mutually acceptable, but it was enforceable nonetheless.

249. Bohannon 1957, esp. 13–19, 28–69 describes the *jir,* the court, among the Tiv of Nigeria. The chief of the subgroup of Tiv Bohannon observed, along with eminent men known as *mbatarev*, would convene for the hearing of cases among the members of the group. The chief and *mbatarev* formed a semicircle, while interested parties from the community would gather before them. The complainant spoke first, followed by the respondent, throughout which the *mbatarev* could engage with the disputants, as could any member of the crowd who was present. Settlement of the dispute, as Bohannon 1957, 65 described it, was reached when "the opinion of the community . . . forces concurrence. Judging . . . consists largely in the timely suggestion of what the majority thinks is right or desirable." See also Gluckman 1973, 15 on the Barotse of Zambia, who allow for the participation of anyone present at the *kuta* to cross-examine the litigants and witnesses.

250. Among the Inuit, disputants engage in singing contests to influence public opinion and to make their adversaries lose face; Rouland 1979, 96–101.

251. As demonstrated by the Shield of Achilles and *WD* 27–29. Also see Lanni 1997 for the continued popularity of watching trials at Classical Athens.

252. See also Bohannon 1957, 13 on the keen interest the Tiv took in hearing disputes.

253. *Il.* 14.243–62.

254. *Il.* 14.257–58.

255. *Il.* 14.258–61.

256. *Od.* 16.409–27.

257. *Od.* 16.424–25, 428–29.

258. *Od.* 16.430.

259. Hesiod's cosmogony makes Nyx the daughter of Chaos (*Theog.* 123) and the mother of Strife, her eldest daughter (*WD* 16–17). See also the powers of Nyx over creation and her primal role in mythological schemes as suggested in later Greek literature (Ar. *Av.* 693ff.; Arist. *Metaph.* 1071b27).

260. Wolff 1946.

261. Penelope accuses Antinoös of forgetting the debt he and his family owed to the house of Odysseus; *Od.* 16.418.

262. Yngvesson 1989.

263. Critics of three-strikes-you're-out laws in the United States routinely offer some variation of the hypothetical case of the individual who has two previous, minor felony convictions, and in a moment of desperation that might affect anyone, say, holds up a convenience store with an unloaded weapon: does such a person deserve life in prison without the possibility of parole? Would that constitute justice?

264. E.g., Thür 1996, 58ff.

265. Schmitz 2004, esp. 27–104 argues that the sort of agonistic impulses I have enumerated here will have applied more to the elite than to commoners who valued solidarity and were less tolerant of deviant behavior. While that may be so, the preceding investigation indicates that community stability was not simply a concern of the nonelites in early Greek communities.

266. Ellickson 1991, 33–39 describes the case of one Frank Ellis in Shasta County, California, who flaunted the norms of the cattle ranchers and ranchette owners, ignoring the established practices of neighborly behavior to the point of precipitating a petition drive aimed at reining him in. Ellis ignored the pressure but moved away from the area soon after the attendant zoning and political issues had played themselves out.

267. Papakonstantinou 2008, esp. 112–25.

268. Chapter 5.1 below.

269. E. Posner 2000, 15–18, 26–32, 88–91.

Chapter 4

1. Plut. *Sol.* 5.1–2.

2. Plut. *Sol.* 5.3.

3. The modern argument finds its genesis in the works especially of Nilsson 1928 and Lorimer 1947, and generally stood until recently. See subsequent note.

4. Latacz 1977; Morris 1987, 197–205; Raaflaub 1997b; van Wees 1998; 2001 (arguing for the absolute and relative wealth of the Athenian *zeugitai*); 2006 (that any hoplite group at Athens at the time of Solon's activity would have more closely identified with the elite landowners than with the mass of marginal landowners and/or laborers); C. Morgan 2001; Schmitz 2004.

5. The term is necessarily a loaded one, both in modern and ancient usage, and scholars have typically meant a variety of ideas when using it to describe the various forms of *polis* government. The one common thread is that when one speaks of "democratizing," one means the inclusion of a greater number of the community's individuals in its political life, however short of an imagined standard such inclusion may remain.

6. For example, Demand 1996, 143–49 views Kylon's attempt at tyranny as the result of popular discontent and Drakon's law code as "the first sign of possible accommodation of the discontents" (143). She goes on to state that, even though Drakon's laws were only the transcription of existing customs (i.e., he introduced no reforms or innovations), his code was still "a significant step forward, for publication in writing gave the aristocratic keepers of the law less chance to 'remember' the laws to their own advantage"; similarly, T. Martin 1996, 82ff.

7. Gagarin 2008, esp. 39–66, 110–21; Papakonstantinou 2008, esp. 45–62.

8. Eder 1986; Gagarin 1986.

9. Among others, Coldstream 2003, 295–302 argues for the rapid spread of literacy

in the eighth and seventh centuries; also, Murray 1980, 94; Vernant 1982, 52; Detienne 1988b, 7–26; Gagarin 2008, 39–66.

10. For example, Calhoun 1944, 22ff; Jeffery 1976, 43; Murray 1980, 173; Vernant 1982, 53. Papakonstantinou 2008, 76–82 tempers this position but still seems to indicate that the use of written instruments as the basis of (or in) litigation will have necessarily had an overall effect of greater fairness.

11. Bonner and Smith 1930, 1.67ff; Jeffery 1976, 43; Vernant 1982, 70; Martin 1996, 60–64, 84; Donlan 1997, 45. With regard to Solonian Athens in particular: O'Neil 1995, 15–21, 34–35; Freeman 1999, 105–6.

12. Murray 1980, 173; Vernant 1982; Donlan 1997, 44: ". . . rule by laws that were arrived at publicly and posted in public naturally worked towards leveling the advantages of birth and wealth and curbing aristocratic excesses." Raaflaub and Wallace 2007b, 22–24, 44–45 argue that the seventh-century law of Dreros regarding magisterial iteration "reflects an effort by a community to gain control over its office-holders and leaders" (23). I offer a different interpretation in Chapter 6.4.

13. E.g., Schmitz 2004, esp. 190–248 understands Solonian legislation as reflective principally of the interests and values of neither hoplites nor elites, but of the village peasants.

14. Murray 1980, 173; Vernant 1982, 74–75.

15. Finley 1970, 103; Stroud 1968, 73f.; Gschnitzer 1981, 75.

16. Jeffery 1976, 91; Vernant 1982, 75.

17. Jeffery 1976, 43; Raaflaub 1997b, 53; Starr 1992, 20. With particular regard to Athens, see Anhalt 1993, 1–8.

18. *WD* 38–39, 202–12, 248–55, 263–64 and Chapter 1.1 above.

19. Most notably Bonner and Smith 1930, 1.46–51; Forrest 1966, 60; S.L. West 1978, 41ff; Gagarin 1986, 85ff., and subsequent note.

20. Contra Papakonstantinou 2008, 36–43, who views the *basileis* as Hesiod's main target, characterizing the aristocracy's grip on the administration of justice (though this runs somewhat counter to his emphasis on the norms of a community as widely recognized and accepted (26) and his overall argument regarding the pluralism of legal narratives). See Tandy and Neale 1996, 20–21, where they discuss the evidence for "good" leadership in Homer and Hesiod and the discussion that follows in the text below.

21. *WD* 636–40.

22. Tandy and Neale 1996, 39–40 suggest that Perses has already lost everything, his *kleros* and *oikos,* in part through his accumulation of *khrea.* I believe that this is certainly a defensible interpretation, based on the evidence of *WD* 37–39 and 404–5, though I do not take it as necessarily inevitable. One could read the former passage as Hesiod's complaint that the *basileis* were complicit in Perses' successful seizure of *ta polla* subsequent to the brothers' division of the patrimony, yet the latter passage does suggest that Perses is now without *oikos.* Thus, Tandy and Neale argue that Hesiod now fears that the same economic and political system that has led to Perses' ruination, his brother will now attempt to use in order to try to gain from Hesiod yet more than he already had. See also the possibilities Gagarin 1974 presents. The main point of my analysis stands in either event.

23. Hom. *Il.* 18.507–8.

24. This was the view of Hirzel 1966, 414, 419ff.; Detienne 1963, 27. See, in addition, Gagarin's discussion 1986, 20–24 of Herodotus' story about Deiokes (Hdt. 1.96–99), which likewise imagines an arrangement of gifts in exchange for judicial pronouncements. Far

from suspecting corruption or prejudice, the Medes so esteemed Deiokes and his judicial wisdom that they made him king.

25. *Theog.* 93. See also Donlan 1997, 42 for the lack of apparent irony or sarcasm in referring to the dues paid to *basileis* as "gifts."

26. Tandy and Neale 1996, 37; Tandy 1997, 207–8, with literature cited.

27. Indeed, if Perses has already lost his *oikos*, Hesiod clearly believes it is his brother's fault.

28. The argument has been variously made that Hesiod and his brother are to be understood as members of the *agathoi*, a prosperous and extensive group of peasants who were excluded from the governing elite but were certainly distinct from the *kakoi*. See Morris 1987, 197–205; Bravo 1977; Adkins 1972, 23–33. Contra: Millett 1984; Tandy and Neale 1996, 26–29.

29. As M. L. West 1978, 3–25, 37–38 argues, Near Eastern wisdom literature enjoyed a profound role in shaping Hesiod's own work, and on more than one occasion examples from the former offer "expostulations and demands for righteousness addressed to the kings and rulers of the people." (37) Thus, contra West's own interpretation, I do not see why Hesiod's various admonitions to the *basileis* must be interpreted as growing out of a long-standing and widespread litany of grievances with the aristocratic judges. On West's own evidence, it seems these warnings are just as likely a refashioned literary trope.

30. *Theog.* 81–87. Gagarin 1992 undertakes a useful discussion that places the connection between poet and *basileus* seen in Hesiod in its wider epic context; see also Murray 1980, 62.

31. *Theog.* 96–103. One might also note, along with Solmsen 1982, 3, that it was not the character of the Muses' gift necessarily to be absolutely consistent from one "performance" to the next.

32. *Theog.* 104–15.

33. Tandy and Neale 1996, 6–7 assume that *Theogony* will have been the type of poem performed in the halls of the powerful, meant to "buttress the position of the elites . . . [that] presents a world that is governed well by gods and men." Therefore, one could argue that *Theogony* does not necessarily reflect how Hesiod felt all along about the *basileis*. I see things differently, as evidenced by the subsequent discussion.

34. The occasion for the victory was the funeral games of Amphidamas (P.-W. "Amphidamas" 8, 1^2.1899.64–1900.23); *WD* 654–57; Plut. *Mor.* 153E-F, and the *Contest of Homer and Hesiod,* 315, describes him as "*basileus*" of Euboea, and in the former named him a hero of the Lelantine War, which fits well with the widely accepted chronology for Hesiod, ca. 750–675 (West 1978, 30–31). See Coldstream 2003, 210, 313, 350; 1976, 15; M. L. West 1966, 439ff.; de Polignac 1995, 130–32; Mazarakis-Ainian 1987.

35. M. L. West 1966, 41ff.; 1978, 32ff.; Janko 1982, 229–31. Tandy and Neale 1996, 7 likewise take it as given that *Works and Days* was the later work.

36. *WD* 216–24, 238–64.

37. Additionally, M. L. West 1978, 33 describes the entire poem as "not a private communication to [Perses], but a public sermon in which he serves as a butt." By extension, the *basileis* might be similarly characterized though again it seems that the real quarrel here is between Hesiod and his brother, not the poet and the elite.

38. Pace, Bonner and Smith 1930, 1.46f., Hesiod did have options in terms of settling affairs with his brother. It is manifest that he and Perses were not required to submit their dispute to settlement in a public forum through the arbitration of the *basileis,* since Hesiod

suggests to Perses that they could simply come to an agreement between themselves (*WD* 33–36). See also the discussion about nonformal means of settling trouble cases in Chapter 3 above.

39. *Il.* 2.225–68.

40. Rose 1988, 6–11 offers an excellent discussion of previous scholarship.

41. Rose 1988, 13–14: ". . . it is impossible to raise the issue of disaffection with the war on the part of even an isolated member of the *demos* . . . without reminding the audience of the real corruption and relative stupidity of Agamemnon and, by extension, the vulnerability of the Achaian social hierarchy to very poor leadership"; Thalmann 1988, 14: ". . . there is nothing particularly shocking by prevailing standards when Odysseus uses force on the soldiers, but there is nothing particularly admirable either. A gap has opened between ideology [*sc.*, that legitimates the position of the *basileis*] and the actual exercise of authority. The soldiers might naturally feel resentment when reality does not measure up to the model that justifies the social hierarchy."

42. Thalmann 1988, esp. 16–25.

43. Thalmann 1988, 5, 25.

44. *Il.* 1.188–224; 2.185–210

45. Rose 1988, 16: "When Odysseus uses Agamemnon's scepter to impose an adherence to Agamemnon's rule which is no longer spontaneously granted by the *demos,* the 'message' is accordingly far from straightforward"; *Il.* 1.234–46.

46. Thalmann 1988, 7–12. As Thalmann further argues, Odysseus, in seizing the scepter and forcing the soldiers back to order, has revealed kingship "brutally stripped of its civil niceties" (12). See additionally Haubold 2008 for the responsibilites of Homeric leadership to the *laos.*

47. Rose 1988, 19. Wilson 2002, makes the case, of course, that Achilles challenges the political authority of Agamemnon generally.

48. *Od.* 2.15–34; Finley 2002, 77–80, 90–92.

49. *Od.* 2.28–32.

50. *Od.* 2.229–41. The language of lines 235–41 is especially telling. (ἀλλ' ἦ τοι μνηστῆρας ἀγήνορας οὔ τι μεγαίρω | ἔρδειν ἔργα βίαια κακορραφίῃσι νόοιο· | σφὰς γὰρ παρθέμενοι κεφαλὰς κατέδουσι βιαίως | οἶκον 'Οδυσσῆος, τὸν δ' οὐκέ τι φασὶ νέεσθαι. | νῦν δ' ἄλλῳ δήμῳ νεμεσίζομαι, οἷον ἅπαντες | ἧσθ' ἄνεῳ, ἀτὰρ οὔ τι καθαπτόμενοι ἐπέεσσι | παύρους μνηστῆρας καταπαύετε πολλοὶ ἐόντες: "Nevertheless I do not feel any grudge toward the manly suitors, that they do violent deeds with mischievousness of mind; for they hazard their own heads as they by force devour the house of Odysseus, whom they say will never return. But now I am wroth with the rest of the people, as you all sit in silence, and still do not say anything accosting to stop a few suitors, you yourselves being many.")

51. *Od.* 2.242–59. See also Chapter 3, n.107 above.

52. *Od.* 16.370–82.

53. See Chapter 3.2 above.

54. Forsdyke 2005, esp. 30–69.

55. For a general discussion of the concerns of "lyric" poets, see Campbell 1983, 84–118; for Solon in particular, Anhalt 1993; Irwin 2005, esp. 175–83, 223–30 on Solon and the theme of justice. Morris 1996 has also argued that within the lyric tradition, broadly defined, one can identify a more "popular" strain; however, one may note that it nevertheless is silent on the issue of aristocratic judicial abuse perpetrated on the

commoners. Solon, of course, makes reference to justice in his poems and the important role it plays in the stability of the community, but as Irwin 2005 and Adkins 1985, 29–31 have noted, there was a very close connection between poetry and rhetoric in the Archaic age, and the testimony of Solon regarding law and justice must be used cautiously. See also Lavelle 2000.

56. [Arist.] *AthPol.* 5.2 for archon and *diallaktês*; Plut. *Sol.* 14.3 and *Mor.* 763D for all three positions; and *Sol.* 16.5 for *nomothetês*. For the date, see Wallace 1983; Cadoux 1948. See Rhodes 1993, 120–23 for further discussion of the literature on Solon's activities.

57. The loci classici: [Arist.] *AthPol.* 5.2–3; Plut. *Sol.* 14.1–15.2; *Sol.* fr.4 (= [Arist.] *AthPol.* 12.1); Hdt. 1.29; Androt. *FGH* 324 F 34.

58. For generally accepted and judiciously framed interpretations, see Sealey 1977, 107–23; Andrewes 1982, 377–82; also, Rhodes 2006, 252–53. Van Wees 2006 argues for an even more extreme position of elite dominance whose competition for power with one another became so debilitating that it provoked a reaction against them. Lavelle 2000 and Wallace 2007 see the *demos* as perhaps more empowered than traditionally thought. Van Wees 2001 has made the case elsewhere that Solon's *zeugitai* could have been by no means poor based on a qualification of 200 *medimnoi*. For doubts on the quantitative thresholds assigned to classes as literal or historical, see Connor 1987 and Ste. Croix 2004, 5–71. For indications that Greeks would not have possessed the requisite numerate skills for such an elaborate scheme ca. 600, see Hawke 2008b.

59. Rihll 1991 has suggested that our understanding of *hektêmoroi* has hitherto been incorrect and argues that before Solon, some people were standing as sureties, a type of collateral in return for their use of public land being worked by slaves; in other words, they were borrowing it in return for a fixed rent involving one-sixth of the produce. If they defaulted, they would be sold as slaves abroad and the *polis* would profit. Under this interpretation, the wealthy were not expanding their holdings at the expense of other citizens, nor should Athenian society be characterized as in some way "feudal" before Solon (itself a misleading and misappropriated label even for the Middle Ages; see Reynolds 1994).

60. There is no reason, however, to think that the *Eupatridai* would have shrunk from the opportunity to victimize their social peers who had fallen on hard times, especially those toward whom they harbored enmity; see also Forsdyke 2005. Still, the culprits were manifestly rich (πλουσίοι) according to Solon (fr. 6.3), though the famous lawgiver nowhere uses the label *Eupatridai*, which has caused no small amount of consternation in modern scholarship. Nevertheless, at the end of the seventh century the majority of the rich would have been those "descended from good fathers"; see Sealey 1960; 1961; 1977, 116–19; Roebuck 1974, 488f.; Donlan 1999, 62–71; Wallace 2007, 49–50, 58. Figueira 1984 has suggested not crediting the existence of the *Eupatridai* as a "caste."

61. For typical interpretations in this vein: Masarrachia 1958, 146–48; Mossé 1979, 89f.; Murray 1980, 180–83; Manville 1990, 125–26; Wallace 2007. Their arguments find support in the *Athenaion Politeia* itself, though for problems with its conclusions, see Rhodes 1993, 169–74; Lavelle 2000, 68–71 for Solon's rhetoric in his surviving poetry. See also Chapter 2.1 above.

62. Sol. fr. 36.18–20.

63. Ruschenbusch 1966 doubted the authenticity of about 40 percent of the "Solonian" legal fragments he identified in his still-fundamental study, and more recently Anderson 2003, esp. 47–52, 57–66, has made a sustained and compelling case against

a major Solonian constitution; see also Day and Chambers 1967, 71–89; Fuks 1953, 14–18. Scafuro 2006, 175–80 has suggested modifying Ruschenbusch's categorization by identifying those laws that could obviously not have achieved their attested form during Solon's time but are likely to have had a Solonian kernel around which details changed due to historical contingencies.

64. Mitchell 1997; Foxhall 1997a; Lavelle 2000.

65. E. Harris 1997.

66. Plut. *Sol.* 25.1–2 discusses the arrangement of Solon's laws and records the controversy over the meaning of *axones* and *kyrbeis*, upon which they were "published." Stroud 1979 has tried to solve the puzzle, but with mixed results. Aelian *VH* 8.10 is one of the few ancient writers to give prominence to the fact of Solon's laws being written, but his account is even later than Plutarch's (late second/early third century CE). Stehle 2006 suggests that Solon's surviving political poetry is too self-conscious and consistent in its portrayal of the lawgiver's persona to be genuinely sixth-century; it must belong to the ideological debates of the fourth century (see also Lardinois 2006). I disagree: while there are elements that are reminiscent of an Isocratean position, the verse, at least as we have it, is so politically vague it is difficult to see how it would have done much to convince fourth-century Athenians of what a properly Solonian *politeia* was supposed to look like. What remains, furthermore, provides short shrift to the law's written nature, odd given the fourth-century Athenian equation of law with written law.

67. Stroud 1968, 66–70 and Gagarin 1981a, 19–21 both argue for the date; see also, Cadoux 1948, 94. Sealey 1987, 115–16 attempted to revive the theory of Beloch 1912–13, 1.2.256–62 that Drakon was not the name of an historical personage but rather a reference to a sacred snake (δράκων) that lived on the Acropolis. Beloch surmised that this divine snake was considered the religious font of the *polis's* pre-Solonian laws, and Sealey followed him in this. The theory runs completely at odds with the ancient testimonia, the full weight of which deemed Drakon a human being. For this reason and others, the thorough dismantling of Beloch's hypothesis by Adcock 1927 is still to be preferred (see likewise, Szegedy-Maszak 1978; and Papakonstantinou 2008, 64, who observes that the activities ascribed to early lawgivers are generally consistent with what survives of Archaic law). One might further note that Drakon and its derivative Drakontides were not uncommon names at Athens (Kirchner 1968, nos. 4542–55).

68. Thuc. 1.126.12 and Plut. *Sol.* 12.1.3 and 13.1–3 both preserve the memory of the disturbances at Athens in the last generation or so of the seventh century. Both Kylon and Megakles belonged to the highest reaches of the elite of Archaic Athens. The best source, but not without complications, is Thuc. 1.126.3–12; cf. the account in Hdt. 5.71, and the comments of Lambert 1986; Rhodes 1993, 79–84. I return to this episode in Chapter 5.4 below; see also the excellent discussion in Forsdyke 2005, 80–90.

69. Gagarin 1981a, 19–21, with 2008, 94–96. Contra: Forsdyke 2005, 84–90, who additionally believes that the law against tyranny may have originated as part of the response to the Kylonian episode and its aftermath.

70. Gagarin 2008, 100–101.

71. The homicide laws in the fourth century were on occasion referred to as "from the Areopagus" (Lys. 1.30, 6.15; Dem. 22.22), and if Wallace 1989, 3–46 is correct in believing that the Areopagus before Solon was principally a homicide court, it would certainly be possible that this body commissioned Drakon at least to draft the homicide law and then deposit it along with any others on the Areopagus hill itself. See Gagarin

1981a, 26–29 for a fuller discussion of the references to the Areopagus as a source of fourth-century homicide law. The official position of Drakon is, of course, a vexed one: he was clearly not *archon eponymos* for the year of his legislative activity, as Aristaikhmos held the post ([Arist.] *AthPol.* 4.1; Cadoux 1948, 92; Stroud 1968, 66–68; Develin 1989, 31). Drakon may have been one of the six *thesmothetai*, but as Stroud 1968, 74–75 argues, the notices of [Arist.] *AthPol.* and Paus. 9.36.8 stating respectively that Drakon "had set the laws" (τοὺς θεσμοὺς ἔθηκεν) and referring to "when Drakon had acted as law-setter for the Athenians" (Δράκοντος Ἀθηναίοις θεσμοθετήσαντος) are not conclusive; see also now the discussion by Sickinger 1999, 8–24. Indeed, the activities of Drakon as a creator and publisher of law (rather than an expounder of learned legal opinion) would have set him apart from the typical *thesmothetes* of the seventh century, if we can put any stock at all in [Arist.] *AthPol.* 3.4; see Rhodes 1993, 102–3.

72. Rihll 1991, 115 with n. 9.

73. [Arist.] *AthPol.* 7.1: Solon set all the laws but retained Drakon's law on homicide; Plut. *Sol.* 17.1: Solon repealed the laws of Drakon, except for those on homicide; Aelian *VH* 8.10: Solon ordered all the affairs of the city and wrote down (συνέγραψεν) the laws still used by Athens up to his own day.

74. Xen. *Oec.* 14.4; Plut. *Sol.* 17.1; Gell. *NA* 2.18.3; Pollux 8.42.

75. [Arist.] *AthPol.* 16.10; see discussion in Rhodes 1993, 220–23. Ostwald 1955 believed that Drakon authored *a* law on tyranny but certainly none of the versions preserved from antiquity; see also Gagarin 1981b; Forsdyke 2005, 87, 92.

76. Arist. *Pol.* 1274b15–21; cf. Gagarin 1981a, 116–18 for a compelling argument highlighting the late and shallow nature of the tradition which earned Drakon his immortality as "draconian."

77. [Arist.] *AthPol.* 4.1–5.1, 7.3–8.5.

78. Rhodes 1993, 113. Wallace 1989, 39–46 underscores the difficulties of the *Ath. Pol.* as a source for pre-Solonian Athens and believes (4–6) that the Areopagus before Solon, as it is presented in [Arist.] *AthPol.* is nothing more than the product of fourth-century speculation based on what the author knew of the council's activities after Solon; see also, Wallace 2007, 64–69. For an account of the invention of Drakon's constitution that still carries conviction, see Fuks 1953, 84–101.

79. Gallant 1982 has gone so far as to question the presence, let alone the group consciousness, of an artisan or commercial element (possibly Solon's *astoi*, e.g., fr. 4.6, at Athens ca. 600), and Lavelle 2000, 68–70 has offered the tantalizing suggestion that it may have been Solon himself who defined this as a rhetorically and politically useful term. Gagarin 2008, 104 may well be right that there is nothing in Drakon's law "to suggest that he aimed to further his own interests or those of a small ruling class by imposing his authority on ordinary people who would not have been able to read his law." For present purposes, however, it scarcely matters whether that was what he intended but rather that "ordinary people" would have been hard pressed to assume that written laws would act to their benefit, given the disintegration of economic and political conditions at Athens over the generation subsequent to the law's publication.

80. An exhaustive analysis of the literature ancient and modern is not possible here; Mühl 1928–29 provides a fundamental study, though subsequent generations have criticized his credulity of the account in Diodorus Siculus. Van Compornolle 1981, who otherwise accepts the tradition about the aristocratic bias of the early laws at Lokris, regards Zaleukos himself as ahistorical, based on Timaeus' own rejection of the lawgiver's

existence (*FGH* 566 F 130; though see Adcock 1927, 105, who argues that Timaeus appears to have simply despaired after attempts to reconcile the varying accounts available to him). Camassa 1988, 134–37 and Link 1992, 11–24 are more sympathetic to Zaleukos' historicity; Papakonstantinou 2008, 64–66 appears agnostic. Against Diodorus' claim (12.20.1) that Zaleukos was an aristocrat, Gagarin 1986, 58–62 presents the notice in an Aristotelian fragment (fr. 548 Rose = schol. Pind. *Ol.* 11.17) that Zaleukos was a shepherd (*poimên*) and thus of humble origin and otherwise argues for Diodorus' unreliability because he also called Zaleukos a Pythagorean, an obvious chronological impossibility. In my opinion, this reconstruction will not do: quite apart from the epic use of *poimên* to describe Agamemnon and other leaders of the folk (e.g., *Il.* 2.85, 2.254, 2.772, 7.230, 16.2, 19.35, etc.), it is difficult to see how Diodorus' report of one part of the confused tradition necessarily invalidates the report of another. It also quite ignores that Aristotle was willing, when need be, to force certain historical "facts" to his particular theories, and the lawgivers were no exception: he asserted (*Pol.* 1269a17–22) humbler origins and outsider status for Solon, Lykourgos, and Kharondas, as well, when the rest of the ancient tradition makes clear that, at least for the first two, such an assertion will not stand.

81. Lokris remained staunchly oligarchic well into the fifth century at least and perhaps as late as 347; van Compernolle 1981; Dunbabin 1948, 70ff.

82. Forsdyke 2005, 84–89, 91; Chapters 5.4 and 6.3 below.

83. Solon himself refers to the ways in which he protected wealth from those who greedily called for a redistribution of land: 4.4–8, 5.1–4, 34.1–6; cf. Plut. *Sol.* 15.1; [Arist.] *AthPol.* 5.2, though the latter has clearly misunderstood Solon's statements regarding *all* those who sought wealth, including the commoners, by ill-gotten means. On the Areopagus: [Arist.] *AthPol.* 8.4; Wallace 1989, 44, 55–64; 2007, 64–69.

84. In addition, see Chapter 4.3 below on the blurred line between the relative importance of written and unwritten laws in the Archaic and early Classical periods, as well as the continued administration of justice by elites.

85. Arist., *Pol.* 1279b1–25.

86. Meyer 1954/1893, 3.512–17; Weber 1968, 3.1352, 1359–60; Nilsson 1928; Detienne 1963, 140; Vernant 1982, 25. Snodgrass 1965 has provided the most lucid and influential formulation in recent decades, and one more reserved than the authorities just cited, arguing for a more gradual change.

87. Bryant 1990; Murray 1980.

88. See n. 4 above.

89. Frost 1984, 293.

90. Whitley 1997.

91. Anderson 2003, 45, 80 has also suggested that the first meaningful inclusion of the hoplites in the guidance of the Athenian polity did not happen until the reforms of Kleisthenes in 507/6. See also van Wees 2001.

92. Tandy 1997, 194–201, 217–21.

93. W. Harris 1989.

94. W. Harris 1989, 3–16 provides a useful discussion of the problem of definitions and modern prejudices when it comes to literacy or literate skill in the ancient world, with literature cited.

95. E.g., Manville 1990, 79–82; Forsdyke 2005, 88–89; Gagarin 2008, 77–80 and passim; Papakonstantinou 2008.

96. H. and M. van Effenterre 1994.

97. R. Thomas 2005, esp. 46.

98. Gagarin 2008, esp. 49–50, 76ff.; Papakonstantinou 2008, 47–63.

99. Arist. *Pol.* 1297b24–28; Gagarin 2008, 88.

100. Gagarin 2008, 56–58, 67–70; Papakonstantinou 2008, 77–81.

101. Gagarin 2008, 56–58; Meiggs and Lewis 1989, no. 8; *Nomima* 1.62.

102. Murray 1980, 94–96, for example, argues for widespread writing in Greece during the century from 750 to 650, using as part of his evidence the inscription of laws in the seventh century. Otherwise, the evidence he adduces is largely confined to simple lists (Olympic victors, Athenian magistrates) or the signatures of potters who owned their work. His argument that erratic letter forms and incorrect grammar indicate a considerable breadth of literacy does not make sense to me; it points rather, I would argue, to a wide distribution of the ability of people to scribble down names or pithy sayings in rough hands (often poorly) but does not suggest in any way a comprehension of more detailed written documents, such as lengthy public inscriptions or literary texts. Coldstream 2003, 301 also assumes the "rapid spread of literacy" from the late eighth century onwards from the "casual nature of the earliest graffiti, all of which are concerned with public life." A similar assumption regarding the sweeping effects of literacy shortly after the appearance of the alphabet occurs in Burns' 1981, 374 discussion of literacy in fifth-century Athens. The influence of Havelock 1963; 1982, 60–88 manifests itself quite clearly in these studies, as does that of Goody and Watt 1963, who saw the alphabetic system of writing as fundamentally transformative, democratizing literacy, and precipitating wholesale changes across Greek society (though Havelock believed the most significant changes took place in the fifth century, not earlier).

103. Slow development: W. Harris 1989, 45; see also Svenbro 1993, 31, who notes that seventeen funerary epigrams from the seventh century comprise "virtually the entire collection of funeral inscriptions from before 600." The work of Jeffery/Johnston 1990 underscores the scarcity of seventh-century material; though one must take into account the accident of survival, the pronounced dearth of seventh-century documents compared to sixth- and fifth-century examples is telling. Jeffery 1982, 3.1.819–33; Jeffery/Johnston 1990, 1–21 supported a date for the introduction of the alphabet somewhere in the first half of the eighth century or, at the earliest, the tail end of the ninth. See also Isserlin 1983, 151n2: while he rejects Jeffery's theory that the various Greek scripts all descended from a single source of Phoenician–Greek borrowing, he nevertheless doubts an origin for Greek alphabets predating 800 (though more recently cf. Powell 2002, 112–25). McCarter 1975, 103ff., while suggesting there was a prehistory in the process of Phoenician influence on the development of Greek alphabetic writing, argues for the independence of Greek alphabetic writing around 800. Additional authorities prior to the late 1970s who favored a date ca. 800–750 may be found in Heubeck 1979, 76 with notes 436–47; Heubeck's study has itself remained influential, and he prefers a date in the second half of the eighth century. Naveh's 1973 and 1982 contention that syllabary-alphabetic writing was introduced to the Greeks by Semitic speakers much earlier has convinced few.

104. W. Harris 1989, 46.

105. Hesiod makes no reference to writing whatsoever and Homer makes but one, that of *Il.* 6.168–69, where the poet refers to "baneful signs, many poisonous things written in a folded tablet" (σήματα λυγρὰ | γράψας ἐν πίνακι πτυκτῷ θυμοφθόρα πολλά). The meaning of this passage has been much debated; to my mind one of the best discussions remains Heubeck 1979, 128–46. Against his interpretation, see Bellamy 1989,

though the latter's arguments have met with considerable skepticism (Goebel 1989–90; Miller 1989–90).

106. W. Harris 1989, 49; see also the remarks of Miller 1989–90, 171: ". . . it can not be overlooked that the only extant examples of early Greek writing are miniscule compared to Homer's nearly 28,000 hexameter verses."

107. The fullest publication and discussion of these graffiti was originally undertaken by Bernand and Masson 1957, including illustrations. See also Meiggs and Lewis 1989, no. 7 and Jeffery/Johnston 1990, 38, 48, 348, 355.

108. See Hdt. 2.160–61 for King "Psammis" employing mercenaries at this time in his expedition against Ethiopia.

109. Bernand and Masson 1957, no. 1 = Meiggs and Lewis 1989, no. 7a; Jeffery/Johnston 1990, 355 with pl. 69 (48a). The writing is fairly neat and uniform, though as Bernand and Masson note, the letters vary in height from four to nine centimeters, and the spaces between lines range from four to eight centimeters.

110. Dillon 1997. Bernand and Masson suggested that the original "Oudamos" should be read "Eudamos."

111. The text reads, "When Psammetikhos came to Elephantine, those who sailed with Psammetikhos son of Theokles wrote this; and they came above Kerkis as far as the river allowed; and Potasimto had command of those of foreign speech and Amasis of the Egyptians; and Arkhon son of Amoibikhos wrote us, and Peleqos son of Eudamos" (translation adapted from Meiggs and Lewis).

112. Bernand and Masson 1957, no. 2 = Meiggs and Lewis 1989, no. 7g; Jeffery/Johnston 1990, 348, 355. The graffito is fragmentary, effaced in several places. What remains reads: "Anaxanor . . . of Ialysos [uncertain verb] . . . when the king, Psammetikhos, alongside Amasis, first led the army." The missing letters from the first line may well be ΕΓΡΑΦΕΜΕ ("Anaxanor of Ialysos wrote me when . . ."). Sufficient space for these letters exists, and this restoration would make sense given the other graffiti at the site.

113. Bernand and Masson 1957, no. 6 = Meiggs and Lewis 1989, no. 7e; Jeffery/Johnston 1990, 355 with pl. 69 (48b): ". . . and Krithis wrote me."

114. As noted by Meiggs and Lewis; it seems, however, given the largely Doric dialect, the missing letter may be better supposed as *phi*.

115. Bernand and Masson 1957, no. 4 = Meiggs and Lewis 1989, no. 7c; Jeffery/Johnston 1990, 348, 355: "Telephos the Ialysian wrote me" (ΤΗΛΕΦΟΣΜΕΓΡΑΦΕΗΟΙΑΛΥΣΙΟ[Σ].)

116. Bernand and Masson 1957, nos. 3 and 5 = Meiggs and Lewis 1989, nos. 7b and 7d; Jeffery/Johnston 1990, 355 with pl. 69 (48c).

117. Bernand and Masson 1957, no. 6 *bis* (based on a description by Lepsius). Bernand and Masson 1957, 19–20 argue that the name Πάβις from the text (ΠΑΒΙΣΗΟϘΟΛΟΦΟΝΙΟΣΣΥΝΨΑΜΜΑΤΑ) should perhaps be read Πάμβιος. Whether "Psammata" refers to the pharaoh or to Psammetikhos son of Theokles who led the company of mercenaries, "Pabis" spelled the name differently than did his colleagues.

118. Bernand and Masson 1957, 20; cf. W. Harris 1989, 48.

119. This is the opinion of Jeffery/Johnston 1990, 355, who attempt to explain the lack of an ethnic for the four names without it. Bernand and Masson 1957, 9–10 believe that Arkhon and Peleqos may also have come from Ialysos, but they do not explain the discrepancy between their graffito and Telephos' (both of which run left to right), and that of Anaxanor of Ialysos (which is boustrophedon).

120. The inscription of Arkhon and Peleqos uses the third person singular form (ΕΓΡΑΦΕ), curious given that both men take credit for its authorship. As nothing indicates a change of hand, presumably the one with the higher degree of scribal skill wrote on behalf of both; though see n. 110 above.

121. Johnston 1983, 67.

122. W. Harris 1989, 52.

123. Stoddart and Whitley 1988; R. Thomas 1992, 57.

124. Powell 1989, 331–32; R. Thomas 1992, 59.

125. Langdon 1976, 11, 17–22 (with nos. 20–35); R. Thomas 1992, 60.

126. R. Thomas 1992, 90 offers useful cautions about making too much even of the more spectacular examples we find from this period. For dedications, see Langdon 1976, 13–17 (nos. 1–19). For a different view of what these finds suggest regarding early literate ability, see Papakonstantinou 2008, 77–81.

127. W. Harris 1989, 52.

128. Cristofani 1981, 177–78.

129. Havelock 1982, 37n42.

130. Beazley 1956, 198; 1971, 69–70; Boardman 1974, 200–201.

131. Boardman 1975, 213.

132. W. Harris 1989, 52, 58–60.

133. Svenbro 1993, 44–63.

134. Knox 1968.

135. Svenbro 1993, 55.

136. Plut. *Arist.* 8.4–5.

137. The institution of ostracism has been construed as evidence of widespread literacy in early Classical Athens: e.g., Nieddu 1982, though other indications undermine such a view. Famously, Broneer 1938 describes the case of the 191 recovered ostraka bearing the name of Themistokles, Aristeides' rival; among these, analysts identified only fourteen discreet hands: perhaps an attempt to "stuff the ballot box" by Themistokles' opponents; see also Forsdyke 2005, 148–49. Havelock 1982, 199–200 argues that the presence of such finds surely resulted from politics and potential vote fixing but more crucially points to the incapacity of most citizens to write or even read names whose written form would be unfamiliar to them. Havelock goes on to suggest, tentatively, that the erosion of ostracism over the course of the fifth century resulted from increasing literacy, as "more people were learning not just to write but to read the names which others might wish to write for them."

138. R. Thomas 1992, 155; cf. Stoddart and Whitley 1988, 751–62.

139. Hdt. 8.128; see further discussion in Svenbro 1993, 55.

140. Svenbro 1993, 56.

141. Meiggs and Lewis 1989, no. 30; Herrmann 1981 provides a useful discussion of this inscription.

142. R. Thomas 1996, 10 registers similar skepticism regarding the reading abilities of the citizens of seventh-century Dreros, the site of the earliest surviving Greek legal inscription. See also Whitley 1997; contra, Papakonstantinou 2008, 77.

143. Meiggs and Lewis 1989, no. 30. See further, Ruzé 1988, who places the Tean law in the context of similar attempts toward the beginning of the fifth century to control members of the community whose skill had made them peculiarly powerful: the *gnomon* at Gortyn in Crete (*ICret* IV 14p), the *thesmothetai* at Athens (although I find her speculations regarding their functions and evolution somewhat problematic), and *prytaneis* at Erythrai

(*IE* 1.1), whom Ruzé 1988, 90 believes "jouent donc pour la cité le role de secrétaires, ce qui ne les empêche pas, par ailleurs, de convoquer les citoyens pour des tâches politiques."

144. They were, however, subject to different rules regarding iteration than other magistrates, which leads Ruzé 1988, 85, 88–92 to characterize them as outside the normal offices of the Greek *polis*. Cf. R. Thomas 1996, 23–25, who sees the power possessed by officials such as *mnamones/mnemones* in Crete and at Athens as constituting authority and responsibility that defined them as important officials of the state. Raubitschek 1970, 156 likewise suggests that the inscription discussed by Jeffery and Morpurgo-Davies 1970 indicates that the scribe at Arkades in Crete was an annual magistrate.

145. Meiggs and Lewis 1989, no. 32.19–22. (νόμωι δὲ κατάπ[ε]|ρ νῦν ὁρκῶ{ι}σ(α)ι τὸς δικαστάς· ὅ τ[ι] | ἂν οἱ μνήμονες εἰδέωσιν, τοῦτο | καρτερὸν ἶναι: "And by custom that the jurors swear oaths just as now: whatever the *mnemones* should know, this will be binding.") Clearly, the *mnemones* at Halikarnassos still commanded substantial political and judicial power as late as 465–50.

146. Hdt. 3.123.

147. *SEG* 29.402.

148. Jeffery and Morpurgo-Davies 1970.

149. The inscription (A 5–10) reads, ποινικάζεν δὲ [π]όλι καὶ μναμονεῦϜεν τὰ δαμόσια μήτε τὰ θιήια μήτε τἀνθρώπινα μηδέν' ἄλον αἰ μὴ Σπενσίθ[ιο]ν αὐτόν τε καὶ γενίαν τὸνυ, αἰ μὴ ἐπαίροι τε καὶ κέλοιτο ἢ αὐτὸς Σπενσίθιος ἢ γενιὰ, [τ]ὸνυ ὅσοι δρομῆς εἶεν τῶν [υἰ]ῶν οἱ πλίες ("No one is to be scribe and recorder for the city neither sacred nor secular except for Spensithios himself and his descendants, unless Spensithios himself should induce and bid the city, or else the majority of his sons, as many as may be adult") (trans. Jeffery and Morpurgo-Davies 1970, 125). See Ruzé 1988, 83–84 for additional discussion. Raubitschek 1970 believes that the annual character of the magistracy described in the decree, itself dated to ca. 500, does not square well with the implication that Spensithios was to serve for life. Thus, he suggests, the information regarding Spensithios and his sons may have dated to an earlier period (the late seventh century), and was copied into a later statute regarding the office of *poinikastas*. However, in light of the other evidence we have examined regarding scribal influence ca. 500, I see no problem imagining that Spensithios might have secured his office for his family in a small community such as Arkades.

150. *IE* 1.1.

151. *IE* 1.17.

152. W. Harris 1989, 50 and n. 23 discusses the evidence for the high status of *grammateis* even at relatively literate Athens.

153. See n. 149 above for text; see further Gagarin 2008, 19–21.

154. Jeffery and Morpurgo-Davies 1970; Edwards and Edwards 1974.

155. *SEG* 31.98; for discussion see Herrmann 1981, 12 and n. 31; Lewis 1982, 71–72; Merkelbach 1982, 212–13. The Tean official in this case perhaps served as secretary to officials known as the *timocheon* and the *tamias*, the latter of which is obviously a treasurer, and these functionaries delegated the *phoinikographeon* to fulfill their task of "reading out" from the stele; Herrmann 1981, 11–12.

156. *IG* xii^{2} 96 and 97.

157. Ruzé 1988, 83–84. On the role of *demiourgoi* as craftsmen but connected to writing, see Burkert 1992, 25–33. Murakawa 1957, 399–403 likewise argues for the higher status of *demiourgoi* in the Homeric and immediate post-Homeric worlds, especially those

who served as heralds and therefore associated closely with the *basileis;* as his study also indicates, however, the term *demiourgos* meant different things in various parts of the Greek world. Roebuck 1974, 491–93 argues that, in Attica, the *demiourgoi* may not have been craftsmen but rather local officials in the demes; against this view, see Figueira 1984, 459–61 and Lavelle 2000.

158. R. Thomas 1992, 62–71. See also Carawan 2008 on the continued role of these officials at Athens.

159. Tiryns: *SEG* 30.380, 34.296; Argos: *SEG* 33.275.

160. *ICret* IV.9.32, IV.11.16, IV.11.53; see the comments of R. Thomas 2005, 48–49, with literature cited.

161. See n. 145 above.

162. *SEG* 34.282.11, 34.283.

163. Ruzé 1988, 84 argues that the oral functions of the herald, now by implication superseded thanks to writing, would have given way to a purely scribal office. I disagree, since one of the clearest examples of scribal privilege, the case of Spensithios, also assumes his important role as a "remembrancer." See also R. Thomas 1996, 22ff., who questions the degree to which we can ever speak of one form of communication superseding another, and Raubitschek 1970, 155, who underscores the dual functions of the "recorder and reciter." Gagarin 2008, 120–21 inclines toward seeing the functions as more discrete.

164. R. Thomas 1996, 19–25. Ruzé 1988, 87–88 views the role of the *thesmothetai* of Athens as similarly based on a combination of written and oral/mnemonic capacities, as they collated the decisions of the past (either in writing or as the *thesmothetai* received them through oral transmission), and then decided how these "precedents" might apply to other cases as the need arose.

165. Athen. 14.619b.

166. Piccirilli 1981, esp. 9–11; R. Thomas 1996, 15, "law-chanter."

167. It makes little difference that in the first century, Strabo tells us of an individual known as a *nomoidos* among the Mazakenoi of Cappadocia, who served as an "exegete of the laws" (ἐξηγητὴς τῶν νομῶν; 12.2.9), likewise informing us that these people used the laws of Kharondas. Whatever the nature of this official's "explanations" by Strabo's day, the etymology of the word strongly suggests that initially the singing of the law was crucial to his duties, a point strengthened by the alleged (if dubious) connection to the famous lawgiver himself. Furthermore, as Svenbro 1993, 109–23, esp. 116–20 notes, there are clear etymological and intellectual associations between law, exegesis, and singing in the Archaic period.

168. Clem. Al. *Strom.* 1.78.

169. See n. 179 below.

170. Ael. *VH* 2.39. Cf. Strabo 10.4.20, whose language is similar (*manthanein . . . ek tôn nomôn ôidas*) but suggests that the laws prescribe certain songs to be performed, not necessarily that the laws themselves are to be learned as melodies.

171. Plut. *Sol.* 3.4.

172. Anhalt 1993; Lavelle 2000, 68–74; Irwin 2005.

173. Stoddart and Whitley 1988.

174. Cerra 1979, 12, 79–91.

175. Thuc. 2.37.3.

176. Humphreys 1988, 473f.

177. Eur. *Suppl.* 433–47.

178. Chapter 2.1 above.

179. Though the Spartans apparently claimed otherwise, it is clear that they did write some laws. See MacDowell 1986, 1–22 for the standard discussion, with Papakonstantinou 2008, 74–76.

180. Willetts 1967, 32.

181. Davies 1996, 53.

182. Arist. *Pol.* 1272a34–6 (ἐνταῦθα δ' οὐκ ἐξ ἁπάντων αἱροῦνται τοὺς κόσμους ἀλλ' ἐκ τινῶν γενῶν). This is confirmed by *ICret* IV 72.5.4–6, where the Great Code of Gortyn refers to an enactment of the time when Kyllos and his colleagues, the Aithalian clan, held the *kosmos*-ship. See also Hawke 2008a.

183. Gagarin 1981a, 66–68, 161; see n.71 above.

184. See n.78 above.

185. Plut. *Sol.* 19.1–4.

186. Wallace 1989, 11–22.

187. Arist. *Pol.* 1274a13–14 (ἀλλὰ μᾶλλον ἀπὸ συμπτώματος); 1274a18–20 (τὰς δ' ἀρχὰς ἐκ τῶν γνωρίμων καὶ τῶν εὐπόρων κατέστησε πάσας).

188. [Arist.] *Ath.Pol.* 4.4, 8.4.

189. Plut. *Sol.* 19.2; Wallace 1989, 55. See Rhodes 2006 on the textual tradition informing both [Arist.] *AthPol.* and Plutarch's biography of Solon.

190. Arist. *Pol.* 1273b40, 1274a1–2.

191. Sol. fr. 5, 33a; Plut. *Sol.* 22.3.

192. Ste. Croix 2004, 82–83.

193. [Arist.] *Ath.Pol.* 8.4; Plut. *Sol.* 19.2.

194. Wallace 1989, 55–69; 2007, 66–69 provides an admirably thorough discussion of the powers of the Solonian Areopagus.

Chapter 5

1. Chapter 3.5, dispute ***A7***.

2. Seaford 1994, 5ff., with other literature at n.24.

3. *Od.* 23.296. The ancient commentators Aristarchus and Aristophanes both testify to this variant ending. See S.L. West 1989.

4. Arist. fr. 507 Rose; Apollod. *Ep.* 7.40; Plut. *Mor.* 284c–d.

5. *Od.* 24.472ff.

6. Bohannon 1967b, 52–53.

7. Nader 1965, 13 notes that when anthropologists had concerned themselves with such questions as the place law takes among other rules of social conduct (e.g., Whiting 1950, Colson 1953, Gulliver 1963), they were usually studying societies where there were "no obvious political institutions concerned in the maintenance of public order." More recently, see the discussion in Rouland 1994, 159–75.

8. Among others, Seaford 1994; 2004, 23–26; Tandy 1997, 84–106; Gill, Postlethwaite, and Seaford 1998.

9. Roberts 1979, 30–35.

10. Rouland 1994, 154, 172–75.

11. Bohannon 1967b, 52–53.

12. For the notion of the early *polis* as a type of microstate, see Davies 1997. Like most scholars working in this field, I do not believe there is much profit in applying

traditional, evolutionary, anthropological hierarchies of state formation to the Greek *polis*, which was certainly a society quite unlike any other. The model here, however, is not diachronic, but rather is broadly descriptive and potentially quite helpful in thinking about Greek communities at the horizon of the emerging protostate. Marx's so-called Germanic mode of production may be instructive here (Marx 1965; Hobsbawm 1965); while I would scarcely argue for the teleological implications of Marx's model, the notion of an atomized, household economy (both in the productive and political sense) requiring some level of communal action and cooperation for social reproduction (Rigby 1987; Gailey and Patterson 1995) is one, I would argue, that fits well with the picture presented by Homer and, especially, Hesiod. Berent 1994 argues that the Greek *polis* even in later periods is not to be understood as a state, but characterizes it as a "stateless political community."

13. For the classic formulation on the stateless nature of Homeric society, see Finley 1981, 242ff. Gschnitzer 1971; 1981, 42 disagrees, arguing the fully developed *polis* was already present in the eighth century.

14. Seaford 1994, 2ff. provides a rich but succinct overview.

15. Qviller 1981, 115–18; Geddes 1984, 36; Rihll 1986.

16. *Od.* 3.7–8; Humphreys 1983, 23 for discussion.

17. Finley 2002, 74–79, 97–98, 104–5; R. Posner 1979.

18. Vidal-Naquet 1986, 26–29; Mossé 1980, 2.8.

19. Finley 2002, 27. Among those who have disagreed are Gschnitzer 1981, 42; Morris 1986, 100–104; Raaflaub 1991, 239–47; 1997a; Scully 1990.

20. Raaflaub 1997a.

21. Davies 1997, 29–30. Seaford 2004, 54–55 argues that the absence of the elements of the *polis* is part of an ideological choice on the part of the poet(s) who did not shape the epics into their final form until well after 700. I do not preclude the possibility of a later date but question the conscious ideological bias of the epic. Cf. Rose 1988; Thalmann 1988; Chapters 2.2 and 4.1 above.

22. Falk Moore 1973.

23. *Il.* 18.501; 23.486; *Od.* 8.236–55.

24. Rihll 1992; Donlan 1979 on the limits of a Homeric king's political and judicial authority.

25. Roberts 1979, 17–29.

26. Bohannon 1967b, 50.

27. The term *aristoi* appears in the epic, but there is real question as to when leading members of Greek communities began to identify themselves consciously as distinctly superior and separate from others. The archaeological evidence suggests a general trend toward stratification of wealth and the desire to use it to distinguish one's self or household from the rest of the community (see Chapter 5.4 below, with literature cited). Donlan 1973; 1999, 77–132 argues that it is only in the sixth century that we have clear literary testimony that hints of a backlash against aristocratic arrogance and privilege, and begins to see the *demos* as separate from the *aristoi* and *kaloikagathoi*. Clearly, though, Homer and Hesiod are aware of and employ evaluative labels: see Adkins 1972. For the fluidity of status and its markers in the archaeological record at Athens, see Morris 1987.

28. Forsdyke 2005, 12.

29. As Donlan 1989a, 8 summarizes, "That the pre-state *oikos* . . . enjoyed considerable political independence also seems clear. Our earliest literary sources reveal only the rudiments of the administrative and judicial apparatus which formed the government of

the later *polis*. Nor is there any evidence that superordinate groups like clans, phratries, and tribes regulated the activities of the early *oikos* . . . Consistently in Homer and Hesiod, a person's primary point of reference is his or her parents, spouse, siblings, children, and property. There is no identification with any broader kin group; in fact, *oikos* is the only formal kinship unit named by Homer and Hesiod." On Donlan's point regarding the lack of superordinate groups *before* the formation of the *polis,* see the excellent studies by Bourriot 1976 and Roussel 1976.

30. Tandy 1997, 94–111 distinguishes between reciprocity and redistribution which, for purposes of understanding the Greek world in the eighth and early seventh centuries, seems to be more technically and theoretically important than to have made much of a practical difference. While his point is well taken that the autonomous *oikos* based much of its organization on a principle of redistributing the wealth controlled by the head, the relationships that determined the collection and outlay of those resources remained, at heart, reciprocal. Furthermore, however redistributive or reciprocal the organization of a particular household may have been, I am again primarily concerned with the relationships that existed *among* the *oikoi* as centers (of networks) of economic and political distribution.

31. Tandy 1997, 94ff.; Seaford 1994, 13–24; 2004, 23–31, 52–60.

32. Seaford 1994, 65ff; 2004, 24, 39–47.

33. Tandy 1997, 98.

34. *Od.* 16.418–33; Chapter 3.7, dispute ***E6***.

35. *WD* 343–45.

36. Finley 1981, 241, 244; Seaford 1994, 16.

37. Gernet 1981, 289–302; Vernant 1982, 45–70; Seaford 1994, 207–20. The most famous example appears in Hdt. 6.127–30, where the Athenian Megakles wins the contest for the hand of the daughter of the Sikyonian tyrant, Kleisthenes.

38. Seaford 1994, 17.

39. Finley 1981, 241; Seaford 1994, 16, with literature cited.

40. Donlan 1979, 51–52.

41. Donlan 1979, 52 with n. 4.

42. Van Wees 1992. Donlan 1979, 52 states that "there is an inherent uncertainty concerning the relative influence or position of standing as determinants of [leadership authority] in any given situation . . . [leadership authority] situations do not exhibit a pattern analogous to a formal chain-of-command or to a conical system of authority." Fried 1967, 33 describes the general, anthropologically observed phenomenon thus: "An egalitarian society does not have any means of fixing or limiting the number of persons capable of exerting power. As many persons as can wield power—through personal strength, influence, authority or whatever means—can do so, and there is no necessity to draw them together to establish an order of dominance or paramountcy." For these reasons, Fried 1967, 83 describes leaders in these types of societies as having authority rather than power, by which he means the ability to coerce and have one's directives followed as a matter of course.

43. Donlan 1989a, 8–10 assembles the epic evidence.

44. Donlan 1989a, 9–10: "Ambition demanded followers; a man's authority depended on, and was measured by, the number of men he could persuade to follow him. What bound all *hetairoi* to their leader was personal loyalty; but beyond the tight circle of boon companions, loyalty was alloyed with self-interest. In return for their aid, followers expected to be rewarded with feasts, booty, gifts; otherwise they, and their families, might choose to support someone else."

45. Donlan 1979, 51; C. Thomas 1983, 1251: "Dark Age *basileis* seem to have been leaders whose position is rested on personal characteristics."

46. Tandy 1997, 106–10, 135ff.

47. Tandy 1997, 107–9.

48. I deliberately follow Tandy in his use of Karl Polanyi's concept of an embedded economy because it seems appropriate here. A few words of exposition will suffice: Polanyi believed that to describe or attempt to understand economic phenomena independently of social ones was impossible. As Tandy 1997, 85 summarizes Polanyi's ideas on the subject, "Economies are almost always 'embedded' in non-economic social institutions and are thereby inextricably bound up in tightly woven fabrics of socially prescribed activities" (following Polanyi 1944, 43–55; 1947; 1953; 1957a, 67–78; 1977, 47–56). For the significance of Polanyi's impact on Classical scholarship, see Humphreys 1978, 31–75.

49. Tandy 1997, 114, with literature cited.

50. For Mycenaean era populations' densities, one of the best detailed regional studies remains McDonald and Rapp 1972, 117–47 (Messenia); for a more impressionistic but also more exhaustive catalog, see Hope Simpson 1981. Dickinson's general statements, 1994, 51–71, are also useful, with literature cited. Classic statements regarding demographic decline in the Dark Age remain Desborough 1972, and Snodgrass 2000, 364–67. While Desborough and Snodgrass disagree on the rapidity of decline (the latter arguing for a more precipitous drop), they concur on its severity. For regional population decline in Messenia, see McDonald and Hope Simpson 1972. Other regional surveys include Jameson, et al., 1994, esp. 229 (Argolid); Bintliff 1985; and Bintliff and Snodgrass 1985 (Boeotia), all of which suggest depopulation on a massive scale. Drews 1993, 21–29 provides an excellent and evocative picture of the extent of the destruction and decline at the close of the Mycenaean period. For theories of civilizational collapse, see Renfrew 1979, 481–506; Tainter 1988, esp. 10–11, 19–21, 44–45, 49, 91–126, 199–204.

51. Purcell 1990, 34.

52. Morris 1987, 23, 72, 156–59, 194.

53. Osborne 1996, 75–83.

54. See the excellent discussion in Tandy 1997, 19–72, with evidence and previous literature cited; also, Scheidel 2003, who sees increases beginning in the ninth and accelerating in the eighth century, though is skeptical of a "population explosion."

55. Donlan 1989b argues effectively for the case that *temenea* which changed hands in epics were not alienated from a third party but rather were arable lands not yet brought under cultivation. Such land would therefore have been open for claim.

56. Tandy 1997, 113. In this, as in much else, Tandy (as well as the present author) owes a great deal to the ideas of Karl Polanyi. Tandy continues, "These markets constituted the third form of economic integration [along with reciprocity and redistribution], which Polanyi called exchange." See also Polanyi 1957b.

57. On the western colonization movement of the eighth century and beyond, see Boardman 1999; Ridgway 1992; Descourdes 1992. On trade and its effects back home, see Tandy 1997, 62ff., with copious literature cited.

58. Tandy 1997, 125ff. Seaford 2004, esp. 34–52 has described Homeric reciprocity as already "in crisis," as revealed in the central complaints that drive the narratives of the *Iliad* and *Odyssey*, namely Achilles' perception of the inequitable (re)distribution of booty and the suitors' consumption of Odysseus' resources without recompense.

59. Seaford 2004, 38–52.

60. Tandy 1997, 126.

61. See also the excellent discussion in Forsdyke 2005, 19–28 for a general overview of the impact of these developments on intra-elite competition, and 36–77 for an examination of the connection between trade, competition, and political instability at Mytilene, Megara, Samos, and Corinth.

62. In Tandy's 1997, 101–6 usage, the reciprocal relationships that radiated from the prominent household as the center of a system of redistributive wealth.

63. Tandy 1997, 126–27.

64. Tandy 1997, 127–35, with quote at 135.

65. Davies 1997, 29.

66. Osborne 1996, 70–136; Tandy 1997, 19–58.

67. Starr 1977, 33; Hammond 1954, 97

68. Snodgrass 1980, 144ff.; see the discussion in V. Parker 1997.

69. Tandy 1997, 39ff.; Osborne 1998.

70. For classic discussions of the Athenian *synoikismos*, see Sarkady 1966; Alföldy 1969; Diamant 1982; Simms 1983. More recently, see Manville 1990, 55–57, and Anderson 2003, who argues compellingly that the Athenian state did not embrace outlying areas of Attica until the age of Kleisthenes' reforms. On the possibility of Dark Age integration of Attica, see C. Thomas and Conant 1999, 60–84.

71. Walker 1995, 3–34.

72. Anderson 2003, 19–21; Manville 1990, 76; Walker 1995, 195ff.

73. These will have remained relatively ill defined; Manville 1990.

74. Chapter 5.4 below.

75. Hågg 1983b, 31.

76. Hågg 1982.

77. Hågg 1983b, 28f., 31.

78. Coldstream 2003, 78–80, 133–34; Anderson 2003, 24–34 on the continued importance of the land holdings of the elite in Attic *khora*.

79. Kelly 1976, 51ff; Antonaccio 1995.

80. De Polignac 1995, 35f., 79f.

81. Kelly 1976, 51–72; A. Foley 1988.

82. Paus. 2.36.4–5, 3.7.4, 4.8.3, 4.34.6; Strabo 8.6.11. Kelly 1976, 64f., dismisses as "oversimplified and erroneous" the tradition that Asinian aid to Sparta during one of its wars with Argos was the cause of Argive anger and thirst for revenge. The Argives, like most inhabitants of the Argolid, considered themselves Dorians, to whom Hera was paramount, while the inhabitants of Asine were "non-Greek" Dryopes who worshipped Apollo above all. Different ethnic identifications among the Greeks were probably more imagined than real, but important nevertheless; Davies 1997, 28; Hall 1997; 2007, 43–55. Whatever the case, it is clear that many of the communities of the Argive plain were banding together, voluntarily or otherwise, and Asine's refusal to participate made it conspicuous and irksome, leading to its destruction. As Kelly 1976, 65ff., notes, after the raid the Argives did not occupy the territory: their aim was punitive.

83. Hodkinson 1997.

84. Thuc. 1.10.2 considers them not to have synoecized as a result.

85. E.g., Thuc. 1.10.2.

86. Forrest 1968, 28.

87. Forrest 1968, 28f. suspects that Pitana and Mesoa were older and might have had priority as they were closer to the acropolis.

88. Forrest 1968, 28.

89. Hodkinson 1997, 88.

90. Hdt. 6.56–58; Carlier 1984, 240–324; Huxley 1962, 44, 49.

91. Finley 1981, 24–40; although see Cartledge 2001, 21–36.

92. So Forrest 1968, 46ff. Later, of course, the Spartans fixed the number of the council at thirty and introduced a minimum age requirement of sixty.

93. Forrest 1968, 34; Huxley 1962, 116, 122–23.

94. Salmon 1984, 24 suggests that, in a sense, "the Corinthia was unified from the start." However, his analysis stems from his acceptance of the existence of a Dorian invasion and Dorian institutions, the reality of which remains an open question with opinion gathering on the negative side of the ledger; see Davies 1997, 28; Hall 2007, 43–55. Furthermore, he claims a reference in the *Suda* (s.v., πάντα ὀκτώ) provides "positive grounds for believing that the tradition knew nothing of such a synoecism"; however, the notice there is confused and cursory. Cf. Roebuck 1972, 104ff., who detects a *synoikismos* on the basis of archaeological evidence and is inclined to date the development to the eighth century.

95. *Suda*, s.v., πάντα ὀκτώ.

96. Nicolaus of Damascus, *FGH* 60 F 2.

97. Will 1955, 609; Roebuck 1972, 114.

98. Roebuck 1972, 115n67 argues that if there had been three Dorian tribes at Corinth, their dissolution would have happened earlier rather than later.

99. Chapter 5.4 below.

100. Seaford 1994, 206ff.

101. For example, the "hero" of Lefkandi, who appears to have possessed singular wealth and or significance ca. 1000. For the excavations, see Popham, Sackett, and Themelis 1980; Popham, Toupoula, and Sackett 1982; Popham, Sackett, and Calligas, eds. 1993, part 2. For interpretations, see Popham and Lemos 1995; C. Thomas and Conant 1999, 85–114.

102. Murray 1980, 38–56, 192–208; 1983a; 1983b; 1994; Schmitt Pantel 1994a; 1994b.

103. Coldstream 2003, 349–52; Tandy 1997.

104. Forsdyke 2005, 21–24. As will become apparent in what follows in this section, I am in nearly complete sympathy with her interpretations regarding violent intra-elite competition, and I have tried to note those areas in which we are in agreement by acknowledging her observations and insights as appropriate.

105. Tandy 1997, 151–55; Morris 1988; Whitley 1988; Antonaccio 1995.

106. Tandy 1997, 166ff., with literature cited. While I agree that the *Iliad* and *Odyssey* were capable of employment in the service of elite ideals and identities, for reasons outlined in Chapter 2.2, I do not think they were fabricated for that purpose. I hold, with Donlan 1999, 1–28, that the poets in the tradition may have elaborated upon and augmented certain elements in the narrative to celebrate certain aristocratic values, but overall the epics themselves reflect the general values of the society that produced them.

107. Tandy 1997, 141–65.

108. E.g., Humphreys 1978, 123ff.; Bravo 1974; 1977; 1984. See now also Forsdyke 2005, 24–29 and passim.

109. E.g., *Od.* 8.159–64.

110. Donlan 1973.

111. For a discussion of the references to tyranny in early Greek literature, Andrewes 1956 remains a classic, though see now McGlew 1993, 52–123 for a more exhaustive

examination of the language of tyranny in Greek thought. Salmon 1997 is also a useful survey of the representation of tyranny in the early *polis*. See Forsdyke 2005, 244–70 on the fifth- and fourth-century ideological currents that complicate later accounts of Archaic tyranny.

112. Forsdyke 2005, esp. 36–78.

113. The Athenians, for example, believed that the annual archonship did not come into being until the early seventh century; Develin 1989, 27–28; on the tradition of life-archons and ten-year archons in [Arist.] *AthPol.* 3.1–4: Hignett 1952, 41–44; Rhodes 1993, 100–102; Harding 1994, 5, 10. Institutions of other *poleis* were, as Forsdyke 2005, 52 notes, "insufficient insurance against attempts at domination by a single elite leader."

114. Hdt. 6.127 is the early locus classicus for Pheidon, though see also Paus. 6.22.2. Salmon 1997, 62–66 provides a discussion of Pheidon's rise to power and its significance.

115. Arist. *Pol.* 1310b26f.; Andrewes 1956, 31–42; Salmon 1997, 61ff.

116. Nicolaus of Damascus *FGH* 90 F 35.

117. As with most dates for this period, this one is conventional, relying on calculations form Aristotle's and Eusebius' chronologies, and that of the Parian Marble.

118. Salmon 1984, 186ff.

119. Andrewes 1956, 44.

120. Forsdyke 2005, 71–72.

121. Hdt. 5.92. While Herodotus certainly embroiders his tale with near-death experiences and oracles, some of the details favorable to Kypselos may have historical merit, especially since the author otherwise regarded the Corinthian tyrant a "monster," consistent with Classical portrayals of tyrants.

122. Hdt. 5.92.

123. Sealey 1977, 48–49. Oost 1972, followed by Forsdyke 2005, 72, identifies Kypselos as a member of the Bacchiadai who held the position of polemarch and killed the "*basileus*," variously named in the same source (Ephorus = Nicolaus of Damascus *FGH* 90 F 57.1, 6) as Patrokleides and Hippokleides. I see no reason to view this state of affairs as mutually exclusive with the tradition of Eëtion as an excluded member of the elite since, as Oost has argued, Bacchiad membership would have passed to Kypselos through his mother.

124. Probably the same Orsippos famously credited with having been the first to have won the Olympic footrace naked (Paus. 1.44.1) and who, at least according to Pausanias, annexed neighboring territory when later serving as a general (*stratêgounta husteron ton Orsippon apotemesthai khôran tôn prosoikôn*). On the date of his victory, see Shaw 1997, 122 with n. 255. On the tradition and the date of the "war" in which Orsippos commanded the Megarians, see Hammond 1954; for cautions regarding the nature, extent, and the belligerents of this war, while agreeing on a date ca. 700, Salmon 1972, 198–200.

125. Thuc. 1.13.4.

126. Forsdyke 2005, 72; Ephorus (= Nicolaus of Damascus *FGH* 90 F 57.6) reports that Kypselos acted in conjunction with his associates (*hetairikon*). See also n. 123 above.

127. Salmon 1984, 195 with literature cited.

128. Forsdyke 2005, 72–74 notes the continuities and further argues that the various figures exiled under the Kypselids all appear to have been Bacchiads.

129. Arist. *Pol.* 1305a.

130. Indeed, Aristotle's brief notice is part of a chapter where he seeks to support a general argument that tyranny is usually established by turning the people against the rich, though see Chapter 2.1 for the effect of contemporary debates on the historical

understanding of those working at Athens in the fourth century. What he does not say is that it was a member of the rich who effected this revolution at Megara. See also the discussion in Forsdyke 2005, 48–52.

131. Thuc. 1.126.3. For further discussion, see Legon 1981.

132. The loci classici for Kylon's failed coup are Hdt. 5.71; Plut. *Sol.* 12.1–9; Thuc. 1.126.3–12.

133. Thuc. 1.126.5. See also Lambert 1986.

134. Megakles' leadership of the anti-Kylonians: Thuc. 1.126.6–11; Megakles as sitting archon: Plut. *Sol.* 12.1. On the history of the Alkmaionidai, see Davies 1971, 368–84.

135. Thuc. 1.126.11.

136. Thuc. 1.126.10; Hdt. 5.71; Ar. *Eq.* 445. On the nature of the exile of the Alkmaionidai, see Anderson 2003, 27–30.

137. Frost 1984, 286ff. and Ghinatti 1970, 24–25 both view with skepticism the claim of Thuc. 1.126.7 that the response was common (as suggested by *pandêmei*). Frost characterizes the coup and the Alkmaionid reaction to it "as evidently spontaneous and the final disposition of a family affair" with the Alkmaionid Megakles leading, according to Herodotus (5.70), their *sunstasiotai* later held accountable for the murder of the Kylonians. Ghinatti, meanwhile, marks the fact that the Alkmaionidai held estates near the Acropolis, in the deme of Alopeke, and thus could have easily mobilized their followers to besiege the Kylonians.

138. Plut. *Sol.* 12.2–9. Forsdyke 2005, 84–90 provides a compelling reconstruction of the immediate aftermath, and we will have occasion to return to this topic in Chapter 6.3.

139. Arist. *Pol.* 1311b27.

140. See Forsdyke 2005, 42–43 for discussion of the literature.

141. Alc. fr. 114.

142. Strabo 13.2.3. Andrewes 1956, 94; Forsdyke 2005, 40–41. For a discussion of the general turmoil, see Boruhovic 1981.

143. Alc. frs. 114, 129; *Suda* s.v., Πιττακός; Diog. Laert. 1.74.

144. Alc. frs. 70, 129.

145. Alc. fr. 129.

146. Arist. *Pol.* 1285a35ff. Aristotle considered this obscure office equivalent to an elective tyranny, but precisely what this signifies in terms of powers or the process of selection is unclear. It may be that Aristotle thought Pittakos' limited term of office, ten years, and his voluntary surrender of power merited him distinction from more typical tyrants. Classical Miletus had a regular, annual magistracy with this title, but Classical Mytilene, as far as we know, did not.

147. Alc. fr. 70.5–9. Forsdyke 2005, 44–45 interprets the election of Pittakos as a response to Alcaeus and his brother Antimenides attempting to return to Mytilene by force.

148. Alc. frs. 72, 129, 348, and followed by Diog. Laert. 1.78.

149. Alc. frs. 70, 428; Hdt. 5.95; Diog. Laert. 1.74; Strabo 13.1.38.

150. Alc. fr. 70.

151. Tandy 1997, 87.

CHAPTER 6

1. Seaford 1994, xvii.

2. Morris 1987; van Wees 2001 on the substantial holdings needed to qualify as a *zeugitês* at Athens, along with van Wees 2006 on the approximate wealth required

to have qualified for the top three Solonian classes. Though see Raaflaub 2006 for important cautions.

3. E.g., Raaflaub and Wallace 2007b; Forsdyke 2005; Chapter 5.4 above.

4. Foxhall 1997a, 120. She refers here specifically to Athens even well after Solon's legislative activity, but as she notes earlier (119), "generally the *poleis* of Archaic Greece were little more than a stand-off between the members of the elite who ran them."

5. All of the evidence pertaining to the "codification" of law in the early Greek context has recently been collected and published by Hölkeskamp 1999. The reader may refer to this extraordinarily useful study for questions pertaining to every type of individual law (*Gesetz*), which Hölkeskamp discovered in the course of his research.

6. More generally, these laws would have concerned themselves not just with the physical house itself, of course, the *oikia*, but with all of the material possessions, land, and obligations associated with it, together making up the *oikos*.

7. Pheidon: Arist. *Pol.* 1265b12–16. Philolaos: *Pol.* 1274b2–5.

8. E.g., Bonner and Smith 1930, 1.80; Will 1955, 317ff.; Zörner 1971, 116; Roebuck 1979, 115f. and n.8; 1980, 1925; Salmon 1984, 57, 63–65.

9. *Pol.* 1274a33–37. One may doubt the details Aristotle provides for Philolaos' exile from Corinth, though any other conclusions regarding his departure will be equally speculative.

10. Salmon 1984, 64n38 doubts such an inference, made also by Will 1955, and Zörner 1971. Despite Aristotle's suggestion that the purpose of the two lawgivers was similar, Salmon argues that Aristotle's language implies otherwise, stating that Aristotle's use of σῴζηται (*Pol.*, 1274b5) to describe Philolaos' intent signifies that he sought "to keep up the number of plots." I believe, however, that Salmon has confused purpose with means. While it is true that these laws concerned themselves with two different aspects of landholding—Pheidon's with the subdivision of *oikoi*, Philolaos' with the adoption of heirs into a childless *oikos* so that it would continue as an independent entity—their effect and underlying intention was the same: the preservation of the current number of households within the communities of Corinth and Thebes.

11. Jeffery 1976, 146; Buck 1979, 95f.; Hölkeskamp 1999, 248.

12. Buck 1979, 92.

13. Salmon 1984, 64 supports this conclusion while admitting other possibilities. Puzzlingly, he rejects the conclusions of Will 1955, 318–19; Roebuck 1972, 115–16; and Oost 1972, all of whom view Pheidon's legislation as not only a stabilization of the status quo for the present, but also for the foreseeable future. Salmon does not believe that Pheidon necessarily concerned himself with the future but then posits that this legislation was part of the impetus for the great Corinthian colonization movement of the eighth century. It is difficult, however, to see how the law could have enticed men to abandon hope of gaining land at home in exchange for better prospects abroad *unless* Pheidon had intended his legislation to establish the current pattern of landholding in perpetuity.

14. *WD* 182ff., 376ff. See also Tandy and Neale 1996, 27–31 on the possible size of Hesiod's farm, and A. Edwards 2004, 84–88 on the number of people a farm such as Hesiod's might support. A surplus of children would have been potentially problematic for *oikoi* of humbler resources.

15. Ephorus *FGH* 70 F 115; 70 F 122a (= Strabo 10.3.2); Arist. *Pol.* 1319a12–15.

16. For discussion, see Gehrke 1985, 52; Hölkeskamp 1999, 97f.

17. *ICret* IV 72.6.2–7; Willetts 1967, 44.

18. There is a possibility that Gortynian law may have been idiosyncratic, if not to Gortyn specifically then to "Dorian" *poleis* and institutions, though Hall 1997 gives us pause regarding the degree to which such identities were real or constructed. As Maffi 1997 has noted at various points, there are substantial similarities between Gortynian and Athenian law with respect to family law, which forms the great bulk of the Great Code of Gortyn. Despite the fifth-century date for the Great Code of Gortyn, I find persuasive the arguments that most of the provisions had much longer histories stretching well back into the Archaic age (e.g., Willetts 1967, 8–9; Davies 1996, 34f.; Maffi 1997, 8 on the relationship between written laws and the much older institutional organization of the family; Hölkeskamp 1999, 118ff.; Kristensen 2004; Papakonstantinou 2008, 60–61 for discussion). Furthermore, a handful of provisions in the Code appear to be explicitly marked as innovative, in that they exclude retroactive application: *ICret* IV 72.5.1–9, 6.9–25, 9.7–17, 11.19–23, and 12.1–5, though only the first of these passages provides a "date," the *kosmos*-ship of one Kyllos. Gagarin 2008, 153 takes this horizon as the effective date for the entire Code, and Maffi 1997, 45–46 surmises that the magistracy of Kyllos—independently unverifiable—will have occurred not more than a generation prior to the Code's publication. It would seem that the need to confront the issue of retroactivity severally, rather than all at once at the beginning of the Code, suggests that remarkable departures from previous practice only inhered in those regulations where the text specifically anticipates the possibility of litigants invoking previous practice or facts on the ground as they may have existed before the publication. As we will see below, earlier statutes from Crete (and Gortyn in particular) are largely consistent (though not identical) with comparable provisions in the Code itself, and therefore even those regulations in the Code with retroactivity clauses may not have been radically different from prevailing practice.

19. *ICret* IV 72.11.34–36.

20. *ICret* IV 72.11.37–39.

21. Willetts 1955, 7–27; 1967, 11.

22. For a fuller discussion of the *apetairoi*, see Hawke 2008a.

23. *ICret* IV 72.2.2–16.

24. *ICret* IV 72.2.21–27; see also Gagarin 2008, 157–58.

25. *ICret* IV 72.2.28–43; for further discussion, see Willetts 1967, 10, 61–65; Maffi 1997, 23–25.

26. *ICret* IV 72.10.39–11.10.

27. *ICret* IV 72.4.39–43; see also Maffi 1997, 35–36.

28. *ICret* IV 72.10.52–11.1.

29. *ICret* IV 20 = *Nomima* 2.37.

30. *ICret* IV 72.10.39–48. Willetts 1967, 12 describes the *epiballontes* as any kinsmen not of the deceased man's *oikos*, except in the special designation the term enjoys when used in conjunction with heiresses, although see Maffi 1997, 77–78 and n. 37 below.

31. *ICret* IV 72.11.11–17. As indicated above (n. 18), one of the retroactivity clauses (11.19–23) of the Code follows closely on these regulations, but given the long-standing distinction between biological and adopted sons at Gortyn (n.29 above), it seems that the regulations in the Code covering this issue more likely represent clarifications of previous practices rather than a substantive change. Compare the apparently similar but unfortunately fragmentary text from the Cretan *polis* of Phaistos dating to before 500 (*Nomima* 2.38), which also provided for the denunciation of an adopted heir before the assembled citizenry.

32. Willetts 1967, 31–32.

33. Cf. the Athenian law, attributed to Solon ([Dem.] 46.14; [Arist.] *AthPol.* 35.2; Plut. *Sol.* 21.3) that stipulated a man could only adopt a male heir in the absence of surviving biological sons.

34. Willetts 1967, 30.

35. *ICret* IV 72.11.33–34.

36. *ICret* IV 72.5.9–22.

37. Following the lines regarding the succession of property through the line of a brother or sister, one finds a stipulation that Willetts 1967, 66 characterizes as "curious": αἰ δέ κα μήτις ἐ͂ι τούτων, | οἶς κ' ἐπιβάλληι ὄπω κ' ἐ͂ι τὰ κρ|ήματα, τούτος ἀναιλλε͂θθα|ι (*ICret* IV 72.5.22–25). Willetts suggests that the phrase means "they are to take it up, to whom it may fall as the source of the property," i.e., other kinsmen who fall under the designation of *epiballontes* but not (obviously) those already named; see also Link 1994, 76, who argues that the term might even comprise anyone beyond the previously delineated successors, including anyone with legal claims against the patrimony, such as creditors. This rendering implies that outside the extensive circle of kin already defined by the preceding lines, other "kinsmen" (and/or claimants beyond ties of consanguinity) would have had the right of succession. However, these applications of the term *epiballontes* would not be consistent throughout the Code. Maffi 1997, 58–59 argues that the word represents the fourth group of potential heirs in the rare event that no one survived among the already named potential successors, thereby indicating the decedent's paternal uncle or uncles and their sons. While understanding *epiballontes* in this way would aid my own argument, this interpretation appears to me to strain the evidence, and I would suggest that the language of this passage intends the preceding list of potential succeeding kinsmen to comprise those individuals eligible to inherit the property in question. In other words, should they (the aforementioned potential successors) not be present, to whom the property should fall, then in this context at least, there are no *epiballontes*, and then follow further arrangements for the disposition of the property in question. This interpretation seems to make more sense, as Willetts' and Maffi's readings would force us to assume that the devolution of the *oikos* to a distantly related and diffuse circle of kinsmen would require less statutory clarification than its succession by the descendants of the dead person's siblings or its devolution to the household servants (see subsequent note). It would follow, rather, that the reversion of the *oikos* to the "clan" would entail more confusion than its succession to people more closely related to the deceased, and it seems odd to assume that the legislator(s) abdicated to private settlement (such as might take place within such units as the clan or tribe) the responsibility of determining the ultimate fate of an *oikos* whose devolution through inheritance he (or they) had otherwise meticulously defined and delineated.

38. *ICret* IV 72.5.25–28 (αἰ δὲ μὴ εἶεν ἐπιβάλλοντε|ς, τᾶς Ϝοικίας οἵτινές κ' | ἴοντι ὀ κλᾶρος, τούτονς ἔ|κεν τὰ κρήματα).

39. *ICret* IV 72.5.44ff.

40. Compare the Athenian law, attributed to Solon and cited by [Dem.] 46.14, that a man could only adopt a male heir if he had no surviving sons; cf. Arist. *AthPol.* 35.2; Plut. *Sol.* 21.3.

41. Arist. *Pol.* 1266b14–18. Aristotle also recognized the futility of such legislation (*Pol.*, 1266b28–32).

42. Arist. *Pol.* 1266b19–21. Aristotle does not name Zaleukos here, but given the context of the passage (the lines appear between references to ancient—*palai*—measures),

it seems quite possible that such a law might date roughly to the presumed period of that lawgiver's activity.

43. Arist. *Pol.* 1266b21–24. Note here that a written law had actually impeded democracy rather than promoted the establishment or guarantee of broader enfranchisement. Further, a fourth-century statute regarding the foundation of the colony of Corcyra Melaina stipulated that half of the land had to remain in the possession of the colonists and their direct descendants and might not be alienated (*SIG* 3.141.7ff.).

44. Arist. *Pol.* 1252b12–15.

45. See also *Pol.* 1274a23; 1296a21; 1297a 23.

46. Adcock 1927; Papakonstantinou 2008, 64. On family law as *the* principal preoccupation of the Great Code of Gortyn, see Maffi 1997.

47. Diod. Sic. 12.15.1–3; 12.18.3; Hölkeskamp 1999, 43, 135; Camassa 1988, 569. Bonner and Smith 1930, 1.80 took the report of Diodorus regarding Kharondas and his laws at face value, but that notice is problematic at best, representing as it does a likely conflation of materials, not all of which belong to the seventh century; see Szegedy-Maszak 1978 for the development of the heroizing legends about lawgivers. Hölkeskamp 1999, 139–41 is probably generally correct in characterizing the remainder of the Kharondas tradition in Diodorus as "historisch wertlos," though see Chapter 4, n.80 above.

48. Diod. Sic. 12.15.2.

49. Diod. Sic. 12.15.3.

50. *ICret* IV 72.8.40–42; 8.53. See Maffi 1997, 100–103 for additional discussion.

51. Sealey 1987, 18–21. See also Hölkeskamp 1999, 140 for the likelihood of similar conditions pertaining in Katana at the time of Kharondas' legislation. The argument for the legal independence of Athenian women in matters of inheritance in the fourth century, if accepted, would surely describe a later development; Gagarin 1998.

52. Diod. Sic. 12.18.4. Diodorus explains that the version of the law as framed by Kharondas had left a certain noblewoman, orphaned by destitute parents, unmarriageable for all intents and purposes. She thus proposed a revision in the law to the assembly (a scenario which in itself strains credulity), and the townspeople voted to redraft the law in such a way that her closest kinsman was forced to marry a penniless wife without dowry. The dramatic embellishments notwithstanding, such a revision would not have altered in any substantive way the law of Kharondas as reported in Diodorus' previous paragraph, 12.18.3. ([Kharondas] ἐκέλευε γὰρ τῇ ἐπικλήρῳ ἐπιδικάζεσθαι τὸν ἔγγιστα γένους, ὡσαύτως δὲ καὶ τὴν ἐπίκληρον ἐπιδικάζεσθαι τῷ ἀγχιστεῖ, ᾧ ἦν ἀνάγκη συνοικεῖν ἢ πεντακοσίας ἐκτῖσαι δραχμὰς εἰς προικὸς λόγον τῇ πενιχρᾷ ἐπικλήρῳ: "For [Kharondas] ordered that the closest kinsman be assigned to the heiress, and ordered likewise that an heiress be assigned to her next of kin, for whom it was necessary to marry her or to pay five hundred drachmae for the dowry of the penniless heiress.")

53. Plut. *Sol.* 20.2–3. Ruschenbusch 1966, F 52a accepts the law as a genuine Solonian measure.

54. The Gortynian Code defined the heiress as the πατρωιῶκον, a construction whose "etymology emphasizes the daughter's relationship in a patriarchal property system, as does the Athenian ἐπίκληρος—perhaps even more forcibly" (Willetts 1967, 71; see also Maffi 1997, 87–106 on heiresses). The appearance of the term in an earlier fragment (*ICret* IV 44 = *Nomima* 2.50) suggests its antiquity.

55. *ICret* IV 72.7.15.18.

56. *ICret* IV 72.7.18–27.

57. *ICret* IV 72.7.40–47.

58. Maffi 1997, 92, 166 takes the *kadestai* to be relatives (*parenti*), but the language of the statute explicitly states that if there is no *dromeus* who is an *epiballôn* (probably to be understood as the paternal relatives as described in n. 37), then responsibility would logically fall to her maternal relatives, which is surely then how we should read *kadestans* in 7.44.

59. *ICret* IV 72.7.47–50 (αἰ δέ κα μὴ ὀπυίηι ἆι ἔγρα|ται, τὰ κρήματα πάντ' ἔκονσα|ν, αἴ κ' ἒι ἄλλος, τõι ἐπιβάλλοντ|ι).

60. *ICret* IV 72.7.52–55; 8.1–7.

61. *ICret* IV 72.8.4–5.

62. *ICret* IV 72.8.7–8 (ἀποδατε̃ται δ|ὲ τω̃ν κρημάτων ἰõι). See Willetts 1967, 71–72 for the identification of the pronoun as masculine.

63. *ICret* IV 72.8.5–7 (ἄλλωι ὀπυίεθ|αι τα̃ς πυλα̃ς τω̃ν αἰτιόντων | ὄτιμί κα λε̃ι). Maffi 1997, 12 argues for the tribe as a geographical categorization.

64. *ICret* IV 72.8.42–46.

65. *ICret* IV 72.8.13–20.

66. *ICret* IV 72.7.50–52. Only when there were no *epiballontes* at all could the heiress enjoy the full use and possession of her property at Gortyn; furthermore, only under such conditions could she marry whomever she wanted among her tribesmen rather than depend on the unsolicited approach of a tribal member, which was required if she had rejected an eligible *epiballôn*, *ICret* IV 72.8.8–12 (αἰ δὲ μὴ | ε̃ιεν ἐπιβάλλοντες τα̃ι {πα|ι} πατρωιω̃κωι ἆ[ι ἔ]γραττται, τὰ κρ|ήματα πάντ' ἔκ[ον]σαν τα̃ς πυ|λα̃ς ὀπυίθ[α]ι ὄτιμί κα λε̃ι). On the tribe at Gortyn, see Kristensen 2002.

67. Plut. *Sol.* 20.4 = Ruschenbusch 1966, F 71a; cf. Pollux, 1.246 (= Ruschenbusch 1966, F 71b) (Σόλων δὲ καὶ τὰς νύμφας ἰούσας ἐπὶ τὸν γάμον ἐκέλευσε φρύγετρον φέρειν σημε̃ιον). Solon's concern to restrict large-scale movements of property outside the kin circle becomes all the more intelligible given recent discussions of the nature of the early sixth-century Athenian state as, in essence, a competitive arena among elite families: Foxhall 1997a; Anderson 2003, 23–56.

68. *ICret* IV 72.2.45–54 defines as "her own" the property with which a wife came to her husband (τὰ Fὰ αὐτα̃ς ἔκεν, ἄτι ἔκονσ' ε̃ιε πὰρ τὸν ἄνδρα: lines 46–48), and there follows a description of her rights to the same. I employ the term "wife's property" even though children could, of course, also have been present, in which case the woman's rights to her property were affected in the event of her widowhood or divorce. See below.

69. *ICret* IV 72.2.45–52 (αἰ κ' ἀνὴρ [κ]ạὶ γυ̣|νὰ διακρ[ί]νωνται, τὰ Fὰ α|ὐτα̃ς ἔκεν, ἄτι ἔκονσ' ε̃ιε π|ὰρ τὸν ἄνδρα, καὶ τω̃ καρπõ τ|άννημίναν, αἰ κ' ε̃ι ἐς τõν Fõ|ν αὐτα̃ς κρημάτων, κõτι | κ' ἐνυπάνει τὰν [ἡμίνα]ν ἄτι | κ' ε̃ι).

70. *ICret* IV 72.3.17–22; *ICret* IV 72.10.15–17 limited to one hundred staters in value the amount of property a son might give to his mother or a husband to his wife.

71. *ICret* IV 72.3.22–24.

72. *ICret* IV 72.3.24–31.

73. *ICret* IV 72.9.9–12.

74. *ICret* IV 72.6.12–23.

75. *ICret* IV 72.3.31–37; 6.31–34.

76. *ICret* IV 72.6.34–36.

77. *ICret* IV 72.6.34–44.

78. For the mother's property, see *ICret* IV 72.6.44–46 (αἰ δέ κ' ἄλλαν ὀπυίηι, τὰ τ|έκνα [τõ]ν [μ]ạτρωίων καρτερὸν|ς ἤμην). The measures cited here are, of course, the best evidence we have for these concerns at Gortyn, but the distinction of maternal goods and the rights of control and inheritance over them had a long history, as indicated by earlier inscriptions from the same *polis* (*ICret* IV 20 = *Nomima* 2.37; *ICret* IV 21 = *Nomima* 2.38). While both of these texts are quite fragmentary, dating to 550 at the latest, there are explicit, restorable references to maternal goods in the former (line 4: τὰ ματρῶια) and paternal goods in the latter (line 5: πατρῶια).

79. Eder 1986.

80. Garland 1985, 26.

81. Garland 1985, 26–27; Rohde 1925, 164.

82. Sokolowski 1969, 77C 15ff.

83. Kurtz and Boardman 1970, 74.

84. E.g., Garland 1985, 21, 121; Morris 1987, 50–52; Seaford 1994, 75–92; Osborne 1996, 223.

85. Sourvinou-Inwood 1995, 440–42; see also Frisone 2000, 96–101.

86. Garland 1985, 41ff., 122.

87. Plut. *Sol.* 12.1–13.3 refers to the continued strife that followed Kylon's abortive attempt at tyranny in 632 and the consequent massacre of his partisans. According to Plutarch, these tensions persisted down to the time of Solon's term as archon. See also [Arist.] *AthPol.* 5.2; Rhodes 1993, 119–20, and Forsdyke 2005, 80–90, who accept the tradition of violence and political turmoil at Athens at this time as largely genuine; see also Chapter 5.4 above.

88. On the clear role of self-help in early Greek homicide cases, see Gagarin 1981a, 5–29; Chapter 3.1 above.

89. *IG* i^3 104 for the copy dating to 409/8.

90. Stroud 1968, 72 and Forsdyke 2005, 80–90 strongly favor a direct connection between the Kylonian affair and Drakon's legislation. Gagarin 1981a; 2008, 93–109 is less enthusiastic, though he concedes in 1981a that Drakon's appointment to draw up the laws was inspired by the turmoil caused by the incident, as was the law on tyranny that Drakon may have established; see Ostwald 1955, 105–8. Sealey 1977, 98–99, 102–3 also doubts a *direct* connection, though he views Drakon's provision of payment to the victim's family as a means of regulating blood feud.

91. *IG* i^3 104.19–20.

92. *IG* i^3 104.20–23.

93. *IG* I^3.104.26–31 (with Stroud 1968, 5) (ἐὰν δ]έ [τ]ις τ|ὸ[ν ἀν]δρ̣[οφόνον κτένει ἒ αἴτιος ε̑ι φόνο, ἀπεχόμενον ἀγορᾶ]ς ἐφο|ρί[α]ς κ̣[α]ὶ [ἄθλον καὶ hιερõν Ἀμφικτυονικõν, hόσπερ τὸν Ἀθεν]αι̑ον κ̣|[τένα]ν̣[τα, ἐν τοι̑ς αὐτοι̑ς ἐνέχεσθαι· διαγιγνόσκεν δὲ τὸς] ἐ[φ]έτα[ς] | [ἐχσ]ε̑[ναι δὲ τὸς ἀνδροφόνος ἀποκτένεν ἒ ἀπάγεν, ἐὰν ἐν] τ̣ε̑ι ἐμεδ̣|[απει̑ . . .). *Atimos* does not appear in the inscription, which becomes increasingly fragmentary at this point, but that was clearly the result within Athens and other restricted areas. See also Gagarin 1981a, 119–20; Ruschenbusch 1960, 147–52, though he concludes elsewhere (1968, 11–15) that Solon, not Drakon, introduced the status of *atimia*.

94. Hölkeskamp 1992b; 1994.

95. Arist. *Pol.* 1274b23–26.

96. Hölkeskamp 1999, 79 also suggests, tentatively, that there may have been some similarity.

97. *Nomima* 1.1. See *Nomima*, pp. 1.9ff. and Hölkeskamp 1999, 174ff. for discussions of the law's provenance and possible connection to Kharondas, with copious literature cited.

98. Arist. *Pol.* 1268b39–1269a3.

99. Arist. *Pol.* 1269a2.

100. Plut. *Sol.* 21.4.

101. Plut. *Sol.* 21.5.

102. Garland 1985, 24, 28ff.

103. Plut. *Sol.* 21.4.

104. Sokolowski 1969, no. 97; Frisone 2000, 58–60.

105. Sokolowski 1969, no. 97.5–6.

106. Frisone 2000, 100.

107. Dem. 43.62.

108. Cic. *de leg.* 2.64.

109. Plut. *Sol.* 12.4. See also the discussion in Forsdyke 2005, 89–90.

110. Plut. *Sol.* 12.1.

111. *Il.* 14.720f.; Aesch. *Ch.* 733.

112. Boardman 1955, 56 believes that the restrictions placed on the *prothesis* were in fact designed to discourage the undertaking of the ceremony "on the scale implicit in the Geometric representations." Rationalistic explanations, such as those Pl. (*Leg.* 12.959a) and Pollux (8.65) posit, have been effectively proven wrong; Zscheitzmann 1928, 36.

113. Kurtz and Boardman 1970, 73–74.

114. Osborne 1996, 223 underscores the volatility of Athenian society in Solon's age, and the likelihood for simple slanders and accusations to lead to conflict among important individuals.

115. Hdt. 1.60. See the discussions in Connor 1987; Lavelle 2000.

116. Kurtz and Boardman 1970, 80.

117. Kurtz and Boardman 1970, 75.

118. Richter 1961, 9; Kurtz and Boardman 1970, 57–58.

119. Kurtz and Boardman 1970, 80.

120. Richter 1961, 9–11, nos. 1–4.

121. Richter 1961, 4–6.

122. Richter 1961, 15, 18–20 nos. 11–21.

123. Capital with squire: Richter 1961, 18–19, no. 21. Examples of stele portraits: Richter 1961, 13 no. 9; 20–21 no. 23; 21 no. 25; 22–24 nos. 27–36; 27 no. 37; 32–36 nos. 45–52.

124. Only two complete sphinxes survive from this period (Richter 1961, 27–29 nos. 37–8), though the capitals still retain the mounting holes, indicating sphinxes remained a regular feature during this phase.

125. Richter 1961, 27–29 no. 37.

126. Richter 1961, 3, 14, 26.

127. I disagree with Sourvinou-Inwood 1995, 290ff. that we should expect to see lengthy inscriptions proclaiming aristocratic values in order to interpret these markers as those of the elite. The expense and design of the marker, in and of themselves, were proclamations of power, wealth, and status, as were depictions of horses, athletes, and the like; all that remained was to signify to whom it belonged.

128. Hölkeskamp 1992a; 1994; 1999.

129. Chapter 5.4 above.

130. See Demargne and van Effentere 1937, 333–48; Meiggs and Lewis 1989, 2–3 no. 2; Willetts 1955, 167–69; Ehrenberg 1943, 14–18; Gagarin 1986, 81–86; 2008, 45–50; Jeffery/Johnston 1990, 311 no. 1a; Hölkeskamp 1999, 90–92; Papakonstantinou 2008, 51–57, 66–69 for discussions.

131. Meiggs and Lewis 1989, no. 2 (ἇδ' ἔϜαδε πόλι· ἐπεί κα κοσμήσει, δέκα Ϝετί ον τὸν ἀ|Ϝτὸν μὴ κόσμεν· αἰ δὲ κοσμησίε, ὁ[π]ε δικακσίε, ἀϜτὸν ὀπῆλεν διπλεῖ κἀ Ϝτὸν | ἄκρηστον ἦμεν, ἇς δόοι, κὄτι κοσμησίε μηδὲν ἤμεν. | (*vacat*) X ὀμόται δὲ κόσμος κοἰ δάμιοι κοἰ ἴκατι οἱ τὰς πόλ̣[ιο]ς (*vacat*).

132. See Willetts 1967, 7f. for the parallels with the Gortynian "constitution" and the duties of the *kosmoi* there.

133. The sense of *akrêston* in the third line of the inscription is unclear, whether it applies only to the right to hold office or is more punitive still.

134. Demargne and van Effenterre 1937.

135. Willetts 1955, 41ff.; Ehrenberg 1943, 14–18.

136. Gagarin 1986, 81–85.

137. Gagarin 2008, 77. Papakonstantinou 2008, 51–57 likewise sees a broader, more communal authority due to the enactment clause, though is cautious about what "the *polis*" may mean, precisely.

138. Gagarin 2008, 77.

139. On Miltiades, archon 664/3 and 659/8, see Develin 1989, 29, with literature cited. On the circumstances and historicity of Damasias, see Hawke 2006.

140. Gagarin 1986, 20–24.

141. As we shall see below, at seventh-century Tiryns a legal distinction applied between the people (*damos*) and the crowd or mob (*oqlos*).

142. *ICret* IV.14 g-p 2. (τρί[ο̂]ν̣ Ϝετίων τὸν ἀϜτὸν μὴ ϙοσμε̂ν, δέκα μὲν γνώμονας, πέντε̣ [δὲ κσ]ενίος: "For three years the same man cannot be *kosmos*, and *gnomon* for ten, *ksenios* for five.")

143. For the provenance of the inscriptions: D. M. Robinson 1943, 191; re-evaluation by Jeffery/Johnston 1990, 208f. Other discussions include Beattie 1947; *SEG* 11.1112, 22.320; Hölkeskamp 1999, 71–72 with nn. 1, 2, 5–9. For the presence of a local sanctuary to Demeter: Paus. 8.15.4, 8.21.3.

144. Beattie 1947, 71f.; Murakawa 1957, 393; Veligianni Terzi 1977, 33f.; Mills 1984, 258f.; Hölkeskamp 1999, 72.

145. Mills 1984, 258ff.; Hölkeskamp 1999, 72.

146. *IvOlympia* 2 (= *Nomima* 1.23); Jeffery/Johnston 1990, 408. See Hölkeskamp 1999, 100n21 for a discussion of further literature and arguments for 580 as the terminus ante quem for these laws.

147. Hölkeskamp 1999, 101 with literature cited.

148. *SEG* 30 380 nos. 1–4. (. . . [τὸν]ς πλατιϜοίνον̣[ς | Ϝεκάστε. αἰ μ' ἐξσθ̣[ο]-ά̣σσαιιεν ὀφλε̂ν ἐν[ς | Δί]Ϝα κἀθαναἐίιαν τριιαάϙοντα μ̣[ε]δίμμνονς α[-|- -]ασιον | [. .]ποσταντον πλατιϜοινάρχον τα δ[- - -] . . . [- - -] | [ἀ]ποδόμεν τοι ἰαρομμνάμονι τὸνς πρα[- - -]ς. τὸν δ' ἰιαρομμναμόν̣[α- - -]εν τ|ὰ δαμόσιια hό|πυι κα δοκεῖ τοι δάμοι ἀλιιαίαν θ̣εν . . . ; plus, *SEG* 30 380 no. 7.2: . . . [τ]ὸνς πλατ̣ιϜοινάρχος [τὰ]ν ζαμιίαν παρσχ̣ε̂[ν] τοον ϙ|ο[ι]νον· αἰ δὲ μὲ hυπερπάρσχ[ο]ιιεν Ϝοίϙοθεν hο ἐπιγνόμον ἐπελ̣[ά]στο τον̣ ὀϙλον. . .). I have followed the translation of Osborne 1997, 75, which seems sensible to me, given the nature and obscurity of the text: ". . . each to the *platiwoinoi* (pourers of libations of wine?). If he does not pay the fine he is to incur a

fine of thirty *medimnoi* to Zeus and Athena . . . if the *platiwoinarkhoi* refuse—to give the *hiaromnemon*—The *hiaromnemon* is to exact the fine/confiscate the property? wherever the people decide to hold the court"; ". . . the community is to provide the penalty for the *platiwoinarkhoi*. But if they do not provide over and above from home, let the *epignomon* impose a fine on the mob . . ."

149. Osborne 1997, 75.

150. Pl. *Leg.* 711c.

Chapter 7

1. Cotterrell 2006, 77–78.

2. Cotterrell 2006, 163–64.

3. See also Morris 1996 regarding the consciously differentiated cultural pursuits of different segments of the elites of the Archaic *poleis*.

4. Contra, Eder 1986. I agree in large measure with Schmitz 2004, esp. 111–26 with 135 that Homeric elites effectively reproduced the values and ideology of elite definition, but of course that ideology was one which stressed competition, giving the elite *less* of a sense of solidarity than that of the commons.

5. Gagarin 2003.

6. Hölkeskamp 1992a; 1992b; 1999.

7. Gagarin 2003; 2008. In the former, Gagarin disagrees with Hölkeskamp, seeing the laws as more encompassing programs of legislation grouped together by category. I would suggest that there is some truth in both positions, particularly once the elite of an individual *polis* had acquired a legislative habit: members of the governing aristocracy may have begun to perceive the interrelated nature of some problems and attempted to address them more comprehensively. But the perceived need was prerequisite to compel the written statute(s) in the first place.

8. E. Robinson 1997.

9. Pl. *Leg.* 711c.

10. Bowman and Woolf 1994a.

11. R. Thomas 1994; Gagarin 2003. Only in cases regarding maritime contracts, in the courts known as *dikai emporikai*, did written evidence outweigh oral testimony and argument; see D. Cohen 2003; E. Cohen 1973.

12. R. Thomas 1994, 34, 39, quote on 49.

13. Svenbro 1993. Contra, Gagarin 2008, esp. 46–66.

14. Bowman and Woolf 1994b, 9.

15. Gagarin 2003, 68.

16. Kahn 2003.

17. C. Thomas 1977; Gagarin 2003, 67–68.

18. Plut. *Sol.* 12.1–3.

19. [Arist.] *AthPol.* 13.1–2. The author refers to two *anarkhiai* and a certain Damasias holding the office for two years and two months before his removal "by force." On the historical reliability of the passage, see now Hawke 2006. For interpretations, see Figueira 1984; Rhodes 1993, 180–84.

Bibliography

Adcock, F. E. 1927. "Literary Tradition and Early Greek Codemakers." *Cambridge Historical Journal* 2: 95–109.

Adkins, A. W. H. 1960. *Merit and Responsibility: A Study in Greek Values.* Oxford.

———. 1971. "Homeric Values and Homeric Society." *Journal of Hellenic Studies* 91: 1–14.

———. 1972. *Moral Values and Political Behavior in Ancient Greece.* London and New York.

———. 1985. *Poetic Craft in the Early Greek Elegists.* Chicago.

Alföldy, G. 1969. "Der attische Synoikismos und die Entstehung des athenischen Adels." *Revue belge de philologie et d'historie* 47: 15–36.

Andersen, Ø. 1976. "Some Thoughts on the Shield of Achilles." *Symbolae Osloenses* 51: 5–18.

———. 1989. "The Significance of Writing in Early Greece: a Critical Appraisal." In Schousboe and Larsen, 1989: 73–90.

Anderson, G. 2003. *The Athenian Experiment. Building an Imagined Political Community in Ancient Attica, 508–490 B.C.* Ann Arbor.

Andrewes, A. 1956. *The Greek Tyrants.* New York.

———. 1982. "The Growth of the Athenian State." *Cambridge Ancient History*^{2} 3.3. Cambridge: 360–91.

Anhalt, E. K. 1993. *Solon the Singer: Politics and Poetics.* Lanham, MD.

Antonaccio, C. M. 1995. *An Archaeology of Ancestors: Tomb Cult and Hero Cult in Early Greece.* Lanham, MD.

Armstrong, A. 1950. "Trial by Combat among the Greeks." *Greece and Rome* 19: 73–79.

Austin, J. 1995. *The Province of Jurisprudence Determined.* W. E. Rumble, ed. Cambridge.

Beattie, A. J. 1947. "Notes on Archaic Arcadian Inscription Concerning Demeter Thesmophoros." *Classical Quarterly* 41.1–2: 66–72.

Beazley, J. D. 1956. *Athenian Black-Figure Vase Painters.* Oxford.

———. 1971. *Parilipomena.* Oxford.

Bekker-Nielsen, T., and L. Hannestad, eds. 2001. *War as a Cultural and Social Force. Essays on Warfare in Antiquity.* Copenhagen.

Bellamy, R. 1989. "Bellerophon's Tablet." *Classical Journal* 84.3: 289–307.

Beloch, K.-J. 1912–13. *Griechische Geschichte.* Volumes 1 and 2. Stuttgart.

Bentham, J. 1988. *Fragment on Government.* J. H. Burns and H. L. A. Hart, eds. Cambridge.

Berent, M. 1994. *The Stateless* Polis: *Towards a Re-evaluation of the Classical Greek Political Community.* Thesis (Ph.D.), University of Cambridge.

Bernand, A., and O. Masson. 1957. "Les inscriptions grecques d'Abou-Simbel." *Revue des études grecques* 70: 1–20.

Bintliff, J. L. 1985. "The Boeotia Survey." In S. Macready and F. Thompson, eds. *Archaeological Field Survey in Britain and Abroad.* London: 196–216.

Bintliff, J. L., and A. M. Snodgrass. 1985. "The Cambridge/Bradford Boeotian Expedition: the First Four Years." *Journal of Field Archaeology* 12: 123–61.

———. 1988. "Mediterranean Survey and the City." *Antiquity* 62: 57–71.

Bleicken, J. 1985. *Die athenische Demokratie.* Paderborn.

Bloch, M. 1989. "Literacy and Enlightenment." In Schousboe and Larsen, 1989: 15–38.

Bloch, M., and J. Parry. 1989. *Money and the Morality of Exchange.* Cambridge.

Blok, J., and A. Lardinois, eds. 2006. *Solon of Athens: New Historical and Philological Approaches. Mnemosyne* Supplement 272. Leiden and Boston.

Boardman, J. 1955. "Painted Funerary Plaques and Some Remarks on Prothesis." *Annual of the British School at Athens* 50: 51–66.

———. 1957. "Early Euboean Pottery and History." *Annual of the British School at Athens* 52: 1–29.

———. 1970. "Orientalen auf Kreta." In Boardman, ed. *Dädalische Kunst auf Kreta im 7. Jahrhundert v. Chr.* Hamburg.

———. 1974. *Athenian Black Figure Vases.* London.

———. 1975. *Athenian Red Figure Vases. The Archaic period.* London.

———. 1999. *The Greeks Overseas*[4]. London.

Boegehold, A., and A. Scafuro, eds. 1994. *Athenian Identity and Civic Ideology.* Baltimore.

Bohannon, P. 1957. *Justice and Judgment among the Tiv.* Oxford.

———. 1963. *Social Anthropology.* New York.

———. ed. 1967a. *Law and Warfare.* Garden City, NY.

———. 1967b. "The Differing Realms of the Law." In Bohannon, 1967a: 43–58.

Bonner, R. J., and G. Smith. 1930 and 1938. *The Administration of Justice from Homer to Aristotle.* 2 volumes. Chicago.

Boruhovic, V. 1981. "Zur Geschichte des sozialpolitischen Kampfes auf Lesbos Ende 7. – Anfang 6. v.u.Z." *Klio* 63: 247–59.

Bourriot, F. 1976. *Recherches sur la nature du genos. Étude d'histoire sociale athénienne, Périodes archaïque et classique.* Paris.

Bowman, A., and G. Woolf, eds. 1994a. *Literacy and Power in the Ancient World.* Cambridge.

———. 1994b. "Literacy and Power in the Ancient World." In Bowman and Woolf, 1994a: 1–16.

Bradeen, D. W. 1963. "The Fifth-Century Archon List." *Hesperia* 32: 187–208.

Bravo, B. 1974. "Une lettre sur plombe Berezan: colonisation et modes de contact dans le Pont." *Dialogues d'histoire ancienne* 1: 110–87.

———. 1977. "Remarques sur les assises sociales, les formes d'organisation et la terminologie du commerce maritime grec à l'époque archaïque." *Dialogues d'histoire ancienne* 3: 1–59.

———. 1984. "Commerce et noblesse en Grèce archaïque: a propos d'un livre d'Alfonse Mele." *Dialogues d'histoire ancienne* 10: 99–160.

Broneer, O. 1938. "Excavations on the North Slope of the Acropolis, 1937." *Hesperia* 7: 161–263.

Bryant, J. M. 1990. "Military Technology and Socio-cultural Change in the Ancient Greek City." *Sociological Review,* n.s. 38: 484–516.

Buck, R. J. 1979. *A History of Boeotia.* Edmonton.

Buckler, J. 2003. *Aegean Greece in the Fourth Century B.C.* Leiden and Boston.

Bureau, J. 1980. "Une société sans vengeance; le cas des Gamo d'Ethiopie." In Verdier, Courtois, and Poly, eds., 1980–84: 1.213–24.

Burkert, W. 1992. *The Orientalizing Revolution.* M. Pinder and W. Burkert, trans. Cambridge, MA.

———. 2004. *Babylon, Memphis, Persepolis. Eastern contexts of Greek culture.* Cambridge, MA.

Burns, A. 1981. "Athenian Literacy in the Fifth Century B.C." *Journal of the History of Ideas* 42: 371–87.

Bury, J. B., and R. Meiggs. 1975. *A History of Greece to the Death of Alexander the Great.* New York.

Busolt, G. 1893 and 1895. *Griechische Geschichte.* Volumes 1 and 2. Gotha.

Busolt, G., and H. Swoboda. 1926. *Griechische Staatskunde.* Munich.

Cadoux, T. J. 1948. "The Athenian Archons from Kreon to Hypsichides." *Journal of Hellenic Studies* 68: 70–123.

Cairns, D. 1996. "Hybris, Dishonour, and Thinking Big." *Journal of Hellenic Studies* 116: 1–32.

Calhoun, G. M. 1944. *Introduction to Greek Legal Science.* Oxford.

Camassa, G. 1988. "Aux origines de la codification écrite des lois en Grèce." In M. Detienne, ed., 1988a. Lille: 130–55.

Camp, J. M. 1994. "Before Democracy: Alkmaionidai and Peisistratidai." In W. D. E. Coulson, ed. *The Archaeology of Athens and Attica under the Democracy.* Oxford: 1–28.

Campbell, D. W. 1983. *The Golden Lyre: the Themes of the Greek Lyric Poets.* London.

Cantarella, E. 2002. "Dispute Settlement in Homer: Once Again on the Shield of Achilles." In *Mélanges en l'honneur Panayotis Dimakis: droits antiques et société.* Athens: 147–65.

———. 2005. "Gender, Sexuality, and Law." In Gagarin and Cohen, eds.: 236–53.

Carawan, E. 1998. *Rhetoric and the Law of Draco.* Oxford.

———. 2008. "What the *mnemones* Knew." In A. Mackay, ed. *Orality, Literacy, Memory in the Ancient Greek and Roman World (Orality and Literacy in Ancient Greece, Volume 7). Mnemosyne* suppl. 298. Leiden and Boston: 163–84.

Carbonnier, J. 1971. *Flexible droit: texts pour une sociologie du droit sans rigueur.* Paris.

———. 1979. *Essais sur les lois.* Paris.

Carey, C. 1996. "Nomos in Attic Rhetoric and Oratory." *Journal of Hellenic Studies* 116: 33–46.

———. 2000. *Democracy in Classical Athens.* London.

Carlier, P. 1984. *Le Royauté en Grèce avant Alexandre.* Strasbourg.

Cartledge, P. 2001. *Spartan Reflections.* Berkeley.

Cerra, G. 1979. *Legislazione orale e tragedia greca.* Naples.

Christ, M. 1998. *The Litigious Athenian.* Baltimore.

Clanchy, M. 1993. *From Memory to Written Record, England 1066–1307*[2]. Oxford and Cambridge, MA.

Clinton, K. 1982. "The Nature of the Late-fifth-century Revision of the Athenian Law Code." In *Studies in Attic Epigraphy, History and Topography Presented to Eugene Vanderpool. Hesperia* Supplement 19. Princeton: 27–37.

Cohen, A. 1985. *The Symbolic Construction of Community.* London.

Cohen, D. 1984. "The Athenian Law of Adultery." *Revue internationale des droits de l'antiquité* 31: 147–65.

———. 1991. *Law, Sexuality, and Society: the Enforcement of Morals in Classical Athens.* Cambridge.

———. 1995. *Law, Violence and Community in Classical Athens.* Cambridge.

———. 2003. "Writing, law, and legal practice in the Athenian courts." In Yunis, ed., 2003: 78–96.

Cohen, E. 1973. *Ancient Athenian Maritime Courts.* Princeton.

Coldstream, J. N. 1976. "Hero-cults in the Age of Homer." *Journal of Hellenic Studies* 96: 8–17.

———. 2003. *Geometric Greece, 900–700 B.C.*[2] London and New York.

Colson, E. 1953. "Social Control and Vengeance in Plateau Tonga Society." *Africa* 23: 199–212.

Comaroff, J. L., and S. Roberts. 1981. *Rules and Processes: the Cultural Logic of Dispute in an African Context.* Chicago.

Connor, R. W. 1987. "Tribes, Festivals, and Processions; Civic Ceremonial and Political Manipulation in Archaic Greece." *Journal of Hellenic Studies* 107: 40–50.

Coombe, R. 1998. "Contingent Articulations: a Critical Cultural Studies of Law." In Sarat and Kearns, eds., 1998a: 21–64.

Cotterrell, R. 2006. *Law, Culture and Society.* Hampshire, UK and Burlington, VT.

Cristofani, M. 1981. "Appendice. Le iscrizioni." In *Materiali per servire alla storia del Vaso François.* Rome: 175–78.

Cross, F. M. 1967. "The Origin and Early Evolution of the Alphabet." *Eretz-Israel* 8: 8–24.

Crotty, K. 1994. *The Poetics of Supplication.* Ithaca, NY, and London.

Dareste, R., B. Haussoulier, and T. Reinach. 1891–95. *Recueil des inscriptions juridiques grecques.* Paris.

David, E. 1984. "Solon, Neutrality and Partisan Literature of Late Fifth-century Athens." *Museum Helveticum* 41: 129–38.

———. 1985. "Solon's Electoral Propaganda." *Rivista storica dell'antichità* 15: 7–22.

Davies, J. K. 1971. *Athenian Propertied Families, 600–300 B.C.* Oxford.

———. 1996. "Deconstructing Gortyn." In Foxhall and Lewis, eds., 1996. Oxford: 33–56.

———. 1997. "The Origins of the Greek *polis:* Where Should We Be Looking?" In Mitchell and Rhodes, eds., 1997: 24–38.

Day, J., and M. Chambers. 1967. *Aristotle's History of Athenian Democracy.* University of California Publications in History 73. Amsterdam.

De Polignac, F. 1995. *Cults, Territory and the Origins of the Greek City-State.* J. Lloyd, trans. Chicago.

Delatte, A. 1922. *Essai sur la politique pythagoricienne.* Paris.

Demand, N. 1996. *A History of Ancient Greece.* Boston.

Demargne, P., and H. van Effenterre. 1937. "Recherches à Dreros." *Bulletin de correspondence hellénique* 61: 333–48.

Demerath, N. J., and R. A. Robertson, eds. 1968. *System, Change, and Conflict. A Reader in Sociological Theory and the Debate about Functionalism.* Glencoe, IL.

Desborough, V. 1972. *The Greek Dark Ages.* London.

Descourdes, J.-P., ed. 1992. *Greek Colonists and Native Populations.* Oxford.

Detienne, M. 1963. *Crise agraire et attitude religieuse chez Hésiode. Latomus* 68. Brussels.

———, ed. 1988a. *Les saviors de l'écriture. En Grèce ancienne*[2]. Lille.

———. 1988b. "L'écriture et ses nouveaux objets intellectuels en Grèce." In Detienne, ed., 1988a: 7–26.

Develin, R. 1989. *Athenian Officials, 684–321 B.C.* Cambridge.

Diamant, S. 1982. "Theseus and the Unification of Attica." In *Studies in Attic Epigraphy, History and Topography Presented to Eugene Vanderpool. Hesperia* Supplement 19: 38–47.

Diamond, A. S. 1971. *Primitive Law. Past and Present.* London.

Dickinson, O. 1994. *The Aegean Bronze Age.* Cambridge.

Dillon, M. 1997. "A Homeric Pun from Abu Simbel (Meiggs & Lewis 7a)." *Zeitschrift für Papyrologie und Epigraphik* 118: 128–30.

Dodds, E. R. 1951. *The Greeks and the Irrational.* Berkeley.

Donlan, W. 1970. "Changes and Shifts in the Meaning of demos in the Literature of the Archaic Period." *La Parola del Passato* 135: 381–95.

———. 1973. "The Tradition of Anti-aristocratic Thought in Early Greek Poetry." *Historia* 22: 145–54.

———. 1979. "The Structure of Authority in the *Iliad*." *Arethusa* 12: 51–70.

———. 1982. "The Politics of Generosity in Homer." *Helios* 9.2: 1–15.

———. 1985. "The Social Groups of Dark Age Greece." *Classical Philology* 80: 293–308.

———. 1989a. "The Pre-state Community in Greece." *Symbolae Osloenses* 67: 5–29.

———. 1989b. "Homeric τέμενος and the Land Economy of the Dark Age." *Museum Helveticum* 46: 129–45.

———. 1993. "Dueling with Gifts in the *Iliad:* As the Audience Saw It." *Colby Quarterly* 29: 155–72.

———. 1994. "Chief and Followers in Pre-state Greece." In Tandy and Duncan, eds.: 34–51.

———. 1997. "The Relations of Power in the Pre-state and Early State Polities." In Mitchell and Rhodes, eds.: 39–48.

———. 1999. *The Aristocratic Ideal and Selected Papers.* Wauconda, IL.

Drews, R. 1983. *Basileus. The Evidence for Kingship in Geometric Greece.* New Haven.

———. 1993. *The End of the Bronze Age: Changes in Warfare and the Catastrophe ca. 1200 B.C.* Princeton.

Dunbabin, T. J. 1948. *The Western Greeks.* Oxford.

Eder, W. 1986. "The Political Significance of the Codification of Law in Archaic Societies: an Unconventional Hypothesis." In K. Raaflaub, ed., *Social Struggles in Archaic Rome.* Berkeley and Los Angeles: 262–300.

Edwards, A. 2004. *Hesiod's Ascra.* Berkeley.

Edwards, G., and R. B. Edwards. 1974. "Red Letters and Phoenician Writing." *Kadmos* 13: 48–57.

Ehrenberg, V. 1943. "An Early Source of polis-constitution." *Classical Quarterly* 37.1–2: 14–18.

Ellickson, R. 1991. *Order without Law: How Neighbors Settle Disputes.* Cambridge, MA.

Evans-Pritchard, E. 1940. *The Nuer.* Oxford.

Falk Moore, S. 1960. "Marxian Law in Primitive Society." In S. Diamond, ed., 1960. *Culture in History: Essays in Honor of Paul Radin.* New York: 642–62.

———. 1973. "Law and Social Change: the Semi-autonomous Social Field as an Appropriate Subject of Study." *Law and Society Review* 7: 719–46.

Farenga, V. 2006. *Citizen and Self in the Greek City-State: Individuals Performing Justice and the Law.* Cambridge.

Ferenczy, E. 1976. *From the Patrician State to the Patricio-Plebeian State.* Amsterdam.

Figueira, T. J. 1984. "The Ten Archons of 579/8 at Athens." *Hesperia* 53: 447–73.

———. 1986. *Aegina, Society and Politics.* Salem, NH.

Finley, M. I. 1970. *Early Greece.* New York.

———. 1971. *The Ancestral Constitution.* Cambridge.

———. 1975. *The Use and Abuse of History.* New York.

———. 1976. "The Freedom of the Citizen in the Greek world." *Talanta* 7: 1–23.

———. 1981. *Economy and Society in Ancient Greece.* New York.

———. 2002. *The World of Odysseus.* With an introduction by Bernard Knox (1978 reprint). New York.

Finnegan, R. 1977. *Oral Poetry. Its Nature, Significance, and Social Context.* London and New York.

———. 1992. *Oral Traditions and the Verbal Arts.* New York.

Fisher, N., H. van Wees, and D. Boedecker, eds. 1998. *Archaic Greece: New Approaches and New Evidence.* London.

Foley, A. 1988. *The Argolid, 800–600 B.C.: An Archaeological Survey.* Gothenburg.

Foley, J. 1997. "Oral Tradition and Its Implications." In Morris and Powell, eds., 1997: 146–73.

———. 2002. *How to Read an Oral Poem.* Urbana, IL.

Forrest, W. G. 1966. *The Emergence of Greek Democracy 800–400 B.C.* New York.

———. 1968. *A History of Sparta, 950–192 B.C.* New York.

Forsdyke, S. 2005. *Exile, Ostracism, and Democracy: The Politics of Expulsion in Ancient Greece.* Princeton.

Foucault, M. 1977. *Discipline and Punish. The Birth of the Prison.* A. Sheridan, trans. London.

Fowler, H. 1925. *Euthyphro. Apology. Crito. Phaedo. Phaedrus.* Cambridge, MA.

Foxhall, L. 1997a. "A View from the Top: Evaluating the Solonian Property Classes." In Mitchell and Rhodes, eds., 1997: 113–36.

———. 1997b. "Appendix 1: Ancient Farmsteads, Other Agricultural Sites and Equipment." In C. Mee and H. Forbes, eds., 1997. *A Rough and Rocky Place.* Liverpool: 257–68.

Foxhall, L., and A. D. E. Lewis, eds. 1996. *Greek Law in Its Political Setting.* Oxford.

Freeman, C. 1999. *The Greek Achievement: the Foundation of the Western World.* New York.

Fried, M. 1967. *The Evolution of Political Society: an Essay in Political Anthropology.* New York.

Friedman, L. M. 1975. *The Legal System: a Social Science Perspective.* New York.

Frisone, F. 2000. *Leggi e regolamenti funerary nel mondo greco. I: le fonti epigrafiche.* Lecce.

Frost, F. 1984. "The Athenian Military before Cleisthenes." *Historia* 33: 283–94.

———. 1987. "Attic Literacy and the Solonian *seisachtheia.*" *Ancient World* 15: 51–58.

———. 1990. "Peisistratos, the Cults, and the Unification of Attica." *Ancient World* 21: 3–9.

———. 1994. "Aspects of Early Athenian Citizenship." In Boegehold and Scafuro, eds.: 45–56.

Fuks, A. 1953. *The Ancestral Constitution. Four Studies in Athenian Party Politics at the End of the Fifth Century B.C.* Westport, CT.

———. 1974. "Patterns and Types of Social-economic Revolution in Greece from the Fourth to the Second Century B.C." In Fuks, 1974. *Social Conflict in Ancient Greece.* Jerusalem: 9–39 = *Ancient Society* 5: 51–81. (Hebrew original: Fuks, 1973. *Proceedings of the Israel Academy of Sciences and Humanities* 5).

Fustel de Coulanges, N. D. 1980. *The Ancient City.* With forewords by A. Momigliano and S. C. Humphreys. Baltimore.

Gagarin, M. 1974. "Hesiod's Dispute with Perses." *Transactions of the American Philological Association* 104: 103–11.

———. 1978. "Self-defense in Athenian Homicide Law." *Greek, Roman, and Byzantine Studies* 19: 111–20.

———. 1981a. *Drakon and Early Athenian Homicide Law.* New Haven.
———. 1981b. "The thesmothetai and the Earliest Athenian Tyranny Law." *Transactions of the American Philological Association* 111: 71–77.
———. 1986. *Early Greek Law.* Berkeley.
———. 1992. "The Poetry of Justice: Hesiod and the Origins of Greek Law." *Ramus* 21: 61–78.
———. 1998. "Women in Athenian Courts." *Diké* 1: 39–52.
———. 2002. *Antiphon the Athenian. Oratory, Law, and Justice in the Age of the Sophists.* Austin, TX.
———. 2003. "Letters of the Law: Written Texts in Archaic Greek Law." In Yunis, ed., 2003a: 59–77.
———. 2008. *Writing Greek Law.* Cambridge.
Gagarin, M., and D. Cohen, eds. 2005. *The Cambridge Companion to Greek Law.* Cambridge.
Gailey, C. W., and T. Patterson, eds. 1987a. *Power Relations and State Formation.* Washington, DC.
———. 1987b. "Power Relations and State Formation." In Gailey and Patterson, eds., 1987a: 1–26.
———. 1995. "State Formation and Uneven Development." In J. Gledhill, B. Bender, and M. T. Larsen, eds. *State and Society: the Emergence and Development of Social Hierarchy and Political Centralization.* London and New York: 77–90.
Gallant, T. W. 1982. "Agricultural Systems, Land Tenure, and the Reforms of Solon." *Annals of the British School at Athens* 77: 111–24.
Garland, R. 1985. *The Greek Way of Death.* Ithaca, NY.
Geddes, A. G. 1984. "Who's Who in Homeric Society?" *Classical Quarterly* 34: 17–36.
Geertz, C. 1983. *Local Knowledge: Further Essays in Interpretive Anthropology.* New York.
———. 2000. *The Interpretations of Cultures* (rev. ed.). New York.
Gehrke, H.-J. 1985. *Stasis. Untersuchungen zu den inneren Kriegen in der griechischen Staates des 5. und 4. Jahrhunderts v. Chr.* Munich.
———. 2000. "Verschriftung und Verschriftlichung sozialer Normen im archaischen und klassischen Griechenland." In E. Levy, ed., 2000. *La codification des lois dans antiquité. Actes de Colloque de Strasbourg, 27–29 novembre 1997.* Paris: 141–57.
Gernet, L. 1938. "Les dix archontes de 581." *Revue de Philologie*[3] 12: 216–27.
———. 1981. "Law and Pre-law in Ancient Greece." In Gernet. *The Anthropology of Ancient Greece.* J. Hamilton and B. Nagy, trans. Baltimore: 141–276.
Ghinatti, F. 1970. *I gruppi politici ateniesi fino alle guerre persiane.* Rome.
Gill, C., N. Postlethwaite, and R. Seaford, eds. 1998. *Reciprocity in Ancient Greece.* Oxford.
Glotz, G. 1904. *La solidarité de la famille dans le droit criminal en Grèce.* New York (1973 reprint).
Gluckman, M. 1965. *Politics, Law and Ritual in Tribal Society.* London.
———. 1973. *The Judicial Process among the Barotse of Northern Rhodesia (Zambia)*[2]. Manchester.
Goebel, G. H. 1989–90. "Bellerophon's Tablet. A Comment." *Classical Journal* 85.2: 170–71.
Goody, J., ed. 1968. *Literacy in Traditional Societies.* Cambridge.
———. 1977. *The Domestication of the Savage Mind.* Cambridge.
———. 2006. *The Theft of History.* Cambridge.
Goody, J., and I. Watt. 1963. "The Consequences of Literacy." *Comparative Studies in Society and History* 5: 304–45.
Graebner, F. 1911. *Methode der Ethnologie.* Heidelberg.

Graham, A. 1982. "The Western Greeks." *Cambridge Ancient History*[2]. Cambridge: 3.163–95.

Grene, D., trans. 1987. *Herodotus. The Histories.* Chicago.

Griffin, J. 1995. *Homer* Iliad *IX.* Oxford.

Gschnitzer, F. 1971. "Stadt und Stamm bei Homer." *Chiron* 1: 1–17.

———. 1981. *Griechische sozialgeschichte von der mykenischen bis zum Ausgang der klassischen Zeit.* Wiesbaden.

Guarducci, M. 1959–60. "Intorno alla legge sacra di Demeter Thesmophoros." *Annuario della Scuola Archeologica di Atene* 37–38: 239–42.

Gulliver, P. H. 1963. *Social Control in an African Society: a Study of the Arusha, Agricultural Masai of Northern Tanganyika.* Boston.

———. 1973. "Negotiations as a Mode of Dispute Settlement: Towards a General Model." *Law and Society Review* 7: 682–705.

Guthrie, W. K. C. 1971. *The Sophists.* Cambridge.

Hågg, R. 1982. "Zur Stadtwerdung des dorischen Argos." In D. Papenfuß and V. M. Strocka, eds., *Palast und Hütte: Beiträge zum Bauen und Wohnen im Altertum von Archäologen.* Munich: 297–307.

———, ed. 1983a. *The Greek Renaissance of the Eighth Century B.C.* Stockholm.

———. 1983b. "Burial Customs and Social Differentiation in 8th-Century Argos." In Hågg, ed., 1983a: 27–31.

Hall, J. M. 1997. *Ethnic Identity in Greek Antiquity.* Cambridge.

———. 2007. *A History of the Archaic Greek World ca. 1200–479 B.C.* Malden, MA, and Oxford.

Halverson, J. 1992. "Goody and the Implosion of the Literacy Thesis." *Man,* n.s. 27: 301–17.

Hammond, N. G. L. 1954. "The Heraeum at Perachora and Corinthian Encroachment." *Annual of the British School at Athens* 49: 93–102.

Hansen, M. H. 1974. *The Sovereignty of the People's Court in Athens in the Fourth Century B.C. and the Public Action against Unconstitutional Proposals.* Odense.

———. 1976. *Apogoge, Endeixis and Ephegesis against Kakourgoi, Atimoi and Pheugontes.* Odense.

———. 1980. "Athenian *nomothesia* in the Fourth Century B.C. and Demosthenes' Speech against Leptines." *Classica et Mediaevalia:* 87–104.

———. 1983. "*Nomos* and *psephisma* in Fourth Century Athens." In M. H. Hansen. *The Athenian Ecclesia. A Collection of Articles, 1976–83.* Copenhagen: 161–77 [= *Greek, Roman, and Byzantine Studies* 19 (1978): 315–30].

———. 1999. *The Athenian Democracy in the Age of Demosthenes* (paperback ed.). Norman, OK.

Hanson, V. D. 1995. *The Other Greeks.* Berkeley.

Harding, P. 1994. *Androtion and the Atthis.* Oxford.

Harris, E. 1995. *Aeschines and Athenian Politics.* New York.

———. 1997. "A New Solution to the Riddle of the *seisachtheia.*" In Mitchell and Rhodes, eds.: 103–12.

Harris, M. 1980. *Cultural Materialism: the Struggle for a Science of Culture.* New York.

Harris, W. 1989. *Ancient Literacy.* Cambridge, MA.

Harrison, A. R. W. 1955. "Law-making at Athens at the End of the Fifth Century B.C." *Journal of Hellenic Studies*: 26–35.

———. 1968–71. *The Law of Athens.* I. *The Family and Property.* II. *Procedure.* Oxford.

Hart, H. L. A. 1961. *The Concept of Law*. Oxford.
Haslam, M. 1997. "Homeric Papyri and the Transmission of the Text." In Morris and Powell, eds.: 55–100.
Haubold, J. 2008. *Homer's People*. Cambridge.
Havelock, E. 1963. *Preface to Plato*. Cambridge, MA.
———. 1978. *The Greek Concept of Justice*. Cambridge, MA.
———. 1982. *The Literate Revolution on Greece and Its Consequences*. Princeton.
———. 1986. *The Muse Learns to Write*. New Haven.
Hawke, J. 2006. "Athenian Politics after Solon." In G. Papanikos and N. C. J. Pappas, eds., 2006. *European History: Lessons for the 21st Century. Essays from the 3rd International Conference on European History*. Athens: 11–26.
———. 2008a. "Written Law and Sub-citizens in Ancient Crete." In K. Hendrickson and N. C. J. Pappas, eds., 2008. *From the Remote to the Recent Past*. Athens: 3–14.
———. 2008b. "Number and Numeracy in Early Greek Literature." *Syllecta Classica* 19: 1–76.
———. 2009. Review of Gagarin, *Writing Greek Law*. *American Journal of Philology* 130: 457–60.
Hedrick, C. W. 1994. "Writing, Reading, and Democracy." In Hornblower and Osborne, eds.: 157–74.
Herrmann, P. 1981. "Teos und Abdera im 5. Jahrhundert v. Chr." *Chiron* 11: 1–11.
Heubeck, A. 1979. *Schrift*. Archaeologia Homerica iii.X. Göttingen.
Hignett, C. 1952. *A History of the Athenian Constitution*. Oxford.
Hirzel, R. 1966. *Themis, Dike und Verwandtes*. Heidelsheim.
Hobsbawm, E. J. 1965. "Introduction." In Marx, 1965: 9–66.
Hodkinson, S. 1997. "The Development of Spartan Society and Institutions in the Archaic Period." In Mitchell and Rhodes, eds., 1997: 83–102.
Hoebel, E. A. 1940. *The Political Organization and Law-Ways of the Comanche Indians*. Memoirs of the American Anthropological Association 54. Menasha, WI.
Hölkeskamp, K.-J. 1992a. "Written Law in Archaic Greece." *Proceedings of the Cambridge Philological Society*, n.s. 38: 87–117.
———. 1992b. "Arbitrators, Lawgivers and the 'Codification of Law' in Archaic Greece. Problems and Perspectives." *Metis* 7: 49–81.
———. 1994. "Tempel, Agora, und Alphabet. Die Entstehungsbedingungen von Gesetzgebung in der archaischen Polis." In H.-J. Gehrke, ed., 1994. *Rechtskodifizierung und soziale Normen im interkulturellen Vergleich*. Tübingen: 135–64.
———. 1999. *Schiedsrichter, Gesetzgeber und Gesetzgebung im archaischen Griechenland*. *Historia* Einzelschriften 131. Stuttgart.
Holoka, J. P. 1991. "Homer, Oral Poetry Theory, and Comparative Literature: Major Trends and Controversies in Twentieth Century Criticism." In J. Latacz, ed.: 456–81.
Hommel, H. 1969. "Die Gerichtsszene auf dem Schild des Achilleus." In R. Starks, ed., 1969. *Politeia und Res Publica: Beiträge zum Verständnis von Politik, Recht und Staat in Antike. Palingenesia* 6: 11–18.
Hope Simpson, R. 1981. *Mycenaean Greece*. Park Ridge, NJ.
Hornblower, S., and R. Osborne, eds. 1994. *Ritual, Finance, Politics: Athenian Democratic Accounts Presented to David Lewis*. Oxford.
Howell, P. P. 1954. *A Manual of Nuer Law*. Oxford.
Humphreys, S. C. 1978. *Anthropology and the Greeks*. Oxford.

———. 1980. "Family Tombs and Tomb Cult in Ancient Athens: Tradition or Traditionalism?" *Journal of Hellenic Studies* 100: 96–126.

———. 1983. *The Family, Women, and Death.* Oxford.

———. 1985. "Law and Discourse." *History and Anthropology* 1: 241–64.

———. 1988. "The Discourse of Law in Archaic and Classical Greece." *Law and History Review* 6: 465–93.

Huxley, G. 1962. *Early Sparta.* Cambridge, MA.

Irwin, E. 2005. *Solon and Early Greek Poetry.* Cambridge.

Isserlin, B. J. 1983. "The Antiquity of the Greek Alphabet." *Kadmos* 22: 151–63.

Jacoby, F. 1949. *Atthis. The Local Chronicles of Ancient Athens.* Oxford.

———. 1980. *Das Marmor Parium.* Chicago (1904 reprint).

Jameson, M. H., C. Runnels, and T. H. van Andel. 1994. *A Greek Countryside: The Southern Argolid from Prehistory to the Present Day.* Stanford.

Janko, R. 1982. *Homer, Hesiod and the Hymns: Diachronic Development in Epic Diction.* Cambridge.

Jeffery, L. H. 1976. *Archaic Greece.* London.

———. 1982. "Greek alphabetic writing." *Cambridge Ancient History*². 3.1. Cambridge: 819–33.

Jeffery, L. H., with A. Johnston. 1990. *The Local Scripts of Archaic Greece.* Oxford.

Jeffery, L. H., and A. Morpurgo-Davies. 1970. "ΠΟΙΝΙΚΑΣΤΑΣ and ΠΟΙΝΙΚΑΖΕΙΝ: a New Archaic Inscription from Crete." *Kadmos* 9: 118–54.

Johnston, A. 1983. "The Extent and Use of Literacy: the Archaeological Evidence." In Hågg, ed., 1983a: 63–68.

Kahn, C. 2003. "Writing Philosophy: Prose and Poetry from Thales to Plato." In Yunis, ed., 2003a: 139–61.

Kakridis, J. 1949. *Homeric Researches.* Lund.

———. 1971. *Homer Revisited.* Lund.

Kelly, T. 1976. *A History of Argos.* Minneapolis.

Kirchner, J. 1968. *Prosopographica Attica.* Berlin.

Knox, B. 1968. "Silent Reading in Antiquity." *Greek, Roman, and Byzantine Studies* 9: 421–35.

Köhler, U. 1867. "Attische Inschriften." *Hermes* 2: 16–36.

Krentz, P. 1982. *The Thirty at Athens.* Ithaca, NY.

Kristensen, K. R. 2002. "On the Gortynian *PULA* and *STARTOS* of the 5th c. BC." *Classica et Mediaevalia* 53: 65–80.

———. 2004. "Codification, Tradition, and Innovation in the Law Code of Gortyn." *Dike* 7: 135–68.

Kullman, W. 1984. "Oral Poetry Theory and Neoanalysis in Homeric Research." *Greek, Roman, and Byzantine Studies* 25: 307–23.

Kurtz, D., and J. Boardman. 1970. *Greek Burial Customs.* Oxford.

Lambert, S. D. 1986. "Herodotus, the Cylonian Conspiracy and the ΠΡΥΤΑΝΕΙΣ ΤΩΝ ΝΑΥΚΡΑΡΩΝ." *Historia* 35: 105–112.

Lamberton, R. 1988. *Hesiod.* New Haven.

Langdon, M. K. 1976. *A Sanctuary of Zeus on Mount Hymettos. Hesperia* Supplement 16. Princeton.

Lanni, A. 1997. "Spectator Sport or Serious Politics?" *Journal of Hellenic Studies* 117: 183–89.

———. 2006. *Law and Justice in the Courts of Classical Athens*. Cambridge and New York.

Lardinois, A. 2006. "Have We Solon's Verses?" In Blok and Lardinois, eds.: 15–35.

Larsen, J. A. O. 1936. "Perioeci in Crete." *Classical Philology* 31.1: 11–22.

Latacz, J. 1977. *Kampfparänase, Kampfdarstellung und Kampfwirklichkeit in der Ilias*. Munich.

———, ed. 1991. *Zweihundert Jahre Homer-Forschung: Rückblick und Ausblick*. Stuttgart.

Lavelle, B. 1993. *The Sorrow and the Pity. A Prolegomenon to a History of Athens under the Peisistratids, c. 560–510 B.C. Historia* Einzelschriften 80. Stuttgart.

———. 2000. "Herodotos and the Parties of Attika." *Classica et Mediaevalia* 51: 51–102.

———. 2005. *Fame, Money, and Power*. Ann Arbor.

Le Roy, E. 1972. "Reflections sur une interpretation anthropologique du droit africain: le Laboratoire d'anthropologie juridique." *Revue juridique et politique, Indépendance et cooperation* 26.3: 427–48.

———. 1978. "Pour une anthropologie du droit." *Revue interdisciplinare d'Études juridiques* 1: 71–100.

Legon, R. P. 1981. *Megara: The Political History of a Greek City-state*. Ithaca, NY.

Lévêque, P. 1978. "Formes des contradictions et voies de développement à Athènes de Solon à Clisthène." *Historia* 27: 522–49.

Lewis, D. M. 1982. "On the New Text of Teos." *Zeitschrift für Papyrologie und Epigraphik* 47: 71–72.

Link, S. 1992. "Die Gesetzgebung des Zaleukos im epizephyrischen Lokroi." *Klio* 74: 11–24.

———. 1994. *Das griechische Kreta*. Stuttgart.

———. 2001. "'Dolos' und 'woikeus' im Recht von Gortyn." *Dike* 4: 87–112.

Llewelyn, K. N., and E. A. Hoebel. 1941. *The Cheyenne Way: Conflict and Case Law in Primitive Jurisprudence*. Norman, OK.

Lord, A. B. 1953. "Homer's Originality: Oral Dictated Texts." *Transactions and Proceedings of the American Philological Association* 84: 124–34.

———. 1967. "Homer as an Oral Poet." *Harvard Studies in Classical Philology* 72: 1–46.

———. 1981. "Memory, Fixity, and Genre in Oral Traditional Poetries." In. J. M. Foley, ed., *Oral Traditional Literature. Festschrift for Albert Bates Lord*. Columbus, OH: 451–61.

———. 1991. *Epic Singers and Oral Tradition*. Ithaca, NY.

———. 2000. *The Singer of Tales*[2]. Cambridge, MA.

Lorimer, H. 1947. "The Hoplite Phalanx with Special Reference to the Poems of Archilochus and Tyrtaeus." *Annual of the British School at Athens* 42: 76–138.

MacAulay, S. 1989. "Popular Legal Culture: an Introduction." *Yale Law Journal* 98.8: 1545–58.

MacDowell, D. M. 1978. *The Law in Classical Athens*. Ithaca, NY.

———. 1986. *Spartan Law*. Edinburgh.

Maehler, H., ed. 1970. *Bacchylides. Carmina cum fragmentis, post B. Snell*. Leipzig.

Maffi, A. 1997. *Il diritto di famiglia nel Codice di Gortina*. Milan.

Maine, H. S. 1986. *Ancient Law*. With foreword by Lawrence Rosen. Tucson, AZ.

Malinowski, B. 1926. *Crime and Custom in Savage Society*. London.

Manville, P. B. 1980. "Solon's Law of stasis and *atimia* in Archaic Athens." *Transactions of the American Philological Association* 110: 213–21.

———. 1990. *The Origins of Citizenship in Ancient Athens*. Princeton.

———. 1994. "Toward a New Paradigm of Athenian Citizenship." In Boegehold and Scafuro, eds.: 21–33.

Martin, R. 1989. *The Language of Heroes: Speech and Performance in the* Iliad. Ithaca, NY.
Martin, T. 1996. *Ancient Greece: from Prehistoric to Hellenistic times.* New Haven.
Marx, K. 1965. *Pre-capitalist Economic Formations.* J. Cohen, trans., with an introduction by E. J. Hobsbawm. New York.
Masarrachia, A. 1958. *Solone.* Florence.
Mazarakis-Ainian, A. 1987. "Geometric Eretria." *Antike Kunst* 30: 3–24.
McCarter, P. K. 1975. *The Antiquity of the Greek Alphabet and the Early Phoenician Scripts.* Missoula, MT.
McDonald, W. A., and R. Hope Simpson. 1972. "Archaeological Exploration." In McDonald and Rapp, eds.: 117–47.
McDonald, W. A., and G. Rapp, eds. 1972. *The Minnesota Messenia Expedition: Reconstructing a Bronze Age Regional Environment.* Minneapolis.
McGlew, J. F. 1989. "Royal Power and the Achaean Assembly at *Iliad* 2.84–393." *Classical Antiquity* 8: 283–95.
———. 1993. *Tyranny and Political Culture in Ancient Greece.* Ithaca, NY.
Meiggs, R., and D. Lewis. 1989. *A Selection of Greek Historical Inscriptions to the End of the Fifth Century B.C.* (rev. ed.). Oxford and New York.
Merkelbach, R. 1982. "Zu dem neuen Text auf Teos." *Zeitschrift für Papyrologie und Epigraphik* 47: 212–13.
Merkelbach, R., and M. L. West. 1967. *Fragmenta Hesiodea.* Oxford.
Merry, S. E. 1988. "Legal Pluralism." *Law and Society Review* 22: 869–96.
Meyer, E. 1954/1893. *Geschichte des Altertums.* 3 volumes. Stuttgart.
Mezey, N. 2001. "Approaches to the Cultural Study of Law: Law as Culture." *Yale Journal of Law and the Humanities* 13: 35–67.
Miller, D. G. 1989–90. "Homer and Writing: Use and Misuse of Epigraphic and Linguistic Evidence." *Classical Journal* 85.2: 171–79.
Millett, P. 1984. "Hesiod and his World." *Proceedings of the Cambridge Philological Society* 210: 84–115.
Mills, H. 1984. "Greek Clothing Regulations: Sacred or Profane?" *Zeitschrift für Papyrologie und Epigraphik* 55: 255–65.
Mitchell, L. G. 1997. "New Wine in Old Wineskins: Solon, *arete* and the *agathos.*" In Mitchell and Rhodes, eds.: 137–47.
Mitchell, L. G, and P. J. Rhodes, eds. 1997. *The Development of the* Polis *in Archaic Greece.* London and New York.
Morgan, C. 2001. "Symbolic and Pragmatic Aspects of Warfare in the Greek World of the 8th to 6th Centuries BC." In Bekker-Nielsen and Hannestad, eds., 2001: 20–44.
Morgan, L. H. 1877. *Ancient Society.* Chicago.
Morris, I. 1986. "The Use and Abuse of Homer." *Classical Antiquity* 5: 81–138.
———. 1987. *Burial and Ancient Society.* Cambridge.
———. 1988. "Tomb Cult and the 'Greek Renaissance': the Past and Present in the 8th Century B.C." *Antiquity* 62: 750–61.
———. 1994. "Everyman's Grave." In Boegehold and Scafuro, 1994: 67–101.
———. 1996. "The Strong Principle of Equality and the Archaic Origins of Greek Democracy." In Ober and Hedrick, eds.: 19–48.
———. 1997. "Homer and the Iron Age." In Morris and Powell, eds.: 535–59.
Morris, I., and B. Powell, eds. 1997. *A New Companion to Homer.* Leiden, New York, and Cologne.

Morris, I., and K. A. Raaflaub, eds. 1998. *Democracy 2500? Questions and Challenges.* Dubuque, IA.

Mossé, C. 1964. "Classes socials et régionalisme à Athènes au début de VIe siècle." *L'antiquité classique* 22: 401–13.

———. 1979. "Les dépendants paysans dans le monde grec à l'époque archaïque et classique." In E.-Ch. Weiskopf, ed. *Terre et paysans dépendants dans les sociétés antiques.* Paris: 77–102.

———. 1980. "Ithaque ou la naissance de la cite." *Annali dell'istituto Universitario orientale di Napoli. Seminario de studi del mondo classico* 2: 7–19.

Motta, R. 1983. "I percosi dell'antropologia giuridica (II): gli studi di Raymond Verdier, negli anni' 80." *Materiali per una storia della cultura giuridica* 13.1: 283–96.

Mühl, M. 1928–29. "Die Gesetze des Zaleukos und Charondas." *Klio* 22: 105–24; 432–63.

———. 1933. *Untersuchungen zur altorientalischen und althellenischen Gesetzgebung. Klio* Beiheft 29. Berlin.

Murakawa, K. 1957. "Demiourgos." *Historia* 6: 385–415.

Murray, O. 1980. *Early Greece.* Stanford.

———. 1983a. "The Greek symposion in History." In E. Gabba, ed. *Tria corda: scritti in onore di Arnaldo Momigliano.* Como: 257–72.

———. 1983b. "The symposion as Social Organization." In Hågg, ed., 1983a: 195–99.

———. ed. 1994. *Sympotica: a Symposium on the symposion.* Oxford.

Nader, L. 1965. "The Anthropological Study of Law." *American Anthropologist* 67.6.2: 3–32.

———, ed. 1969. *Law in Culture and Society.* Chicago.

Nagy, G. 1990a. *Pindar's Homer: The Lyric Possession of an Epic Past.* Baltimore.

———. 1990b. *Greek Mythology and Poetics.* Ithaca, NY.

———. 1996. *Homeric Questions.* Austin, TX.

———. 2003. *Homeric Responses.* Austin, TX.

Naveh, J. 1973. "Some Semitic Epigraphical Considerations on the Antiquity of the Alphabet." *American Journal of Archaeology* 77: 1–8.

———. 1982. *The Early History of the Alphabet.* Leiden.

Nelson, S. 1998. *God and the Land: The Metaphysics of Farming in Hesiod and Vergil.* Oxford.

Nieddu, G. 1982. "Alfabetismo e diffisione sociale della scritture nella Greca arcaica e classica." *Scrittura e civiltà* 6: 233–61.

Nilsson, M. P. 1928. "Die Hoplitentaktik und das Staatswesen." *Klio* 22: 240–49.

Ober, J. 1989. *Mass and Elite in Democratic Athens.* Princeton.

———. 1996. "The Athenian Revolution of 508/7 B.C.: Violence, Authority, and the Origins of Democracy." In Ober, 1996. *The Athenian Revolution: Essays on Ancient Greek Democracy and Political Theory.* Princeton: 32–52.

———. 1998. "Revolution Matters: Democracy as Demotic Action (a Response to Kurt A. Raaflaub)." In I. Morris and Raaflaub, eds.: 67–85.

———. 1999. *Political Dissent in Democratic Athens.* Princeton.

Ober, J., and C. Hedrick, eds. 1996. *Demokratia: A Conversation on Democracies, Ancient and Modern.* Princeton.

Oliver, J. H. 1935. "Greek Inscriptions: Laws." *Hesperia* 4: 5–32.

Ong, W. 1982. *Orality and Literacy.* London.

O'Neil, J. L. 1995. *The Origins and Development of Ancient Greek Democracy.* Lanham, MD, and London.

Oost, S. I. 1972. "Cypselus the Bacchiad." *Classical Philology* 67: 10–30.
Osborne, R. 1996. *Greece in the Making, 1200–479 B.C.* London and New York.
———. 1997. "Law and Laws: How Do We Join up the Dots?" In Mitchell and Rhodes, eds.: 74–82.
———. 1998. "Early Greek Colonization? The Nature of Greek Settlement in the West." In Fisher, van Wees, and Boedecker, eds., 1998: 251–70.
Ostwald, M. 1955. "The Athenian Legislation against Tyranny and Subversion." *Transactions and Proceedings of the American Philological Association* 86: 103–28.
———. 1969. *Nomos and the Beginnings of the Athenian Democracy.* Oxford.
———. 1986. *From Popular Sovereignty to the Sovereignty of Law: Law, Society, and Politics in Fifth-century Athens.* Berkeley.
Page, D. L. 1955. *The Homeric Odyssey.* Oxford.
Palmer, L. R. 1950. "The Indo-Europeans Origins of Greek Justice." *Transactions of the Philological Society* 49: 149–68.
Papakonstantinou, Z. 2002. "Written Law, Literacy, and Social Conflict in Archaic and Classical Crete." *Ancient History Bulletin* 16: 135–50.
———. 2008. *Lawmaking and Adjudication in Archaic Greece.* London.
Parker, R. 1996. *Miasma: Pollution and Purification in Early Greek Religion.* Oxford.
Parker, V. 1997. *Untersuchungen zum Lelantischen Krieg und verwandten Problemen der frühgriechischen Geschichte.* Stuttgart.
Parry, J., and M. Bloch. 1989. *Money and the Morality of Exchange.* Cambridge.
Parry, M. 1928. *L'Epithète traditionelle dans Homère.* Paris.
———. 1930. "Studies in the Epic Technique of Oral Verse-making I: Homer and the Homeric Style." *Harvard Studies in Classical Philology* 41: 73–147.
———. 1932. "Studies in the Epic Technique of Oral Verse-making II: the Homeric Language as the Language of an Oral Poet." *Harvard Studies in Classical Philology* 43: 1–50.
———. 1971. *The Collected Papers of Milman Parry.* A. Parry, ed. Oxford.
Parry, M., and A. B. Lord. 1954. *Serbocroatian Heroic Songs.* Volume 1. Cambridge, MA.
Paulsen, T. 1999. *Die Parapresbeia-Reden des Demosthenes und des Aischines.* Trier.
Pestalozzi, H. 1945. *Die Achilleis als Quelle der Ilias.* Zurich.
Phillips, D. 2008. *Avengers of Blood. Homicide in Athenian Law and Custom from Draco to Demosthenes. Historia Einzelschriften* 202. Stuttgart.
Piccirilli, L. 1981. "'Nomoi' cantata e 'nomoi' scritti." *Civiltà Classica e Cristiana* 2: 7–14.
Plommer, W. H. 1969. "The Tyranny of the Archon List." *Classical Review* 19: 126–29.
Polanyi, K. 1944. *The Great Transformation.* New York.
———. 1947. "Our Obsolete Market Economy." In G. Dalton, ed., 1968, *Primitive, Archaic and Modern Economies. Essays of Karl Polanyi.* New York: 59–77.
———. 1953. "Anthropology and Economic Theory." In M. Fried, ed. *Readings in Anthropology.* New York: 2: 216–38.
———. 1957a. "Aristotle Discovers the Economy." In Polanyi, et al., eds., 1957: 64–94.
———. 1957b. "The Economy as Instituted Process." In Polanyi, et al., eds., 1957: 243–70.
———. 1957c. "Marketless Trading in Hammurabi's Time." In Polanyi, et al., eds., 1957: 12–26.
———. 1966. *Dahomey and the Slave Trade.* Seattle.
———. 1977. *The Livelihood of Man.* H. W. Pearson, ed. New York.
Polanyi, K., C. Arensberg, and H. W. Pearson, eds. 1957. *Trade and Market in the Early Empires.* Glencoe, IL.

Popham, M., and I. Lemos. 1995. "A Euboean Warrior Trader." *Oxford Journal of Archaeology* 14: 151–57.

Popham, M., L. H. Sackett, and Calligas, eds. 1993. *Lefkandi II:the Protogeometric Building at Toumba.* Athens.

Popham, M., L. H. Sackett, and P. G. Themelis, eds. 1980. *Lefkandi I: the Iron Age.* London.

Popham, M., E. Toupoula, and L. H. Sackett. 1982. "The Hero of Lefkandi." *Antiquity* 56: 169–74.

Posner, E. 2000. *Law and Social Norms.* Cambridge, MA.

Posner, R. 1979. "The Homeric Version of the Minimalist State." *Ethics* 90.1: 27–46.

Pounder, R. 1984. "The Origin of *theoi* in Inscription Heading." In W. T. Loomis, et al., eds., 1984. *Studies Presented to Sterling Dow on his Eightieth Birthday. Greek, Roman, and Byzantine Studies* Monograph 10. Durham, NC: 243–50.

Powell, B. 1989. "Why Was the Greek Alphabet Invented? The Epigraphical Evidence." *Classical Antiquity* 8: 321–50.

———. 1991. *Homer and the Origin of the Greek Alphabet.* Cambridge.

———. 1997. "Homer and Writing." In I. Morris and Powell, eds.: 3–32.

———. 2002. *Writing and the Origins of Greek Literature.* Cambridge.

Primmer, A. 1970. "Homerische Gerichtsszene." *Wiener Studien* 83: 5–13.

Purcell, N. 1990. "Mobility and the *polis.*" In O. Murray and S. Price, eds., *The Greek City: from Homer to Alexander.* Oxford: 29–58.

Qviller, B. 1980. "Prolegomena to the Study of the Homeric *demiourgoi* (Murakawa's Theory Re-examined)." *Symbolae Osloenses* 55: 5–21.

———. 1981. "The Dynamics of Homeric Society." *Symbolae Osloenses* 56: 109–55.

Raaflaub, K. A. 1991. "Homer und die Geschichte des 8. Jahrhunderts v. Chr." In Latacz, ed.: 205–56.

———. 1996. "Equalities and Inequalities in Athenian Democracy." In Ober and Hedrick, eds.: 139–74.

———. 1997a. "Homeric Society." In Morris and Powell, eds., 1997: 624–48.

———. 1997b. "Soldiers, Citizens, and the Evolution of the Early Greek *polis.*" In Mitchell and Rhodes, eds.: 49–59.

———. 2006. "Athenian and Spartan *eunomia,* or: What to Do with Solon's Timocracy." In Blok and Lardinois, eds.: 390–428.

Raaflaub, K. A., and R. W. Wallace, eds. 2007a. *The Origins of Democracy in Ancient Greece.* Berkeley.

———. 2007b. "'People's Power' and Egalitarian Trends in Archaic Greece." In Raaflaub and Wallace, eds., 2007a: 22–48.

Raubitschek, A. 1970. "The Cretan Inscription BM 1969.4–2.1: a Supplementary Note." *Kadmos* 9: 155–57.

Reay, M. 1974. "Changing Conventions of Dispute in the Minj Area." In A. L. Epstein, ed., *Contention and Dispute.* Canberra: 198–239.

Renfrew, C. 1979. "Systems Collapse and Social Transformations: Catastrophe and Anastrophe in Early State Societies." In Renfrew and Cooke, eds.: 481–506.

Renfrew, C., and K. L. Cooke, eds. 1979. *Transformations: Mathematical Approaches to Culture Change.* New York.

Reynolds, S. 1994. *Fiefs and Vassals: the Medieval Evidence Reinterpreted.* Oxford and New York.

Rhodes, P. J. 1985. "*Nomothesia* in Fourth-century Athens." *Classical Quarterly* 35: 55–60.

———. 1991. "The Athenian Code of Laws, 410–399 B.C." *Journal of Hellenic Studies* 111: 87–100.

———. 1993. *A Commentary on the Aristotelian* Athenaion Politeia (paperback ed.). Oxford.

———. 2006. "The Reforms and Laws of Solon: an Optimistic View." In Blok and Lardinois, eds.: 248–60.

Richter, G. M. A. 1961. *The Archaic Gravestones of Attica.* London.

Ridgway, D. 1992. *The First Western Greeks.* Cambridge.

Rigby, P. 1987. "Class Formation among East African Pastoralists: Maasai of Tanzania and Kenya." In Gailey and Patterson, eds.: 57–80.

Rihll, T. E. 1986. "'King and Commoners' in Homeric Society." *Liverpool Classical Monthly* 11: 86–91.

———. 1989. "Lawgivers and Tyrants: Solon frr. 9–11West." *Classical Quarterly,* n.s. 39.2: 277–86.

———. 1991. "ΕΚΤΗΜΟΡΟΙ: Partners in Crime?" *Journal of Hellenic Studies* 111: 101–27.

———. 1992. "The Power of the Homeric βασιλεῖς." *Homer 1987. Proceedings of the Third Greenbank Colloquium.* J. Pinsett and H. Hurt, eds. Liverpool Classical Papers 2. Liverpool: 39–50.

Roberts, S. 1979. *Order and Dispute.* Oxford.

Robertson, N. 1978. "The Myth of the First Sacred War." *Classical Quarterly* 28: 38–73.

———. 1990. "The Laws of Athens, 410–399 B.C.: The Evidence for Review and Publication." *Journal of Hellenic Studies* 110: 43–75.

Robinson, D. M. 1943. "A New Arcadian Inscription." *Classical Philology* 38: 191–99.

Robinson, E. 1997. *The First Democracies: Early Popular Government outside Athens. Historia Einzelschrift 107.* Stuttgart: Franz Steiner.

Roebuck, C. 1959. *Ionian Trade and Colonization.* New York.

———. 1972. "Some Aspects of Urbanization at Corinth." *Hesperia* 41: 96–127.

———. 1974. "Three Classes (?) in Early Attica." *Hesperia* 43: 485–93.

———. 1979. *The Early Greek World: Collected Essays of Carl Roebuck.* C. Thomas, ed., 1979. Chicago.

———. 1980. "Stasis in Sicily in the Seventh Century B.C." In M. J. Fontana, M. T. Piraino, and F. P. Rizzo, eds., *Miscellania di studi classici in onore di Eugenio Manni.* Rome: 1921–30.

Rohde, E. 1925. *Psyche: The Cults of Souls and Belief in Immortality among the Greeks.* W. Hillis, trans. London.

Rosaldo, R. 1998. *Culture and Truth: the Remaking of Social Analysis.* Boston.

Rose, P. 1988. "Thersites and the Plural Voices of Homer." *Arethusa* 21: 5–25.

Rouland, N. 1979. "Les modes juridiques de solutions des conflits chez les Inuit." *Etudes Inuit* 3 (suppl)." 5–168.

———. 1994. *Legal Anthropology.* Ph. Planel., trans. Stanford.

Roussel, D. 1976. *Tribu et cite: études sur les groupes sociaux dans les cites grecques aux époques archaïque et classique.* Paris.

Rudolph, F. 1891. "Die Quellen und die Schriftstellerei des Athenaios." *Philologus* Supplement 6: 109–62.

Ruschenbusch, E. 1958. "Πάτριος πολιτεία. Theseus, Drakon, Solon und Kleisthenes in Publizistik und Geschichtsschreibung des 5. und 4. Jahrhunderts v. Chr." *Historia* 7: 398–424.

———. 1960. "ΦΟΝΟΣ. Zum Recht Drakons und seiner Bedeutung für das Werden des athenischen Staates." *Historia* 9: 147–52.

———. 1966. ΣΟΛΩΝΟΣ ΝΟΜΟΙ. *Historia* Einzelschriften 9. Wiesbaden.
———. 1968. *Untersuchungen zur Geschichte des athenischen Strafsrecht.* Cologne.
———. 1982. "Der Ursprung des gerichtlichen Rechtsstreits bei den Griechen." In J. Modrzejewski and D. Liebs, eds., *Symposion 1977: Vorträge zur griechischen und hellenistischen Rechtsgeschichte.* Cologne: 26–33.
Ruzé, F. 1988. "Aux débuts del'écriture politique: le pouvoir de l'écrit dans la cite." In Detienne, ed., 1988a: 82–94.
Salmon, J. T. 1972. "The Heraeum at Perahora, and the Early History of Corinth and Megara." *Annual of the British School at Athens* 67: 159–204.
———. 1984. *Wealthy Corinth.* Oxford.
———. 1997. "Lopping off the Heads?: Tyrants, Politics and the *polis.*" In Mitchell and Rhodes, eds.: 60–73.
Sarat, A., and T. R. Kearns, eds. 1998a. *Law in the Domains of Culture.* Ann Arbor.
———. 1998b. "The Cultural Lives of Law." In Sarat and Kearns, eds., 1998a: 1–20.
Sarkady, J. 1966. "Attika im 12 bis 10 Jahrhundert Die Anfänge des athenischen Staates." *Acta classica Universitatis Scientiarum Debreceniensis* 2: 9–27.
Scafuro, A. 2006. "Identifying Solonian Laws." In Blok and Lardinois, eds.: 175–96.
Schadewaldt, W. 1959. "Kleiderdinge. Zur Analyse der Odyssee." *Hermes* 87: 13–26.
———. 1966. *Iliasstudien*[3]. Berlin.
Schapera, I. 1938. *A Handbook of Tswana Law and Custom.* London.
Scheidel, W. 2003. "The Greek Demographic Expansion: Models and Comparisons." *Journal of Hellenic Studies* 123: 120–40.
Schmitt Pantel, P. 1994a. "Sacrificial Meal and *Symposion:* Two Models of Civic Institution in the Archaic City?" In O. Murray, ed.: 14–33.
———. 1994b. *La cite au banquet: histoire des repas publics dans les cites grecques.* Rome.
Schmitz, W. 2004. *Nachbarschaft und Dorfgemeinschaft im archaischen und klassischen Griechenland. Klio* supplement 7 (n.s.). Berlin.
Schousboe, K., and M. T. Larsen, eds. 1989. *Literacy and Society.* Copenhagen.
Scribner, S., and M. Cole. 1981. *The Psychology of Literacy.* Cambridge, MA.
Scully, S. 1990. *Homer and the Sacred City.* Ithaca, NY.
Seaford, R. 1994. *Reciprocity and Ritual.* Oxford.
———. 2004. *Money and the Early Greek Mind.* Cambridge.
Sealey, R. 1960. "Regionalism in Archaic Athens." *Historia* 9: 155–80.
———. 1961. "Eupatridai." *Historia* 10: 512–14.
———. 1977. *A History of the Greek City-States, 700–338 B.C.* Berkeley.
———. 1982. "On the Athenian Concept of Law." *Classical Journal* 77: 289–302.
———. 1987. *The Athenian Republic.* University Park, PA.
———. 1994. *The Justice of the Greeks.* Ann Arbor.
Shaw, P.-J. 1997. *Discrepancies in Olympiad Dating and Chronological Problems of Archaic Peloponnesian History. Historia Einzelschriften* 166. Stuttgart.
Shipp, G. 1978. *Nomos 'Law.'* Australian Academy of the Humanities Monograph 4. Sydney.
Sickinger, J. 1999. *Public Records and Archives in Classical Athens.* Chapel Hill.
Simms, R. 1983. "Eumolpos and the Wars of Athens." *Greek, Roman, and Byzantine Studies* 24: 197–208.
Smithson, E. L. 1968. "The Tomb of a Rich Athenian Lady, ca. 850 B.C." *Hesperia* 37: 77–116.
Snodgrass, A. M. 1965. "The Hoplite Reform and History." *Journal of Hellenic Studies* 85: 110–22.

———. 1974. "An Historical Homeric Society?" *Journal of Hellenic Studies* 94: 114–25.
———. 1980. *Archaic Greece: the Age of Experiment.* Berkeley.
———. 1993. "Homer to Solon—the Rise of the *polis.* The Written Sources." In M. H. Hansen, ed. 1993. *The Ancient Greek City-State.* Historisk-filosofiske Meddleleser 67. Copenhagen: 41–105.
———. 2000. *The Dark Age of Greece.* (1971: reprint with foreword to new edition). New York.
Sokolowski, F. 1969. *Lois sacrées des cites grecques.* Paris.
Solmsen, F. 1982. *Kleine Schriften 3.* Hildesheim.
Sourvinou-Inwood, C. 1995. 'Reading' Greek Death. Oxford.
Starr, C. 1977. *The Economic and Social Growth of Early Greece, 800–500 B.C.* New York.
———. 1986. *Individual and Community.* Oxford.
———. 1992. *The Aristocratic Temper of Greek Civilization.* Oxford.
Ste. Croix, G. E. M. de. 2004. *Athenian Democratic Origins and Other Essays.* D. Harvey and R. Parker, eds. Oxford.
Stehle, E. 2006. "Solon's Self-reflexive Political Persona and Its Audience." In Blok and Lardinois, eds.: 79–113.
Stoddart, S., and J. Whitley. 1988. "The Social Context of Literacy in Archaic Greece and Etruria." *Antiquity* 62: 761–72.
Strauss, B. 1986. *Athens after the Peloponnesian War.* London and Sydney.
Street, B. V. 1984. *Literacy in Theory and Practice.* Cambridge.
Stroud, R. 1968. *Drakon's Law on Homicide.* Berkeley.
———. 1978. "State Documents in Archaic Athens." In W. A. P. Childs, ed., *Athens Comes of Age.* Princeton: 20–42.
———. 1979. *The Axones and Kyrbeis of Drakon and Solon.* Berkeley.
Svenbro, J. 1976. *La Parole et le marbre. Aux origines de la poétique grecque.* Lund.
———. 1989. "Phrasikleia. An Archaic Greek Theory of Writing." In Schousboe and Larsen, eds.: 229–45.
———. 1993. *Phrasikleia. An Anthropology of Reading in Ancient Greece.* J. Lloyd, trans. Ithaca, NY.
Szegedy-Maszak, A. 1978. "The Legends of the Greek Lawgivers." *Greek, Roman, and Byzantine Studies* 19: 199–209.
Tainter, J. 1988. *The Collapse of Complex Societies.* Cambridge.
Tandy, D. 1997. *Warriors into Traders. The Power of the Market in Early Greece.* Berkeley.
Tandy, D., and C. Duncan, eds. 1994. *From Political Economy to Anthropology.* Montreal.
Tandy, D., and W. Neale. 1996. *Hesiod's Works and Days.* Berkeley.
Thalmann, W. G. 1988. "Thersites: Comedy, Scapegoats, and Heroic Ideology in the *Iliad.*" *Transactions of the American Philological Association* 118: 1–28.
Thomas, C. 1970. *Homer's History.* New York.
———. 1976. "From *wanax* to *basileus:* Kingship in the Greek Dark Age." *Hispania Antigua* 6: 187–206.
———. 1977. "Literacy and the Codification of Law." *Studia et Documenta Historiae et Juris* 43: 455–8.
———. 1983. Review of Drews 1983. *American Historical Review* 88: 1251.
———. 1984. "Mycenaean Law in its Oral Context." *Studi micenei ed egeo-anatolici* 25: 247–53.
———. 2005. *Finding People in Early Greece.* Columbia, MO.

Thomas, C., and C. Conant. 1999. *From Citadel to City-State: The Transformation of Greece, 1200–700 B.C.* Bloomington, IN.

Thomas, R. 1989. *Oral Tradition and Written Record in Classical Athens.* Cambridge.

———. 1992. *Literacy and Orality in Ancient Greece.* Cambridge.

———. 1994. "Literacy and the City-state in Archaic and Classical Greece." In Bowman and Woolf, eds., 1994a: 33–50.

———. 1996. "Written in Stone? Liberty, Equality, Orality and the Codification of Law." In Foxhall and Lewis, eds.: 9–32.

———. 2003. "Prose Performance Texts: *epideixis* and Written Publication in the Late Fifth and Early Fourth Centuries." In Yunis, ed., 2003a: 162–88.

———. 2005. "Writing, Law, and Written law." In Gagarin and Cohen, eds.: 41–60.

Thür, G. 1970. "Zum *dikazein* bei Homer." *Zeitschrift der Savigny-Stiftung* 87: 426–44.

———. 1984. "Hans Julius Wolff zum Gedenken." *Zeitschrift der Savigny-Stiftung* 101: 476–92.

———. 1996. "Oaths and Dispute Settlement in Ancient Greek Law." In Foxhall and Lewis, eds.: 57–72.

Todd, S. C. 1993. *The Shape of Athenian Law.* Oxford.

Trimborn, E. 1927. "Grundsätzliches zur Methode der historischen Rechtsforschung." *Zeitschrift für vergleichende Rechtswissenschaft* 42: 1–7.

———. 1928. "Die Methode der ethnologischen Forschung." *Zeitschrift für vergleichende Rechtswissenschaft* 43: 416–64.

Van Compornolle, R. 1981. "La législation aristocratique de Locres Epizéphyrienne, dite législation de Zaleukos." *Antiquité Classique* 50: 759–69.

Van Effenterre, H. and M. 1994. "Ecrire sur les murs." In H.-J. Gehrke, ed., *Rechtkodifizierung und soziale Normen im interkulturellen Vergleich.* Tübingen: 87–96.

Van Velsen, J. 1967. "The extended-case method and situational analysis." In A. L. Epstein, ed., *The Craft of Social Anthropology.* London: 129–49.

Van Wees, H. 1992. *Status Warriors: War, Violence, and Society in Homer and History.* Amsterdam.

———. 1998. "A Brief History of Tears. Gender Differentiation in Archaic Greece." In L. Foxhall and J. Salmon, eds., 2006. *When Men Were Men: Masculinity, Power and Identity in Classical Antiquity.* London: 10–51.

———. 1999. "Introduction: Homer and Early Greece." In I. J. F. de Jong, ed., *Homer: Critical Assessments.* London and New York: 1–32.

———. 2001. "The Myth of the Middle Class Army: Military and Social Status in Ancient Athens." In Bekker-Nielsen and Hannestad, eds.: 45–71.

———. 2006. "Mass and Elite in Solon's Athens: the Property Classes Revisited." In Blok and Lardinois, eds.: 351–89.

Vansina, J. 1973. *Oral Tradition. A Study in Historical Methodology.* Harmondsworth, UK.

———. 1980. "Memory and Oral Tradition." In J. C. Miller, ed., *The African Past Speaks: Essays on Oral Tradition and History.* Folkstone, UK: 262–76.

Varhelyi, Z. 1996. "The Written Word in Archaic Attica." *Klio* 78: 28–52.

Veligianni Terzi, C. 1977. *Damiurges. Zur Entwicklung einer Magistratur.* Thesis (Ph.D.), University of Heidelberg.

Verdier, R. 1980. "La système vindicatoire." In Verdier, Courtois, and Poly, eds.: 1.13–42.

———. 1981. "Premières orientations pour une anthropologie du droit." *Droit et Cultures* 1: 1–23.

Verdier, R., G. Courtois, and J.-P. Poly, eds. 1980–84. *La Vengeance.* 4 volumes. Paris.

Vernant, J.-P. 1982. *The Origins of Greek Thought.* Ithaca, NY.

Vidal-Naquet, P. 1986. *The Black Hunter: Forms of Thought and Forms of Society in the Greek World.* Baltimore.

Wade-Gery, H. T. 1931. "Eupatridai, Archons, and Areopagus." *Classical Quarterly* 31: 1–11, 77–89.

———. 1933. "Studies in the Structure of Attic Society: II. The Laws of Kleisthenes." *Classical Quarterly* 27: 17–29.

———. 1952. *The Poet of the Iliad.* Cambridge.

Walker, H. 1995. *Theseus and Attica.* Oxford.

Wallace, R. W. 1983. "The Date of Solon's Reforms." *The American Journal of Ancient History* 8: 81–95.

———. 1989. *The Areopagus Council to 307 B.C.* Baltimore.

———. 2007. "Revolutions and a New Order in Solonian Athens and Archaic Greece." In Raaflaub and Wallace, eds., 2007a: 49–82.

Weber, M. 1968. *Economy and Society.* Guenther Roth and Claus Wittich, eds., E. Fischoff, et al., trans., New York.

West, M. L. 1966. *Hesiod.* Oxford.

———. 1978. *Works and Days.* Oxford.

———. 1997. *The East Face of Helicon. Asiatic Elements in Greek Poetry.* Oxford.

West, S. L. 1989. "Laertes Revisited." *Proceedings of the Cambridge Philological Society* 35: 113–43.

Whiting, J. W. M. 1950. *Paiute Sorcery.* New York.

Whitley, J. 1988. "Early States and Hero cults. A Reappraisal." *Journal of Hellenic Studies* 108: 173–82.

———. 1991. *Style and Society in Dark Age Greece.* Cambridge.

———. 1997. "Cretan Law and Cretan Literacy." *American Journal of Archaeology* 101: 635–61.

Will, E. 1955. *Korinthiaka: Recherches sur l'histoire et la civilisation de Corinthe des origines aux guerres médiques.* Paris.

Willcock, M. 1997. "Neoanalysis." In Morris and Powell, eds.: 174–89.

Willetts, R. F. 1955. *Aristocratic Society in Ancient Crete.* London.

———. 1967. *The Law Code of Gortyn. Kadmos* Supplement 1. Berlin.

———. 1974. "Cretan Law and Early Greek Society." In *Antichità cretesi: studi in onore di Doro Levi.* Catania: 22–31.

———. 1982. "Cretan Laws and Society." *Cambridge Ancient History*^{2}. Cambridge: 3.324–48.

Williams, R. 1983. *Keywords: a Vocabulary of Culture and Society* (rev. ed.). Oxford and New York.

Wilson, D. 2002. *Ransom, Revenge, and Heroic Identity in the* Iliad. Cambridge.

Wolff, H. J. 1946. "The Origin of Judicial Litigation among the Greeks." *Traditio* 4: 31–87.

———. 1975. "Greek Legal History: Its Functions and Potentialities." *Washington University Law Quarterly* 53: 395–408.

———. 1980. "Vorgeschichte und Enthstehung des Rechtsbegriff in frühen Griechentum." In W. Fikentscher, ed. *Entstehung und Wandel rechtlicher Traditionen.* Munich: 557–79.

Wolpert, A. 2002. *Remembering Defeat. Civil War and Civic Memory in Ancient Athens.* Baltimore.

Wood, I. 1986. "Disputes in Late Fifth- and Sixth-century Gaul: Some Problems." In W. Davies and P. Fouracre, eds., *The Settlement of Disputes in Early Medieval Europe*. Cambridge: 14–22.

Worthington, I. 2000. *Demosthenes, Statesman and Orator.* London.

Yngvesson, B. 1989. "Inventing Law in Local Settings: Rethinking Popular Legal Culture." *Yale Law Journal* 98: 1689–1709.

Yunis, H., ed. 2003a. *Written Texts and the Rise of Literate Culture in Ancient Greece.* Cambridge.

———. 2003b. "Introduction: Why Written Texts?" In Yunis, ed., 2003a: 1–14.

———. 2005. "The Rhetoric of Law in Fourth Century Athens." In Gagarin and Cohen, eds.: 191–208.

Zörner, G. 1971. *Kypselos und Pheidon von Argos. Untersuchungen zur frühen griechischen Tyrannis.* Thesis (Ph.D.), University of Marburg.

Zscheitzmann, W. 1928. "Die Darstellungen der Prothesis in der griechischen Kunst." *Athenische Mitteilung* 53: 30–38.

INDEX